1632231

SEEDING
CIVIL WAR

SEEDING CIVIL WAR

KANSAS IN THE NATIONAL NEWS,

1854-1858

CRAIG MINER

UNIVERSITY PRESS OF KANSAS

All photographs are from Corbis except where otherwise designated.

Published by the University Press of Kansas (Lawrence, Kansas
66045), which was organized by the Kansas Board of Regents and is
operated and funded by Emporia State University, Fort Hays State
University, Kansas State University, Pittsburg State University,
the University of Kansas, and Wichita State University

Library of Congress Cataloging-in-Publication Data

Miner, H. Craig.
Seeding Civil War : Kansas in the national news, 1854-1858 /
Craig Miner.
p. cm.
Includes bibliographical references and index.
ISBN 978-0-7006-1612-1 (cloth : alk. paper)
1. Kansas—Politics and government—1854–1861. 2. Kansas—Press
coverage. 3. Journalism—United States—History—19th century.
4. Rhetoric—Political aspects—United States—History—19th century.
5. Sectionalism (United States)—History—19th century. 6. United
States—History—Civil War, 1861–1865—Causes. I. Title.
F685.M666 2008
973.7′11—dc22
2008014480

British Library Cataloguing-in-Publication Data is available.

Printed in the United States of America

10 9 8 7 6 5 4 3 2 1

The paper used in this publication is recycled and contains
30 percent postconsumer waste. It is acid free and meets the
minimum requirements of the American National Standard for
Permanence of Paper for Printed Library Materials Z39.48-1992.

For they have sown the wind,
and they shall reap the whirlwind.

HOSEA 8:7

CONTENTS

Chapter 8
Lecompton
210

Conclusion: The Fires Go Out
236

A photograph section follows page 164

PREFACE

The idea for this book came to me while I was doing research at the Kansas State Historical Society on my history of Kansas. One of the first acquisitions of that society after its founding by a group of newspaper editors in 1875 was the Thomas W. Webb collection, purchased in 1877 for $400. Webb was the chief administrator of the New England Emigrant Aid Company, that famous—to some, infamous—Boston corporation that in the 1850s dispatched settlers of free-state sentiment to Kansas Territory during the tumultuous struggle over whether slavery would be established in the new state. Among the records acquired with this purchase were seventeen volumes of scrapbooks. These represented what we might now call a clippings service concerning events and the doings of the company in Kansas Territory from March 1854 to September 1856. The first Biennial Report of the Historical Society noticed in 1879 that the scrapbooks were "a complete reflection of the sentiments of the press and of the public men of the whole country, North and South, upon the Kansas question, during those years of agitation." As such, they constituted "a collection of Kansas historical material the worth of which can scarcely be estimated in money."[1] Reading the scrapbooks convinced me that it was worthwhile to study public opinion on Kansas as expressed in the national press with a sweep and depth greater than had been done previously.[2]

Historians have perhaps not so directly linked the press to the coming of the Civil War as they have connected "yellow journalism" to events culminating in the Spanish-American War. However, there has been clear recognition of the press's importance and its influence in agenda setting in the 1850s. There was a shift in that era from individualism to a commercial culture, which could sell not only goods but also ideas through a national network of standardized knowledge and information.[3] A Virginia editor in 1860 went so far as to say, "Newspapers and Telegraphs have ruined the country. Suppress both and the country could be saved now." Historian David Reynolds commented that while that statement was an exaggeration, "without the press, the task of those who divided the nation would have been infinitely more difficult."[4] In 1829 a Vermont newspaper wrote, "Our citizens need to study more the history of the revolutionary struggle—not of its battles and sufferings, but of the *reasonings* which nerved men's souls to endure them."[5] The same might well be said of the Civil War and its causes.

What emerged from the Webb materials and to a much greater degree in my further research was sometimes significant nuance, but also, often, fundamental arguments about approaches to and interpretations of Kansas that have been relatively or entirely neglected in published literature. And what a rich mine of quotation there was, almost none of it published since its original appearance.

It turned out, however, that the Webb clippings, 3,000 pages plus, were hardly the "complete reflection" advertised. They ended in 1856, and though they contained a good sample of Southern papers, they tended, as one might expect, to best represent the New England and the Republican press. The clipping process itself was selective, as I found reading the complete files of such papers as the *New York Daily Times* and the *New York Daily Tribune*, which, although sampled in the scrapbooks, were richer in Kansas coverage than those volumes indicated. Over time, keeping the microfilm machine warm as I read newspapers (often execrably printed and indifferently filmed) and accessed the new electronic databases of historical newspapers as they became available, I multiplied the range of papers considerably. I read hundreds of thousands of articles on Kansas from papers of every political stripe and from every section of the United States, to which I added magazines, pamphlets, and the debates of Congress.

The newspapers were the core. Almost all the congressional material, often verbatim, and much of the pamphlet literature appeared first in the newspaper press. Newspapers in California and in the far West generally took relatively little interest in Kansas, probably because of their physical isolation, but from Kansas City east the concern and the coverage was intense. The North had the advantage of having more newspapers than existed in the South. In 1860 the newspaper and periodical circulation of the South was 103,041,346, while the corresponding number in the North was 824,910,112. One in three Americans lived in the South, but only one in eight newspapers and magazines originated there. The *New York Daily Tribune* had a daily circulation that was greater than the total circulation of the sixty-six dailies in the South.[6] Still, many small towns everywhere had more than one newspaper, and newspaper reading was a regular habit nationwide.

There was remarkable variety in view, dictated somewhat by party and section but also driven by the particular sensitivities of the editor, and no doubt by the editor's sense of the local audience. Yet even in the same city there could be deep divisions, as evidenced by the contrasting coverages of the *Daily Missouri Democrat* and the *Daily Missouri Republican* in St. Louis. Southern papers were hardly of a piece. One might expect border papers such as the *Louisville Journal* to be moderate, but so was the *Richmond Enquirer*, and both contrasted with "fire-eating" papers such as the *Charleston Mercury* and the *New Orleans Daily Delta*. The *New Orleans Daily Picayune* had quite a different take than did the *Delta*, while the *Detroit Daily Free Press*, a newspaper in the orbit of Michigan's senator Lewis Cass, contained some of the strongest racist arguments I found anywhere. The New York newspapers, of course, were a universe unto themselves, running the whole gamut from the near sympathy with the South of the *Herald* to the extreme abolitionist stance of the *Tribune*. The *Washington Union* was an administration organ, putting out the official line, but that line changed as administrations and circumstances changed. Sometimes I chose a paper because of the fame of its editor, such as Samuel Bowles at the *Springfield Daily Republican*, John Forney at the *Philadelphia Press*, or Horace Greeley at the *New York Daily Tribune*. But one of the joys of the research was the discovery of how articulate many obscure editors were and how tellingly they engaged their readers, pushing them to a perspective, to be sure, but hardly unaware that in a democracy one must persuade more than bludgeon. Achieving political balance was important in my selection, and given the complicated politics of the 1850s, that involved choosing not only Democratic and Republican papers but also ones that represented the Whig and Know-Nothing factions. I tried to represent smaller towns—such as Natchez, Mississippi; Concord, Massachusetts; Bangor, Maine; Dayton, Ohio; and Macon, Georgia—along with the metropolitan media centers. Also, particularly in the chapter on religion, specialized newspapers and magazines proved useful.

While I have intervened and commented regularly in this text, I have also sometimes allowed the newspaper editorialists to speak for themselves at the abstract and interpretive level where the words of the modern scholar are usually employed. Highly intelligent people, who distinguished themselves by their powers of observation and communication, created my primary materials. They did not have the advantages of distance or hindsight, but they did not have their disadvantages either. They were constrained by crisis and a certain responsibility for the future in what they said, but often what they said went closer to the core of things as they unfolded at the time than would my mere paraphrasing and employing "bottom line" data from these sources. I have therefore tried to present the whole cloth, with its patchwork and blemishes, its grandeur and its disgust.

Parallel, dueling arguments are presented from different perspectives and through different lenses. Readers may be convinced either by the whole argument, or by certain details of a presentation made by people with whom they may in general be out of sympathy. Fanaticism and reason, invective and persuasion, knew no politics and no section.

I was influenced from diverse directions over the years to take an interest in the making of popular opinion, directions including the musings of St. Augustine on imagery in our memory and the insights of British historian J. G. A. Pocock on the significance of language variations that developed around, and influenced thinking about, political issues in the eighteenth century.[7] An especially strong impact came from Walter Lippmann's book *Public Opinion* (1922), with its adaptation of the printing term "stereotype" to refer to the "pictures in our heads" that the media used to move masses.

In a 1975 article I identified eight stereotyped arguments used in newspaper editorials and stump speeches of the 1850s. The purpose of this literature was to convince the public to regard the Pacific railroad (as the transcontinental railroad project was then called) as practical, necessary, and desirable.[8] I thought about writing a book expanding that study to include public thinking about other late-nineteenth-century issues, such as the currency question or the nature of insanity, but moved away from that research into several books on the history of Kansas. It did not occur to me then that eventually the two interests (the rhetoric of opinion making and the history of Kansas) would combine.

That the Civil War began in Kansas is a bromide (Missouri claims something similar). But there is truth in it. And whatever underlying economic or political forces were driving the nation inevitably over the brink to war, the public had to be brought along. The information to which that public was privy came largely from newspapers. Newspaper writers had an agenda, readers had preconceptions, and everything mixed in a terribly emotional brew. But out of that brew came public support of certain positions, however distorted or stereotyped they might seem, that were strong enough to lead many people eventually into fights to the death. Therefore, at the center of this book is an extensive presentation by category and purpose of what contemporary newspapers had to say about the Kansas issue. There is also a considerable illustration of just exactly how they said it: the funny and the profound, the hysterical and the cynical, the sophisticated and the crude.

Historians of journalism understand that newspapers do not conform to the factual model often advanced for them in the Progressive Era. Instead, they "frame," and in some ways umpire, a debate with and among readers. "All journalism can do," James Carey wrote, "is preside over and within the conversation of our culture." David Nord added, "Newspaper stories, like poems, do not have fixed meanings. Meaning occurs not in the text but in the reading of it."[9] Newspaper accounts were part of what social scientists have called "the social construction of reality."

Not only has this type of literature on Kansas as a national issue never been read so extensively before, but surely few have fully realized what a deep obsession to the United States Kansas really was—how thoroughly it dominated the press in cities large and small, North and South, for several years. Study of such a single riveting issue is revealing of how the press functioned, and functions, in trying to influence public opinion in a free society. Some of the conclusions one is forced to come to are encouraging; some are not. The issues were neither simple nor trivial, extending as they did not only to the meaning of good government but to the nature and duties of mankind itself. In looking at Kansas and its troubles, the rest of the nation well sensed, as to some degree it has ever since, that it was looking into its own heart.

I acknowledge the help of the library staff at Ablah Library at Wichita State University and at the Kansas State Historical Society in Topeka. The Department of History at Wichita State provided a microfilm reader for the duration of this project, which was vital. As often, I appreciated the honest and wise advice of Fred Woodward at the University Press of Kansas. Without the continued love and support of my wife Susan, to whom this book is dedicated, I would have to get into a more practical, but less personally rewarding, line of work than writing history.

SEEDING
CIVIL WAR

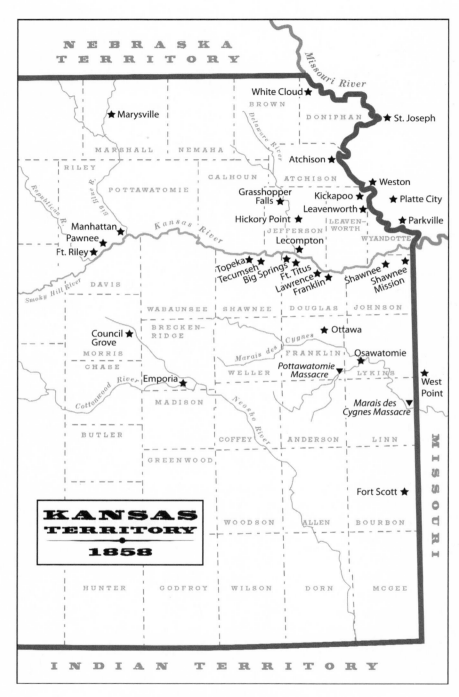

Kansas Territory, 1858. Map by David Rohr.

INTRODUCTION: THIS FAR-FAMED LAND

This book is not about Kansas per se, but about a debate during four years (1854–1858) concerning the nature and destiny of the American Republic occasioned by the creation, under peculiar circumstances and elevated passions, of Kansas Territory. Events in Kansas Territory were the reason for the editorial and political commentary studied here, but the comments were not exclusively *about* those events. Kansas was, and was known at the time to be, a "test," or a battleground, to determine, as Abraham Lincoln later memorably said, whether a Republic founded on the principles of the Declaration of Independence and ordered under the rules of the Constitution could survive in the world as it was in the middle nineteenth century. Three times—in 1854, in 1856, and in 1858—the Kansas issue dominated an entire session of Congress, and at no time during the era was it far from the center of attention. A correspondent of the *Boston Liberator* observed in 1855 that Kansas Territory was a "far-famed land," a subject of conversation all over America, and to some extent around the world.[1] Kansas, wrote a contemporary observer, "was born in trouble, and has lived in a storm. She has not been left to manage her own affairs. All the States have taken a hand to keep the excitement at a fever heat."[2]

My overarching thesis is that Kansas was more important to the coming of the Civil War than has been hitherto recognized, and that it was important more because of how events there were talked about in the national press than because of the significance of those events themselves. As a long-running spectacular issue with legs, as we would now say, it drew to itself arguments and passions one would imagine to be far beyond its ken. The rhetoric surrounding Kansas events, the seeming "tangents" it caused editors and readers to follow, were not just the setting, not just the coloring, but also the main event in influencing cultural understanding and political behavior. Choices were framed more in reading than in acting—the one was the province of the many, whereas the other was the venue of the few. Historians have studied politics and events in Kansas and in Washington, D.C., but have addressed the medium in between much less. Arguably, editors, forming

public opinion as they did, providing frames with which people could identify and in which they could find a home for their inchoate thinking, were as
important as politicians and the actual actors in the drama. Then as now,
players were influenced by the publicity concerning them. No modern public figure is more aware of image, more aware of being an actor on a national
stage, more cognizant of how his or her behavior and statements will play in
Baltimore than were the characters exploiting the Kansas issue in the 1850s.
Words became an intermediate reality, formed the warring cultures, and led
to dire consequences.

Therefore, it is important to make a comprehensive study of exactly what
was said about Kansas. This must include not just the *Squatter Sovereign* and
the *Herald of Freedom*, the Kansas propaganda organs so regularly quoted, but
newspapers across the United States. They must be quoted in extenso and
day by day, year by year, not just at a highlighted moment. That it was important to read a balance of newspapers in the North and the South was obvious;
that there was so much variation within the sections was a surprise. So was
the degree of drama, sophistication, and terrible, earnest intensity in the
editorials and stories on the Kansas issue.

Some of the illustrative incidents presented here will be familiar to
scholars and students of the history of Kansas. Some of the events that were
made much of by the contemporary national press, and that are therefore
given significant attention in this book, have appeared only briefly or only in
the most specialized, or ancient, of the academic literature. Some incidents
and many details have probably never been discussed in the published literature at all. Of course, the broadened context inevitably has its effect on the
fundamental story. Even the familiar stories gain depth, nuance, salient detail, humor, drama, realism, and interpretive context when examined from
the points of view and through the descriptive powers of numerous editors
and correspondents across the nation. I have not ignored the standard fare.
Certain events, issues, and people have been often talked of because they
were genuinely important. But I have always aspired to make the parameters
and style of the presentation sui generis without venturing into anything
unauthentic. Therefore, I make the disclaimer that while this is not a new
history of Bleeding Kansas, it does make a considerable contribution to that
fundamental genre.

The causes of the Civil War were complex. To posit that the Kansas issue
was a factor in the coming of the war would be to state the obvious, and to
imagine that Kansas or the press it got was the sole or principal cause of the

war would be to push a thesis too far. However, the extent of the national obsession about Kansas, and therefore its significance as a collector of national passions and arguments, has never before been as thoroughly studied and illustrated as it is here.

The Kansas debate was not the only contemporary media subject of its kind: There were, for example, the discussion of the Dred Scott decision, John Brown's raid on Harpers Ferry, the Lincoln-Douglas debates, the reception of *Uncle Tom's Cabin*, and various incidents concerning enforcement of the Fugitive Slave Act. But Kansas was, it can be argued, *the* major collector in the 1850s of arguments, *the* most important focus for the complex sectional argument, *the* issue that drew in the most elements that concerned people about the nature and survival of the Union, and *the* single matter to which the most ink was devoted by the national press and the congressional reporters in the crucial center of the 1850s. This importance played out more in the media and opinion capitals of the eastern United States than in the tiny towns on the plains of Kansas.

The Kansas issue was long-running and wearying. The continual shifts, the ups and downs over whether Kansas would be slave or free, frustrated and damaged the nation's psyche. It provided characters people loved to hate. One might defer with some grace to Daniel Webster, John Calhoun, or Henry Clay. But that was hardly possible with Franklin Pierce or James Buchanan, and not possible with Stephen Douglas, Lewis Cass, Charles Sumner, or Alexander Stephens, nor with the nearly comic governors of Kansas—Andrew Reeder, Wilson Shannon, Robert Walker—or such extremist leaders as James Lane, Charles Robinson, David Atchison, and Benjamin Stringfellow. Instead of meliorating the situation, these often aggressive, testy folks offended and divided. The big issues tending to the division of the Union—slavery, the differences between the societies and economies of the North and the South—had been there for decades. So why did the Civil War come in 1861 just as Kansas became a state? That had a great deal to do with the process by which that troubled state entered the fragmenting Union. If one were forced to give a single proximate cause for the Civil War, the failure to find common ground on the Kansas issue would be a strong candidate. Kansas was the test of the matter of the extension of slavery into the territories, and that was a prime sticking point even among those who were willing to ignore the past and allow slavery to continue where it existed.

One can think that the causes of the Civil War form a broad topic and that the Bleeding Kansas debate is a narrow one. However, no other state or territory has had such a burst of significance as did Kansas in the middle 1850s. There was enormous exaggeration in the press at the time of the significance of Kansas, comparing the battles there to those at Lexington, Concord, and even Thermopylae, and averring that the issues were the most important not only in the history of the United States but in the history of civilization. But even without exaggeration, Kansas was indeed overwhelmingly important. Seen in proper context, the history of Kansas in this period is hardly regional history at all. It was part and parcel of the whole, and no student of the causes of the Civil War can avoid dealing in detail with the Kansas struggle. An account of the Civil War published by Denton Snider in 1906, *The American Ten Years' War: 1855–1865*, considered the Kansas troubles and the Civil War proper all of a piece. So did I in my chapter "Trampling Out the Vintage," in *Kansas: The History of the Sunflower State, 1854–2000*.[3]

Newspaper editors and political pundits did as much to *create* the events and the characters of the Kansas imbroglio in the minds of their readers as Congress had done in 1854 to create Kansas Territory itself as a political unit. Kansas, as portrayed in the press, occasioned an intense, multifarious, ever-present, repetitive, passionate public discussion. This discussion came to exclude nearly everything else, day after day in newspapers all over the nation, and it drained away the possibilities for accommodation in 1850s America. It was the touchstone for everything else, polarizing opinion and hardening factions in a wearying, discouraging way that made cynics of former idealists everywhere. No one was deceived that the Kansas crisis, or the emotion swirling around it, was laid to rest by the awkward "solution" of the cobbled-together English Compromise or by the failed vote on entry under the Lecompton Constitution in 1858. Instead, the laughable compromises about Kansas presaged the end of compromises and of the foundations of the civilization, culture, and political system that Americans thought they had shared. Lecompton left a bad taste in the mouth, gave compromise itself a bad name, and was so humiliating, awkward, and unsatisfactory that people concluded there were worse things than resolution through war. In debating Kansas, it seemed everything had been tried, ad nauseam, ad infinitum, and each try was less satisfactory than the one before. Yes, Kansas largely disappeared from the radar until it entered the Union just as the Civil War broke out in 1861. Yes, Abraham Lincoln and Stephen Douglas, debating in Illinois in 1858 about the subjects that had long been argued about with reference to Kansas, took the place of Kansas itself in the national media. But Kansas was the ghost of Banquo at the feast, the specter that could not be exorcised, the embarrassment that could be neither forgotten nor forgiven.

Some at the time did see that after Kansas was admitted to the Union, compromise was no longer possible. James Lane and John Brown in Kansas thought so. Many in the South thought so. They regretted the necessity of breaking the Union but considered it their destiny, a dire necessity for the sake of principle that might, by a long shot, save them. But, ironically, most in the nation underestimated the impact on long-range behavior of the media circus over Kansas. Many considered it a sideshow that, with its pettiness and name-calling, had become too extreme in its rhetoric to be taken seriously by sensible people. On the surface, there actually seemed to be consensus. Everyone believed in "freedom," "law and order," "popular sovereignty," and "the Union." Events in Kansas would eventually run their course, newspaper readers would flock to some other sensation, the country would escape the noose, and the Union would survive, turbulent, but short of the civil war and dissolution that headlines were always predicting.

The pundits were mistaken. As people read and talked about what they meant by "freedom" and applied it to the situation in Kansas, suddenly nothing was obvious or assumed or understood any more. It was the part of the Kansas debate that contemporaries, and to some extent historians since, took least seriously—namely, the descriptive language and the stereotyped arguments presented in the national press—that made the difference in the slide toward civil war, not the relatively local struggles in Kansas that were their occasion.

For that reason I have viewed Kansas more from the perspective of New York City and Richmond than from that of Lawrence and Topeka. I have concentrated not on every detail of the well-known story of "Bleeding Kansas" but on key events that acted as "collectors" of national opinion, which resonated strongly and provoked intense interest and reactions in the sections. Sometimes this results in a different estimate of importance than is common. John Brown himself, for example, was hardly a factor in generating national publicity during the 1854–1858 period, nor was much attention paid to details concerning his sons, his opinions, or his military role. James Lane was far more interesting to the press then, although Brown indeed became a key media figure at the time of the Harpers Ferry raid in 1859. I have approached things extensively and inductively and let the story unfold as it unfolded for Americans at the time, taking their information largely from their local morning paper. Not only was Kansas a major cause of the Civil War, but so also was the modern print culture in which it was played out.

Edward Ayers, the Hugh Kelly Professor of History at the University of Virginia, is one of a new generation of insightful thinkers about the coming of the Civil War. He sees the war not only as the result of many causes, but also as a disagreement, not between a modern society (the North) and a premodern society (the South), but between two modern societies. And not only was the war a conflict within modernity, it was a conflict *about* modernity, brought about by the tools of modernity, especially newspapers and print culture and their inevitable concomitant, popular politics. These, Ayers argues, "created the necessary contexts for the war." Print "permitted people to cast their imaginations and loyalties beyond the boundaries of their localities, to identify with people they had never met, to see themselves in an abstract cause. People learned to imagine consequences of actions, to live in the future. Print shaped everything we associate with the coming of the Civil War."[4]

Newspaper people wrote thousands of editorials on Kansas based on raw data from correspondents, telegraphic reports, and speeches by national and regional politicians. Here is where most of what a modern media analyst would call spin or framing took place. Here, in the nexus of "print capitalism," occurred what Walter Lippmann called "stereotyping" and what Stephen Harnett called the formation of "cultural fictions," or the "paradoxes of democratic representation."[5] There arose Lippmann's "pictures in our heads," simplified images that influenced behavior in people unable to handle the complexities of undigested reality (all of us to some degree and on most issues). As Paul Starr has said in his book *The Creation of the Media*, technological advances in the nineteenth century shaped communication for "both instrumental and symbolic purposes."[6] The *Charleston Mercury* put it more directly: "They first invent the facts, and then invent a remedy for them."[7]

There is no question that the newspaper was the "monarch of public opinion" in 1850s America. "There is no book so instructive as a newspaper," said the *Daily Richmond Enquirer*, "no knowledge so necessary to be acquired as that which may be gleaned from its columns."[8] The press, said an observer in Chicago, "is one of the few units of power existing in the world to-day; one of those rare things that can project and accomplish from its own volition. It moves through and moulds the passions and interests of the States, and is to American social life what Mohammed was to Oriental faith." It was plagued by shallow commentary and manufactured opinion. "Yet these 'fripperies,'" one editor observed, "are the chief matter of men's minds." They lived on bread, faith, and the morning paper.[9]

Ayers recognized the overarching importance of the juxtaposition of the Kansas issue and journalism in this process. "Although Bleeding Kansas was far removed from the East, and John Brown's raid freed no slaves, these events gained critical significance because they were amplified and distorted by newspapers. Without the papers, many events we now see as decisive would have passed without wide consequence. With the papers, events large and small stirred the American people every day. The press nurtured anticipation and grievance."[10] That was an important insight. But Ayers advanced it in a brief essay. I intend to document and illustrate it fully and in detail from contemporary primary sources.

Some of the greatest American historians have written about the 1850s. Among them were Allan Nevins, David Potter, Arthur Schlesinger Sr., Carl Sandburg, and Roy Nichols. In writing about the "Impending Crisis" (Potter), "The Ordeal of the Union" (Nevins), or "The Disruption of American Democracy" (Nichols), they considered the Kansas struggle a main contributor to the Civil War. More recently, such scholars as Mark Neeley, Tracy Campbell, Richard Striner, Susan Mary Grant, Nicole Etcheson, Gunja SenGupta, and David Reynolds have added depth to our understanding of events in Kansas and the reaction to them.

In addition, there has been fascinating literature on the role of rhetoric and propaganda generally and on framing in the media presentation of political issues. The literature is extensive and profoundly interdisciplinary. Michael Shapiro wrote in *Language and Politics*: "All stories and accounts, no matter how much their style might protest innocence, contain a mythic level—that is, they have a job to do, a perspective to promote, a kind of world to affirm or deny."[11]

Hearing on the nightly news in 2006 such phrases as "cut and run," "bottom line," "wake-up call," "pro-choice," "tax relief," "weapons of mass destruction," "antisocial," "faith community," "surgical strike," "freedom fighter," "flip-flopper," and "death tax" reminded me of the contemporary relevance of framing of alternatives and control of tools of discourse. Steven Poole collected many of these modern epithets in his book *Unspeak*, where he reminded us that it is not necessary to invent new words to give old words new significance. A stereotyping epithet brings with it a series of assumptions of which the reader may not be aware. And, Poole claimed, "as a phrase becomes a widely used term of public debate, it tends to saturate the mind with one viewpoint and to make an opposing view ever more difficult to enunciate."[12]

Historians have studied rhetoric for some time, moving away from the "debunking" school, which prided itself on ignoring unrealistic newspaper accounts of things in order to get at the underlying "truth." It was a revelation to me to read Henry Nash Smith's *Virgin Land: The American West as Symbol and Myth* (1950), with its serious analysis of the impact of such verbal constructs as "the Passage to India" on such projects as the building of the Pacific railroad. Among other books with particular influence in informing my thinking about a new type of approach to history were Leo Marx, *The Machine in the Garden: Technology and the Pastoral Ideal in America* (1964); R. W. B. Lewis, *The American Adam: Innocence, Tragedy, and Tradition in the Nineteenth Century* (1955); and John Stilgoe, *Metropolitan Corridor: Railroads and the American Scene* (1983).[13]

Dealing with my period for study here and emphasizing the importance of imagery and rhetoric were the article by Aaron Wildavsky and Richard Ellis, "A Cultural Analysis of the Role of Abolitionists in the Coming of the Civil War," David Davis's *Slave Power Conspiracy and the Paranoid Style*, Stephen Harnett's *Democratic Dissent and the Cultural Fictions of Antebellum America*, Gunja SenGupta's *For God and Mammon: Evangelicals and Entrepreneurs, Masters and Slaves in Territorial Kansas, 1854–1860*, and Nicole Etcheson's *Bleeding Kansas: Contested Liberty in the Civil War Era*.

Wildavsky and Ellis employed cultural-functional theory to help explain ideological and partisan coherence and realignment, and they applied it to the breakdown of America's political and cultural system in the 1850s. They argued that in the South of the 1850s, slavery was infused with cultural value for the first time and became not a mere economic device but a symbol of the slaveholders' sense of cultural identity. Compromise, even rational discussion, became difficult.[14]

Davis examined one overarching stereotype, that of the slaveocracy, or slave conspiracy. Davis concluded that truth and falsity were often relative. Framing was important in creating a slavery that was a "giant parasite, a plague, a poisonous plant, a dragon, a monster," and an angel of death for the Christian Republic, rather than merely an alternative form of labor. It was uncertain how many believed in a slave conspiracy, but Davis was sure that in times of great internal conflict and uncertainty, "the line narrows between respectable ideology and what might normally be dismissed as the ravings of screwballs and nuts."[15]

Harnett's study of "the glorious and maddening paradoxes of democracy" looked at the relationships between abolitionism, capitalism, race, and slavery. His topic, as Harnett described it, was the "stories, norms, explanations, icons, justifications, and sustaining myths"—that is, the "cultural fictions"—that people used as coping mechanisms in a changing, confusing, often frightening world. An image like that presented by Stephen Douglas—"A horrible reptile is coiled in your nation's bosom"—had nearly the power of a spell. Such images, Harnett argued, were a form of "representational conflation in which essentially inexpressible concepts are reduced or condensed into a more recognizable object or category of perception." Opinion was less dominated by local elites as "print capitalism" developed during the period, and the national molders of rhetoric became ever more important. Choices were likely to be made "on the basis of the lure of eloquence."[16]

SenGupta's book emphasized, as do many recent scholars, that the Kansas battle was not a simple fight between good and evil or even between two clearly defined and unified positions: "Yankee and Southern in Kansas did not inhabit mutually exclusive, homogeneous worlds." The mediator among these various interests was imagery, advanced mostly through newspapers. "Bleeding Kansas," SenGupta emphasized, "paved the path to the Civil War with compelling public images in the free states of civilization and savagery, freedom and dependence, North and South locked in mortal combat."[17]

In a recent historiographic essay on Bleeding Kansas, SenGupta called for a reconciliation of the "politics of sectional conflict with the social and cultural insights of the new history." She suggested that it was "time to break free of the tradition of simply narrating in ever greater detail the sequence of political events that constituted the Kansas conflict and asking instead, what did these events *mean?*" That would involve studying the dynamics between East and West, between politics and culture, and between popular ideology and sectional violence.[18] I have taken that to heart.

Etcheson also wrote specifically about Kansas. She covered the basics from Kansas-Nebraska to Harpers Ferry in a sophisticated way (it was the first thorough scholarly history of the subject in thirty years), but she also went beyond a catalog of the battles, deaths, and labyrinthine politics of Kansas Territory. Hers was at root an intellectual history with the thesis that the conflict in Kansas was talked about by both sides as being not so much about freedom for slaves as about freedom for white people. The issues in the territory turned on voting rights and on the rights of the sections in the Union. She asked also a most broad question: whether "Bleeding Kansas" itself was not an absurdity, in which blood was shed over slavery in a place where there were few slaves and where almost no one thought slavery could really exist. Her insight was that it was a battle more about principles than about real interests, and that those principles were defined by opinion leaders and framers.[19]

Allan Nevins referred to the "Melodrama in Kansas."[20] David Potter, in *The Impending Crisis*, noted of the 1850s: "For purposes of understanding what took place in the nation, it is possibly less important to know what happened in Kansas than to know what the American public thought was happening in Kansas." Instead of reacting to each other as they actually were, the people in each section responded to a "distorted mental image" of the other side.[21] James Malin spoke of "the power of fanatical propaganda—unending repetition of unscrupulous falsehoods—syllogizing in semantic confusion—intolerance masked under moral and religion symbolism—all leading the public to frustration and defeatism, which at long last found escape from stalemate in Civil War."[22] The political campaigns of the 1850s, wrote Roy Nichols, "focused public attention too sharply upon conflicting attitudes, exaggerating them to perilous proportions. . . . They aroused passion to such a pitch that only blood letting . . . could relieve the tension."[23] Like a free-market economy, laissez-faire politics has both an attractive vitality and a frightening hazardousness about it.

But did irresponsible rhetoric actually cause the Civil War? Could more responsible leadership have avoided it? Most historians writing after about 1950 concluded that those earlier scholars, from James Randall forward, who had blamed a "bungling generation" for stumbling into war from stupidity, venality, poor judgment, and "false images and fictitious issues" were making too much of an obviously unsatisfactory tone of discourse.[24] Historian Paul Gates argued in 1954 that the problems in territorial Kansas were not primarily due to the ideological battle over slavery at all. They arose from confused federal land and Indian policy, a premature political organization of Kansas, and a struggle over patronage.[25] Analysis among historians generally moved away from the study of public address toward that of private motive, from biography to economics, from quotation to statistics. That, and the insights emerging from the discoveries about genocide coming out of World War II and about the intransigence of racism that became so obvious during the American civil rights movement of the 1960s, made it seem much more likely that a bloodbath had been coming over slavery in America in the

1850s no matter what anyone said. Impersonal forces were leading to a conflict that no mistake could cause nor wisdom prevent.

That analysis, however, only put the bungling in a different relative context. It did not eliminate bungling as a serious complicating factor, particularly in creating the aroused public feeling that must go along with any crusade, however pedestrian some of its underlying causes. In the second volume of William Freehling's *The Road to Disunion*, published in 2007, there was again serious emphasis on the importance of individuals and the way they talked about things. "The following history," Freehling wrote, "shows that personal emotions exploded past impersonal drives. . . . Portraits of angry confrontations, not dissections of abstruse concepts, best lead to empathy with insulted combatants. Moreover, a dissection of detached forces, barren of accident or coincidences of personalities, erases too much of the human condition." When Preston Brooks beat Charles Sumner with his cane in the U.S. Senate chambers in 1856, it was not just because Sumner represented a political and sectional opponent. It was what Sumner specifically said in a speech and how he phrased it.[26] Learning to speak with one another in a civilized and respectful way may not be the key to ending the troubles of the human race, but it could not hurt.

Louis Menand, in his prize-winning study of Gilded Age ideas, *The Metaphysical Club*, emphasized the effect of war and wounds on Oliver Wendell Holmes Jr., the son of an 1850s literary idealist and himself later a Supreme Court justice. Holmes blamed his father and his father's generation, especially their idealistic talk, for the descent into a war, which he found quite non-redemptive. "It was not a matter of choosing sides," Menand concluded. "It was a matter of rising above the whole concept of sidedness." But it was no wonder that the majority of the country could not accomplish that feat, moved as they were by warring journalists and polarizing politics. The younger Holmes's pragmatic approach to the law rejected absolutes for the brand of sociological jurisprudence that emerged in his practice and in his classic text *The Common Law* (1881). To Holmes—largely, Menand thinks, due to the shock of his war experience—terms like "justice" and "fairness" became only "slogans, propping up particular strategies, not eternal principles."[27] That change in attitude must be calculated as a cost of war, of the preface to war, and of the language surrounding both.

Recently, in a review of works by Hannah Arendt on the "banality of evil," reviewer Jeremy Waldron noted the predominance of unsatisfactory rhetorical patterns still. He wrote in 2007: "The paraphernalia of thoughtlessness is legion. Clichés and jargon, stock phrases and analogies . . . the petrification of ideas—these are all devices designed to relieve the mind of the burden of thought, while maintaining the impression of intellectual cultivation." Arendt, he noted, "understood the insidious and nonspectacular aspects of practical and moral deterioration."[28]

Clearly, the masculine bravado, the libelous ad hominem tone of the press of the 1850s when reporting on Kansas Territory, precluded the "face-saving" that is the essence of successful diplomacy. Wrote a journalist in 1858: "The truth is, Human Nature is apt to be intolerant, and Human Nature has a good deal to do with the issues of the Press. . . . Men who are engaged in a struggle for a great object ought to be a little forbearing towards each other—watch over each other for good—tolerate opinions not at war with the Idea that combines them for a single purpose—beware of exalting every point of difference into a question of overshadowing importance, raising issues calculated to divide and embarrass."[29]

Any history is a selection and a simplification. "In the great experiment of democratic government that we are making," wrote a reporter at the *Boston Daily Advertiser* about Kansas in the summer of 1856, "there is so much of good and evil; so many destructive forces to cause alarm, and so much conservative power to inspire hope; so much license given to ignorance, falsehood, error and selfish passion, and so much intelligence and virtue to resist them, that the mind wavers as it contemplates the varied picture, hesitates to form a judgment, and ends in doubt as to the future; a painful and depressing feeling when related to a subject of so much magnitude and interest." The writer hoped that in the future, things would be clearer. "Opinion rules the world," he concluded, "and opinion is modified by advancing culture, so that the maxims and habits of one age become barbarisms in the next."[30]

However, the passage of the years has not lessened the dilemma for the historian. In 1857 there was a popular exhibit in St. Louis showing the whole of Kansas Territory and Indian Territory, complete with towns and bison-hunting sites, portrayed on about 12,000 square feet of canvas. The advertising claimed that it showed all the events that had transpired in Bleeding Kansas, including the burning and sacking of cities and the capture of prisoners.[31] One could wish that such a satisfactory and inclusive diorama could be contained between the covers of a book, but one must select.

At the core of the conflict was the Kansas-Nebraska Act, passed in amended form by a close vote in May 1854 following one of the most extensive, emotional, and well-publicized debates in American history. Many of the rhetorical themes that were to characterize the entire four-year mania about Kansas arose during this debate and were discussed in newspapers, magazines, and pamphlets. I therefore start with it, organizing at first by time rather than topic. The Kansas-Nebraska Act was the "organic law," the founding statute, for Kansas Territory as long as it remained a territory. During that time, the governor and the judicial administration were appointed by the federal administration, and the legislature was elected by the residents.

After a discussion of the role of the media in forming opinion and an illustration of how this worked with the Kansas-Nebraska debate, the middle of this book separates issues topically, and then returns to the final debate on Kansas, the one over the Lecompton Constitution. There, the goal is to reintegrate the issues and techniques that have been treated in detail separately.

Chapter 3 concerns the forced emigration to Kansas and the consequent national discussion of how representative the various votes in Kansas were or were not. How, in short, does one practically determine the will of the people in such a volatile situation? Chapter 4 is about religion, which all the warring Kansas factions used in their arsenal. The questions here are how one determines the will of God and how one applies it. Chapter 5 concerns the stereotyping and apotheosis of those few who lost their lives in Kansas. The military details in Kansas were tremendously magnified and their significance was remarkably exaggerated, with the result that the "civil war" imagined in Kansas eventually became real for the nation. Chapter 6 concerns views of slavery and of the relation of slavery to proper constitutional government and to a proper understanding of the origins and nature of the federal Union. Slavery was in, through, and behind all the debates on Kansas, whether in the foreground or only obliquely. Chapter 7 is about leadership and about the failure of leadership so emphasized by the "bungling generation" school of historians. Not only were the presidents and the Congress in Washington widely excoriated by all factions as nincompoops or worse, but a number of men, of various degrees of talent, dispatched to Kansas Territory as governors, had their careers and reputations ruined by their brief and painful tenure there. Could even a Lincoln have governed Kansas, or was it being driven by events and passions out of the control of any individual?

Because this is not another history of the raw facts at the scene, I provide here a quick sketch of the key events in and concerning Kansas Territory from 1854 to 1858 that evoked a substantial national media response. This short and strictly chronological account is for reference, makes no pretense of originality, and has no notes except insofar as something may be introduced that is not well known from multiple published sources.

The most salient element of the Kansas-Nebraska legislation was its effective repeal of the Missouri Compromise of 1820. The compromise had dictated that new territories north of 36 degrees 30 minutes latitude would enter the Union as free states, and those south of that line, as slave states. Largely through the efforts of Stephen Douglas, the concept of popular sovereignty took its place. This was an almost universally popular principle, though it was interpreted variously. In practice, it turned out to be enormously problematic. The principle held voting to be at the core of a republican form of government. Voting, one assumed, would determine the will of the people. That will, once determined, would be respected by the minority, whose rights in turn would be honored by the electoral winners. These assumptions were tested and failed in Kansas Territory. No frame is more prominent or more heatedly or regularly debated throughout the period than popular sovereignty in principle and practice.

Following the debates over the Kansas-Nebraska Act and as a direct result of opening the new territory of Kansas to a sort of competition to determine its "domestic institutions" (a euphemism for slavery), there was an escalation of organization by the sections to dominate the new region politically. Kansas meetings became standard fare throughout the eastern part of the United States. At first these meetings were primarily for the purpose of organizing and equipping actual emigrant parties. Later they included appeals for the relief of suffering settlers in Kansas. They were a feature of both North and South, and they sometimes involved state as well as private funding. Both sides claimed that this "artificial" organization and funding of emigrant groups was the original and fundamental source of the problems in Kansas Territory, as contrasted with the more peaceful progression in Nebraska Territory. Each section charged the other with being the instigator of this forced development, as contrasted with the "natural" and slower growth that would have taken place had actual settlers been allowed to wander in without encouragement.

The most common villain in regard to organized emigration was the New England Emigrant Aid Company, organized in 1854 in Massachusetts. This organization was perceived as embodying all the negative stereotypes of uptight New England reformist Puritanism and moneybags capitalism capable of buying an issue. While it has been demonstrated that the company was not very effective and that New Englanders constituted a very small part of the emigration to Kansas, here was a case where a demonizing stereotype was effectively created, manipulated, and communicated by the South and by the Democratic Party. Whether or not the Missouri Blue Lodges or Kickapoo Rangers were created earlier as intervening organizations was of little importance in framing the contemporary debate. Massachusetts and the Aid Company were on the defensive from the beginning.

However, Aid Company or not, emigration of people with a free-soil philosophy from Northern states was relatively slow. Therefore, the initial elections in Kansas Territory—for territorial delegate in November 1854 and for the territorial legislature in March 1855—were victories for the proslavery faction. This would probably have been the case even had the elections been fair, but they clearly were not. Investigating the facts of the March 1855 election especially became a real industry for those hoping for a free-state Kansas, but it was clear that nonresident Missourians intimidated voters and cheated at the polls. Few seats, however, were formally contested at the time on the grounds of fraud. The territorial governor, Andrew Reeder of Pennsylvania, certified most of those that were contested as valid and seated the legislative members.

This produced another watershed moment, as it led the free-state settlers in Kansas to declare this legislature "bogus" and to take the revolutionary, some even said treasonable, step of resisting its laws and decrees. They voted to do this at the Big Springs Convention in December of 1855, and from that time forward they solicited support from the East for their policy of mostly nonviolent resistance to what their side considered an illegitimate government.

The problem was that the territorial government was technically legal. All the forms had been followed. That gave the proslavery group, which took to calling itself the Law and Order Party, its own high moral ground from which to argue. No group, it said, was entitled, because it had lost an election, to flaunt the law. Such behavior would mean the end of civilization as it was then known in the United States and would lead to anarchy, disunion, or civil war.

The free-state faction not only opposed the existing legislature but established its own "state" legislature, wrote and adopted a "state" constitution (the so-called Topeka Constitution, after its place of origin), and elected a "governor," Charles Robinson. The faction regularly held elections in which only its own people voted and regularly boycotted the authorized territorial elections, which therefore overwhelmingly went to the proslavery faction. This naturally raised the issue of the legal status of groups refusing to participate in the electoral process. Were charges of widespread fraud true? And if they were true, was that sufficient justification for civil disobedience? By January of 1856 the two governors and two legislatures that characterized Kansas Territory in this era were in place. Two delegates with competing claims went to Congress from Kansas. In the end, amid an enormous national frenzy of backbiting, neither was seated.

There followed a series of what were sometimes called wars, but they hardly amounted to that. The so-called Wakarusa war during the winter of 1855 was initiated by the murders of free-state men by proslavery men. The killings were probably motivated by something other than politics, but they fed perfectly into the political hysteria that was building. A threat to the Free State Party and Emigrant Aid Company headquarters at Lawrence from about 1,000 militiamen, consisting mostly of Missourians, was averted by a "treaty" between Free State Party leaders Robinson and James Lane and then territorial governor Wilson Shannon in December 1855. Robinson said that instead of giving their arms to the Missourians, free-staters would give them the rifles' contents.

A second quasi-military action at Lawrence, creating much national publicity, took place in May 1856, a month of intense activity. A congressional investigation committee (the so-called Howard Commission) went to Kansas in March to take testimony concerning potential fraud in the 1855 elections. While they were there, Charles Robinson was imprisoned on a charge of treason, Senator Charles Sumner was beaten senseless in the U.S. Senate for giving an incendiary speech on the Kansas issue, and there was a militia attack on Lawrence, leading to the destruction of its main hotel and its outspoken newspaper, the *Herald of Freedom.* A salient subfeature, from the perspective of the national publicity it generated, was the shooting of Douglas County sheriff Samuel Jones while he was trying to serve warrants in Lawrence a few weeks before the attack. Jones was criticized in the Northern press for his abrasive personality and for having the temerity to try to arrest men who had forcibly "rescued" a prisoner from his custody. Jones survived the shooting and led the militia triumphantly into town to at last take his prisoners under the eyes of the whole nation. Late in the month John Brown and a group of followers took several individuals of proslavery persuasion from their homes in southeast Kansas and killed and mutilated them with short swords.

After that, the floodgates seemed to open on controversy, violence, and publicity. The number of newspaper articles concerning Kansas increased exponentially and stayed high for the next two years.[32] A raft of books on Kansas appeared, mostly generated in the Northern publishing centers. The national press talked of a civil war in Kansas. Congress argued over the contested delegate election, spent a great deal of time debating various bills for the possible admission of Kansas as a state, and carried on an acrimonious and controversial debate about denying the U.S. Army any appropriation unless the bill contained a provision that U.S. troops would not be used to quell so-called sedition by the free-state faction in Kansas. The army appropriation bill that year passed only after a special session was called. Meanwhile, private militias of both persuasions roamed the territory looting and burning. U.S. troops dispersed the Topeka legislature but did not quash its support. Both factions claimed to be the innocent victims of rape and pillage, to have been attacked without provocation by demented fanatics while peaceably putting in their crops and tending their firesides. Missourians blockaded the Missouri River and boarded steamboats to search emigrants from the Northern states for arms and to intimidate them generally. A new route through Iowa brought James Lane back to the state after an absence fund-raising in the East, and with him came another flood of emigrants. Stories of "martyrs" became standard fare, and the gorier the better. It mattered little that voting fraud was endemic all over the United States or that far fewer people were killed during the whole era of Bleeding Kansas than died in the Louisville or New Orleans election riots during the same period. The murders and the cheating and the pitched battles at "forts" and at little Kansan towns like Palmyra, Franklin, and Osawatomie were the fuel for manufacturing the "outrages" that kept the sensation alive.

The summer and fall of 1856 were marked by various small battles among militias in Kansas Territory. This phase ended with the more effective use of U.S. dragoons and the policy of still another territorial governor from Washington, D.C., John Geary, to disband the private militias. People seemed to turn for a time to land speculation as the Indian reserves in the area began to be sold at auction and the price of town lots increased. Robinson temporarily resigned as free-state governor.

In 1857, however, several developments heated things up again. William Sherrard, who, over Geary's objection, was to replace Jones as Douglas County sheriff, threatened a meeting of the legislature with a firearm and was shot and killed. This led to Geary's resignation. His replacement, Robert

Walker, was the most famous individual to serve as Kansas governor, and his eloquence, nerve, and attempts at evenhandedness made him a lightning rod for publicity. Walker convinced the free-state faction that there could be a relatively honest election in Kansas. Consequently, free-staters voted in the October elections for territorial legislature and won a majority. The old legislature, however, had authorized a constitutional convention, whose delegates were chosen in an election free-state voters boycotted. The product of that convention, which was held at the territorial capital of Lecompton, was the infamous Lecompton Constitution, whose erratic career caused the arguments and the rhetoric concerning Kansas to peak.

There were numerous debatable issues concerning the Lecompton Constitution. Was the legislature that authorized the Lecompton constitutional convention itself legitimately elected? Should the entire constitution be submitted to the people of Kansas for confirmation or rejection before it went to Congress? Who were the people of Kansas for the purposes of voting? Was Congress free to go behind the official process, or must it accept whatever constitution the process created under the official nonintervention policy of the Democratic Party?

The facts of the process complicated it further. There was a vote on the constitution in Kansas Territory in December 1857. The vote was not, however, on the whole constitution, but only on the slavery clause. Voters got the Hobson's choice of voting for the Lecompton Constitution with slavery or without slavery, but not of voting down the constitution itself. Some claimed that in either case slavery would be a de facto fact of life. Free-state voters boycotted that election, and the "constitution with slavery" provision passed overwhelmingly. But then, on January 4, 1858, came a second election, authorized by the "new legislature," meeting in a special session whose very authorization led to the dismissal of a temporary territorial secretary. This election allowed an up-or-down vote on the Lecompton Constitution as a whole, and at the same time on state officers under the Lecompton Constitution if it survived. The proslavery faction boycotted that election, and the vote went overwhelmingly against the Lecompton Constitution. The constitution and both votes went forward to the U.S. Congress, which was supposed, somehow, to hash it out. Meanwhile there were new guerrilla activities in southeast Kansas and one last horrific outrage, the shooting of a group of unarmed free-state farmers rounded up along the Marais des Cygnes River. The complications and the emotions were extreme.

Territorial Governor Walker, who thought that the new U.S. president, James Buchanan, backed him, went out on a limb by supporting the submission of the full Lecompton Constitution to a vote of the people. Buchanan, who decided to back Lecompton to appease the South and because at least the forms of popular sovereignty had been followed, subsequently dismissed Walker, who then gave out interviews and went on a speaking tour.

In Congress another lengthy debate on Kansas took place, resulting ultimately in a compromise measure, created by a conference committee, called the English bill. It provided for a vote in Kansas on the Lecompton Constitution. Should the people pass it, Kansas would be admitted immediately as a state and would get the federal lands and offices that went with that status. Buchanan's view was that the people of the new state could then immediately revise the constitution to eliminate slavery, despite some provisions in the document itself preventing that. Should they reject the constitution, Kansas would have to wait, as was the general rule for territories, until it had a population of about 93,000. At the election in August 1858, the Lecompton Constitution was soundly defeated, and the Kansas issue suddenly and almost completely disappeared from the national news. Instead, people were interested in debates between Illinois senatorial candidates Stephen Douglas, hurt as he was by the failure of popular sovereignty, and newcomer Abraham Lincoln. People in Kansas turned their attention either to their farms or to the goldfields discovered in what was then far-western Kansas Territory, up against Pike's Peak.

Such were the main facts.[33] They were much filtered in the public understanding, and any one observer had an incomplete and biased view of them. The purpose here is to examine the views that were conveyed through the media and the images and stories that constituted them. The *St. Louis Daily Missouri Republican* expressed in 1858 the by-then forlorn hope that newspaper readers would be sophisticated enough to avoid "that volatility, which is impatient of ordinary restraint and flies for relief from evil, whether real or imaginary, to the first remedy, which is suggested by the cunning of the designing few to the passions of the less considerate many."[34] The public, it turned out, was not that sophisticated.

CHAPTER 1
MANUFACTURING OPINION

———•◦•———

Some Americans thought that New York City in 1858 bled more than Bleeding Kansas and that the eastern philanthropists raising money to clothe, feed, and house the pioneers for freedom in that western territory should be turning their attention to the waifs and beggars on the streets of Gotham. The Kansas issue, the cynical said, was a "humbug," a "stalking horse," cranked up by the office-seekers in Washington who in 1854 had destroyed the Missouri Compromise. It was sustained by a media machine, North and South, that manufactured hyperbole and falsehood faster than it conveyed reliable information. The United States in 1858 could focus on promising marvels of a wondrous age—the Atlantic telegraph, the Pacific railroad, oceangoing steamers, a flood of California gold, Admiral Matthew Perry's opening of Japan, the building of the Suez Canal, even the modest projects of restoring George Washington's Mount Vernon, finishing the Washington Monument, or planning Central Park—rather than wallowing in such emotional and dead-end distractions as the Free-Love issue, the Nicaragua filibuster, and the Kansas imbroglio.[1] Wasn't it the better part of wisdom to avoid conversations about politics and religion, dangerous topics that filled every editorial on Kansas? After all, what a fraud the outrageous events surrounding Kansas elections and constitutional conventions had made of the promise of popular sovereignty contained in the organic act that formed the Territory! In the light of harsh recent history in the field, what an insult the idealism of the earliest proposed Kansas Territory motto had come to seem— "Populi voce nata" (Born of the popular will).[2]

People in the rest of the country had grown tired of hearing about Kansas, so much so that newspaper editors apologized for bringing it up again. Wrote an editor in Columbus, Georgia, in the spring of 1857: "The frequency with which this subject has been pressed upon the consideration of our readers is excused and justified by its overshadowing importance to the South."[3] Farming magazines, literary journals, business publications, Christian newsletters, fashion sheets, even the *American Phrenological Journal* ran articles on Kansas more or less constantly. The *New York Herald* alone had by 1858 published 4,042 articles and 635 editorials on Kansas in the four years since the passage of the Kansas-Nebraska Act. By contrast there had been no articles during the period on New Yorkers Herman Melville or Walt Whitman. Melville wrote *Moby Dick* in 1851, and Whitman in 1855 published a little volume of poetry called *Leaves of Grass*, which subsequent ages seemed to regard as of more importance than some of the details about Kansas.[4] The *New York Daily Times* did have a casual little piece on the "brawny, rough and original" work of Whitman in November 1856, after a copy of his book, left at its office, had languished for a year waiting for a break in the political news.[5]

Attention to Kansas did eventually fade. In the next four years, between the debate on the Lecompton Constitution in 1858 and the admission of Kansas Territory as a state in 1861, the *Herald* ran only 198 news and 41 opinion articles on the subject. Kansas had not changed in physical area, but the shadow it cast on the national consciousness was suddenly greatly diminished.

The 1858 season had promised well for sensation. It produced "as astonishing a crop as was ever forced, under glass, in a hot house, under the . . . influence of steam." But its potential was, a reporter noted, nipped by a killing frost in that an unusual percentage of the reports were simply not true. "What would [Horace] Greeley [editor of the *New York Daily Tribune*] do without his outrages—their brown toasted free State men and hung clericals—which they are accustomed to partake of for breakfast?"[6]

The reason for the change was partly that the news from Kansas Territory was less exciting. An observer kidded that the "outrage crop" had failed in 1858 when some of the rumors of war between the Free State militia and U.S. dragoons in southeast Kansas fizzled. Many Kansas martyrs, it turned out, had been killed by "computation" and then were resurrected.[7] Kansas, said a journalist in Dayton, Ohio, had "become a synonym of bloodless wars, and bloody telegraphic dispatches."[8] Some reports, such as the one that Jim Lane, head of the Kansas Free State militia, was a Mormon spy in direct contact with Brigham Young, were a little much for any newspaper reader to swallow whole.[9]

Boredom with the Kansas phenomenon contributed to the decline in the number of stories and in the intensity of reaction to them. "Kansas has occupied the field long enough," the *Herald* editors wrote. "The people of the United States are a practical people, and when a great political question is

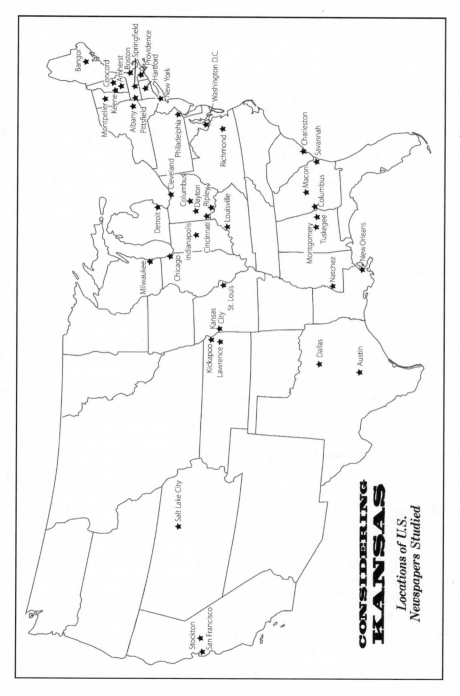

Considering Kansas: Locations of U.S. Newspapers Studied. Map by David Rohr.

settled they drop it. They do not care to waste their time in fighting mere shadows and empty abstractions."[10]

True, the struggle itself was not quite over. The so-called Marais des Cygnes massacre, a cold-blooded shooting of unarmed free-state men by proslavery marauders, occurred in May 1858. Survivors' accounts, detailing how they had been marched into a ravine, lined up, and shot, again filled newspapers nationwide with a late-blooming, but authentic, Kansas "outrage."[11] Jim Lane, the free-state leader all loved to hate, killed a neighbor over rights to a well and was tried in the national press as well as a local court. True, William Tomlinson's 1859 book *Kansas in Eighteen Fifty-Eight* did not generate an interest parallel to that in William Phillips's 1856 volume *The Conquest of Kansas by Missouri and Her Allies*, but the guerrilla actions in southeast Kansas in 1858 were still filled with evocative incident. More significantly, the hopes that the Kansas issue had really been "settled" by the political compromises of that year and that the broader sectional issue for which Kansas was an early battleground would be resolved without blood proved chimerical. And it was unquestionably true that Kansas was important. "Events occurring directly under our eyes do not assume that greatness or grandeur which belong to them, and with which the future so fully invests them," wrote a Chicago newspaperman. "But wearisome as these events may be . . . they must be detailed, dwelt upon, elaborated, until the public sees their importance, and grasps hold of them in earnest."[12]

The Kansas drama, many averred, had ended in comedy. It was time for those who wept for her to wipe their eyes "and smile upon the world once more."[13] People begin to weary, wrote a Richmond observer, of such exclusive attention to the "intrusive and importunate squabbles of a remote territory."[14] "What is Kansas," asked Indiana congressman William English in 1858, "that she should have caused all this turmoil and confusion throughout the land for the past four years?"[15] President Buchanan agreed. "Kansas," the president said in 1857, "has for some years occupied too much of public attention. It is high time that this should be directed to far more important objects."[16] The *Providence Daily Post* wrote that reporting on Kansas was "unpleasant work, and we would gladly avoid it; for the reader must know that we are quite as sick of Kansas headings, and Kansas histories, and Kansas quarrels, and Kansas gabble, as we can possibly be." There was "a sickening, senseless, soulless" cry of "Kansas! Kansas! Bleeding, suffering, groaning, shrieking Kansas! Enslaved Kansas! Outraged Kansas! Who is not sick of this sickening, senseless, soulless cry! When shall it have an end?" The editor in

Rhode Island had had "a surfeit of Kansas speeches. . . . We are tired of paying for the trash that is sent to us over the wires, from Washington. We are
tired of devoting our columns to Kansas, to the exclusion of more interesting
matter. We are tired of waiting for the business of the people to be attended
to."[17] The "harps of a thousand strings" that played always the dreary Kansas
tune, were, wrote a reporter in Concord, New Hampshire, creating the impression that New England should be more interested in the "knavery and
humbuggery" of people in Kansas than in their own taxes and public im-
provements.[18] Newspapers and magazines, said a writer to the editor, had
"freighted whole cargoes of lies, and loaded down huge trains of cars from
the far West, with Kansas hobgoblins and ghosts of freemen by border ruffians slain, and have employed a whole horde of political cannibals in the land
to concoct curses by the acre, to pour out upon devoted democratic heads."[19]
It was wearing, this hysteria. "We have lived," wrote one editor, "for four
years, as it were, under the peals of an alarm bell."[20]

Be that as it may, at its height the Bleeding Kansas phenomenon was a national obsession. It is certain, the *New York Daily Tribune* had claimed during
the high excitement after a militia raid on the free-state stronghold of
Lawrence, Kansas Territory, in 1856, "that these are historical times, and
that Lexington and Concord are not more familiar names in our history than
will hereafter be that of Lawrence."[21] The Kansas conflict was seen not as a
local matter but as one of national, perhaps universal, human significance,
involving as it did the issues of slavery, constitutional law, and sectional
identity.

Said a journalist in Georgia early in 1856: "Kansas is now the focal point to
which the whole nation is directing its attention. There, now, lies the struggle for supremacy."[22] For the South, it was often said, Kansas was of no less
import than the pass at Thermopylae had been for the ancient Greeks defending against an invasion from Persia.[23] "This idea," wrote an Alabama
editor a year later, "was the fuel which made the political cauldron boil over
in this section. Bass, tenor and treble all sang the same eternal chorus—
Kansas, Kansas, Kansas!"[24]

It was the same in the North. An 1857 editorial in the *Daily Cincinnati
Commercial* said, "The news from Kansas is eagerly read throughout the
Union. Many affect a total indifference to the stories told of 'Bleeding
Kansas,' and assume to be exceedingly incredulous relative to anything said
pro or *con* the pro-slavery or anti-slavery parties in the disputed territory,
but all persons of ordinary intelligence know full well that the contest in

progress in that quarter is of importance beyond the reach of exaggeration."[25] Said L. S. Foster of Connecticut in the U.S. Senate chamber during the 1856 debates on Kansas: "The territory of Kansas still continues painfully to absorb the public attention. It so overshadows all other subjects, foreign and domestic, that it can almost be said to be the only question before the country."[26] Samuel Cox, a member of the House of Representatives at the time, thought that then and later "the whole country became a Kansas."[27]

Strangely, although some stories were invented out of whole cloth and other minor incidents were much exaggerated in the reporting, the outrage that later received the most attention was little mentioned by the contemporary press. In May 1856 John Brown and a company of others killed five proslavery settlers, in cold blood in the dead of night with short swords, along Pottawatomie Creek in southeastern Kansas Territory. The Pottawatomie Creek massacre would seem ideal fuel for the propaganda machine of the South. Yet at the time it was hardly mentioned. It appeared in correspondents' letters now and then, but it seldom reached the level of editorial comment.

David Reynolds, in his recent biography of Brown, has suggested that the "real horror" of the Pottawatomie incident did not stand out amid the wild reporting of general mayhem. Ironically, the newspaper reader could hardly tell the real from the artificial, and perhaps preferred the latter.[28] It was not so obvious then as it was later that Brown was "on the right side of history" and therefore fitted to heroic rather than criminal status.[29]

But although the propaganda machine seems to have missed Brown at first, it did not miss much. Nor did it neglect any story from squeamishness. It seemed smart to say bold things, mean things, insulting things. Sensation circulated newspapers, as did an obsession with an issue that everyone was talking about and that grew until it was nearly unstoppable.

Political simplification through the creation of epithets and catch phrases became a fine art in conveying the Kansas issue to what was called "the public mind." Some of the phrases, such as "Bleeding Kansas" or "Beecher's Bibles" (the Sharps rifles sent to free-state partisans), are familiar to readers of national history a century later. But these do not begin to span the field of phrase making. There were policy mantras, like "nonintervention" and "popular sovereignty." There were references to supposed practices, such as "hireling labor," "howling," "clap-trap," "infernal abortion," "imbroglio," "hireling clergy," "bug-bear," "political ding-dong," "demagoguism," "fanaticism," "humbug," and "slaveocracy." There were designations aimed at enemies. Those hoping that Kansas would enter the Union without slavery were called by their detractors "Black Republicans," "nigger-worshippers," "Lords of the Loom," "Mongrel Adventurers," "higher-law proponents," "screechers," "croakers," and "freedom shriekers." The other side marched through newspaper columns as "border ruffians," "bowie knife gentry," "slave drivers," "Sham Democrats," "bogus legislators," "fiends," "Lords of the Lash," and "Barons."

It all seemed a kind of play in masks, a "theatre of strife and tumult," as one politician called it.[30] One traveler to Kansas, a bishop in the Methodist Episcopal Church South, wrote that he had been "perplexed" by what he had read about the place but became "confounded" by what he heard on the steamboat going there. "The honest did not know what was true, and the designing manufactured to order. There was no limit to tales but the power of invention; and the public mind, excited and exasperated, was credulous to weakness. . . . The thread of history became more knotty and tangled."[31]

The name-calling, exaggeration, and outright irresponsibility were all part of scooping the competition and of a kind of manly and vigorous journalism. The editor of the *Daily Cincinnati Commercial* observed in 1855, "The attentive reader of the public journals of the day cannot, if he is free from prejudice, escape a knowledge of the fact that there is a pro-Slavery fanaticism at the South which, like the anti-Slavery fanaticism of the North, is constantly laboring to stamp its own features upon the popular mind, and to infuse its spirit into every manifestation of the will of the people. Gifted with intense activity, it is ever ready to take the initiative in the political movements of the time, and to impress upon them its own extreme and violent character."[32] That character came largely through the press in the words of political and opinion leaders quoted there.

Many people eventually realized that some bitter words could not be taken back, and that there were positions so extreme that compromise would never again be a possibility. But there was the hope that all of a sudden there would be a breakthrough in negotiations, the audience would become bored, and the whole issue would be yesterday's stale news. Few saw how deadly the disagreement was until the Union actually came apart in a bloody civil war.

When the editor of the *New York Herald*, James Gordon Bennett, entered his office in New York City in 1858, it was most often to write an editorial about the Lecompton Constitution, a proslavery document for the organization of the potential state of Kansas that had been cooked up in the tiny hill town of Lecompton, on the Kansas River west of Lawrence. Bennett did not have to explain to his readers where Lecompton was or why it was important. Kansas provided much of the copy fed to the *Herald*'s ten-cylinder Hoe press for distribution to the paper's 90,000-sheet local circulation.[33] "For the next week or two," Bennett wrote late in 1857, "the news from Kansas will be of greater importance to the American people than all the intelligence from the rest of the world."[34]

While the *Herald* opposed the extension of slavery into the territories, it professed to be willing to abide by the decision of the residents there. It did not support the extreme egalitarian views of some abolitionists and some Northern newspapers. The U.S. Constitution, Bennett wrote, was an Anglo-Saxon document, and there was nothing in it suggesting it favored the "amalgamation" of the races.[35] The country, as another editor once put it, was "for Sam and not for Sambo."[36] The African race, the *Herald* wrote, was an inferior one, marked so by the creator, and had to remain in an inferior position even when free and living in a white society. In that the *Herald* agreed with even the most virulent Southern editors. The cry about the horrors of slavery, Bennett thought, was a "mockery and a snare" that would lead to civil war and/or race war. "And all these ultimate consequences are interwoven into the treacherous web of this Kansas controversy. The sectional agitations, jealousies, and revenges of half a century, are concentrated in this Kansas question."[37] People bought the *Herald* for a penny. It was read by urban crowds and pleased readers of the little weeklies across the country that copied its pieces.

Not that there was not plenty of criticism in the Northern journals of Southern society and the slave institutions that poisoned it. Henry Ward Beecher, the charismatic pastor of the Plymouth Church in Brooklyn, wrote in 1856 that on the battlefield in Kansas were arrayed on the one side the representatives of civilization and on the other those of barbarism. "On the one side stand men of liberty, Christianity, industry, arts, and of universal prosperity; on the other are the waste and refuse materials of a worn-out Slave State population—men whose ideas of society and civilization are comprised in the terms, a rifle, a horse, a hound, a slave, tobacco and whiskey." Northern men came to Kansas with books, built towns, and converted the wilderness to a garden. Southern men introduced a "leprosy" that "sucks the blood from everything it touches." Nothing could fatten on the slave system, Beecher intoned, "except the cunning few that sit upon the middle of the web—swollen spiders—while the rest swing in the edges thereof, mere skeleton insects." The Northern emigrants to Kansas, the preacher thought, were

on the best errand and the Southern emigrants on the worst that ever engaged humankind.[38]

Similar sentiments, expressed in less highfalutin prose, were legion in
the North. A Chicago man thanked God that his city did not and could not
have any trade with the South. He wrote that Chicago would rather work with
the small towns that freedom would create along its railroads than have all of
rival Cincinnati's commerce with neighboring slave state Kentucky.[39]

Even though the *Herald* was far from taking the most radical of Northern
positions, editors of Southern newspapers did not copy Bennett's pieces
much, except to sneer at them. Nor was the South pleased at the rumor late
in 1857 that Bennett might be appointed governor of Kansas Territory.[40] Another sort of opinion factory was operating in the South. How oppressed the
South felt, and at the same time how superior to the North, where the grasping, pecuniary Yankee groveled for coins in his polluted, crime-ridden
cities! "Imagine the hirelings of Boston, Salem, New Haven, Concord and
other dens of Abolitionism crowded together in one indiscriminate jam, all
living by the excitement they make; and then ask yourself where the trouble
they depend on for bread will end."[41]

Wrote the *Richmond South:* "The iniquities of New York can be compre-
hended only by an imagination familiar with vice and crime in every con-
ceivable shape and in every possible excess." The "hideous deformities and
depravities" of society there were characterized by worship of fashion, prostitution of the pulpit, and obsession with murder.[42] A Georgia editor commented, "This Babylon of the United States is always in a bubble and a stew.
Murder, Robberies, Burglaries, and Adulteries form the staple of its editorial news. Soon as one billow of excitement breaks and subsides, another
follows in its wake. It is said, every dog has its day and the converse in New
York is true—every day has its dog."[43] Yet New York City was only concentrated Northern America, and Northern America illustrated the foibles of
freedom. Commented a writer for the *Muscogee Herald* in Alabama: "Free Society. We sicken of the name. What is it but a conglomeration of GREASY ME-
CHANICS, FILTHY OPERATIVES, SMALL FISTED FARMERS and moonstruck THEORISTS?
All the Northern and especially the New England States are devoid of society
fitted for well-bred gentlemen. . . . This is your free society which Northern
hordes are endeavoring to extend into Kansas."[44]

More extreme still were comments in the *New Orleans Daily Delta,* a newspaper representing the most extreme of Southern opinion. New York, its editor wrote in 1855, was celebrating the "saturnalia of fanaticism and

humbug," and the "quid nuncs?" (what nows?) of the nation gathered at its museums, baby fairs, and monkey shows, where a "thoughtless herd of loafers" could sightsee. Glib speakers and irresponsible newspapers fed the "stupid geese," and "insane and criminal convocations" were held on such topics as women's rights.[45] Never had there been such "nervous excitability" caused by "intellectual vagaries" as now. Vegetarians and meat eaters, churchmen and spiritualists, "hards" and "softs," prohibitionists and immigrants—all were at each other in the "universal rolling and tossing of society in a trough of opinion, like a dismasted ship in a tempest."[46] "Philanthropy," the paper claimed, was the most abused word in the language: "It has no longer a mild . . . face, but is merely a grinning mask, under which every scoundrel can shuffle his prayers or mutter his hypocritical petitions." Could not Horace Greeley leave the South alone? Did not the editor of the *Tribune* have enough spectacular material writing about his own city "with its pestiferous inhabitants—its children drinking brandy from the mother's breast—its 'free' negroes sweltering in steaming passes of plague and filth—its rot-gut carouses and its dung-hill delights . . . stinking in the nostrils of God"?[47] It was time, New Orleans writers thought, "that the land of chivalry and tolerance should raise its voice and hand against the growth of bigotry and moon-struck fanaticism in its midst."[48]

The editors of the *Richmond Enquirer*, William F. Ritchie and Robert Pryor, held forth often on the same theme. Just as Northern editors regularly downplayed any abolitionist opinions in their zealous promotion of the rule of popular sovereignty for the territories, so Southern newspapers tended to talk obliquely about the enormous issue of slavery in reference to Kansas. Instead, they harped on the general inferiority of the North.

The North had a culture of "superficial refinement," the Richmond editors said, that had come from a system of "incomplete and irreligious education." Instead of fitting citizens for the discharge of their obligations to society, their education bred a feeling "of uneasy discontent . . . and instructed them in the mischievous arts of social agitation." That word, "agitation," so much used by the South to characterize the activity of the Northern abolitionists about the Kansas issue, is telling. Restlessness supposedly arose from the urban centers in the North. They were the "pseudo-free" states, the editors concluded, really only free for chaos, change, discontent, and disorganization.[49] There was no fixed policy there, nothing that anyone believed for more than two years running. The "extraordinary activity of the human mind" had in that atmosphere turned on itself and become a "chronic disease."[50] People pried into the affairs of their neighbors, which were none of their business, and into the systems of distant states, where they had even less legitimate compass, out of an endless, destructive curiosity.[51] Thus, any serious moral questions posed by the North were reduced in much of the Southern press to sociopsychological symptoms.

The "Red Republican Party" of the North, which had by 1856 turned the Kansas issue into a "Fremont and Freedom" campaign, was, according to the Richmond newspapermen, "a mere combination of the thousand Isms that infect its society," from Fourierism to spiritualism to Free Love–ism. Greeley, they noted, talked about evaluating everything from the perspective of "passional attraction." No wonder he flitted from fad to fad. No wonder the "political preacher" Henry Ward Beecher eventually ended up in court charged with adultery. "Cut every human relation which has anywhere grown uneasy, sheer asunder; reduce whatsoever was compulsory to voluntary, whatsoever was permanent among us to the condition of nomadics; in other words loosen by assiduous wedges in every joint, the whole fabric of social existence, stone from stone, till at last all now being loose enough it can . . . be overset by sudden outbursts of revolutionary rage." That was the "Kansas agitation" in a philosophical nutshell. It was a symptom of the failure of free society generally. The best representative of such a people was not the president of the Republic but rather P. T. Barnum.[52] People who would believe anything would believe everything.

It was no surprise that the columns of the *Richmond Enquirer* often contained attacks on Bennett's *New York Herald*. Everyone knew, the *Enquirer* said, that the conduct of the *Herald* was controlled by the "basest instincts of personal corruption" and that the *Herald* supported any party "that addresses the strongest appeal to its venal passions" and to those of its readers. The *Herald* had been "born of the brain of the most dastardly and degraded villain that ever dishonored humanity," and it was "nursed in its infancy by the ruined reputation of innocent women." Its crime and infidelity stories gave it "the vigorous growth of the fungus offshoot of rotten matter," which soon "satisfied the sordid appetite of the blind-eye ghoul who pocketed the profits." Thus, the newspaper "born in a brothel" began to have higher ambitions, yet it continued in pursuing these causes to exhibit "the same cruel contempt of human sensibility, the same sordid impulses, and utter prostitution of principle" that had always been its central characteristic.[53]

The *Herald*'s readers, "trained to regard hyperbole as eloquence, and extravagant abuse as satire," in reading about Kansas as much as about crime,

looked for "beastly gratification."[54] Kansas, associated as it was with "turbu-
lence, lawlessness, assassinations and strife" fed the fever, the "omnivorous
appetite of the age." It provided "a source of apparently inexhaustible sup-
plies to the newsmongers and caterers for the repast of such intellectual
cannibals as luxuriate on railroad accidents, frightful conflagrations, bloody
reencounters, civil commotions, famine, pestilence and plague."[55] Progress
itself was a mixed blessing: "We are in the midst of the mightiest intellectual,
moral, and social movement that the world has ever known, whether we consider the ability of its leaders, the zeal and number of its proselytes, or the
destructiveness of its purpose."[56]

The *Enquirer,* for all its broader philosophy, did address the question of
slavery and the "dragon of abolition" bluntly enough now and then.[57] It
quoted Aristotle, John Locke, and the Bible in justifying slavery.[58] It took
note of Northern racism and of the hypocrisy of advocating freedom for a
people to whom most Americans, even among the free-state faction in
Kansas, were not willing to grant social or political equality.[59] Why should
blacks in the North be any more happy, better employed, or better dressed
than the immigrants living in slums and ghettos in its cities? "Ours is a far
more ancient and common form of society than that at the North—justified
alike by human and Divine authority."[60] African slavery, the *Enquirer* held,
fed and clothed the world and had done more for civilization than the discovery of North America.[61] What kind of society, the paper asked, would the
South be if its white chivalric knights, the members of a master race, were
forced to "clean the streets, work the roads, stand behind the chairs of gentlemen at table, brush their clothes, black their boots, and hold their
horses"?[62] None but a madman would be ready to dissolve the Union in civil
war to emancipate the Negro.[63]

The *Herald* and the *Enquirer* were only representative, not unique. One
could quote to the same effect other Northern papers, such as the *New York
Daily Tribune* or the *Detroit Daily Free Press,* or other Southern sheets, such as
the *Charleston Mercury* or the *New Orleans Daily Delta.* It is, however, true also
that at any level of nuance and detail, the range of opinion was considerable,
even within sections or factions. And, as we shall see, the emotional, even
mythological, filters through which such information passed were many and
finely grained.

Sometimes words seemed to come loose from their moorings, to be used
in all sorts of unaccustomed and dangerous ways. The *New Orleans Daily
Picayune* commented in 1858 that Kansas rhetoric had become "a perilous

abuse of words . . . when they can have no application but one of contumely and no effect but one of irritation." There were too many "cant words" that stigmatized anyone who disagreed as an inveterate enemy. The *Picayune* compared such language to that used in the intestine discord at Jerusalem when it was under siege by Titus in AD 70.[64] Northern books, led by Harriet Beecher Stowe's best seller *Uncle Tom's Cabin*, tended toward sensational and sentimental romance. Young women threw off "saucy paragraphs" in a smart style reflecting on private character and "heart-burnings," which were none of the public's business. And this same style, short on facts and long on passion, became a model for political discourse. "They hang out their sign; flaunt their banners, with its detestable mottoes and shibboleths."[65]

The great weapon of what was called "stereotyped slang" was the "epithet," or simple, vivid, metaphoric word or phrase.[66] "To damn with an epithet," wrote the *New York Daily Times*, "is the shortest form of political logic." It was easy to call advocates of any truth or opponents of error fanatics and thus to dismiss their points. "Dissenters may expose your fallacies, refute your arguments but by the well chosen and oft-repeated epithet, as by a talisman, all the glory of the contest remains your own." There was no secret to this technique; it was used every day. "It acts like an opiate on all the otherwise decided movements of the day. It crushes enterprise, condemns the earnest and patriotic to obscurity, and leaves the stage of politics for knaves and fools, the Punches and Judies of routine to caper upon."[67]

The appeal did not have to be simple or unsophisticated. By "perversion of terms" and a "Jesuitical casuistry" in argument, black could be changed to white and evil to good. "The infamy of crime," the *Louisville Daily Journal* concluded, "is increased in proportion to the intelligence and education of its perpetrators." The most sophisticated and most effective Northern journals were of smooth address. They were humble and mild, in contrast to the "coarse epithets and abusive denunciations of the less wily and more intemperate."[68] These "plausible sophistries," contributed their part to the fever.[69]

The *Washington Union* called all such speech "propagandism." That was not an intellectual word, the editor said, but it expressed a force that was endowed with the power and authority of truth. The national capital was filled with those who had great visions, who had acquired an abstract conception of what was right, "without reflecting that the affairs of society are not, like a desk or wardrobe, made to be taken to pieces and again put together, with such alterations as may suit the mechanic." Crusades were always tyrannical.

"We have no faith," the editor wrote, "in the efficacy of political ethics which are thus propagated, like poultry, by artificial heat—hot-house productions of sickly constitution and life. They may have the form and features of those of natural growth, but they contain little of the vital principle, and at most serve to feed pampered and depraved appetites." The newspaper recommended a careful reading of Edmund Burke's reflections on the French Revolution as an object lesson in the dangers of unchecked enthusiasm and self-righteousness.[70]

The *St. Louis Daily Missouri Democrat*, close to the conflict in Kansas, spoke of "fierce excitement" and a "stormy conflict of minds." According to the paper, the spirit of the Puritans had ascended to the pulpit as in the days of Cotton Mather, and lecturers were perambulating around the North raising subscriptions for Kansas. "Every item of intelligence, every floating rumor, every reported affray in that far off territory is sought by news-gatherers, and made to flash along the telegraphic wires from Independence to Boston." In Congress there was a "heavy swell" caused by "every ripple" in Kansas.[71] Newspapers contained mean and relatively unvarying names for free-staters in Kansas, repeated ad nauseam: "abolitionists," "damned Yankees," "negrophilists," "God-forsaken traitors," or "nigger thieves." A Kansas territorial governor could comfortably be called an "unscrupulous and pig-headed toady," a "tool," or an "inebriate."[72] "Anyone who had ever read these journals," an editor commented, "by shaking the foregoing epithets among a moderate quantity of monosyllables, disyllables, and trisyllables, will form an accurate conception of their editorial articles. Be careful, however, not to throw in a single truth and to mix with the nicknames a sufficient quantity of ungrammatical expressions."[73] The Kansas issue was a "foolish frenzy" and an "absurdity" that was being forced by a "race of political crusaders" on a nation that should have more common sense.[74] It would be tragic should "patriotism" become a meaningless word, but, like so many other words, it was being devalued by overuse in the "ebullitions of the political cauldron" stirred by the Kansas issue. It seemed that "smothered and pent-up volcanic fires" would explode and damage the economy of St. Louis and many other commercial cities. Citizens must guard against "specious pretense," "fallacious reasoning," and "unreflecting sympathy" advanced by "political harlequins." They must guard against joining the "swell of popular passions" driven by words.[75] The alternative was that history itself, the history of their own times as viewed by the future, might be resolved into a "gigantic myth, into a congeries of subjective fancies and daydreams, a brilliant but baseless phantasmagoria, a shadowy procession of unrealities which but cheat the senses and make a bitter mockery of our rational nature."[76]

Northern papers used different examples but did not disagree about the cant. The *Philadelphia Public Ledger & Daily Transcript* commented in 1856 on what it called "the literature of disorder." The revolutions of 1848 in Europe had communicated their spirit of individual self-gratification to American newspapers, "filtered free of its grosser and more sensual ideas, but still chemically poisoned with its denial of duty." Once newspapers convinced their readers that there was a "higher law," violence and disorder began, for example, with the vigilance committees in San Francisco and the militia battles in Kansas.[77] Too many "poison darts" were being flung, and it was impossible "that the criminations and recriminations which are now bandied back and forth can pass away and leave no scars behind."[78] "It seemed," said a writer for *Putnam's Monthly Magazine of American Literature, Science & Art*, "as if all the warring winds of opinion were loose."[79]

This verbal mania on Kansas seemed a species of terror. "We are in the midst of it," wrote a journalist in Detroit. "It overshadows—it surrounds us. Its agents, its servants, its ministers, its allies, its armies, its officials, its priests, its police, are everywhere around us and among us, whispering, persuading, appealing, warning, threatening, driving, 'subduing' to its purposes, a long-suffering, too credulous, and too selfish people." The "whole machinery of terror" was in operation in Kansas and rode "rampant and blaspheming over the land. . . . It sneers at humanity, tramples on moderation, scoffs at religion, and defies everything. It answers argument by abuse; reason by the bludgeon; opposition by murder." Terror blinded men: "They mistake shadow for substance and, seeking salvation, rush upon destruction."[80]

The "raw" news of Kansas came down the Missouri River to St. Louis, where it first went out on the "tell-lie graph," as it was jokingly called, and where it appeared in the city's big dailies, the *Democrat* and the *Republican*. The news filled columns of tiny print in these papers, which exercised only an amateur degree of "spin." But soon enough that material was cooked by more expert stirrers in other urban centers.[81]

An important study of the influence of the telegraph in early-nineteenth-century America, Menahem Blondheim's *News over the Wires*, has suggested that the telegraph and the Associated Press created a national community, which could share exciting news and dramatic scoops in real time. However, telegraphy in the 1850s was severely truncated, and the instantaneous text was not only unreliable but also dreary. As Blondheim admitted, "The reports were uniform in all newspapers that had wire services privileges, and, from a literary perspective, they were quite boring. Studying the columns on nineteenth-century Associated Press telegraphic news is a chore only as interesting as verbatim accounts of filibusters in Congress, assorted stock quotations, and pages from the ledger of a compulsive clerk in a seaport can be."[82] Thus, it seems from the evidence in Blondheim's book that extreme compression and lack of literary verve made the telegraph per se of limited significance to the Kansas issue. The real newspaper debate generally began with the arrival of letters from correspondents, and it began in the St. Louis dailies and spread eastward.

The field correspondence was detailed, some of it invented of whole cloth but much authentic enough, although undigested. "Kansas topics continue to be all pervading," wrote the *Chicago Daily Tribune* correspondent RANDOLPH in May 1857, "and no newspaper bears its own passport without a fresh chapter from some Kansas pen."[83]

Southern papers tended to rely on random missives from travelers or locals who had moved to Kansas. That was true early of Northern newspapers and magazines as well. Charles Stearns, a friend of William Lloyd Garrison, the editor of the *Boston Liberator,* sent early letters back to the *Liberator* in which he criticized the New England Emigrant Aid Company and suggested that New England free-soilers had not much influence in Kansas and that emigrants should come with plenty of money and as individuals rather than in groups. That hardly fit the general program and caused a falling out between Stearns and Charles Robinson, leader of the free-state forces. But it was an authentic expression of individual opinion.[84] However, the larger Northern newspapers soon introduced a more partisan slant into their correspondence and made a science of the letter from Kansas. They either hired a resident to write regular letters or sent a professional journalist to incorporate himself into the events, often as much an actor as an observer.

Some of those journalists, such as William Phillips of the *New York Daily Tribune,* James Redpath of the *St. Louis Daily Missouri Democrat,* Thomas Gladstone of the *London Times,* or Douglas Brewerton of the *New York Herald,* gained wide enough notoriety to in time turn their quotidian observations into books to feed the frenzy of curiosity about Kansas. Others remained anonymous, either for literary reasons or for considerations of personal safety.[85] So there were LITERAL, RANDOLPH, TRIMMER, HAIL, JUNIUS, OBSERVER,

JACOBIUS, X, and a host of others filling the panoply of Kansas correspondents.[86]

Still others who became writers for that same market were merely there, or were associated with high-level players in Kansas. One such was Sara Robinson, wife of Dr. Charles Robinson, the "governor" elected by the free-state faction. Her book *Kansas: Its Interior and Exterior Life* (1856) was one of the popular polemics of that tense season. Other women, such as Clarina Nichols and Hannah Ropes, also participated in the sending of public correspondence. Eventually some of the major actors wrote memoirs. "Governor" Charles Robinson himself did so, as did Eli Thayer of the New England Emigrant Aid Company. However, the biweekly or so missives to the home papers had a fresh vividness, passion, and unedited volubility that made them a special element in shaping the events they described.

The focus in this study is on the higher-level processing done by editorial writers at a distance from the scene, writers who had less involvement with the players and more time for reflection. It was here that most of the framing was done, most of the compelling simplification was advanced, and most of the tenacious imagery was created. Still, there is no mistaking that to the literate citizen of the 1850s following the Kansas issue, a major element of the filtered atmosphere from Kansas would have been the minimally reflective, sometimes convoluted, often overexcited, but voluminous, enthusiastic, and fresh missives from the field correspondents. Their letters were set quickly, often in atrocious type, column after column and day by day, regular as clockwork.

These newspaper field correspondents—"pensioned letter writers," they were sometimes called—were, despite the everyday purpose of their prose, criticized for exaggeration, fabrication, and bias. They were universally guilty.[87] One man complained, "The Kansas Question assumes from day to day as many different phrases as there are Telegraphic correspondents."[88] Said one paper in 1858: "No territory or state ever suffered so much from misrepresentation and slanders of letter writers and political adventurers, as has Kansas."[89] Many correspondents, one journal concluded, belonged to the "sensation school." Their goal was to excite and bewilder. "One must examine a score of accounts before he can arrive at any *true* conception of things as they are." Particularly, there was a bias against the more boring aspects of party organization and the doings of moderate people in organizing at the polls. There was also awareness in the national press that these correspondents created a vicious circle of distortion in the national circulation of their stories. "They pervert Opinion in the States," said a writer for the *Washington National Era*, "and hail the reaction of this perverted Opinion upon the People of Kansas." Thus, events were to some extent influenced by reaction to other events, and history fed on its own publicity.[90]

Many correspondents were simply not up to the task professionally. An editor in Indianapolis wrote in 1856 that there were three classes of lying correspondents in Kansas. First were the hired newspaper correspondents proper. "They are paid by the line, and the bigger the lies they can tell the bigger price they can command." This might not pay well in the long run, "but for the present, as the public pulse now beats in relation to Kansas, lying pays much better than truth." The second class was made up of missionaries who corresponded with religious newspapers. They did not intend to lie, but they were easily hoaxed by rumors. They did not inquire into the truth of the stories they heard; instead, "they sit down and write in a high falutin' style, in bad grammar and worse taste" about things they did not understand. The third class was the failed politicians who had gone to Kansas to restore their fortunes. These men could not be elected constable in any town where they were known, but they went to Kansas "with the hope of being floated into position by some chance wave." They were willing to exaggerate and distort if it served them.[91]

There was an impression that the town of Lawrence was such a hotbed of radicalism (the "gall bag of the Territory," the proslavery faction called it) not only because the threats of war had interrupted regular urban and rural occupations but also because a great number of the otherwise unemployed people became newspaper correspondents. "Editors and letter-writers," Brewerton said, "are like lawyers, very apt to tell but one part of the story, and that in their own way."[92] But a story there must be. "A Settler" wrote to the *Boston Post* in 1856 that he saw little trouble in Kansas, but then he had come there "for business purposes, and not to dabble in her affairs . . . , I seek no newspaper notoriety, nor do I wish to become a correspondent of any."[93] Perhaps that was the way it looked to most residents of Kansas Territory. To some Kansas Territory residents, however, a quiet day was an occupational hazard.

The United States, wrote the Reverend Theodore Parker, had a great intensity of life: "All that we do we overdo." Americans showed rashness, haste, and superficiality, but also great intuition and spontaneity. "How we crowd into cars and steamboats; a locomotive would well typify our fuming, fizzing spirit." But this "scamper," so evident in American cities, was hardly reflected at all in the nation's "tame, and weak" permanent literature. Rather, it shone forth in the "evanescent" literature found in newspapers, speeches, and pamphlets. Parker called newspapers a thoroughly American medium, in which were reflected the real morals and manners of the country. It was not a flattering picture one saw there, but a true one, showing the details of "that vulgarity, that rant, that bragging violence, that recklessness of truth and justice, that disregard of right and duty" that were part of everyday life at midcentury. Editors were like orators: "a little turgid, hot, sometimes brilliant, hopeful, abounding in half truths, full of great ideas; often inconsequent; sometimes coarse; patriotic, vain, self-confident, rash, strong, and young-mannish."[94]

Editors and newspaper owners were aware of their responsibilities and delighted in analyzing their own virtues and their competitors' shortcomings as purveyors of responsible journalism. At one level the production plant of the 1850s newspaper partook of the great revolution that steam and steel had created everywhere. The people at the *New Orleans Daily Picayune* thought that "steam has become the great agent of modern revolution, as well as modern stability, the foundation in many ways of all power." Its introduction had changed the current of human thought as much as it had the speed and direction of travel and had broken the influence of authority over the mind of the public as effectively as it had overcome the impact of distance on human relations.[95]

The type in the newspaper offices of the 1850s looked much like that of Johannes Gutenberg in the fifteenth century, and the composition process, in that pre-Linotype age, was also similar to the hand-setting techniques of centuries earlier. But the press itself had undergone recent and revolutionary changes, mostly due to the innovations of an American corporation called Robert Hoe & Co. The Hoe patent press, which printed from a continuously revolving cylinder rather than from the plates moving up and down of the traditional screw press, speeded and automated printing marvelously, especially when several cylinders were tied together in a single huge machine. Newspapers that had been expensive, few, and purchased on credit were now cheap, numerous, and purchased for cash.[96] The *Daily Cincinnati Commercial* boasted in 1854 that it had acquired a four-cylinder Hoe press, capable of about 2,500 impressions per hour on each cylinder. It was the only such press in the United States west of the Allegheny Mountains at that time, but there were bigger Hoes to the East. "In a race so full of wonders," a writer commented when the press arrived, "it is difficult to say which is most to be admired—the march of periodical literature or the magic speed with which it has created its instrumentalities."[97]

Newspaper after newspaper installed a new press. The *Philadelphia Public Ledger & Daily Transcript* moved in its Hoe rotary cylinder press in the summer of 1856. To be thus able to distribute 60,000 newspapers a day created a "new power in civilized communities," giving them "the greatest combination and concentration of forces known in the intellectual world." That newspaper writers could impress their own thoughts and feelings "spontaneously and simultaneously upon as many thousand minds, proximate to each other, as in a large city like Philadelphia and New York, is a power of such magnitude, that it is not surprising the public mind generally has no adequate conception of it." An orator at a mass meeting might reach a few thousand people, and a preacher many less, but here was a medium for reaching the entire literate community every morning, provided only that each had a penny to spend for a newspaper. The *London Times* had ordered a ten-cylinder Hoe, but even the smaller ones, like the two four-cylinder presses on which the *Ledger* was printed, had done for newspapers what Robert Fulton's steamboat had done for transportation: It made the newspaper cheap and universal.[98]

The obvious influence caused newspapers to wax poetic about their own operations. No institution of society, argued a writer at the *Washington Union*, could compare with "this great engine—this great organ of the human mind. . . . It is a statesman, a lawyer, a physician, a clergyman, a teacher, a mechanic, a farmer, a manufacturer. . . . It controls the State and it controls the Church—it directs the family, the legislator, the magistrate and the minister. None rise above its influence, none sink below its authority." In 1858 the *New York Herald* alone published enough pages every day to fill 20,000 volumes of 500 pages, or 10 million pages a year. The fearsome thing was that it was impossible to "wield an engine so complicated and powerful—to drive a machine of such gigantic proportion" without offense or distortion.[99]

Similar sentiments were expressed by writers at the *Louisville Daily Journal*. The newspaper, they said in 1854, was destined to become the "most influential form of popular literature." It appealed to and informed all classes, who looked to it not only for facts but also for "thought applied to the facts." Civilization had reached the point at which the newspaper was "its best and most efficient ally" in advancing the progressive work of the age. The editor must therefore appreciate his mission by purifying his heart and subduing his passions in order to carry out civil and honest discourse even with an opponent.[100]

Ladies should read newspapers, the *Natchez Daily Courier* intoned, and should not limit their attention to the fashionable literature of the day. If women were to be suitable conversationalists, they would have to find something to talk about, and there was nothing better than the actual world and its events. "History is of some importance; but the past world is dead and we have nothing to do with it. . . . Let the gilded annuals and poems on the center table be kept part of the time covered with weekly and daily journals."[101]

Naturally, the new influence gave newspaper editors and publishers a sense of dignity, along with a feeling of responsibility. The editor of the *Charleston Mercury* called the responsibility of operating a paper of its reputation a "grave" one. But he thought the "day of mere hacks" was over. Editors were no longer under the thumb of a politician or party; rather, they were the "creators, not the creatures of the Administration."[102] The same seemed to be true of private interests. "What our great men are," claimed the *New York Herald*, "the New York press has made them."[103] According to the *Philadelphia Public Ledger & Daily Transcript*, the newspaper had replaced the pulpit as the director of the public mind. It "rules the tempest" in times of crisis and therefore must not be "venal or ignorant." It was "a serious mistake, if not a grave crime, in a newspaper, to indulge in coarse vituperation." A strong argument did not require such aids, and some publishers felt that irresponsible practices would eventually destroy circulation.[104]

Samuel Bowles, the visible editor of the *Springfield Daily Republican*, advised editors to identify themselves and their opinions in order to "give each leader or communication a paternity."[105] The press should never use its freedom, a writer at the *Washington Daily Union* asserted, to "sink the attributes of the judge in the feelings of the vindictive prosecutor." He worried that "defamation is becoming a necessity of life, insomuch that a dish of tea in the morning or evening cannot be digested without this stimulant."[106]

The *Daily Cincinnati Commercial* saw the newspaper as a kind of conscience that approved right and condemned wrong by cultivating the mind. The civil character of a people depended on the state of the popular conscience, which in turn depended upon information and understanding. Therefore, the question of how the public understanding was to be cultivated was "of all others, to a self-governing people, the first in importance." Newspapers had taken their place among "the great instrumentalities for the moral education of mankind." Therefore, it was "no small thing amid the multiplicity of events, great and small, to make up a right newspaper." It would be better to take a fool into one's household than a foolish newspaper. "The lightness of the one is, indeed, more tolerable than the stupidity of the other, and less liable to be contagious."[107]

Large cities were becoming ever more pivotal in national affairs, partly because they were media centers, and newspapers were crucial to that role. The *New York Herald* and the *New York Daily Times* both commented on their role in May 1854 as the Kansas-Nebraska bill was making its way through Congress, with results for the West and the nation that could not then be accurately estimated.

The *Herald* was at that time sending correspondents all over the world to get accurate stories, and, it claimed, was making public opinion and imposing its law on those who used to censor it. New York, it asserted, was the focus of public opinion formation in the United States, illustrating perfectly through its newspapers the tendency of civilized man toward "intellectual centralization." There were half a dozen leading journals in New York City, and some, like the *Herald* and the *Times,* had circulations upward of 50,000 daily, far more than the 3,000 of the most popular paper twenty years earlier. These metropolitan dailies, the writers said, "give the most faithful reflection of the minds, of the focus of the country; it is now merely a sort of arena where the ideas of the New York press are discussed, and acted upon. The great mind of the country is here."[108]

The *Times* was also sanguine about the beneficence and scope of its power. Congress, its columns asserted, had lost all pretension of leadership of public opinion. The newspaper was the new statesman. "It discusses all great questions far better—with more range—with deeper subtlety—with much more exhaustiveness." The *Times* writers invited readers to compare its prose with the debates in Congress and "see where the intellectual forces of the world are marshalling themselves." Congress was a debating society, and its members gave lectures as though they stood before a college classroom. Newspaper writers, by contrast, were "pressed at the start into the heart of things." If they expected to be heard "in the roar of omnibuses, in the confusion of business," they had to speak "so as to possess the ear." The most talented would in future go into the newspaper business, for it was there that the national mind would be formed. "It is rapidly becoming as absolutely necessary to the energy and enterprise of human life (especially city and commercial life) to be supplied every morning with a map of the world and a commentary on its current facts, as it is to have the divisions of day and night, or the laws of appetite and assimilation."[109]

At the highest level of abstraction generated by the Kansas debate, there was seeming consensus. Everyone was for freedom! But what a tangled and entangling web that term wove for its disparate and polarized devotees. James Malin, the pioneering historian of what he called "the Nebraska question," noted that the people of the 1850s were captive to "traditional concepts and semantic forms" and were therefore blind to what events were telling them about the illusory or delusive role of such concepts as progress, egalitarianism, democracy, and freedom in relation to the new realities of a "mechanized society." Old words took on new meanings, and readers, occupied in a "pathological outburst of excitement," sometimes did not know it.[110] Lewis Cass, in a speech before the Senate in 1856, called propaganda about Kansas a "terrible national malady" that "prostrates the judgment and almost paralyzes the conscience, and prepares the excited mind for strange delusions and dangerous deeds."[111]

One does not have to take such a grim view to see the point about what the *Washington Union* in the 1850s called "the varied and studied forms of phraseology."[112] A reviewer of Sean Wilentz's *Rise of American Democracy* noted that one of the work's contributions was its sense of the irony of American history. The book showed how the sections in the antebellum period had developed two different systems of democracy while appealing to the same ideas and values. The "spread of democratic politics in both the North and the South . . . made it impossible to solve the problem of slavery peaceably," and "the triumph of democracy nearly destroyed the United States."[113]

Freedom surely has its endemic weaknesses. Thomas Hobbes, perhaps their most eloquent student, in the seventeenth century regularly pointed to the corruption of public opinion through manipulative phraseology as the primary flaw in republican forms of government. "Man's tongue," he wrote, "is a trumpet to war and sedition." He added, "*Stupidity* and *eloquence* unite to subvert the commonwealth." In his book *Leviathan* he proposed that the ideal society should ban the use of metaphor. He also warned against tendencies to make private judgment sacred. He considered metaphor "the tool by which the word conscience had been turned into a justification for obstinacy." False analogies and false prophets abounded, and always would, so long as "men stand in awe of their own imaginations."[114]

Studies of Bleeding Kansas have demonstrated that one of the flaws of freedom is that voting is an unsatisfactory way to resolve moral issues.[115]

Also, the very practice of freedom, with its attendant responsibility, is at times so frustrating to the human psyche that one may desire to escape it altogether.[116] Henry Ward Beecher described well some of the inherent weaknesses of freedom in his religious paper the *New York Independent*. Liberty was so rich, he wrote, that it had a tendency to ferment and was filled with divisions. Slavery, by contrast, had "but a single selfishness" and was an efficient unit in ambition and council, however "imbecile" it might be in creative force.[117] A commentator on the election of the first Kansas legislature in March 1855 observed that despotism appealed more directly to selfish material interests "and can more readily than freedom marshal its trained bands to defend its citadels."[118]

But was there no legitimate place for persuasion? Some observers in the 1850s believed there should be. Moderates, who often called themselves conservatives, existed in both sections. They were represented by many newspapers, whose editors were appalled at the partisanship and the escalated rhetoric concerning Kansas and freely predicted that editorial irresponsibility, not the intractability of the issues themselves, would bring the nation to ruin.

"What has a newspaper a right to publish?" asked an editorial writer for the *Daily Cincinnati Commercial* in 1854. Was there some system of ethics editors were bound to follow in the public interest and despite the profits to be gained from sensationalist circulation? All too often, he thought, the press had been guided by "men of like passions with others—equally blind to truth, equally prone to the bias of interest, party and faction; equally liable to deduce rules of action from isolated circumstances, rather than fundamental principles; equally dull to perceive the beginning of an abuse, and equally wanting in that prudent foresight which alone can render it a safe umpire in opinion or guide of conduct." Newspaper errors were the errors of society, the editorial continued: "In its false pictures, its unsound doctrines, its causeless resentments, and groundless loves; its indiscriminate censures and laudations, its conventional estimates of good and evil, its inflation, trumpery, tumid eloquence, misplaced pathos, diseased sentimentality, and bare balderdash, it is only painting with greater vividness, the picture of that mankind of which it is the symbol. . . . In a community where all were just, wise and exemplary, a bad press could not exist." A newspaper "diffuses the atmosphere it breathes," and it drew its character from its surrounding circumstances. Would that the journalist could always rise to an unerring balance of justice.[119]

Many moderate editors felt that some standard of realism was required and that newspapers had to make an effort, even if short of perfection, to calm the storm rather than compete for attention by adding to the rhetoric. The staff at the *Columbus Daily Ohio Statesman* thought in 1858 that there were too many "desperate controversialists" in the world peddling "trash" in an attempt to "cajole or to brow-beat honest men." In Washington, D.C., the *Statesman* averred, people talked "as flippantly about rebellions by a million or two of the people, as [they] would of a revolt among the clerks and porters of one of the public departments." The national press manufactured too many deities and too many devils, and it was silly, the paper continued, to speak about every event in Kansas as though it were an evil and a fraud unprecedented in history.[120]

Many observers saw that there needed to be more realism, more tolerance, if the danger were to be averted. Surprisingly, perhaps, some of the most moderate opinion came from the South. The *New Orleans Daily Picayune* ran a piece in the spring of 1858 called "Political Quackery." The South was like the doctor who had a panacea for fits and therefore tried to convince all patients that they were subject to the disease and therefore amenable to his cure. This was, said the paper's writers, typical of the "convulsive" school of journalism. Many newspapers in the South seemed to think that the question of slavery was the only question. This simplified things dangerously: "Every malady of the state, or disorder of the times, is resolved into some premonitory or symptom of Abolitionism; and the infallible nostrum is disunion. Setting out with this idea, they are very dogmatical on signs and symptoms." Everyone who did not agree was getting the Northern disease and must be treated for fits.[121]

This "summary and dictatorial style" replaced the complexities of reality, and the journalists at the *Picayune* thought its motivation was partly notoriety and partly profit. There was too much, they said, of "this system of browbeating and dragooning, this hurrying up of doubtful issues and extreme measures . . . because they get notoriety—and sometimes only notoriety—demanding them to be received as tests, and fulminating denunciations against all who are not convinced, or who ask time to think." The South gained nothing by this "intolerant forcing of issues." It was a "perilous abuse of words, where words are substantial things." It could have no effect but irritation, and it debased the language. Words too often and carelessly repeated in questionable applications became "mere cant words, which lose their significance when applied . . . on real and practical issues." It was folly "to bring the tactics of hostile camps into the controversies about social questions," as though the struggle were some sort of sports contest in front of cheering and jeering fans. A look at history would show how well those strategies had worked in other conflicts: "The charlatans may throw us into the desired 'fits,' but their panacea is quite as likely to kill as to cure."[122]

Northern moderates felt the same. The *Daily Cincinnati Commercial* believed that thoughtful people must be constantly asking themselves whether the state of civilization, maybe even of human evolution, was sufficiently advanced for self-government. Was there enough virtue, popular intelligence, or tolerance to handle it? Was there enough of the conservatism that grew out of independent thought and a feeling of responsibility, or would such restraint simply be seen as "old fogeyism" by the radicals? Where was the thoughtful person to acquire sound information in a world where most speech was "flatulency" and windy emissions? Such language, the *Commercial* held, appealed to class prejudices and deep emotions, which should not be roused lightly.[123]

Congress could not be expected to escape such influences. Was it any wonder, the moderates asked, that when Charles Sumner gave a particularly rude and incendiary speech on Kansas in the spring of 1856, he was beaten unconscious by another senator who had taken offense? The speech was only words, and words no more dangerous than those flung with abandon at each other by editors. But these words drew blood. After a fistfight in the House of Representatives during a debate about Kansas early in 1858, a Southern paper commented on the spectacle of grown men swinging at each other in the open space before the speaker's chair and the clerk's table and in the midst of the hoary and glorious architecture of the Capitol building. "The House is full of inflammable material, which may, by a slight spark, be at any time exploded. The prevailing tone of the press, and of political meetings, throughout the country, is so harsh, not to say brutal, that it cannot fail to be imitated in Congress. . . . Bleeding Kansas will be lost sight of when the bad passions of men, now forcibly repressed, shall have found vent in the capitol."[124]

The *Washington Union* was considered an organ of the administration. As such, it bore special responsibility for the impact of its own rhetoric, and it tended, as power often does, toward moderation and compromise. On April Fool's Day, 1857, a writer at the *Union* ruminated about the survival of the American Union and of civilization. He wondered whether the American people, "who can cope with the world in arms, in arts of industry, in everything that contributes to make a nation strong, a people great, are able to survive the shock of continuous collisions among themselves; whether our government is equal to an assuagement of the prejudices and passions which are fostered under its own beauties and blessings as poisonous plants and noxious weeds rankle under oaks or among roses, cherished and sustained by the same laws of light and vegetation, which are the essence of the existence of both."[125]

It was a complex and paradoxical dilemma. The human mind, wonder that it was, could create dangerous phantasms, which the body then acted on. And the images with which it dealt were all too simple. "It is only in the mind," the philosophers at the *Union* said just a year later, "that violent remedies are applied and violent revolutions sought." Thousands of people saw moral principles as trees in the forest, each standing alone, rooted and drawing independent sustenance. The reality was that the moral universe was a unit under which "operated the complex machinery of human life." It was dangerous to abstract things from the whole and debate them in isolation.[126]

The *Daily Albany Argus* addressed the same issues from the same moderate perspective in 1855, when Kansas had just begun to dominate national discussion. Could there not be more "sense" and less "spirit" in public discussions? The questions before the country required "solemn discussion," not "[the] flaunting of banners and the blaring of trumpets." Asking for "cool investigation" and "moderate but resolute action" did not mean advocating an "owlish respectability" that was afraid of its shadow. But too much of public debate seemed to reduce itself to simple *"meum et tuum"* (mine and thine), accompanied by a lot of emotion and surrounded by a great deal of "childish clap-trap." Party meetings could be particularly offensive, with their mass chanting of slogans. So could the "frivolous drivel" that appeared in journals. Such activity was "masquerading," but the audience could not leave quietly when the bombast of the play was finished. It was particularly ironic, the writers at the *Atlas* thought, that all this silliness was advanced in the name of freedom. The principle of freedom, they held, should be no one person's or one party's or one journal's private property. Honor and truth should have nothing to do with vested interest. To advance freedom required forbearance with one's fellows, assuming that at base they were loyal to many of the same principles.[127]

Two adages were regularly quoted in articles about Kansas through the 1850s. One of them was the Latin admonition "Fiat justitia, ruat caelum" (Let justice be done though the heavens fall). The other oft-cited adage was the biblical warning that those who sowed the wind could expect to reap the whirlwind.

Withal and in all, there was the great question of the significance of the obvious pain in Kansas. The nation struggled, right up to the time Lincoln drafted the Gettysburg Address, to extract from the death, sacrifice, and suffering some sense of mission, some feeling of gain for the Republic. And there were cynics, too, who wondered if the meaning of it all was not just the obvious depressing one.

In the fall of 1855, when the battle for emigration and for political dominance in Kansas was just underway and when the press was heating up with charges and countercharges, one of the chief abolitionist journals of the country, the *Washington National Era,* ran a series of articles by Seth Webb using a semifictional setting to communicate powerfully the tone of the debate.

Webb, the cynic, was sitting alone after dinner one evening in his Wall Street office with a cigar and a volume of Thomas De Quincey. At that point, according to his account, an office mate from across the hall entered holding a newspaper detailing the physical attack in the executive offices of Kansas Territory on the territorial governor Andrew Reeder by the border ruffian Benjamin Stringfellow. It had excited him no end. It was, he said, a crisis in civilization. "Let the dead East bury its dead. Kansas is a career!"

Webb tried to shut him down. Remember Achilles, he said, and his vulnerable heel. But there was no slowing the rhetoric, now in full hyperbolic mode. "The Kansas emigrant," his friend went on, "at the present time is the prominent object of notice on this planet. Sebastopol is the seat of a skirmish; but Lawrence is the seat of a war." In all history, the speaker averred, there had been "some enterprise, some idea . . . to which all earthly eyes involuntarily turn, in which all the interest of the great drama centers, and over which all bright and dark angels hover as the Pagan immortals hung over Troy." And such was Kansas. It was as much a turning point as had been the battles of Poitiers or Thermopylae or Bunker Hill, as significant as St. Paul on Mars Hill, Luther before the Diet, or Columbus on the quarterdeck of the *Santa Maria.* "There is no element of the moral sublime, which the position of the Kansas emigrant does not fulfill."

At this Webb lighted another cigar and sneered. Oh, I know what you are thinking, his friend said. "You would say that these cadaverous Yankees and brandy-soaked vagabonds who squabble now in Kansas are neither more nor less than other soldiers of fortune, mere scramblers for a living, or in for a drunken row." That is partly right, the friend admitted, but the spirit of the whole was different from the actions of a few. Kansas was special. "I count it as one of the few signs extant in this age, that we are not altogether given over to Mammon and materialism." His language, the friend claimed, was not inflated: "It just clothes the beautiful fact, no more." The Kansas emigrant was a "pilgrim; more than a pilgrim; he is a crusader." Like the Pilgrims of New England, the people coming to Kansas from the North were "stern, solid, majestic, colossal." They represented no less than what humankind had learned over 6,000 years of recorded history, which the United States at its best represented.

The conversation at last wound down, and Mr. Abel Bison, as Webb called his friend, went to the window and looked forlornly over the city. He then returned to Webb's desk and set down a miniature depicting an attractive young woman. It seemed to change his mood as he departed with the words: "My friend, if Peter the Hermit had had a wife and two children, there would have been no crusade."

Webb sat alone again in his armchair with his cigar and book and mused on the complications of the whole affair. Perhaps more than emigrant aid societies or sawmills or acts of Congress or money, Kansas did indeed need a certain kind of people. But where exactly would they be found?[128]

CHAPTER 2

THE ALL-ABSORBING QUESTION

The creation of Kansas seemed at first a simple enough task. It was a political act, an artificial, formal procedure, such as the antique process of "creating" someone a duke or an earl in "Merry Old England." It had often been done before. The steps were clear. First a U.S. territory was made, which existed for a time in a colonial relationship to the federal government proper. It had a hybrid government: Washington appointed the major officers, and the local population elected the legislature. In time, the residents of the territory formed a constitution and applied to Congress for admission to the Union.

The process had been dull and bureaucratic. There had been some acrimonious debates over the possible spread of slavery into the West. However, many Americans thought that the Missouri Compromise of 1820 and the Great Compromise of 1850 provided rules of thumb on that issue, which could be followed more or less mechanically. So when proposals surfaced to create Nebraska Territory, little controversy was expected. What happened, however, was an explosion. "An apparently innocent bill to organize a territorial government west of the Missouri river," wrote historian Orman Ray in 1909, "provoked a gigantic and picturesque parliamentary duel in the Senate Chamber of the United States."[1]

Congressman Charles Hughes of New York noticed the change in the session of 1854, the first of the Thirty-third Congress. Day after day at first, he said, senators discussed and disposed of ordinary subjects of legislation. Then, about January 1, Senator Stephen Douglas of Illinois proposed what developed into the Kansas-Nebraska Act. Leaving aside its ill-planned proposal to displace Indian tribes, who had been removed to the region with treaty guarantees that whites would not organize governments there, the bill contained two bombshells. The first was the repeal of the Missouri Compromise, and the second was the institution of the principles of popular sovereignty and congressional nonintervention. The result was that the tenuous lid that had been put on slavery agitation in 1820 by the Missouri Compromise was out the window. Each new territory, North or South, would be up for grabs vis-à-vis slavery, as its "actual inhabitants" might express themselves through the wonderful and supposedly unambiguous democratic process of the ballot box.

That, said Hughes, changed everything. For weeks before the bill came up formally, it was brought up for discussion on the floor every day. These speeches, printed as pamphlets on the high-speed presses of the newspaper offices, circulated through the land. "We are now," Hughes commented, "once more afloat upon a wild sea of agitation. Crimination and recrimination have gone forth from this Hall to fester in the hearts, and gall the souls of our various constituencies, and heartburnings and reproach now occupy the places so lately filled with amity and good will."[2]

Eventually the bill evolved to propose two territories instead of one. From the moment the combination of letters "Kansas" or "Kanzas" appeared in print, that territory became "the All-Absorbing Topic of the Day."[3] The *New York Herald* called the new bill a "slumbering volcano." This time the slavery issue could not be disposed of with "any temporary make-shifts or ephemeral compromises—it must be probed to the bottom. . . . The question itself is the greatest problem which the destiny of the United States presents."[4] The Kansas-Nebraska question, said Senator Charles Sumner of Massachusetts, had become an issue of "gigantic proportions," the question of questions "by the side of which Senators and Presidents are but dwarfs." It could destroy the Union by becoming the equivalent of the magnetic mountain in an Arabian story: Attracted by the mountain, the iron bolts that held together the timbers of a ship were drawn out until the whole fell apart and became a scattered wreck.[5] "Pass this bill," said Congressman Israel Washburn of Maine, "and you kindle a fire which will need all the rain in the sweet heavens to extinguish. . . . If the fire shall not blaze up at once, and fill the sky, it will burn the more intensely when it does break out."[6]

The extremes were evident right away, and they became more fixed and passionate as the congressional debate extended over months and spread across close to 1,000 pages of the *Congressional Globe.*

Laurence Keitt of South Carolina, speaking on March 30, 1854, in the House, represented one end of the spectrum. He worried that power would be concentrated in the federal government, an eventuality he hoped the Kansas-Nebraska bill would prevent. Consolidate the government in Washington, "shut from the extremities the pulses of the heart, and stifle the returning pulsations, and whatever name you give to the regime under which the people agonize or slumber, it is a corrupt tyranny."[7]

What of the slavery issue? That, thought Keitt, was simply a matter of property. If one form of property were endangered, all eventually would be, and the result would be anarchy. Slaves were content, not vexed by care, and protected in their old age and disability. Shipping African Americans back to Africa would bankrupt the government, while freeing them would make U.S. society a "moral hell, ringing with agony and blasphemy, smoking with crime and suffering."[8]

At the other pole was Congressman Gerrit Smith of New York. Rising from his place just a week after Keitt's address, Smith spoke in opposition to the proposed bill. Slavery in the territories must not be allowed in any guise. Slavery, he said, "is the baldest and biggest lie on earth. In reducing man to a chattel, it denies that man is man; and in denying that man is man, it denies that God is God." There was a higher law to which all human law must conform. "Essential wrongs" could not be legalized. To call a man a thing was antilaw and insanity. It was time to remove the cancer in the polity. "A bastard democracy accommodated to the demands of slavery, and tolerating the traffic in human flesh, is our national democracy; and a bastard Christianity, which endorses this bastard democracy, is the current Christianity of our nation." Both were shams.[9]

Perhaps, Smith concluded, it would be more "gentlemanly" of him to speak of the issue in terms of economics or politics. That would be fine if he were speaking of horses or oxen. "But I have been speaking of men—of millions of immortals." Would the agitation destroy the Union? Smith hoped not, particularly if the fall were to be violent. But there were two Unions, one of which he prized for the wisdom and piety in which it had been begotten, and the other that had emerged now amid compromises. Would the nation repent? Would Americans hear the voices in the wilderness and understand with their hearts?[10]

Perhaps the many interleaved and nuanced technical questions of the Kansas-Nebraska controversy seem antique to the modern mind. Surely, the defense of slavery as a positive good goes beyond sophistry in the direction of a shocking, though intellectualized, brutality. But the broad questions of the proper balance between freedom and authority, centralized and dispersed power, the rights of majorities and minorities, the proper means for determining the authentic will of the people, and the place of moral versus legal considerations in a republican form of government—all of which were turned over seriously in Washington and the rest of America in those dramatic months of the spring of 1854—remain and will remain difficult challenges of systematizing freedom.

James Malin argued that the popular sovereignty question "was fundamental to the mid-nineteenth century problem of equilibrium and freedom." Steam and electricity were amoral powers, he thought, that were shattering the traditional social structure. They were also changing the reality behind "traditional cultural concepts and semantic forms" more quickly than those forms themselves could change. The political victory went to nationalism and abolition. But the broader ideological and cultural setting in which the struggle took place—consisting of ideas about progress, liberalism, egalitarianism, and universal suffrage—was, according to Malin, largely a "delusion." These frames bore little relation to the facts of a centralizing, homogenizing, mechanized society, whose implications are still being worked out over a century later.[11]

The politics might seem straightforward. The construction put upon it by the winners was that the Kansas-Nebraska bill, even though introduced by Douglas, a Northern Democrat, was a scheme of the South. Senator David Atchison of Missouri did have some discussions with Douglas about the terms, but the reality was not so simple. It was not a matter of proslavery groups favoring Kansas-Nebraska and antislavery groups opposing. Nor was the bill strictly a party measure, with Democrats promoting and Whigs and Know-Nothings opposing it. Instead, the politics of it were labyrinthine, with constantly shifting alliances, and great pressure put upon individuals in Congress to attract votes in what would be a close decision. The Whig Party, early bulwark of a viable two-party system, was in the process of dissolution, and the Republican Party, to be formed partly out of the fusion of antislavery sentiment, was not yet born in 1854.[12]

The tension was extreme because there was such uncertainty and such fear. Wrote a columnist in New York: "As the last flicker of a dying lamp seems to derive unusual brilliancy from the approach of death, so the prospect of the final close of the quarrel appears to lend new virulence to the disputants and fresh acrimony to the debate."[13] Like dealing with a large telescope, which is at the same time heavy and awkward, expensive and delicate, every move here, every adjustment, every change was dangerous—potentially and perhaps suddenly disastrous. The sections of the country were metaphorically on a teeter-totter. Each was represented in Congress by an equal number of states, a situation that would change one way or the other unless all future states were admitted in pairs with opposite laws on slavery. The South felt that once the tipping point was reached, the momentum would be irresistible, and the balance would never return. To use another metaphor, it was as though there existed a high watershed ridge. It might seem of small moment whether the modest headwaters of a tiny stream went one way or another, but it could be of great moment when the river it eventually became reached the sea. Kansas was nothing. Kansas was everything.

The so-called Nebraska question consisted of many questions and sub-questions, with considerable nuance attached to each. And each of these questions opened a Pandora's box that released Harpies to complicate the process of state making in Kansas.

The full implications of many of these questions were not grasped. The author of the Kansas-Nebraska bill, Stephen Douglas, had what Allan Nevins called a *"gaudium certaminis"* (joy in struggle), with "a whole broad complex of reasons, half-reasons, and quarter-reasons" reinforcing that instinct. But when the bill entered the sphere of public opinion, neither the "Little Giant" nor anyone else could control it. Douglas was a practical man of action, who, Nevins wrote, "was never disposed to give prolonged meditation to the complexities of a situation, or to undertake a careful weighing of forces and futurities." Douglas may have been thinking mostly about rail routes to the Pacific. The issues of the bill he introduced, however, reached "the feelings, the prejudices, the religious and political principles of men."[14]

Douglas was not the only political leader so limited in vision and focused on one particular interest. A writer at the *Charleston Mercury* observed in February 1854 that the weather in Washington was changeable. On February 3 it was "as bright and bland as a day in the tropics." The next morning opened with a whirling snowstorm. So it was, the paper thought, with careers in Congress, with their "practiced, controversial gladiatorship" and the "scathingly severe" and often irresponsible rhetoric of the members. "What a farce!"[15]

The controversy became primarily a question of the fate of Kansas. There was a general understanding that Nebraska's climate was unsuited for slavery to be successful. A good number considered that true of Kansas also, and thought that to struggle over the status of slavery there was to struggle over a moot point. Many people at the time and a good number of historians since have therefore concluded that the slavery issue was a screen for other economic or political interests, from land speculation to railroads to patron-age.[16] However, principles were involved, namely, the right of Southerners to carry their "property" into the territories, and the right of the settlers in those territories to decide for themselves whether or not to institutionalize slavery. "If Nebraska were a barren rock," one editor wrote, "the principle would be the same, and the controversy would not be altered."[17]

There were plenty of opinion makers who thought the balance of power in the Union must be preserved by allowing Kansas to enter the Union as a slave state and Nebraska as a free state. They thought the South would fight for that real interest as well as for abstract principle. And the South had a chance. Would it not be natural that under a rubric of popular sovereignty, Kansas, bordering as it did slaveholding Missouri, would attract more proslavery than free-state voters? That possibility led to a serious reaction on the part of the free-soil North. And, it must be said, the Kansas issue as it developed over the next four years showed that the proslavery alternative for the south-ernmost of the new territories was much more viable than the climatological scoffers imagined. Thus, though the debate in 1854 concerned two new ter-ritories, the national battle was to be over just one.

In including the repeal of the Missouri Compromise specifically in the Kansas-Nebraska bill, its proponents could be accused of violating a sacred compact, thus calling into question all governmental promises and agree-ments.[18] And, however attractive in theory was the policy of referring all lo-cal questions, including the status of slavery, to the will of the majority of the "bona fide settlers" in the area, how would it work in practice? Throughout 1858 newspaper editorials and magazine articles on Kansas harked back to the irregularities in the passage of the act that had officially created it.

The Missouri Compromise had been, according to the *Richmond Enquirer,* a "fatal concession" for the South, an "unequal compact" in which South-erners had acquiesced for the sake of Union and peace. Southern journals claimed, however, that the North had itself jettisoned the Missouri Compro-mise when in 1850, in the debate over the admission of California as a free state and the territorial organization of New Mexico and Utah without any reference to the establishment of slavery, the idea of popular sovereignty had been broached as a substitute for the old Missouri Compromise line. Even the failed Wilmot Proviso, which would have had Congress dictate freedom in the area, would have been an unnecessary initiative had the Mis-souri Compromise still ruled. Douglas in 1854 said that the formal repeal of the Missouri Compromise and support of popular sovereignty in the

Kansas-Nebraska Act only confirmed the principles already established in 1850.

Many in the South felt that the new arrangement could be more beneficial to their section than the Missouri Compromise had been. Whether slavery really established itself in the Northwest or not, the new bill would release the South from "Congressional tyranny" that might in the future use abolitionist congressional majorities to prevent the establishment of slavery in territories with local majorities favorable to slavery that might form in Cuba or Central America. It would give the South the chance to restore its position of equality in the Union.[19] Emphasis on decentralization and local freedom was philosophically palatable to all sides.[20] It would withdraw from the congressional arena "the most dangerous subject which can enter into our political discussions."[21]

Writers in this vein found it appalling that much Northern opinion regarded the Kansas-Nebraska bill as a Southern plot. The South argued that the territories were the common domain of the states, for they had commonly shed blood in the Revolution, and that it was improper to ban anyone or his or her property from free emigration and settlement there. Now the opportunists were taking this latter legal ground as well. How, asked a Southern newspaper, could Northern abolitionists, whose strategy "rests upon resistance to law and comity, and laughs at the binding force of constitutions," now appeal to the Missouri Compromise as a reverenced agreement? Was not the general principle of these groups to support the right of the North to appropriate all the public domain, and to insult the South while doing it? Were the Northern abolitionists not devotees of the higher law and natural religion? Why their sudden scruple about the Missouri compact?[22] "It is a prodigious fall from the clouds, for such high-reaching spirits as the Free-soilers."

There was a strain of public opinion in the North that agreed. What was the Missouri Compromise, anyway, but a human law, "one of those temporary palliatives with which timid political quacks seek to cure a deep seated and dangerous disorder"?[23] A writer at the *New York Herald* thought that the truce of 1820 and 1850 was over and that events would come crowding "as wave rolls over wave under the lashings of a heavy gale." That time of compromise was over. "The day for mixed concessions between abolitionists and the propaganda of slavery has passed by. No more hybrid mulatto compromises will avail—no more schemes of Africanization and free soil, share and share alike." The U.S. Constitution was for Anglo-Saxons, the *Herald* thought, but there would be an ordeal to face over what was to become of the other major race present. "We have the beginning," a reporter wrote in January 1854, "but the end is yet to come."[24]

Both sections saw themselves as victims of an aggressor, who was magnified by their fears into a unified, purposive monster with deep-laid plans. Readers of history are more familiar with the image of the rampaging "slaveocracy" than with the descriptions of the depredations of the psychopathic abolitionists. But the contemporary press was filled with both. The spirit of abolitionism, based in the certain righteousness of religion, would, a Washington correspondent wrote, soon be "exhibited in all its deformity."[25] The *Richmond Enquirer* commented, "If experience had not made us familiar with the arrogant and aggressive character of Northern Abolitionism, the violent opposition which the Nebraska bill encounters would fill us with astonishment and indignation."[26] A New York observer agreed that the movement against the Kansas-Nebraska Act in the North "springs from feeling, unadulterated by reason. The language used by the free soil and abolition organs is that of senseless anger; they cannot condescend to argue the point."[27]

The Missouri Compromise issue received editorial attention around the country, but particularly in the North, where the newspaper press demonstrated early its talent for organizing an effective propaganda campaign based on framing an issue and inventing the language with which to speak about it. The editorials followed some expected lines, but with a good deal of subtle variation. Samuel Bowles at the *Springfield Daily Republican* called the Kansas-Nebraska bill "a huge stride backwards," on the grounds that the Missouri Compromise had kept the lid on agitation. The moral forces of the North would meet head-on the "insanity" of the slave interests.[28] The *Amherst Farmer's Cabinet* felt the same. The repeal of the Missouri Compromise, it claimed, had taken the country by surprise, coming from an administration that had promised to abide by the great compromises crafted by the wise statesmen of a prior generation.[29] The *Milwaukee Daily Sentinel* contemplated the change with "great repugnance" and thought it "ill-judged and ill-advised."[30] The *Chicago Daily Tribune* felt that Douglas was "misrepresentative" of Illinois and that in his defense of the Compromise repeal he had advanced a "sophistical, question-begging tirade in the guise of an argument."[31]

As often in creating propaganda, a common device was the analogy, imperfect as it could sometimes be. The *Daily Cincinnati Commercial* used a homely parable: There was a difference between driving one's hogs into a neighbor's cornfield, and pulling down the bars to let them walk in themselves, but it was a technical difference only; the result was the same.[32] Another farming analogy appeared in the *Milwaukee Daily Sentinel:* Two men owned a farm together. Each worked a third, planting different crops and using different modes of cultivation. The final third was left open to be cultivated and enclosed by either as needed. One man grew wheat and corn. The other man produced Canadian thistles, "fancying that the business is profitable; but whether profitable or not, insisting upon his right to cultivate the nuisance." For the sake of fellowship, they wrote out an agreement that the open lands should not be planted with thistles. The time came when the man planting grain wanted more ground and the partner repudiated the compact. He bribed judges and got decisions that he had a right to put thistles where he pleased. Would that not be scandalous? Was the analogy with the Nebraska bill not clear?[33]

When the bill passed in May, Cincinnati writers commented again. With the Missouri Compromise gone, "in the name of Heaven, what bulwark of human liberty is next to be mined and demolished."[34] Greeley's *New York Daily Tribune* chimed in. The Kansas-Nebraska bill was "a wanton and unprovoked outrage; it is a lion turned loose by the drunken keepers among the crowd of helpless men, women and children, who have just been feeding and fondling him."[35] But what did the country expect? "If any of our retired merchants, or any ancient fogy anywhere, is rocking himself to sleep with the notion that a doctrine *can* be established respecting Slavery, that the South will not aim to subvert the instant it is discovered that it will operate to her disadvantage . . . let him discard it as quickly as possible."[36] There should be no illusion that there could be business and profits as usual amid political compromises. Even in far-away California, which expressed little interest in Kansas over the years, people saw that the opposition to slavery was grounded in religious fervor, "demanding the immolation of its victims on the altars of its superstitions or its zeal."[37]

The efficiency of the Northern press in creating and propagating its spawn of anti-Nebraska rhetoric impressed Southerners. The hostility to the repeal of the Missouri restriction, the *Richmond Enquirer* noted, was "brought out with the utmost emphasis and power of expression. The opponents of the Nebraska bill have set in motion every engine of popular agitation. The public press, popular meetings, the pulpit and the State Legislatures have been employed as a means for kindling the passions of the mob and coercing the action of Congress."[38] The *New Orleans Daily Delta* too was glad that the era of compromises was over, as the Missouri Compromise seemed to have "added fuel to the strife which it was framed to extinguish." The South needed to acquire some territory, which would "arrest the growing preponderance of the North." The paper suggested the South take up the motto "Cuba—the South—the Union."[39] If history were read right, the *New Orleans Daily Picayune* thought, it would be seen that the Missouri Compromise had not been a real mutual bargain with concessions on both sides. But what chance was there that anyone in the atmosphere of 1854 was interested in reading history aright, or indeed in reading history at all?[40]

What was happening instead seemed to be nothing less than a revolution.[41] Bostonians took to the streets in May 1854, just as the Kansas-Nebraska bill passed, to "rescue" Anthony Burns, who had been captured under the Fugitive Slave Act section of the old compromise system. That shocked the *Boston Post*, a Democratic paper. Was the Fugitive Slave Act not the law of the land? Did civil resistance not open up an unbridgeable abyss? What should the conservatives who ran the newspaper make of "the continuous flood of handbills and placards, the actual presence of hundreds of abolitionists from abroad, and the seditious course of the city abolition press" that had been added to "the mad appeals of journals of other places?"[42]

What of liberty? It was subject to abuse. Said Senator Andrew P. Butler of South Carolina in the Senate chamber in February: "Liberty is like fire, which may be used either to warm and preserve the temple in which it is kindled, or to be the means of its destruction."[43]

The phrase "popular sovereignty" was an epithet of particular genius—a massive simplification, subject to any variety of interested interpretation, and with reach and legs. But who were the people? When and where were they the people? And what would be the neutral instrumentality for the expression of their true will? The issue of how the people's will would be discovered presented an authentic dilemma. Popular sovereignty was often perceived as a two-edged sword, as unsure in application as it was ambiguous in expression.

The *New York Daily Tribune* addressed the voting problem right away. On whom did the Kansas-Nebraska bill devolve the decision for the future of millions of inhabitants on the issue of slavery or freedom? Was it the first twenty-five squatters that arrived, or the first thousand? What about free blacks? What about foreigners? And how was the voting to be regulated?[44]

But the voting mechanism had defenders. The *Washington Daily Union* argued that the popular sovereignty principle was "so palpably democratic and unquestionably sound" that it would end the slavery debate in the public mind.[45] "If sixty, or a hundred thousand of the people of Nebraska, or of Kansas, who are alone concerned in the question, cannot determine whether slavery ought, or ought not to be introduced into these territories," a writer from Missouri said, "we submit that a set of fanatical and desperate politicians . . . are wholly disqualified to legislate upon the subject."[46]

Opinions varied on the advisability of intervention or nonintervention by Congress. On the one hand arose the argument that the territory was common to all the states and the claim that Congress regulated the territories in many ways already, including appointing their governors and justices with veto power. Why should the question of slavery be different? When did full sovereignty inure to the benefit of the regions? Was it immediately upon territorial organization, or only upon the formation and ratification of a state constitution and admission by Congress to the Union? The *St. Louis Daily Missouri Republican* argued this with its cross-town counterparts at the *St. Louis Daily Missouri Democrat* until the *Democrat* was moved to write, "It is difficult to impart the elements of instruction to those who have grown gray in stupidity."[47] Both papers were in a slave state, but they were also in a substantial commercial city, which had close ties to Northern trade and a population with a wide range of interests.

The *Washington National Era* argued that the question was one of agent and principle. Was not Congress merely the agent of the people? Were not the antislavery people who objected to the Kansas-Nebraska Act, and who argued that Congress should intervene to prevent slavery, being, for all their vaunted love of freedom, essentially aristocratic and elitist?[48] The *Detroit Free Press*, the Cass organ, needed to establish a position that was both Democratic and free-soil. So it added that whether or not Congress could constitutionally legislate for the territories, as a practical matter nonintervention was the only common ground upon which the friends of sectional harmony could meet.[49] Popular sovereignty would result in free states. The bill, the Detroit editor wrote, was "the greatest advance movement in the direction of human freedom that has been made since the adoption of the Constitution."[50]

The *Daily Albany Argus* made a similar argument. The alternative to having the people decide would be to leave the deciding to Congress. That might be fine were Congress composed of wise and high-minded people. But members of Congress were more likely than the masses of people to heed the "breezes of expediency" and to be deceived by the "tricks of clap-trap and deception."[51]

There were passionate responses to the promotion of popular sovereignty from all combinations of political direction. The doctrine of popular sovereignty, said a free-soil paper in Chicago "is the very height of demagoguism." It only sounded like democracy. In fact, it transferred what belonged to the many to the hands of a few—that is, from the American people as a whole, represented by Congress, to a few "adventurers" who happened to make it to the local polls first. There would be "gigantic schemes of fraud and plunder" both in land taking and in voting in Kansas, and the aggressive emigrants who went there were likely to "defy the efforts of the general government to direct and restrain them." It would become a kind of "domestic filibuster" operating independently of the rest of the country. Mockingly, the newspaper claimed that the Kansas-Nebraska Act was a kind of new religion, and that "whenever two or three are gathered together in its name, they are entitled to sovereignty." "This is democracy, precious and privileged; and it enables the enterprising few to throw off the rule of the many."[52] The real question, of course, was what faction on the slavery question would get the most people on the ground early in Kansas Territory, and how and to whose benefit they might manipulate public opinion, the polls, or both. That, in 1854, was a disturbing unknown.

Each perspective advanced its own interpretation; every political philosopher claimed his forum. A writer at the *Richmond Enquirer*, while supporting the bill in general, complained of a "deplorable confusion of ideas" in the press concerning its details. He called the idea of absolute territorial squatter sovereignty "a novelty and an absurdity." Congress could intervene in certain conditions. What was the Kansas-Nebraska bill itself but an intervention to allow the ingress of slaveholders into an area forbidden to them by a former congressional edict, the Missouri Compromise? Would Congress be required to admit any state having a republican form of government, no matter how bizarre its institutions? Could Utah apply for admission with polygamy in place because the people there voted for it?[53]

All commentators returned eventually to the problem that the people, as defined by voting in the field, might be the wrong people from the point of view of the faction doing the commenting. A Philadelphia newspaper reminded its readers that it was common to dignify mere mob proceedings by sects or parties as authentic expressions of the public will. How could one be certain that the voice of the people in Kansas would be the "voice of the majority legitimately expressed," and not the voice of a faction "passionate, illegal, or revengeful?" Even the best people were subject in moments of excitement to "inequalities of temper."[54] And the opening of Kansas might be a long and intense moment of excitement.

Maybe the high-sounding idea of the "will of the people" would turn out to be a kind of farce, one of the "popular errors" of the day. Maybe it had been worthwhile in the time of the American Revolution, when independence was "not an ambitious, selfish idea in a leader's brain, but a living feeling in the popular heart." Then, it seemed, the Union was "spoken into being by the almost divine power of the *vox populi*." But it was otherwise in 1854, chary editors thought. "Instead of having public servants to do what we bid them, we have public masters who bid us what to do; and from being a mirror to reflect, legislation has become a mould to shape public sentiment." Partisans were in more demand than patriots these days. "Ballots have become a sort of lottery ticket; public distinction and ability are measured by the rule of salaries; men have come between the public eye and principles, causing a total eclipse of the latter; right has yielded to expediency, and merit to availability." Even God's laws could be modified or ignored. Fortuna of the pagan pantheon may have already taken the place of the Judeo-Christian deity. "Every politician fully believes that the god of chance who has regulated these matters for some years past, may make him president, which is undoubtedly true, provided he is sufficiently corrupt and hasn't too many brains."[55]

These newspaper debates on the Kansas-Nebraska issue were examples of framing. They set up simplified, maybe even false, emotion-filled dichotomies, speaking to the common culture as well as to special sectional and party sensibilities. They created the feeling that there was in each case a stark choice between good and evil and that the alternate choice was unthinkable.

There were subframes as well: The proper place of religion was questioned. Theorists examined the implications of the new legislation for the Indian tribes now resident in Kansas. The stereotypes concerning regional identity and the strategies for regional defense were strengthened. Commentators newly and more intensely examined the morals and ethics of the times and the quality of contemporary leadership. And each of these was played out not only in the press but also on the real stage for this initial drama, the halls of Congress.

The political issue of freedom and authority, of centralization and decentralization, of the will of the people versus the will of representatives had its parallel in the discussion among religious writers of the place in this debate of the higher law of God as it was, or should be, reflected in human law and morality. Early in the Kansas-Nebraska debate, it was said in the U.S. Senate that there was no higher law than the Constitution. While there were many using that as a rough guide to behavior, few would tolerate such a bald statement. According to an article in the *Providence Daily Post:* "None but atheists deny the providence and paramount law of God. . . . The law of God, his revealed will, is the source from which inferior laws are improved, elevated, and carried forward to the highest purposes of utility." But who was to know what the will of God was? This particular writer thought slavery was wrong, but noted that God had let it exist for ages, and it was legal. What to do?[56]

Some were not so hesitant. Greeley and his *New York Daily Tribune*, providing a model of abolitionist fanaticism to the moderates on both sides, argued that compromises should not be observed when they did not correspond to the higher law as revealed through its columns. How could people say that to deliver up fugitive slaves was a necessary part of the compact that bound the Union? The paper compared the founding fathers' compromises on slavery to the beheading of John the Baptist: "Human liberty has been beheaded to gratify the dainty courtesan, Slavery. . . . We are despised for it all over the planet." There were compromises enough in Christianity adapted to the age of steam, but supporting slavery in the West, where it would blight the land and degrade labor, was too much. "Our commercial Christianity may sacrifice its humanity to Slavery for dollars and cents, but sacrificing dollars and cents to Slavery is another matter."[57]

Henry Ward Beecher took up the theme from his pulpit at Plymouth Church in Brooklyn. Both he and Unitarian divine Theodore Parker went on the lecture circuit with an anti–Kansas-Nebraska message. Beecher argued that to say the South had the right to slaves was equivalent to saying a man had the right to be drunk.[58] Parker told a large audience at the Tabernacle auditorium in New York City over a period of nearly two hours that the area of freedom had been shrinking and that its diminishment must stop. If the South were successful in extending slavery into Kansas, then Mexico, Cuba, Puerto Rico, even South America would be next. He claimed, to loud cheers, that Jesus was a "child of Liberty" and that the country must follow Jesus rather than money or political expediency. The Constitution's legalization of slavery had been a covenant of selfishness between the sections. Slavery had to come to an end, and the North should apply all its industrial power and, more, "the gigantic strength of educated intellect" to tread down the monster. "The blessing of Almighty God," he intoned to a crowd huge despite the

February storm raging outside, "will come down on the noblest people the world ever saw—who have triumphed over Theocracy, Monarchy, Aristocracy, Despondency, and have got a Democracy—a Government of all, and by all—a Church without a Bishop, a State without a King, a Community without a Lord, and a Family without a Slave."[59]

The local press noted that three months earlier such an "extraordinary diatribe" given by a minister would have been applauded by only a few, but "the public temper is undergoing a great change in this respect."[60] The next month 3,000 New England clergymen signed a petition opposing the Kansas-Nebraska bill as a violation of the will of God. Hundreds of sermons were preached against it across the country, invalidating, one editor thought, the "threadbare case" that the pulpit should have nothing to do with politics. "It is not," said Samuel Bowles of the *Springfield Daily Republican*, "a question of expediency, nor of commercial or manufacturing prosperity, nor of political economy, as ordinary political questions are, nor of constitutionality *alone*; but it involves important principles of natural law and right;—of moral law and right." The new bill went too far in proposing a compromise with honor in order to enslave and degrade people whom God made free. It was therefore every person's duty to raise his or her voice "whether it interferes with the peace and quietness of churches or not."[61] What historians identify as the age of the social Gospel was many decades in the future, but in effect that was exactly what these preachers put forward.

There were divisions, but the churches became engaged. The *Tuskegee South-Western Baptist* had refrained from participating in discussion of the bill on the ground that a religious journal was not the venue for such a discussion, but by March 1854 it had changed its editorial policy. Although the Prince of Peace never directly interfered with the political institutions of his time, the Northern religious journals were in the fray and left the Southern ones no choice.

The journal went on to argue that the people who put together the Missouri Compromise were no wiser than politicians of the present and that the doctrine of nonintervention was best. The time for the Missouri Compromise line was gone, "and all the indignation meetings which the Beechers and Garrisons, and the noisy tribes of agitators who catch the key note from these vandal spirits, and vociferate it with the energy of Baal prophets upon Mount Carmel cannot *galvanize* even a momentary vitality into that which is 'twice dead.'" The editors did not hope that their fellow Baptists in the North would become proslavery men, but they trusted that as Christians they would leave the slavery question in the hands of the people where the Constitution left it.[62]

The fanaticism of the "political priesthood" in the North became a stock part of Southern editorials. The *Richmond Christian Advocate* noted, "This is a sad affair, not for the country, but for Christianity, so shamefully outraged in 'the house of its friends.'" Jesus had said his kingdom was not of this world, but here were his ministers crusading against the rights of the South, "trailing their priestly garments in the dust to accomplish objects not mentioned in their commission, and never dreamed of in the acts and writings of the apostles."[63] The *Macon Georgia Telegraph* criticized the "pseudo Ministry" that was corrupting youth and adults. It would take fifty years to unwind the falsehoods preached in the pulpits and taught in the schoolrooms of the North during the previous twenty-five years.[64]

Northern spin about Jesus and his ministers was often different. A minister speaking to a large crowd in Providence, Rhode Island, said that Christ had died that mankind might escape deserved punishment for its transgressions, and that he had died for the "ignorant and downtrodden African, as much as for the haughty Anglo-Saxon oppressor." While on earth, Jesus had chosen the lot of the poor man. The black and the red men, whose rights were violated by the Kansas-Nebraska bill, were the brothers of those who were being asked to support it.[65] Kansas, said another minister, was "consecrated to freedom," and religious people could not be indifferent.[66] Although Senator Douglas was highly critical of the petitions of clergymen, many publications argued that clergymen had the same right to free speech as other citizens.[67] Even so, there was surprise when Beecher prayed for Nebraska and freedom and when ministers printed and distributed their "seditious sermons" as pamphlets.[68] "The politicians are stunned and bewildered," said the *Washington Daily Union*, "by the clamors of a new estate that has suddenly appeared in the land. The intimidation of the press is nothing to the intimidation of the pulpit."[69]

The moral fervor spilled over into the Indian question. Just as it is a myth of the cynical young that few in the United States of the nineteenth century cared about the state of the slaves, it is likewise a myth that there was little passion spent in defense of the Indians. As Paul Gates has pointed out in his classic *Fifty Million Acres*, there was at the time of the passage of the Kansas-Nebraska Act no land legally available for white settlement in Kansas. It had been pledged to perpetual reserves for Indian tribes, not only those indigenous to the area but also those who had been forcibly moved from the Southeastern and Great Lakes portions of the Union to allow white expansion into their former hunting and farming grounds.[70] Arguments over the terms of the treaties, the execution of those terms, and the rights of Indians contrasted with those of settlers went on in parallel and intertwined with the arguments over slavery and town sites in Kansas Territory through the next years. Like so many things, these problems could be traced back to lack of specificity in the Kansas-Nebraska Act.

Many observers recognized early the injustice of organizing a territory in Kansas and thereby encouraging rapid emigration of especially aggressive and politically savvy whites into Indian Territory. What was going to happen to the Shawnees, Delawares, Kickpoos, Pottawatomies, Kanzas, and Osages living in the proposed Kansas Territory? Where could they be removed? How could they be civilized or brought the Gospel when they were in such a state of insecurity about their future?[71] "To coerce them to alienate their possessions," wrote the *Austin Texas State Gazette*, "would show an utter disregard of the faith of treaties, while to establish a territorial government over them, thus bringing their tribal homes within the precincts of the white settlements, would, as all experience demonstrates, be to hasten with cruel rapidity the time when the 'last syllable' of their recorded history shall be uttered." It was no "sickly sentiment" to be saddened by that. "If we cannot stay the relentless march of the destroying angel among this doomed race, we should at least do nothing to hasten their descent into an irrevocable oblivion."[72] The idea of exterminating a half million Native Americans, a Louisville newspaper wrote, "is calculated to shock the moral sense of all just men."[73] Even if a decree of nature doomed the Indian, the white men of the United States should contemplate any part they played in it with "pain and humiliation."[74] Would it not be particularly ironic should the rapid removal of the tribes and the breaking of plighted faith with them be done in the wake of the breaking of the Missouri compact, and for the purpose of extending slavery and the Southern slave empire?[75] Was this what was meant by "Let the People Rule?"[76]

As with the other questions, there was an alternative frame here, another choice subtly justified. The relation of the United States to the Indians was, thought a Louisville writer, "anomalous." The United States had assumed the duties of a guardian over the "imbecility and weakness of a minor," and now the Indian presence in Kansas was an "embarrassment." Frontier life was characterized by daring, and no law could restrain the white frontiersmen from entering the region. Statesmen must think of assimilating the Indian and must look beyond the "ignorant present" to a better future.[77] The fate of the tribes was "melancholy," but necessary. No philanthropic plan could be devised that would much modify "the law of this advance of power and civilization, and this decay of ignorance and weakness."[78] There was no reason why "such an extent of the surface of our country should be left and wasted for them to run over in the idle life of hunters."[79]

Ironically, this second choice of peaceful but firm removal and assimilation was advanced strongly by the Southern press, which even proposed the creation of a slave state south of Kansas composed largely of Indians. After all, there was a second irony here: Many of the tribes just to the south of Kansas, where Kansas Indians might be removed, were themselves slaveholders.

Other complications abounded. Indian "floats," that is, titles given to individual Indians, would be the legal basis for the first Kansas towns even while the representatives of the Office of Indian Affairs were negotiating the removal treaties. Claims associations would interfere with the auctions designed to at least get the Indians a good price for the lands they left; the associations were motivated not only by the claim that squatters had rights, but also by the fact that some of the large, moneyed bidders, with their deeper pockets, were of the proslavery persuasion and were envisioning hemp plantations where the Shawnees had of late lived. Everyone recognized that the Mexican War had put the Indians of Kansas, formerly on the border with a foreign country, in the middle of an expanded United States. And it was a United States with a railroad technology capable of building straight across the former Indian Territory to connect the burgeoning Mississippi River valley with booming California. Perhaps the smart money had seen these possibilities all along. But the rhetoric got out of hand.

Amid all these specific arguments to and fro, there grew an undercurrent of Northern and Southern nationalism, of a strong attachment to section, made stronger by the fear and the challenges. When it was said that supporters of the national administration's position on the Kansas-Nebraska Act were "crawling at the feet of the slaveocracy" or were "hewers and drawers of water for the task masters in the South," did that not go beyond hyperbole? The *Boston Post* wondered what words could be better calculated to create sectional strife and break down any common bond that had existed.[80]

The mean epithets for the sections came in a torrent in the early months of 1854 as the Kansas-Nebraska bill moved through Congress—the source of a river of invective to come. A "little knot of Slavery propagandists" in the

U.S. Senate, claimed the *Chicago Daily Tribune*, had prevented the organization of Nebraska in the last session on the grounds that the Indian title had
not been extinguished and that they should honor the Missouri Compromise. But those were not the real reasons, the writers intimated. There was a
"secret history" too in which organized proslavery forces planned to "trample genuine democracy and real freedom ruthlessly under its feet."[81] The
other side was just as harsh. Northern rhetoric, said a Louisville newspaper,
was only "vaporings," sound and fury. Politics was no place for religion, "nor
is the ballot-box the exact tribunal for the decision of points of conscience."
The slave question was damaging the Union, and it was time to "[change] the
game, by throwing out this card" and return to the "more wholesome spirit
of the earlier days of the Republic."[82]

There was agreement that things had grown serious and that the differences seemed intractable as the positions of the sections hardened and individuals were marshaled by propaganda. Yes, slavery was an evil, observed a
writer at the *New York Herald*. But what was gained by that discovery?
Hireling labor in the North was an evil. Cold, hunger, and disease were evils,
all inseparable from the human condition and its way in the real world
through history. Perhaps a greater evil was all the higher-law moralizing
about it. "It is outside of the question. We must stick to the compact of the
States, and the sovereignty of the popular will."[83]

That scenario, however, became increasingly unlikely. We love the South,
said a writer at the *Chicago Daily Tribune*. "But we love the North, bleak land
and cold as it is, but the chosen home of Liberty and Right . . . far better."[84]
Compliments became backhanded. "There stands the South," wrote the *New
York Daily Tribune*. "Look at her! Virginia, the birth place of Washington,
sunk to the level of a mere negro-breeding territory."[85] The Kansas-
Nebraska bill, Greeley wrote, was the first "great effort of Slavery to take
American freedom directly by the throat."[86]

And from the other side: "We perceive that some of the less discreet and
ferocious of the Northern presses are proclaiming that the South will submit
to any humiliation and degradation rather than go out of the Union, but this
is silly language, calculated and intended only to provoke, exasperate, and
insult the feelings of the South. It no more deserves to be heeded than the
language of a drunken blackguard in the street addressed to the passers-
by."[87] Northern newspapers had been made increasingly extreme and unfair, according to the Southern press, by the Kansas-Nebraska debate. Even
when they tried to present the Southern point of view by quoting Southern

newspapers, they interpreted them with "feelings willfully perverse."[88] The "incomplete and irreligious" education of the North led to a "superficial refinement" that bred only discontent and mischief. The whole area needed to be quarantined, as one would do with a patient having a fever.[89]

Why did such division have to happen? A newspaper in Texas noted that the alienation between the sections had started in Congress, spread to churches, and then invaded social circles and colleges. The "diseased state of public opinion" meant that Southern families would as soon send their son or daughter to a brothel for education in morality as to Yale.[90]

The *Daily Albany Argus* thought that during the Kansas-Nebraska debate, sectionalism had grown, almost week by week, to be the "seductive siren" of national politics. A more advanced future would be appalled at the malice of leaders in 1854 and the credulity or timidity of their followers. "Men will read the passionate and childish appeals to prejudice and irrational hatred with which the press of to-day teems, with surprise." But the meanness seemed to grow. The editor could only hope that the common sense of the masses would overcome the manipulations of irresponsible leaders in politics and in the press. The people in both sections should be able to see their dependence upon one another. "No portion of them propose to take up arms and march against their brethren—to bellow forth high-sounding maledictions—or to rush, torch in hand, to the destruction of the capitol." These threats were "the ravings of men who make money or get office by raving, and who know well enough how far they dare to go." The "eternal jargon" about North and South was detestable. What was needed to counter it was only education to true interest. A permanent popular alienation, the newspaper thought, "can never be compassed among the educated, well informed and newspaper reading American public."[91]

Would that it were so! Would that some of the leadership had, as a Southern editor suggested, dipped their heads in ice water to cool their fiery brains.[92] Instead, there was every indication that Kansas-Nebraska was only the commencement of an ever-greater struggle. "Old parties will be disorganized; new combinations formed; the Press will thunder; sectional Discord lift its horrid front. . . . Conservatism will turn pale."[93]

There was some consensus in a negative view of the political leadership of the United States. It was particularly against these pygmies, tiny compared to their forebears, that newspaper columnists warmed their pens in invective. Fomenting disrespect for individuals was entertaining, but it was undoubtedly not helpful. Yet nearly no one of prominence escaped it. It was rare to

give credit for trying or to recognize that the challenges were indeed difficult. Instead, the newspaper-reading public was treated to a picture of a pack
of fools ignoring obvious solutions and escalating the conflict for their own
sordid and selfish purposes.

No wonder nothing got done in Washington, with all the hacks there
floating on the tide accompanied by an "inebriated political morality."[94] The
profitable lecture circuit attracted "exalted itinerants" who excited an already disturbed audience further, taking the role of the missionaries of
old.[95] "Most assuredly," wrote the *Springfield Daily Republican*, "very stupid
men get to Congress."[96] Speeches in Congress were described as "tirades"
that were "petulant," "pettifogging," or "sophistical."[97] A bill or an idea became, in journalistic description, a "sham," "bunkum," "a bore," "tedious,"
"twaddle," "a hollow pretense," "a farce," "a device." The times were called
"degenerate."[98] A "universal spirit of corruption" seemed to pervade the
parties and cliques in the nation's capital. Patent agents and railroad lobbyists formed a "mighty and unscrupulous conspiracy" for attracting the weak
and venal to the feast. "States' rights, the right of the South, the principles
which hold the Union together, are all moonshine with this hungry army of
spoilsmen." There was a "foggy looseness" at Washington, which bode ill.[99]
One would think, watching the debates in Congress, that "half a dozen flocks
of geese had been occupying the hall."[100] One man likened the members of
Congress and the "idle writers" who described their doings to naughty boys
breaking glass.[101]

Such language made the writers and the readers feel worldly-wise and sophisticated—practical men of affairs able to cut through the devices of those
out to fool them. There was a "no-nonsense" stance, a critical mien that took
the easy path of destroying measures for their association with men rather
than the harder one of suggesting positive alternatives. Where were the great
leaders of old? Where were Henry Clay, John Calhoun, and Daniel Webster?
Where were the likes of George Washington and James Madison? Had the
prophets departed?[102] Oh, yes, said the shallow, looking around the surface.
Surely they had.

And so in this context, the solons of Congress, limited as they were to
one-hour set speeches, consumed huge blocks of time debating the Kansas-
Nebraska bill. It passed by the narrowest of majorities late in May, just as
there occurred a rare annular eclipse of the sun.[103] Many observers found
the bill unimpressive. In the view of a writer from Louisville, it was "as disgraceful as it is novel," in that it had been "adjusted to all shades of public

opinion, until, at last, upon reflecting the hue of every faction, it is notoriously destitute of consistency and principle."[104] A writer in Natchez quoted the story of a man who purchased a pie from a boy crying out "Hot Minced Pie." When he tasted it, he found it frozen hard as ice. "You scoundrel," he told the boy. "Why do you call this hot minced pie?" The seller replied, "Because that is the *name* of it."[105]

The *New York Evangelist* took the debates more seriously. Its commentators thought that the bill had removed "ancient landmarks" but admitted that the speeches had been wonderful, with much that "lays hold of the heart." The legislation itself was "a great fact for history."[106] However, most newspapers were not willing to give the proceedings much dignity or respect. That was not what their readers wanted.

There developed almost a cottage industry in describing the scene in the Senate and House chambers during the debates, reinforcing in its tone the impression of startling crisis and of pandemonium, double-dealing, and fear. Senator Salmon Chase commented, looking at the "thronged lobbies" and the "crowded galleries," that the heavy attendance proved "the deep, transcendent interest of the theme."[107]

A spectator at debates in the Senate in March had just come from a call on a large delegation of Nebraska Indians visiting Washington and wondered whether they were much different from the people he saw on the floor and in the galleries of the Capitol. The debate this reporter witnessed went through the night, as debates often did in those days. Lewis Cass spread an old blue and yellow handkerchief on his desk; Sam Houston whittled. Salmon Chase and Charles Sumner had drawn their chairs close and watched intently, while John Weller of California spoke in a "coarse, vulgar manner." When Douglas spoke at 1 A.M., Senator William Seward of New York was frequently on his feet to interrupt. A man sitting next to the reporter said, "If he spoke to me as he does to Sumner, I would get up and knock him down." The reporter wore out at 4 A.M. and left, but the galleries were still filled. Many of the spectators were women.[108]

Another glimpse of the hall came in mid-May as debates wound down. This time the scene was in the House. The members had been thirty-six hours without meals or regular sleep, and many dozed at their desks. The members, wrote a Southern reporter, looked "tired, dirty and clammy; somewhat like men who have slept for six hours in a gutter after being 'on a bust' for four days and nights. Their eyes are blood-shot, their beards long, and their hair tangled and matted." The speaker cried, "Order." The members cried, "Order." There was a threat of fights, with members taking off their coats in readiness. "The contest was kept up, amid the monotony of forms, with here and there a gleam of light to relieve the somber clouds of darkness all around." Parliamentary tricks disgusted the reporter, who thought there was a "skulking behind rules." Why should there be more speeches, after there had been a hundred already? Did the people want speeches?[109]

Whether they wanted them or not, they got them. And the newspapers printed them, selectively to be sure, but often rather extensively, for readers who must have had excellent vision or good glasses. The themes discussed in the press appeared in the debates also: the concern about the Indians, the fear of growing sectionalism, the concern about minority rights in an unbalanced confederation, the awareness of the mix of faith and politics, the concern about the loss of the tenuous peace of the compromises. But there were comments, too, on something broader. Members were aware of their own style and tone and of the extent to which it was replicated in newspapers, pamphlets, and magazines, perhaps to the hazard of the Union. And they were conscious, also, of some destiny that seemed to be driving the country either to progress or to doom almost independently of what any speaker or writer or politician could do.

The rhetoric was dangerous. Senator Archibald Dixon of Kentucky complained that many of the speeches were designed to produce rather than to allay excitement, which was not in keeping with the Senate's mission to promote calm and deliberate consideration of measures.[110] Senator George Badger of North Carolina thought the debates created and reinforced a stereotypical impression of the South. "That we have slaves among us, if it be a fault, God knows it is not our fault. They were brought here in the times of your fathers, and of our fathers." What could anyone do now? "I blame those at a distance from us who take up false and mistaken impressions respecting us. I know that efforts, the most wicked and persevering, have been made to produce these impressions, and to present us to the minds of our northern fellow-citizens as monsters of cruelty and oppression. . . . They have been trained to entertain these sentiments and feelings."[111]

The ministers were among those spreading such misimpressions. Congressman Alexander Stephens of Georgia spoke of the "evil spirit of pride and ambition" they engendered even in the halls of Congress. "Those conventions at the Tabernacle and at Chicago, and elsewhere—the ravings of the infidel preacher Theodore Parker, and all his weaker followers—are but the repetitions of the Pandemonium scenes." They were the "ravings," "howl-ings," and "hissings" of factionists and malcontents.[112]

The propagandists, said Senator John Weller of California, "have taken possession of the press; they have taken possession of a large portion of the light literature of the day. They have even taken possession of the theater."[113] The result, said Senator Andrew Butler of South Carolina, was that the Sen-ate was giving up the "controlling power" granted it by the Constitution and allowing itself to be swept along with public opinion as though the United States were a sort of Athenian direct democracy, trusting in the "simple des-potism of a majority." The Senate's abdication would allow "the masses—un-der the influence of popular leaders—to control the judgment that should come from an organized *will*, duly expressed with sound and disposing memory." The current debate would "afford oil to the lamps of a wild and distracting fanaticism."[114] Senator Lewis Cass of Michigan agreed but noted, "Popular feeling is a power hard to resist."[115]

There were hopes to counter these fears, hopes that the current pain was part of the price of a progress that would either rid the growing country of the incubus of its sinful past or allow some accommodation to emerge of its own accord. Senator William Seward of New York, as so often, was in the van on that issue. He regarded the change as desirable and inevitable. "You may sooner, by act of Congress, compel the sea to suppress its upheavings, and the round earth to extinguish its internal fires, than oblige the human mind to cease its inquirings, and the human heart to desist from its throb-bings."[116] Senator Robert Hunter of Virginia agreed but thought the benefi-cent workings of destiny were a reason for the government to let the process well enough alone. Government should only protect the basic rights of peo-ple and then leave it to them to develop their own moral and material re-sources. Free enterprise had made the United States the wonder of the world, and it had been done through "self-acting and self-adjusting" prin-ciples working through "unseen forces." Worry over the slavery question was a distraction to a country that, united, could dominate the world. Hunter supported the Kansas-Nebraska bill, not, he said, because it was of any prac-tical benefit to the South, but because it recognized the benefits of untram-meled freedom to choose.[117] Senator Charles Sumner of Massachusetts did not dissent about that, but he disagreed on what the signs of the times por-tended. The "great omens," he said, of developing civilization were all with the antislavery side. "Art, literature, poetry, religion—everything which ele-vates men—all are on our side. The plow, the steam engine, the railroad, the

telegraph, the book, every human improvement . . . gives new encouragement to the warfare with slavery."[118]

But whatever the result, there was agreement that the country would move
into an unfamiliar future quickly. Said Congressman John Millison of Virginia: "Young America cannot wait. It is perpetually screaming 'Progress!
Progress!' The course of nature is altogether too slow." The country was
"shallow, saucy, headstrong, and foolhardy," seeing no danger and avoiding
none.[119] Young America, said, Congressman Richard Yates of Illinois, was
wiser than an earlier public. "With ruthless hand," it was "obliterating all the
old and time-tested landmarks, names, and ideas, and . . . going forth with
the flaming sword of innovations, laying waste to the antiquated superstruc-
tures of our simple-minded fathers." Why waste time on "sickly sentimentality" when such an adventure was at hand?[120]

The final bill certainly started rather than ended something. It was, a
journalist thought, "one of those great events which, in a nation's history,
inaugurate a political revolution, and a new cycle in political affairs."[121] But it
was also a mishmash. It was, said Congressman William Sapp of Ohio, a bill
to "delude men who may be carried off by mere names."[122] It was, said Senator Thomas Hart Benton of Missouri, "a bill of assumptions and contradictions—assuming what is unfounded, and contradicting what it assumes." It
was a "see-saw" bill, an "amphibological bill" that was "stuffed with monstrosities, hobbled with contradictions."[123] Terms like "popular sovereignty" and "nonintervention" were, thought Congressman Charles Hughes
of New York, "mere catch-words . . . a mere decoy duck, a sugaring over of
the devil."[124] According to Congressman Presley Ewing of Kentucky, anyone
could see the vague political construction as he wished it to be, just as Polo-
nius in Shakespeare could see a cloud as resembling a whale or a weasel, as
his interlocutor suggested.[125]

The sections organized to see that their own take on the bill would become
reality. Local elections all over the country turned on the Nebraska question.
The Blue Lodge and the Kickapoo Rangers organized in Missouri to influence the initial votes in Kansas Territory in favor of slavery, while the Massachusetts (later New England) Emigrant Aid Company began raising capital
to ensure that, at least eventually, Kansas would enter the Union as a free
state.

Why had Congress not been more specific, asked a writer at the *New York
Daily Tribune*? Why leave so much to the "construction of contingency?" If
the members meant freedom, they should have said so. If they meant slav-

ery, that should have been the message. "Men, if you cannot afford to do right, at least muster the courage to be manfully wrong! If you will fire your blunderbuss at the Rights of Man, do not shut your eyes and pretend that you cannot see what you are aiming at."[126] The bill was, said a Missouri journalist, "swathed and bandaged in the corruptions of Washington City; linked with the hopes and schemes of the plunderers of the national treasury; fondled as the darling child of those who seek to sow broadcast the seeds of disunion." There was peace, but now a new man had arisen in Israel and set up unknown idols, and the people must decide whether to worship them.[127]

Perhaps, however, things were in the hands of fate—of Providence, people hoped. A Southern doggerel went:

This wonderful Nebraska bill has wrought,
A miracle that ne'er was seen or thought.
Three thousand priests of pure New England breed,
Who never in one point of faith agreed,
And never will again—that I'll be sworn—
Have tuned their throats to one harmonious strain,
And draw together both by bit and rein.

Religion ne'er could bind them in one tether
But politics has brought these saints together.[128]

John Greenleaf Whittier wrote a poem that became the "Emigrant's Song" sung at Kansas organizing meetings throughout the East. Went one verse:

We cross the prairie as of old
The pilgrims crossed the sea.
To make the West, as they the East,
The homestead of the free. . . .
Upbearing like the Ark of old
The Bible in our van,
We go to test the truth of God,
Against the fraud of man.[129]

The *Washington Daily Union* thought that in 50 years the United States would have a population of 100 million, and in 100 years, 400 million, and would laugh at the "low and narrow lines of reasoning" about national destiny typical of the 1854 Kansas debates. The nation had been and would be guided by "unsuspecting ways and unconscious agencies" into its destined greatness despite the blunders of men.[130] The *New York Daily Times* thought that "Young America" was not just a phrase, but a concept that "involves ideas, thoughts, sentiments, instincts and practical tendencies of the greatest significance in the political and social sphere." God approved of the noble and progressive ideas suggested by that epithet and frowned on the Old Fogeys, who would put too fine a point on law and history. "It is wise and reverent," the *Times* said of the phrase, "not ignorant or arrogant."[131]

Perhaps so. But the editor at the *Detroit Daily Free Press* attributed the Kansas-Nebraska bill to the "father of lies" rather than to the Lord of Hosts.[132] There was a cloud looming up in the West, the *Charleston Mercury* observed, that was already larger than a man's hand and promised to grow quickly.[133] A Virginia correspondent of the *New York Daily Times* wrote, "You Northern people don't understand the difficulties of the case."[134]

CHAPTER 3

VOX POPULI

—•◦•—

In the wake of the Kansas-Nebraska bill, there was certain to be a battle, either at the ballot box or with rifles and bowie knives, or perhaps both. People seemed to know that the fight would shape the future Union, setting precedents that would either reassure or further frighten and annoy the sections. The bill, wrote a New Haven paper, broke down the confidence in slavery compromises, and the only consolation was "that there is a Providence that shapes the destiny of the country . . . and that he will bring good out of this monstrous evil."[1] The *Charleston Mercury* writers thought that if the federal government were "shorn of its symmetry and robbed of its spirit," it could become the instrument of a tyrannical majority—"a mere football for narrow minded and mean demagogues."[2] However, a newspaperman in Natchez thought that the masses of the people might be proven wiser than their leaders, if only their voices could be honestly heard: "Mississippi politicians may change with each mutation of Court and Cabinet—ever like the sunflower, watching the face of the great dispenser of political light and heat—but the people cannot be so fickle."[3]

However attractive that idea was in the abstract, voting was hardly the automatic salvation of the South. First, public opinion was running against the South, as the propaganda engines of the North gained purchase on the issue and devoted increasing quantities of ink to it. "Errors of opinion" and the "plague" of anti-Southern abolitionism, wrote an observer in Columbus, Georgia, early in 1855, had infected the whole body of Northern society.[4] Second, Northerners were more restless and more entrepreneurial than Southerners, and their property was portable. "While the planter is collecting his 'people' and preparing for their removal," a New Englander commented, "the free laborer, whose only help is his own stalwart arms, is there with his axe on his shoulder and his rifle by his side, building his shanty on his 'claim,' and preparing the soil for his crop."[5] While farming, he would be voting. Third, the North would be likely to devote more money to the cause in Kansas than would the South. It was a wealthier region and was well known both for organizing prosperous corporations and for raising considerable money for philanthropies at public meetings. The New England Emigrant Aid Company contributed a relatively small percentage of the early population and resources of Kansas. However, as a Yankee corporation—a sort of successor to the Massachusetts Bay Company that had taken such a role in the planting of the original colonies—and backed, as it was, by big names in Northern business, it cut a larger figure rhetorically than materially.[6] While all factions pretended to be ready to respect the will of the people, none actually was unless the result suited their predilections. Amid the rhetoric of idealism, the practice was cynical, leaving all parties open to charges of hypocrisy and inconsistency.

Certainly, the results and significance of voting were intimately related to the organization of emigration into Kansas, and that organization was controversial from the start. The *New York Herald* objected to aid organizations, as "immigrants are not to be cooped like fowls, or driven in flocks like sheep," but thought it was appropriate for the struggle to take place in Kansas rather than in Boston, Charleston, or Washington.[7] Without a struggle at the polls in the field, the arguments became so abstract as to be irrelevant and impractical. The lecture season in the East was an abomination, observers said. The "peripatetic humbug" went around the Union "diffusing borrowed lights and plagiarized rhetoric . . . like gamblers and thimble riggers at country fairs."[8] Perhaps the theorists, both North and South, would find it more difficult to weather a Kansas winter than to address a crowd. "At all events, let the agitators who are going into spasms concerning slavery in Kansas, bundle up and move there without delay. . . . There can be no repeal of the sovereignty of the people."[9]

Be that as it may, populating Kansas with voters was hardly the panacea that some had hoped it would be. From the time of the controversy over the first Kansas elections in late 1854 and early 1855, the legitimacy of the electoral process there was in serious question. As with other issues, the emotion the elections generated was related to the perception that although the stage was in Kansas, the drama affected every citizen of the United States.

The first Kansas electoral issue to emerge nationally was whether the voting population of the new territory was the natural one—that is, the settlers— or was made up of select groups of political enthusiasts who had been marched into a potential war zone. On this front, the Southern propagandists had an advantage. Northern capitalist enterprise had brought settlers of antislave sentiment to Kansas from a great distance and at an accelerated rate. The reaction of the South—not only in organizing its own emigration groups and asking its own state legislatures for funding but also in using violence to intimidate and disarm these Northern interlopers—could be viewed as a defensive action against a well-funded aggressor.

Eli Thayer, who founded the predecessor of the New England Emigrant Aid Company in May 1854, was often described as an impractical visionary, involved in what he later himself described as a "crusade." However, the South took his $5 million capitalization of the company, and its potential for publicity as well as profit, seriously.[10] The Emigrant Aid Company, wrote a reporter in Richmond in 1855, "is the sole author of the deplorable broils in Kansas." Massachusetts itself was an abomination—a state that had "exhibited from her first settlement, a haughty, intolerant and dictatorial spirit, never equaled by any other people." Its people, especially those moved to go to Kansas, were "[a] little, waspish, narrow-minded band of pseudo-philanthropists."[11]

The North, Southern writers intoned, had organized a society with branches in all Northern cities. This "nefarious movement" planned to buy up immense tracts of land, which the Aid Company intended to donate "to the refuse of foreign and domestic 'hirelings,' to be paid for by abolition votes." This company was the "motive power" by which the South was to be deprived of its rights.[12] To call these people emigrants, went a broadside sent out from Missouri in 1855, was "a sheer perversion of language." They were enthusiasts, "men with a single idea," who had been "picked and culled from the ignorant masses, which Old England and New England negro philanthropy has stirred up and aroused to madness."[13]

Or was that too generous an interpretation of a movement that was perhaps primarily economic at its base? Was the Aid Company not just another rapacious corporation? "What care the stockholders, so long as the 'quarter sections' are retained, 'best water rights' secured, 'steam and grist mills' leased in their name, and 'comfortable dividends in prospect'?" While the pioneers were battling weather and Indians in the wilderness, "the stockholders will be enjoying the comforts of Boston civilization, and the exhortations of Brother [Henry Ward] Beecher or Brother [Theodore] Parker, a thousand leagues away."[14] Thayer, the Latin-quoting thirty-five-year-old self-made businessman who ran the company, predicted that someday the national capital would be in Kansas,[15] a prediction that moved Missouri partisans to offer a $200 reward for his capture, dead or alive.[16]

The supporters of the New England Emigrant Aid Company naturally disagreed with these unfavorable characterizations. The *Boston Christian Register* commented that the company was the prime vehicle for a "great Exodus to this New Land of Promise."[17] The company's objectives, claimed the *New York Daily Tribune*, were of the "most disinterested and lofty character."[18] The Northern settlers, said the *Boston Journal*, were special: They had "a fixed purpose aside from securing a home in the wilderness, and they are not the men to be turned aside from their object."[19]

Thayer had taken his inspiration from William Seward's speech during the Kansas-Nebraska debates accepting the challenge of a battle between slavery and freedom, with the greatest numbers at the polls to prevail. Such a legal contest was the essence of democracy, and it was as appropriate to organize for it as for any national presidential campaign. Thayer's goal was to create a "new method of bringing two hostile civilizations face to face upon the disputed prairies of Kansas in such a way as to unite in its support the entire Northern people of whatever parties." The North should go, Thayer wrote, "with all our free labor trophies: churches and schools, printing presses, steam-engines and mills," and thus peaceably prevail. Such a method was far superior to staying home and worrying about slave auctions and manacles while millions remained in chains.[20]

Thayer was aware of the importance of publicity to his cause. Accordingly, he met with Horace Greeley and formed a firm connection with Greeley's newspaper, the *New York Daily Tribune*. Thayer, on his first visit to New York City, visited Greeley in his office in a grimy building at Spruce and Nassau streets and there, amid the din of chattering telegraph machines, the smell of ink and hides, and the roar and rumble of the presses, laid the case before the editor.[21]

Greeley was as eccentric as Thayer, as determined, and far more influential. He had his finger on the collective pulse of the nation and was, a biographer wrote, a "gatherer, transmitter and reflector of ideas, a kind of switchboard for international republicanism." In 1855 the *Tribune* purchased a ten-cylinder Hoe press, which cost $25,000 and was the largest in the world at that time. That it could do so and that it needed to do so had much to do with the Emigrant Aid Company and its project in Kansas. Greeley was a "philosophical incendiary with a vision of universal freedom," and the struggle in Bleeding Kansas was just the kind of forum for him.[22] Yet he emphasized that he only represented a trend and that attacks on his peculiarities would be to no avail in stopping the movement. Journalism would gain dignity only by disassociating itself from party and from personality and attaching itself to causes and to truth.[23]

There was no question that the *Tribune* thrived financially by emphasizing the Kansas issue. By the middle of 1856, at the height of the Kansas controversy, the newspaper paid semiannual dividends of 125 percent per year on the stock. In the summer of that year it purchased a new building, paying 25 percent of the purchase money down. It acted as a clearinghouse for Kansas aid donations and itself contributed heavily both to the New York Kansas Aid Committee and to the new Republican Party.[24]

The *Tribune* started its Kansas series with a string of editorials late in May 1854 as the Kansas-Nebraska Act passed Congress. "The Revolution is accomplished and Slavery is King," Greeley wrote. "How long shall this monarch rein?" The answer must come from the people who were willing to go to Kansas and to farm and fight there. It was time for an "earthquake" to create a change in the material world. Calmness, practicality, organization, and unity were important—all things the Aid Company could provide. "The cause of Freedom in Kansas must be strengthened by the immediate migrating thither of faithful, intelligent, high-principled settlers from New York, New England, Ohio and the Free West." There should be branches of the New England Emigrant Aid Company in every state. There should be new journals. Clergymen of the "right stamp" should go to Kansas. Pioneers should establish towns without encroaching on the rights of the Indians and without expecting any help from a federal government dominated by the Democratic Party. "Our adversaries will set up their standards in the territory in the panoply and pay of the Federal Government, while the soldiers of Freedom must look out for themselves." It would require 5,000 picked men "for whom the plains have no terrors," and at least $1 million to start. It would not be easy, and the momentum was currently wrong. "There is rejoicing around the auction-blocks of Richmond, and slave-pens of Charleston; and a wider revelry in the midnight orgies of the dealers in human sinews generally, at the prospect of new markets opening for their merchandise at once in the South and in the West." But there were forces "silently maturing" that in time would ensure that the sun no longer looked down on any American slave.[25]

The West was the place for these changes, as "everything whatever connected with this marvelous and gigantic region rises at once to gigantic dimensions." The more the eastern American penetrated there, "the more free is his action, the less he is encumbered by an obnoxious past, the easier are his movements, and the greater, therefore, and purer the social outlines and forms which are shaped by him."[26] The prairie of Kansas was a monotonous and "wearisome" landscape to some, but its regular forms and wide horizon seemed to others a tablet upon which American civilization and enterprises might write.[27]

The first party of emigrants sponsored by the Aid Company went to Kansas in July 1854 and established a town site on three sections of land laid out into 600 lots with ninety-nine acres reserved for parks. The emigrants had big plans for this "Yankeetown," or "New Boston," soon named Lawrence.[28] Their mantra was that the Emigrant Aid Company provided an opportunity to "be good and grow rich at the same time." The company expected returns of 25 percent on its investment in town sites and farms in Kansas, coming particularly from buying Indian and government lands in large tracts at low prices and reselling to individual settlers.[29]

Lawrence was a primitive place at first, consisting mostly of tents and a common dining room.[30] In December 1854 a visitor found fifty "huts" and a boarding house that charged $2.50 a week. Women and children were exhausted when they reached Lawrence, and the settlers faced controversy over claims, questions about Indian title, and a hard-to-plow virgin grassland.[31] In a letter to Brattleboro, Vermont, a man, sitting on a three-legged stool, described the twelve-by-fifteen-foot sod-and-hay-bale house in which he and his brother and their wives lived. Many houses in Lawrence, he said, were "built in a shape similar to hencoops," with a roof of cotton cloth.[32] The town, said another writer, presented a "dreary aspect—the Indians roamed uninterrupted through the forests," while the emigrants lived "in miserable canvas tents, with scarce room enough for one man to stretch himself."[33] Things were not much better a year later. In the fall of 1855 a visitor said that Lawrence had "a celebrity . . . unproportioned to its size." Imagine, he wrote, a few stone buildings of the penitentiary or cotton factory style of architecture "looking eternally down on a hundred . . . log cabins and frame houses . . . which seem built on no premeditated plan. . . . place three saw mill pipes, puffing out steam, in the background to the right, and a cabin on top of the hill to the left, and the 'sum total of the whole' will be the little Yankee city of Lawrence."[34]

Clarina Nichols, however, wrote in January 1855 that Kansas was lovely. It "outromanced" all description. "It is as if the Almighty had spread wide the heritage of humanity to indicate its inherent right to freedom." It seemed to her the perfect place for a crusade.[35]

The group at Lawrence, whatever their attitudes, were in a political minority in the territory in 1854–1855. Charles Robinson, one of the agents of
the Aid Company at Lawrence and eventually the first governor of the state of
Kansas, compared the arrival of the New England parties on the prairie to
the situation of the Hebrew scouts in the land of Canaan, who quailed before
the giants in the earth and rent their clothes. Even some of the leading abolitionists predicted that Kansas would "eat up" the little cadre of free-state
settlers in short order.[36]

Strong stereotypes of the Northern and the Southern emigrants emerged
in the press. Readers of Kansas history from the time of the Kansas-Nebraska Act are familiar with the border ruffian image promulgated in the
Northern press through its descriptions of William Quantrill's 1863 raid on
Lawrence. Equally ubiquitous were the word portraits in the Southern, and
sometimes Northern, Democratic press of the fanatic abolitionists from
New England moving into the region with their Bibles and rifles and not
amenable to order or reason. The wild descriptions were as much a part of
the campaign to get out the vote and to influence the vote as any strictly political argument about the issues.

The Missourians crossing the line to vote in Kansas or to take up small
homesteads or plat out towns, were, according to a Boston writer in 1854,
"scum" who were "roving about like ruthless savages, drinking like beasts,
swearing like furies." They supposedly tried to convince the Indians that
slavery was a boon, while at the same time prostituting and intoxicating Indian women in the indulgence of their "dirty passions."[37] They represented
a descent to barbarism in the country. "Heaven spare us from the infection—
not the bullets," wrote a fearful New Yorker. "For in no other civilized land
can there be found so obscene, depraved, brutish a race of beings, as inhabit
the border counties of Missouri." What a spectacle that the president of the
United States should take sides with the "hellish designs" of these "demons
of the night," who dreamed of ravishing Northern women carried off to their
"bestial dens."[38] Congressman Gerrit Smith compared the Missourians to
wolves. If a farmer found a wolf in the sheepfold, he would not make a compromise that let it take half the flock. "No, he would deem the wolf a gentleman entirely incompetent to make a bargain—would insist, that as a wolf, he
had but one right—and that, *the right to be killed.*"[39]

It was said that every person whose idea of popular sovereignty did not include the establishment of slavery would be mobbed, maimed, or put to
death by ruffians waiting for him at the Kansas border.[40] The Southern parti-

sans thought of themselves as chivalrous knights and so were easily carica-
tured as Don Quixotes out of their proper time. "We are to have the Middle
Ages over again in Missouri," wrote a journalist. "We are to be booted and
spurred, clad in steel and robed in ermine, to mount war horses and amuse
ourselves with tilts and jousts."[41] The motto of these antique types, the
Northern press reported, was "knives to the hilt, and bullets to the muzzle."[42]

The style of the ruffians supposedly corrupted the entire country. It led
the members of Congress, once gentlemen, to speak in the manner of desperadoes and to descend to blows. Stump speeches as well as formal addresses were no longer the mature opinions of statesmen but "ravings" born
of an exaggerated self-importance. "Has the Senate no staff to strike down
the irreverent barbarism that plucks them by the very beard? Has decency
no spokesman, where violence and disorder have a score at least? Will no
one interpose to save the vanishing dignity of the highest deliberative body
in the world?"[43]

Northern emigrants characterized the Southerners in Kansas as arrogant
braggadocios, accustomed to lording it over slaves and acting the aristocrat.
A minister living in Lawrence wrote to a religious paper in 1857 that it was
possible to forgive the murders and house burnings in the interest of peace
in the future. But there was something less easy to bear, namely, that "devilish, overbearing, slave-driving spirit, which lowers upon and cracks its lash
over free men. It is the constant, petty, irritating exercise of tyrannical, ar-
bitrary power which eats into the soul and goads on to madness."[44]

David Atchison, the former U.S. senator who led the Missouri militias in-
filtrating Kansas Territory, was often misquoted and was regularly described
as the very type of the Southern ruffian. He broadcast "exhortatory, imprecatory, inflammatory epistles" recruiting vile men. His every act, the *New
York Daily Times* claimed, was treason, and he threatened slaughter with
every breath. He was a "modern Cataline," a leader of a filibuster more dangerous than any foreign adventurer.[45] His kin was found in every bar room
or political meeting—small lawyers "of democratic professions, and vile
habits; affecting vulgarity of dress, manners and association." They always
had a quid of tobacco or a huge flaming cigar. "They may be heard swagger-
ing and blustering wherever a lazy village audience can be gathered together,
unsparing in profanity, and as ready with a blow or a bowie-knife as with the
tongue." Atchison was only an example of the "noisy and brawling type." His
election to the Senate was as much an insult to democratic government, a

New York paper said, as the onetime appointment to the Roman Senate of the emperor's horse.[46]

Atchison's reputation varied with the viewer, always, however, tending to one or another extreme. "The reckless, dram-drinking pettifogger of the Abolition print, is the hero of the slaveholder, the Godfrey of the new crusade, the redeemer of a virgin territory from the low, brutalizing, blighting influence of Freedom and free labor."[47] A newspaper in Detroit noticed that extremes met, and that the monomania of an Atchison was not unlike that of a Greeley. "Atchison agrees with the foaming abolitionists of the North that the whole question of slavery hinges upon the events of the Kansas controversy. Thus, two extremes, with jaundiced vision, see the same object from different standpoints, and both strive for the advantage by extraordinary means. The spectacle is monstrous."[48]

Epithets about the Southerners were legion. They were "myrmidons of border ruffianism," examples of "gigantic wickedness," who had committed some of the "most execrable crimes recorded in history."[49] The proslavery apologists at Washington were "Catalines," and the settlers from Missouri, "savages," "ferocious blackguards," "drunks," "burglars," "imbeciles," "pirates," "highway robbers," "devourers of widows' houses," "cannibals," and "midnight assassins."

There was no rhetorical journey a reporter would not undertake for spectacular effect. A particular target was the small town of Lecompton, which, although it became the capital of Kansas, was nondescript enough to serve as a case study of the way in which proslavery sentiment diminished individual character and retarded economic and social development. In September 1857 a Chicago correspondent described a "Night at Lecompton" in terms designed to paint a vivid and negative picture in the minds of his readers of the fate of Kansas should the proslavery faction ultimately prevail there. At the center of the "horrors" of his visit was the hotel and the dinner served him there: "On the ringing of the gong we floated into the dining room with a tide of hungry cormorants. The room was long and dark—darkened with clouds of lazy swarms of house flies; and as each guest would take his place at the board a full thousand of the undrowned and unentangled ones would rise in clouds to seek a more quiet retreat. . . . The waiters upon the table were white and colored slaves, who were the subjects of constant imprecations and damning. . . . One gentleman sitting near was so ponderously drunk as to be entirely unable to hold his head up while eating, and lay on the edge of the table with his chin, sucking up coffee from the saucer."[50] In a similar article entitled "Daguerreotypes of Lecompton," published in December 1857, the observer gave an anything-but-neutral photograph of the Kansas capital and its residents. Concerning the clerk of the constitutional convention, then meeting there, he wrote, "Imagine a regular built Philadelphia or Baltimore Plug Ugly, and then dash in a little of the pirate slave-trader and Border Ruffian, and it will give but a faint idea of this fellow." He was, the reporter concluded, "a cross between a bull and a jackass."[51]

Editors were as extreme as correspondents. "Better, ten thousand times better," wrote one in Wisconsin in 1856, "would it be that every Northern press were burned, than that it should be an accomplice to tyranny or a pander to barbarism."[52] It had become habitual, one editor said, for Northern papers to stereotype Missourians and exaggerate their deeds, so much so that "a letter is hardly thought worthy of publication unless it contains a little of the horrible."[53] Such a celebration of wild hyperbole was hardly adequately countered by the assertions of visitors and conservative editors that the proslavery people in Kansas were, in their experience, as "civil as mice."[54]

Northern emigrants did not escape the sting of the stereotype. So many stereotypes were directed specifically at the New England Emigrant Aid Company that it published an "Address" to the people of Missouri in the fall of 1855 as a corrective. The company only helped settlers with their transportation to Kansas, the address claimed; it did not interfere with Indians' lands and was not in the propaganda business.[55] However, few newspaper and magazine readers in either section believed that. For all the company's denials of a direct connection between itself and the *Lawrence Herald of Freedom*, it was generally understood that the paper was the organ of the Emigrant Aid Company, that the company had financed the movement of its editor George W. Brown from Pennsylvania to the Kansas plains, and that Brown's mission there went beyond publishing the price of corn and documenting local deaths and marriages.[56] The Southern press accused the Aid Company of hiring writers and correspondents to "manufacture a false public opinion" both in newspapers and in books.[57]

The cant of the "Abolition Pharisees of the North" was said to create a "mass of disorder, crime and misery which is shocking to contemplate."[58] New England, from the perspective of New Orleans, was a "huge witches' caldron into which every ingredient is flung."[59] Philanthropy, it was said, was the "disease of America," and people in the North treated every public question sentimentally. They seemed, in the words of Charles Dickens, "all mind and nerves." Common sense was not to be had. "In Parker's Church, in Emerson's parlor, in Garrison's office—in public life, in private life, in loafing life, at the table where 'aesthetic tea' is poured out for a select few of powerful mind and miserable nerves, . . . the sentiment precedes the shriek, and the shriek is the necessary complement of the sentiment."[60] The antislavery emigrants were "insects" that had deposited their eggs in Kansas and that "generate a brood of crawling political maggots to be winged and to buzz through the country as public sentiment." Why was every trifling disease of the American system "being fly-blown by this bite of fanatical vermin?"[61] The "Molochs" who controlled the North were the "wizards" who invoked the tempest in Kansas. They wanted to "impale" the U.S. Constitution on "faggots" and plunge the Union into civil war from their safe desks in New York City.[62] The Northerners in Kansas were painted as insatiable beasts, "godless and insane," deaf to reason, insensitive to pity—bedlamites, tigers who, tasting a drop of a victim's blood, howled for the whole carcass.[63]

The most baneful result of ignorance, wrote a Charleston editor, was the folly it engendered, "dragging in its train the concomitant evils of presumption, prejudice, fickleness, intolerance and vice." The insolent pragmatists of the North, so positive they knew what they were doing, thrust their "blank visage" in anyone's face and "belched" with discordant noises at wiser people. Could orderly self-government come from such bigots, asked the editor, or would they want instead a polity that they could easily manipulate?[64]

The Emigrant Aid Company was not without its critics among Democratic newspapers in the North. The *Providence Daily Post* noticed late in 1855, as violence escalated in Kansas, that there was no such news from Nebraska. The difference was the Aid Company. "Its lecturers, its newspapers, and its letter-writers, have edified us with violent abuse of the friends of slavery in Kansas and its neighborhood—representing them as ignorant, degraded, vile, sensual and savage, in character and habits; as drunkards, liars, perjurers, blasphemers, cutthroats and devils." More than that, the company had framed the Kansas emigration as a battleground for freedom and had armed its representatives as soldiers in the fray. Although the company had officially advised moderation, and although civil war would certainly not be in keeping with its economic aims, was it any wonder that among the "more excitable and less intelligent" of the masses, both North and South, the language it used should have produced hatred, bitterness, and violent action?[65]

While Southerners were being accused of being pirates, Northerners were being called "effeminate Greeks," "frogs," "lice," "Philistines," "lizards," "pimps," and "peddlers."[66] Antislavery emigrants were said to really be in Kansas not to oppose slavery but to make money.[67] None of them were real settlers.[68] Lawrence, said a Richmond correspondent lying low there in 1856, was "peopled by a set of hired assassins; men sent on by Beecher . . . Robinson, and other fanatics."[69]

The average emigrants sent by the New England Emigrant Aid Company were, Southern writers said, not suited for menial labor and not prepared financially to be the owners and operators of profitable farms. They tended to be short, with "sallow complexion[s], lean and stringy, suspicious looking, nervous movements, presumptuous, inquisitive, cold and hungry . . . [the] sleeves of their coats, and the legs of their pantaloons too short."[70] They were less than manly men, dandies "who were doubtless clerks on living salaries, with nice ruffled shirts and perfumed handkerchiefs," who cursed the day they went to Kansas.[71] They were "white-fingered clerks" sent from Boston "to plague the frontiersmen and thwart the natural course of events." They were fanatics who "Mahomet-like would proselyte by fire and sword."[72]

They were not to be trusted. "They presume upon any indulgence. Blinded by fanaticism which springs from the one idea of self-righteousness, they rival in audacity the Prince of Darkness; and as they sound their watch cry, Freedom! Freedom!! Freedom!!! would govern us with a rule more despotic than that with which his Sable Majesty governs his imps." They stole peoples' servants. They practiced "vile machinations and deceptions" and murdered with "Machiavellian smiles."[73] No wonder! Some of them came from Massachusetts, where "they may have hung old women for witches . . . and been guilty in a thousand ways of the most fanatical, incendiary, lawless, offensive, and absurd acts ever known of a civilized and intelligent community."[74] One Southern official in Kansas said he would "rather be a painted slave over in Missouri or a serf to the Czar of Russia than have the Abolitionists in power."[75] If the free-soil people succeeded in Kansas, with their "wild heresies," who, asked another commentator, would "arrest the career of the Goths and Vandals and knightly pilgrims of the North" from sweeping over the entire South?[76] Many objected to any comparison of these mobs sent to Kansas to fight against slavery with the Puritan fathers of the colonies.[77] Mothers in the far West, a congressman claimed, hushed their crying children by telling them that if they did not stop, the New England Aid Company would be after them.[78]

There *were* those who saw these sectional stereotypes as exaggerated in the interest of newspaper circulation. They saw, too, that the newspaper stories that created the circulation also brought forth the rough types that they then proceeded to describe. We disapprove of border ruffians, wrote a reporter in Georgia, "but we also highly disapprove of that want of sense, want of temper, want of all power of comprehending the true interests of society, which lead men of education and ability, to inflame and stimulate the passions of those classes of society who always have been and always will be the most excitable and difficult to control."[79] There was too much beating of the drums and waving of the red flag in Kansas, wrote a Cincinnati newspaper. "You have more excitement in Cincinnati and in Washington about Kansas than there is in all that territory, the people of which are innocent of any knowledge of three-fourths of the trouble imputed to that pandemoniomized Eden." Every private feud, from dog fights to hog stealing, every impromptu drunken quarrel, was imputed to the battle between slavery and freedom.[80] Calm thinkers were appalled that the country was "permeated with a current of nervous excitability. . . . Society is divided into cliques, each of which proscribes the other."[81]

Notwithstanding the instructions of wise people, wrote a columnist in St. Louis, that the golden mean was best, the country was tending to extremes. People were like planets that, when the balance of power that retained them in their orbits was destroyed, "fall in ruin upon the central sun, or are hurled away and lost in the abyss of unknown space." Too many men neglected their own businesses to stir in that of another. Their intellects were acute, "but their temperaments impulsive, eccentric and unbalanced; so that, like the keen but indolent Athenians, they are continually seeking something odd, novel, or unnatural." Slavery encouraged extremes, all "rabid," disorganizing, and destructive. "Moderation, candor, and expediency" were "scoffed at" by both the Northern fanatic and the Southern fire-eater.[82] Did these men, asked a writer from Ohio, think the people "are a set of brainless fools, reeking and panting for each other's blood, and that they have no better pastime than to go a thousand or two miles into the prairies of Kansas to cut each other's throats"?[83] Apparently so. There was, wrote a reporter in New Orleans, "no spirit, no idea, nor desire so absolutely contagious as that of war." Public opinion was no longer a "mere chatterer and caucuser; it is a tall man, 'with a helmet on its head and a long sword by its side!'"[84] Few could see the dire ultimate result of all this loose talk, this lack of temperance, forbearance, and common sense. "The poisoned dart is flung, it enters, it rankles, and it will fester and fester many a weary day."[85] One paper likened the conflict to the religious wars of the Puritans and Cavaliers come again to the American plains.[86]

Perhaps the whole business of squatter sovereignty was a myth, a fad, a media creation, like "the last new bonnet from Paris, or the most senseless opera from Italy." Would-be statesmen seemed to think the voting doctrine was some sort of revelation and "confounded it with the Koran," which would make the territories as "perpetual paradise." It was the "squatter sovereign courtesan," said some moderates, an ugly idol that "should be kicked off the pedestal, where it sits in mock majesty and courts the adoration of fools and demagogues."[87]

Events soon showed that attempts to practice popular sovereignty in Kansas had real effects, which were manifest in territorial elections. The first such election, held in November 1854 for territorial delegate, occasioned some waves and a strange anomaly. The second, in March 1855, caused a local revolution and an ongoing national sensation.

The first Kansas territorial governor, Andrew Reeder, made his way deliberately to the West from his home in Easton, Pennsylvania, and was slow in establishing the census and the electoral machinery. Indian treaties were in the process of negotiation, but much of the best farmland either was not yet legally available or had a suspect title. In Kansas Indian lands were not transferred to the public domain and then sold subject to federal land law; rather, they were sold at auction to the highest bidder, as the treaties with the tribes provided.[88] This was irksome to settlers, both because they wanted land at the lowest possible price and because they feared that bidders at the Indian sales might be railroads or, worse, speculators of the opposite persuasion on the slavery issue.

There was not even full certainty that the Indians would be removed at all. George Manypenny, the commissioner of Indian affairs and author eventually of the reform-minded book *Our Indian Wards*, had the idea that the tribes might remain on diminished reserves, taking advantage of the prosperity white settlement would bring.[89] That seemed odd to a writer in Philadelphia. Orators might regret it, but it seemed a fact of history that "races, like orders of plants, have their periods of existence, and that after they have fulfilled their mission, they gradually disappear." Manypenny should remove the natives immediately "and exclude even the possibility of collisions between the savages and the intruding immigrants."[90]

The Indian plan, wrote the *New York Daily Times*, was benevolent in its intention but imperfect in execution. Instead of the Indians benefiting from the arrival of the whites, "their wigwams became the refuge of the unprincipled and desperate, fleeing from abodes they could no longer pollute with impunity. . . . Missionaries preached to leaden ears."[91] When a delegation of Kansa Indians visited Washington, D.C., in the summer of 1855, they shocked the commissioner of Indian affairs with their "dirty and uncouth appearance." Before they visited the president they had to wash the paint off their faces and dress in clean shirts. They returned to Kansas Territory aboard a steamboat in their new clothes.[92]

The period was one of chaotic cultural interchange. The editor of the *Kansas City Enterprise*, near the scene, commented, "it is manifest to every one, that millions of money . . . might have been saved by effecting Indian treaties at the right time" rather than waiting for the "unpleasant circumstances," which came with the arrival of the whites en masse.[93] There were regular reports of "drunken Indians" adding to the chaos of the early territorial election days.[94] When Indian lands did begin to be sold, the auctions came off poorly for the tribes because of collusion among settler claim groups, who threatened violence if bidding were allowed to go above the $1.25 an acre prices standard for the public domain.[95] Some journalists thought the Indians' rights "should be respected even if they are red men," but most concluded that since either Indians or squatters must be cheated, better that it were Indians.[96] A. B., from Alabama, visited the Pottawatomies in September 1854 and found them "a particularly strange people," wearing feather ornaments and animal skins and painting like New York society women, but in a most different style. They were, he said, "a most hideous looking people" who were amused that the whites consulted books when they had a problem. Their views of the world, he said, "were not without interest," but neither he nor the other settlers had time to be interested.[97]

In the end the Indians disappeared from Kansas and were compensated in money, though not at the rate projected in the treaties. A Philadelphia paper, commenting in 1857 on "Our Fatal Indian Policy," thought the problems were corruption in Washington and a basic philosophic mistake of "trying to do justice to them by a system of pecuniary compensation." Could not the whites spend more time trying to understand Indian culture?[98]

The answer, of course, was no, and particularly not in Kansas with factions forming and all the political energy and focus on the slavery and the

Union questions. While the Indian question was an important element of the Kansas-Nebraska bill debate, it was quickly eclipsed by the issues of the status of slavery and of states' rights. National newspaper coverage of Indian affairs was minimal compared to that on other Kansas matters, even though the regional Indian removal process took nearly twenty years.[99] The Indians were a sideshow, sad but insignificant.

The election for territorial delegate to Congress took place on November 29, 1854. J. W. Whitfield, a former Indian agent residing in Missouri, was the proslavery Law and Order Party candidate, and Robert Flenniken, who had been a congressman and minor official in the Polk administration, the Free State Party candidate.[100] These ideological factions were, for most of the history of Bleeding Kansas, the relevant identifications in all local elections, national parties playing a small and distant role. Whitfield won, as, to use contemporary language, "the game was in the hands of the fire-eating Missourians." There were immediate concerns about fraud and about the honesty of the well-armed Missourians who behaved badly at the polls. A reporter estimated that at least 1,500 voters, most with no real claim to a residence in Kansas, arrived from Missouri.[101]

The news of the election, often exaggerated for effect, led to a "universal howl" around the country. It would not do to approve violence and intimidation by nonresidents at the polls; the sanctity of the ballot was too much a national icon for that. However, some Northern Democratic Party papers said what historians have said since: that the proslavery faction doubtless had a majority on the ground and therefore would have prevailed, fraud or no fraud. Also, both sides cast many fraudulent votes, and voting fraud and intimidation was common in U.S. elections at the time. The Democratic press went further and argued that the free-state group had "invented" the invasion by Missourians to "cover their mortification" at losing. Territorial Governor Reeder had a chance, at this point and at the legislative elections the next spring, to refuse to issue certificates of election on the grounds of fraud. But, to his everlasting blame from the Northern press, he did not. Part of the reason was that there were few formal challenges to the results as reported.

The claim originated in November 1854 that this and other Kansas elections were not about slavery versus freedom at all. That scenario, said a Detroit writer, was a kind of artificial framing, which played into abolitionist propaganda. The real issues, it was said, was how popular sovereignty under the Kansas-Nebraska Act was to be administered, and whether Congress would respect the decision of the residents of the territory, whatever it might be.[102]

A typical Southern reaction was that the fraud was exaggerated, that the South deplored electoral fraud as much as anyone, and that bowie knife–wielding Missourians, insofar as they were a factor, were acting on their own and were not part of a larger sectional conspiracy.[103]

Northerners hardly qualified their criticism. A Massachusetts man thought the fraud in the Kansas delegate election was too "gross" to ignore. "Base" and "treacherous" politicians who prated about popular sovereignty had failed to defend its primary institution, the ballot box.[104]

Benjamin F. Stringfellow, who would edit the notorious proslavery newspaper *Squatter Sovereign* in Kansas, said early in 1855 that any who thought after this election that Kansas could not be won for slavery were "dumb as dogs." If anything, he argued, those so eager to keep slavery out of Kansas had, by their aggressive organization, forced a counterreaction that was to bring it in. Missourians, he said, were not invaders, but people who wanted to make their homes in a state better adapted to plantation crops than to small grains.[105]

The other shoe fell at the legislative election, which took place on March 30, 1855. The proslavery faction again prevailed. It won so convincingly that the few Free-State candidates who received certificates of election quickly resigned from the new legislature in disgust.[106] "A most extraordinary and interesting result," wrote the *Charleston Mercury*. The "scheming North," the paper thought, had outsmarted itself by challenging the united South to a trial of strength on an issue close to its core. "They have fought the first battle, and the result is ominous of the final issue."[107]

In 1856 Congress appointed a special committee, the Howard Commission, to carry out a massive investigation of the troubles in Kansas. The resulting 1,206-page report, filled with testimony and statistics, helped make this election a particular cause célèbre in the national debate over Kansas.[108] It immediately caused the free-state faction to refuse to recognize the newly elected "bogus" legislature. And the electoral process, however honest or dishonest, became the basis upon which the proslavery faction (which, aware of the battle of language, took the official name Law and Order Party) based its claim that unless legal electoral processes and the institutions they established were recognized, the entire system of self-government would fall into anarchy.

Recriminations about the election were passionate, widespread, and strongly sectional in their orientation. The *New York Daily Tribune* editorials said that Kansas Territory had been overrun with "unmitigated villains" who aimed to attract the support of moderates in the entire South. If they succeeded, Kansas might become an area for slave breeding.[109] The *Bangor Daily Whig & Courier* commented that the Kansas election showed "the overbearing and violent spirit of the slave power," more than anything yet in American history.[110] The journalists at the *Washington National Era* thought it showed there must be more physical counterforce applied. "A thousand armed ruffians may overpower a few hundred peaceful men, women, and children; but when a few thousand sturdy farmers from the West, who know how to use a rifle as well as the axe, have established themselves in Kansas, they will protect themselves by means that the bowie knife gentry understand."[111]

From Montgomery, Alabama, came the report that the *Squatter Sovereign* newspaper was underway in Kansas to counter the propaganda of the "Hessian mercenaries" who ran the *Herald of Freedom*.[112] Who cared about the intense reaction in the media, the "howl," wrote the *Charleston Mercury*, that was like that of the damned in Dante? From the perspective of the *Mercury*, the recent election was just a case of the "hardy Missourians" driving "hireling" Negro stealers away from their front doors. What if they had intimidated voters or cheated? Why was Kansas suddenly so important to the North? Was it not being created by their propaganda machine to be more than it was in the wake of an election that "disturbed their lust of domination"? "It was a case of honor, of home, of property and life, against a remorseless and bloody invader." Could the South not use the higher law as well as the North? Who was to criticize them if "they respected not the forms of law, when forms and substance had been ever, and were now, perverted for their destruction?" The time for "shallow and temporizing expedients," for forms and ceremony, had passed, and the time for courageous, physical action had arrived.[113] The stakes were high. "Our property and our institutions depend on the fate of Kansas," wrote a South Carolina man. "If we make Kansas a slave territory we carry our institutions to the Pacific; if we fail, Missouri, Arkansas and Texas will be abolitionized—to say nothing of the effect upon other Southern States; and there is nothing in the other scale but the Union—which is and will be only an instrument of oppression."[114]

As usual, there were more moderate responses. A Cincinnati newspaper blamed "stories of a most distorted character" for the national outrage. Its editor thought the *New York Daily Tribune* reporter must have written his dispatches "when in an awful condition of excitement, his hair crisping with the heat of his brain, and his neck almost out of joint from sheer wolfishness." The truth of the election, when known, would not be as bad as that "meddlesome man," with his selective polling-place interviews and sensationalist descriptions, had made it seem.[115] The *Chicago Daily Tribune* called the stories of election fraud "a moral mirage" cultivated by abolitionists who wanted to start a fight.[116] Most reasonable people hated the mob, wrote an observer in Dayton, Ohio. Mobsters should not be taken as the type of whole sections. Many people knew how to regard "that class of restless wretches who devote what little sense they possess to the fomenting of mischief."[117] Even the *New York Daily Times* thought that equipping free-state settlers with Sharps rifles was a bad idea.[118] Some observers hoped the public excitement over Kansas was "evanescent" and that in time it would be seen that there was "no occasion for making this Kansas matter *the* great question of the day."[119]

But many editors saw that these controversies involved more than Kansas. Wrote a Buffalo, New York, newspaper: "Everything that the political thinker and patriot hold dear, is more or less implicated in the occurrences there passing; the prevailing tone of our politics for years to come, will be dictated by the issue; and to attempt to smother the embers of discussion now, will only increase the fury of the flame which will then burst out a year or two hereafter." This was not a "legislative quibble," not mere political "mummery," but something affecting every individual. "If Americans have a right to rule America, Kansans have a right to rule Kansas."[120]

The abyss widened not only in print but also in the physical layout of the territory. By 1855 Kansas had proslavery and free-state newspapers and proslavery and free-state towns. This separation increased the likelihood that the residents of those homogeneous towns would reinforce their own prejudices and would accept any characterization of the enemy that was offered. Leavenworth and Lecompton were proslavery towns; Lawrence and Topeka, free-state ones.[121]

These towns became local centers for the generation of public opinion and for its dissemination throughout the country. As early as May 1855, one Southern paper expressed the opinion that the Kansas issue had been "worn out" through overexposure. Every newspaper in the East, it claimed, had one or two correspondents in Kansas, each of whom was writing a letter or two every week.[122] A newspaper correspondent from a Democratic or Southern paper was hardly likely to be interviewing people in Lawrence or Manhattan;

nor was an abolitionist sheet likely to seek news in Tecumseh, Kickapoo, or Franklin.[123]

Late in August 1855, the free-state faction in Kansas Territory began meeting with a view not only to renounce the "bogus" legislature and refuse obedience to its laws but also to refuse to vote in any elections it called. Instead, this faction, which represented itself as the true "people" of the territory, would hold its own elections, elect its own legislature and officers, and write its own constitution. The Topeka government, as it came to be called after its designated capital city, claimed it was not an alternative territorial government but, rather, a state government, organized against the day that Kansas would be admitted to the Union as a free state under its constitution. The faction made the policy formal at a convention held at Big Springs on September 5, 1855.

Understandably, many who hoped for peace and accommodation were less than impressed by the free-staters' logic or motives. An editorial published in St. Louis called it hypocrisy. "It is a curious commentary upon the course of those who have talked so glibly about the violation of compromise, and disregard of law and good order, and 'border ruffianism' and all that kind of slang—it is curious to hear preachers, and journals pretending to more purity than patriotism and devotion to Christian and other duties of good citizens, applauding these declarations of an intention to resist all law."[124] A Maryland congressman commented, "Sir, if the occasion were not a most solemn one, this whole proceeding, known as the Topeka transaction, would be characterized as a complete farce."[125]

There was good support, however, in the North for the course taken. The territorial legislature had passed the Missouri code of laws and added some particularly offensive limitations on basic civil rights, such as free speech. Violations had draconian penalties attached, of which few, even in the South, approved. So dramatic had been the seeming victory of the proslavery faction in the election that it had contributed to an arrogance that knew no compromise. Therefore, it could be argued that as long as the "bogus" legislature controlled the territorial electoral process, and as long as the only recourse was an appeal to territorial governors, who were beholden to a Democratic administration in Washington (itself entangled with the slave power in the South), there could be no such thing as neutral administration of a Kansas election. If the free-state people tried to vote, they would be denied victory by chicanery and then accused of having recognized the existing government by their participation.

Until the fall of 1857, when the free-state faction participated in the regular election and achieved control of the regular legislature of the territory, the separate elections were no contest. Whoever sponsored an election won it overwhelmingly, and the rest of the population refused either to participate or to honor the result.

In this atmosphere came a second election for delegate, or, rather, two elections. The standard election occurred on October 1, 1855, and the free-state version, on the ninth. The results were foreordained, as was the sectional press's reaction nationally. The correspondent in Leavenworth for the *Cleveland Leader* wrote a lurid description of the polling there in the regular election. The proslavery group had carried it, of course. They voted, a writer said, "almost before the Missouri mud was dry upon their boots. With rifles in their hands, knives in their belts, bottles in their pockets, and whiskey in their bellies, they swaggered around the polls."[126] The Southern press referred to the later voting by free-state people as a "mock" election and asked, "Was there ever anything more ridiculous?"[127]

Two territorial delegates claiming to be duly elected from Kansas arrived in Washington, D.C., that fall to ask for a seat in Congress. The delegate elected at the first election, boycotted by the free-state faction, was John W. Whitfield, and the one elected at the rump election was Andrew Reeder, the former territorial governor. President Franklin Pierce had dismissed Reeder from his gubernatorial post because of a land-speculation scandal, and Reeder had joined the free-state cause. In the end, Congress rejected both claimants. But there intervened a lengthy and highly partisan debate, which created another national Kansas spectacle.[128] Both men claimed to represent the true voice of the people of Kansas.

Late in October, the free-state faction held a convention and drafted the Topeka Constitution. There was nothing unusual about it, except that it existed at all. The only irregularity in the proceedings was a vote to recommend to the first state legislature that it exclude free blacks from the new state.

Right away some Northern papers began defending the Topeka government, and they continued right through 1858 to recommend that Kansas be admitted to the Union immediately under this Topeka Constitution. Kansas, wrote the *New York Daily Times*, was the first practical realization of a state of things "which philosophers have dreamed of," namely, it was "virgin soil for governmental experiments." It was a tabula rasa for a political artist. And the people at the Topeka gathering were, according to the *Times*, honest intellectuals, quite unlike the regular legislature, then meeting at the Shawnee Mis-

sion. "There is, in fact, as much difference between the *animus* of the Legislature at Shawnee and the Convention of Topeka as between the Forty
Thieves and the Forty French Academicians."[129] By contrast, the St. Louis
press called the Topeka delegates "filibusters" urged on by their "insane
counselors" in the East to an "unholy project."[130]

Reeder and Whitfield attracted enormous attention in Washington, both
in presenting their formal cases in Washington and in casual meetings at the
National Hotel among all the factions and interest groups of the time. While
the House struggled to select a speaker, the public rooms at the hotel filled
with people "perpetually forming clusters of from three to half a dozen persons facing inward for a moment's earnest converse on the events of the day
and the chances of the morrow; then dissolving to form new clusters, with
endless fermentations, as individuals drop off to their rooms, their meetings, or their evening calls, and others drop in to fill their places." There
were editors, correspondents, and lobbyists, all forming a "moving, shifting, jostling crowd." Whitfield and Reeder circulated among them. "How vitally," wrote one correspondent who was there, "must the struggle of '55 and
the future character and destiny of our country be influenced by their conflicting fortunes!"[131]

The delegate contest and the formation of the Topeka government also
represented the beginning of an ambitious fund-raising and propaganda
campaign around the nation, both by the free-state people themselves and
by their backers in the East. Speakers and pamphlets circulated, and they offended some members of their audiences. At Dayton, Ohio, when it was reported that a representative from the free-state faction of Kansas would
appeal to the state of Ohio for aid, the *Dayton Daily Empire* ran a series of editorials emphasizing the necessity of nonintervention in the Kansas struggle
by the rest of the country. The editor hoped that any representative from
Kansas would be sent home "with a flea in their ear," as the situation in
Kansas was none of Ohio's business. "Let them have their trouble. . . . They
may fume and fret, if they please, at the mention of Slavery, or establish it;
they may hang and murder or threaten to hang and murder, if it so please
them . . . and they may manufacture great men out of scant material, or do
any other outrageous action for all that we care in Ohio—all that we want is
that *we are not asked to care.*"[132] Nor should Ohio buy the propaganda. To
think that the "Free State party is immaculate, and that Free State leaders are
pure, patriotic men, and saints ready for speedy translation to heaven . . . is
so simply absurd as to need no refutation." It seemed, however, that far-off

affairs had their appeal to the sympathetic: "We propose next that a meeting be held to procure a red flannel shirt for each negro baby on the Timbuctoo Coast of Africa."[133]

But again, as with the formation of the Emigrant Aid Company in 1854, these actions in the North provoked reactions in the South. Early in 1856 major organized groups started for Kansas from the South under the leadership of Jefferson Buford and E. B. Bell.[134] Appeals for funds were made to Southern legislatures.[135] Meanwhile, in the House of Representatives, Alexander Stephens of Georgia asked the questions that were on many minds: "How far in this business do you intend to proceed? Are you going to back those deluded men in Kansas whom Governor Reeder represents here, while they stand with arms in their hands?" What would happen when they met federal dragoons and there was a battle? "Ought we to do anything calculated to inspirit or encourage any misguided portion of the people of this country to put themselves in open, hostile, armed resistance to the laws? What is this but treason?"[136] One New Orleans writer considered the whole thing theater. The Free-State "governor," Charles Robinson, had sent messages to the chief executives of other states, just as though he were a real governor. "Thus far these have been harmless amusements, of which no person can complain any more than they can of the representations in a theater where actors personate Presidents, Governors, and Generals, and play revolutions." But, he warned, Robinson's farce could turn ugly.[137]

The sectional conflict had begun to seem serious. In the spring of 1856 men were boarding steamboats on the Missouri river and confiscating arms being brought to Kansas from the North and East.[138] Large fund-raising and organizational meetings were held throughout the South to rescue Kansas from the "frogs, and lice, and locusts" with which she was threatened. Southerners suggested they needed to subsidize the press as the North did and to arm and organize emigrants as the North did. The North had used the press to disseminate falsehood, and the South should take that weapon from them and use it for better purposes. It should not shy away from other weapons either. "Let there be rifle for rifle from the South, knife for knife, blow for blow, blood for blood."[139]

Similar rhetoric in the North escalated daily as new emigrants arrived in Kansas. Will the free-staters be "subdued by this black sea of despotism," asked a letter writer to a Chicago paper? Not likely. "I see here men whose blood has never been turned to water. I see here men whose fathers made tea in Boston harbor, and crimson streams down the sides of Bunker Hill. I see here the Saxon soul against whose rocky strength every system of tyranny has been shivered for the last three hundred years. Does any man between the oceans imagine for an instant that the people of Kansas are going to set the first example of tame submission to a horde of savages, either in Platte County, Mo., or Washington D.C.? Depend upon it, the men of Kansas are of sterner stuff."[140]

The bill to admit Kansas under the Topeka Constitution, which appeared in 1856, had little chance to pass, certainly not in the Senate.[141] Congressional investigations and reports, a Louisville editor concluded, were "in the existing frame of the public spirit . . . simply engines of sectional agitation. . . . Their only effect is to complicate the unhappy question in dispute, to intensify prejudices, to inflame resentment, and to sever the hearts of the people."[142]

That view seemed confirmed by the career of the congressional Howard Commission. Although the members were, it was said, "men of prepossessing manners," observers feared that even if they did come to some definite conclusions, Congress would not accept them.[143] The only real alternative to simply offending one side or the other with no change in the status quo was somehow either to remove the current Kansas legislature on the grounds that it had been elected by fraud, to negate the legislation that it had passed, or both. Given the momentum and the remaining power of the proslavery faction in Kansas and the country, such action seemed unlikely. How could the dissenters expect "any government to become partisans of a revolution to overthrow authority sanctioned by the same laws to which it owes its own powers and means of interposition?"[144]

The Howard Commission arrived in Kansas and began taking testimony on possible fraud in the 1855 elections in late April 1856, and in the midst of considerable factional violence in the territory. "It appears," wrote an observer, "that they are greatly at a loss where to begin, what to do, and where to go to do it."[145] So disturbed had matters there become that a Democratic editor in Ohio wrote that the only people who went to Kansas anymore were those curious to see "imaginary battles" and the "miserable fanatics who fancy that they have the destinies of the world, and the cause of freedom, upon their shoulders."[146]

Some newspapers close to the proceedings of the Howard Commission were contemptuous of them. The commissioners were appointed, a Kansas City, Missouri, newspaper wrote, for partisan reasons "over hosts of men, their superiors in ability," and the procedures used were flawed, biased in favor of free-state witnesses. The evidence, the editor thought, was "a mass of absurdities," and the report itself was "an exhibition held in unmitigated contempt by every man of unbiased mind who has witnessed the proceedings."[147] Far from being a respected document with a calming influence, the Howard report created more controversy.

Not only, as shall be seen, were the militias in the field making provocative moves, but so too were the territorial courts. The latter indicted and arrested "Governor" Robinson and others on charges of treason. On July 4 U.S. dragoons dispersed a meeting of the Topeka legislature.[148] The free-state faction was in "embarrassing, almost overwhelming circumstances." If its people submitted to the territorial laws, they were "poltroons and slaves," but if they resisted, they were traitors and liable to hang.[149]

There was a move toward direct action, both in the field and on the stump. Gerrit Smith, speaking late in July 1856, said, "Political action is now our greatest evil—our greatest danger. We are looking after ballots, when our eyes should be fixed on bayonets. We are counting votes when we should be mustering armed men."[150] The same spirit came out of the South. Gen. Isaac Morse said at a Kansas meeting in New Orleans in August that he was against compromise. "He was sick of that physic. Fling it to the dogs!" Morse said he would fight in Kansas whether it was worth a damn or not, and he would fight regardless of the "puling and sickly cant about the Union."[151]

James Lane, who headed the Free State military forces, threatened to "rescue" Robinson by force. Lane, a mesmerizing orator, went about the country giving incendiary speeches in defense of the Topeka movement. The *Dayton Daily Empire* thought it was a shame he should appear there, since he was the "evil genius" of a revolutionary faction. His rhetoric, the editor thought, would appeal only to weak minds.[152] People were more impressed by him in Milwaukee, where the "gallant Col. Lane" drew a large crowd. Lane said he had once been a Democrat and a supporter of slavery but now stood for and would fight for freedom. Was there a man in the audience who would obey the despotic laws of Kansas Territory? It was President Pierce and Senator Douglas, Lane said, who "have thrown the ship of State on the verge of this maelstrom. . . . Remember, laboring men, that you are, in the society of slave states, the lowest in the scale. Do you want Kansas, and the States west of it, to be Slave States?"[153] Lane was even more effective in Chicago, where he raised $15,000 after a single speech.[154] Thomas Wentworth Higginson, a professional writer himself, heard Lane on that occasion and gave him credit for being a master with a crowd. "Never did I hear such a speech," he wrote.[155]

The blockade of the Missouri River in the summer and fall of 1856 forced Northern emigrants to come to Kansas through Iowa and Nebraska on the "Lane trail." They were accompanied by wives and children and farm implements, and, yes, firearms. And they presented a grand spectacle, marching in trains sometimes a mile long, with men dressed in red, white, and blue.[156]

The victory of Democrat James Buchanan over Republican John Fremont in the presidential election of 1856 did not settle anything in Kansas. Neither did another series of separate elections in Kansas, one for delegates to the legislature, in which only proslavery partisans voted, and the other for a state organization, in which only free-staters voted.[157] The expected and meaningless results caused some to wonder whether elections could ever quiet the issue that divided the nation on Kansas. "We have indeed fallen upon strange times," said a writer in Louisville. "The very institutions established to guard rights have been perverted and made instruments of their demoralization." Elections were shams, not to be trusted. They were supposed to show the sober judgment of people with common sense, but had instead degenerated into a contest among demagogues.[158]

And what had it come to now? Maybe there would be war. The *New York Daily Tribune* quailed at the thought. "Yes, there is something fearful in revolution under such circumstances, and well might the timid shrink. The frowning rows of United States artillery, the serried lines of bayonets and flashing lines of sabers, and behind this pride and panoply of war, a ruffian horde, filled with hate, and scrupling not to touch blood; and still behind these the Pro-Slavery Courts; friends of Freedom languishing and dying in filthy prisons, or convicted of heinous crimes for loving Freedom; Bogus Sheriffs riding about the country with pockets full of writs. Yes, there is something fearful in revolution."[159]

Still, the free-state group stuck to its position of not voting. Most significantly, they refrained from voting in the election held under the auspices of the regular territorial legislature in June 1857 for delegates to a convention to form a constitution for a proposed state of Kansas. This convention, which framed what was called the Lecompton Constitution, arrogated a number of powers to itself, arguing that all people had had their chance to vote in June to participate in the constitution-making process and that they should have done so then or forever hold their peace.

A good number of newspapers with free-soil sympathies agreed and thought that the free-state revolutionaries in Kansas made a big mistake at that spring 1857 election. There was evidence, these newspapers said, that those elections would have been relatively fair, and even if they hadn't been, one did not have standing to protest or contest an election if one hadn't voted in it. Would a representative elected by law be any less authorized to discharge his duties because the majority of people in his district refused to vote? Would his actions be less binding on his constituents? Could any person of even limited intelligence fail to see this?[160]

What could failure to participate avail the free-state people? Could they fall back on the Topeka Constitution, which had no force without the sanction of Congress and was created entirely extralegally? The *Washington National Era*, sympathetic as it was to the free-state position, wrote prophetically that realistically the battle would be fought over the constitution then being formed at Lecompton. Massive free-state emigration had given that faction a sizable majority in Kansas, and it was high time they were exercising it through the regular electoral machinery. To continue to argue about the legitimacy of the Lecompton legislature could have no practical result, especially when the territorial governor, with federal troops at his disposal, was required to enforce the de facto law.[161] Were the free-staters ready to fight the U.S. government? Would they ignore reality? "The enemy has chosen his own position—he has the advantage—he will not abandon it—he will not place himself on a fair field—we must fight him where he is."[162] Preserving party consistency in the face of changing public opinion was disastrous.[163] "We have little patience," the *New York Daily Times* wrote, "with aimless and undecided obstinacy. For obstinacy without decision, unintelligent obstinacy, is an attribute, not of strength, but of weakness."[164] The force of the free-state numbers and influence must be felt in some way. Why not at the polls?[165]

Abraham Lincoln, an up-and-coming politician for the new Republican Party, when asked about the validity of the Kansas-Nebraska Act and the question of the Kansas Free State Party's refraining from voting, was "silent as the grave" on the former question and "Delphic in his oracular vagueness on the latter." Free-staters should vote in Kansas, Lincoln said, if the election were fair. He would not say whether he thought it would be.[166]

As so many scholars have shown, Lincoln was a politician and also an attorney, concerned about freedom and morality and concerned also about law and constitutionality. Wrote Orville Burton, discussing Lincoln's leadership: "A great lie encompassed all generalizations about American freedom. . . . Revolutionary America had been born of commerce, expropriation, war, and slavery. Its premises were grounded in ruthless ideas of inequality, war, and slavery." Any realist of the 1850s, no matter how much he might have quoted Thomas Jefferson's language about the equality of all men before God, must have recognized that reality. When Lincoln spoke of the necessity for a "new birth of freedom," he meant literally that. The old idea and practice was worn out and unsatisfactory. Burton called one of his chapters "Kindred Spirits and Double-Minded Men"—a most appropriate way of describing the dilemma the Kansas voters were in vis-à-vis the nation and its debating sections.[167] According to Richard Cawardine, that Lincoln hoped for moral suasion, a way of bringing change that would come "gently as the dews of heaven, not rending or wrecking anything," was a consummation only to be wished even by a leader of his consummate ability, determination, and unerring plumbing of the public will. Yes, Lincoln could speak of an appeal to the "mystic chords of memory" and the "better angels of our nature," which, given time, might take hold among a thoughtful and frightened majority. And, yes, the news from Kansas was important, however moderate his public statements about it might be in helping "keep the steel in Lincoln's soul" about the battle over freedom.[168] However, appointed governors and hangers-on about the centers of power in Kansas, not to mention voters torn between battles, crops, and the weather, could hardly be expected to rise to the occasion with any untoward vision, insight, or courage.

Southern papers felt the free-state faction should vote. To a surprising degree, editors there were restive with the thought of accepting a fait accompli with a due process that was only technical in its execution. The result would be a Pyrrhic victory probably not in the long-term interest of the section. And they regularly emphasized that the violation of the rights of anyone would lead ultimately to the ignoring of the rights of everyone. The conscientious opponent of slavery, claimed the *New Orleans Daily Picayune*, had a common interest with the slaveholder in putting down "the disorganizing doctrines and pernicious practices that set up the creature of a squatter mob as an authoritative form of government for a new State." Only zealots could approve the mob law represented by the Topeka Constitution.[169] The absurdity of the Topeka position, said a columnist at the *Washington Union*, was such that free-state people following it would only "suffer themselves to be made the tools of a faction to the prejudice of their own interests and tranquility."[170] The Topeka rebels, a Louisville editor said, were acting a "desperately false and silly part."[171] The U.S. Supreme Court had recently decided in *Dred Scott v. Sandford* that slavery was valid nationally. Carrying a slave into a free state did not free him, nor was resistance to the Fugitive Slave Act to be tolerated anywhere. Therefore, it seemed that in the nation there would be an agreement to let Kansas decide on slavery and to abide by the result. But to decide, all residents had to participate.[172]

The free-state faction had a different perspective about freedom and about the will of the people and how it was and should be expressed. And at base, it was a higher-law position freed of technicalities or even overt legalities. "Governor" Robinson addressed the Topeka legislature in June 1857. "The bitter experience of the past has brought nothing with it that could relieve you of your responsibility," he said. The Topeka group must "with calmness, wisdom and determination prepare those bulwarks on which the people may rest their constitutional rights as American citizens, and keep that state government in readiness for admission into the Union." The present territorial government was only an "inanimate frame-work," while the Topeka Constitution and legislature represented "our inherent rights as *men*." All the official pronouncements of presidents and territorial governors did not constitute law, for nothing was law "save the legitimately expressed will of the people." That was the purpose of the struggle. "The rights of the people, the glory of republicanism on earth, the integrity of our government, are all wrapped up in this issue." The hope was to establish in the new state of Kansas "a government not unworthy of this civilized age and our republican institutions." Robinson's address was printed in a pamphlet, of which 5,000 copies were distributed nationally.[173]

So the delegates to the constitutional convention were elected by default, setting the stage for the national debate over the Lecompton Constitution in 1857 and 1858. All the while emigrants poured into Kansas, overwhelmingly from the North. A Washington paper estimated in May 1857 that they were arriving at a rate of about 1,000 a day. "Before the onward march of the PEO-PLE, politicians must quail, and be swept from sight, like the dry grass before our prairie fires; and these ruffian plans and bogus enactments be like a dam of rushes in a Missouri freshet."[174] There came, too, the news that free-state capitalists were actually buying former proslavery towns, such as Doniphan, and were changing newspapers there to free-state sheets.[175] The *Squatter Sovereign* in Atchison ceased its proslavery propaganda. The story was often repeated of James Lane and the notorious border ruffian Col. Henry Titus sitting down to lunch together to discuss land and town-lot speculation. There was evidence that the South had given up. "The era of force and personal outrage is at an end," thought a Cincinnati editor.[176] This was not so, nor was the eventual political victory of the Free State Party as much of a foregone conclusion as many thought.

The final event in the cycle of double governments, which had begun at the meeting at Big Springs in September 1855, was another meeting of the Free State Party at Grasshopper Falls, Kansas Territory late in August 1857. There, after considerable acrimony, they made the momentous decision to vote in the legislative elections that October. At Grasshopper Falls Robinson said that he thought "this thing of politics" was a dirty business and that un-yielding principle was not always expedient. The party had to "grapple with these things as they could be won."[177] Jim Lane was more colorful. He felt, he said, like a man in prison whose only escape was through a sluice by which the filth was washed out. In order to escape he had to lie down in the sewage, and that is what, in proposing that free-staters vote, he was advising them to do.[178]

There were some irregularities in the election, whose correction led to the demise of yet another territorial governor. However, it was relatively fair as 1850s elections went, and consequently the Free State Party elected a ter-ritorial delegate of their persuasion and won control of the regular territorial legislature. A *New York Daily Times* editorial writer concluded, "Hereafter Kansas politics will be matters mainly of local interest and concern."[179]

While that was certainly not true, the October elections in Kansas Terri-tory represented the end of an electoral era that had tested the concept of popular sovereignty. It did demonstrate, as Burton has put it, that when it came to popular sovereignty, "rhetoric was one thing, details another." It also revealed a deep philosophical divide amid seeming consensus. All were for reform and improvement, personal and social, but was salvation to be achieved "by reining in and carving out man's lower propensities, or was the millennium possible only if the holy light within the human heart was al-lowed to shine forth in free abandon? Was the soul of the nation ultimately good or evil? . . . Was the project of bringing America to Christian perfec-tion within grasp or a dangerous delusion?"[180]

However, these late elections also seemed to show, at least to contempo-raries, that in the end, and despite difficulties, voting would be the key to a peaceable resolution. What, asked one journalist, had the violence of the free-staters and border ruffians really accomplished "except to make a noise and excite ill blood"? The free-state faction had been wrong to refrain from voting. "They labored under the insane idea that public meetings, hot-headed speeches and violence were somehow to keep slavery from the soil of Kansas." But the real magic was in voting, and "each vote was a magician to charm away the spirit of discord."[181] In October 1857 everything finally seemed to come together in a way it was hoped all could respect. "In Kansas," said a writer for the *Washington National Era*, "as we expected nothing, we have been agreeably disappointed."[182]

One would have thought it might be the end, too, of the proslavery chances. A columnist for the *New York Daily Tribune* thought so: "We have seen the Slave Democracy of Kansas, though drenched in Federal patronage, backed by a large Federal army, and reinforced by two or three thousand bal-lot-box stuffers from Missouri, fairly beaten out of Kansas by the over-whelming Free-Soil sentiment of her People."[183]

Perhaps the Kansas factions would disappear altogether, and regular nonviolent party politics, as practiced in the rest of the country, would emerge. Many in the rest of the country were contemptuous of the leader-ship there. Each faction had "acted as badly as it possibly could," said a De-troit paper, and their leaders should have their ears cut off and be sent out of the territory.[184] A state, wrote another newspaper, was not a mere expanse of land. One could not make a state by putting down 5,000 or 100,000 "strag-gling, interloping speculators from every point of the compass." It had to be a community, a society, with some network of neighborhoods and some sense of common identity and commonweal. Perhaps this took more time than Kansas had been given. It seemed a "hot bed state" gotten up "in shorter time than is required to mature an asparagus bed." What would George Washington and Benjamin Franklin have thought of "precocity like this"?[185]

The Kansas elections seemed another illustration of the endemic prob-lems of democracy in 1850s America. A Boston editor quoted Shakespeare's *King John:* "The present time's so sick, / That present medicine must be ad-ministered, / Or overthrow incurable ensues." What was lacking in the American democratic system, this writer said, was a measure of security and permanence. There was much of good and evil in a democratic government, "so many destructive forces to cause alarm, and so much conservative power to inspire hope; so much license given to ignorance, falsehood, error and selfish passion, and so much intelligence and virtue to resist them, that the mind wavers as it contemplates the varied picture . . . and ends in doubt as to the future." No doubt opinion ruled the world, but opinion was modified by a changing culture and expressed imperfectly through political forms.[186]

The ultimate test was practical. New country, like Kansas, needed filling up by the right sort of person "whatever crotchets he may have in his head." Opinions, abstract theories, and media stereotypes would slowly "wear out in the struggle of life." Ten years of ordinary farming in Kansas, said a St. Louis philosopher, "will do much to mitigate the leanest, longest and most crotchety Yankee." The colors of the newspaper columns would fade and meld into a rather pleasing, if less spectacular, daily reality.[187] When that happened, elections in Kansas would no longer be national news.

CHAPTER 4
FIRST PURE, THEN PEACEABLE

The Sharps rifle was a large-caliber, rapid-firing piece of 1850s high technology that was said to be deadly at 1,000 yards. It could bring down a bison and inflict grievous harm on the human body. It was perhaps a myth that Missourians were deathly afraid of it, but it was a plausible myth.[1] A reporter for the *St. Louis Daily Missouri Democrat* commented in 1855: "It is the most efficacious and terrible firearm in existence."[2] A visitor to the factory agreed: "Such weapons as these, employed in obstinate conflict, would do fearful execution."[3]

Yankee entrepreneurs manufactured the gun in Hartford, Connecticut. Kansas aid groups often purchased rifles in quantity, then disguised them in their crating and labeling in order to run the Missouri River. It was common at meetings held in the North to raise funds for Kansas to solicit cash subscriptions in $25 segments to provide settlers with these rifles. "Any man who can afford the luxury," commented the *Hartford Courant*, "may well exult in his secret heart of hearts to think that, if he is not himself directly in the field for the good cause, he has nevertheless put a good tool into the hands of a good substitute."[4] One rifle, given by a philanthropist and sent to the West, was reportedly christened in a church with the name "Son of Thunder."[5] Another was inscribed: "Ultima Ratio Liberarum" (The last resort of freemen).[6]

The gunrunning was enough to create controversy. But there was more. The writer for the *Courant* suggested that in addition to the rifle, the donor should send along antislavery literature. The rifle alone was "good for nothing without . . . moral backing." That sentiment escalated in the hands of a class that came to be known as "political preachers," ministers who held forth from the pulpit on current affairs and particularly on the moral issues at stake in Kansas. And, that topic being so popular, others crept in. "If a boiler bursts, or a rail-car breaks down, or a hangin' takes place, or any other dreadful thing happens they preach sermons on them and advertise 'em and so keep up with the times." The papers carried ads for sermons: "One is to preach on Kansas, one on Uncle Tom's Cabin, one on Wall Street frauds, one on Railroads . . . and so they 'pile up' the agony on every new thing that happens."[7] One wag joked that a man asked his friend about some current political issue. The friend said he was not up to date on that, as he had not attended church the previous Sunday.[8]

Rev. Henry Ward Beecher and Rev. Theodore Parker were likely to say that the rifles themselves were not just practical necessities but moral agents.[9] "A battle is to be fought," said Beecher in an 1856 sermon. "If we are wise, it will be bloodless. If we listen to the pusillanimous counsels of men who have never shown one throb of sympathy for Liberty, we shall have blood to the horse's bridles." Kansas was "the Territory given to Freedom by the God who made it." The key to peace was to "stand firm" and be prepared for war. The danger was in listening to those "who never rebuke violence on the side of power, and never fail to inveigh against self-defense of wronged Liberty." That weakness would lead to aggression and civil war. One should not expect protection from a federal government whose "veins . . . are filled with black blood, and [whose] heart and every artery beat with the fatal current of Slavery." The minions of slavery—"hordes of wild and indolent fellows, that hang about the cities and towns of the slave states, as gigantic vermin"—must be resisted as they came into Kansas. "It is a spark now. A foot may tread it out. But if it kindles, it will sweep the prairies in sheets of flame." It was true in history that "the rifle brought peace," and it would be true now. If war came, Beecher said, "on the skirts of false peace will its blood be found."[10] Critics, with tongue in cheek, called such ministers "pacificators."

Beecher's prominence from his bully pulpit at Plymouth Church in Brooklyn led to the creation of an epithet to designate ultra-abolitionists of a religious stripe: "Beecher Screechers."[11] It was rumored that at least one case of the rifles was marked "Bibles," leading to the phrase "Beecher's Bibles," which has survived among the icons of the popular imagination about Bleeding Kansas. "Think of it!" wrote an outraged editor of a Democratic newspaper in Detroit. "A meeting held in a church, conducted by ministers, assembled for the purpose of putting arms into the hands of men with which to shoot down other men! Are these the weapons of the religion of Christ?"[12]

Southern journals especially often remarked that ministers not only had demeaned themselves by straying from their Gospel message and their congregational business, but had created a kind of heretical idolatry, where "wizards and Molochs" worshipped mammon.[13] Abolitionism was a faith, wrote BRUTUS in the *Charleston Mercury*, and to the "vultures" and "dark spirits" that practiced it, Sharps rifles were part of the new liturgical paraphernalia.[14] Was there no danger, a writer in Dallas, Texas, demanded, "when you turn to the North and see thousands of politico-religious ministers desecrating the temples of God by preaching sedition and revolution from the pulpits?"[15] The times were out of joint. The *Washington Union* claimed that all sorts of absurd doctrines had sprung from the "corrupt state of political profligacy and religious infidelity which thrived together." These ministers had "set up standards and guides of their own. They have learned to read the works of creation by a new alphabet, and to interpret the laws of Providence and Nature by methods of their own invention."[16]

Some Northerners were critical also. The *Indianapolis State Sentinel* called political preaching the "great delusion" of the times. Instead of sticking with the "simple doctrines" of the Gospel, ministers rushed into politics. As a result, "their sacerdotal garments become soiled with the dust and smoke of the contest; they give and receive wounds, which . . . are never regarded by the public judgment as in harmony with the sacred calling of the ministers of Christ."[17] These ministers had politics on their minds. "They preach, talk, write and pray partisan politics, and upon all occasions and under all circumstances, they intrude it upon those who come within their influence; and this, too, under the garb and sanctity of religion."[18] Political priests, added a writer in New Hampshire, "convert the sanctuary of angels of light and life into a mere gambling saloon of political quacks and knaves."[19] One hour in Beecher's "politico-religious laboratory," a journalist in Boston thought, would be enough "to fill the mind with visions of 'fantastic devils.'"[20]

Parker was a spiritual descendent of William Ellery Channing, the Unitarian who had shocked the clerical establishment with a humanistic sermon in 1819. The intermediary was Ralph Waldo Emerson, whose Divinity School Address at Harvard in 1838 led Parker to question traditional views. The equivalent for Parker was his 1842 sermon "The Transient and the Permanent in Christianity," in which he categorized a good deal of beloved church doctrine as "transient." The "higher criticism" of the Bible moved away from literalism, and many liberal ministers emphasized the necessity of consulting one's inner conscience and feeling as a guide to action. One's conscience, not the creeds of the church, became the relevant moral standard. Parker defended John Brown's right to kill on behalf of God-given rights, rights that he, Parker, had arrived at privately and, it could be argued, subjectively.[21]

Pious learning, some observers thought, was not real education. Such education as the clergy had was only enough to reach "a very extraordinary pitch of narrowness." Ministers knew enough Hebrew to read the first five chapters of Genesis with the aid of a dictionary, and enough Greek to wade through a few pages of the New Testament. They then felt qualified to hold forth on all sorts of subjects. Newspaper editors, at least according to newspaper editors, were better qualified to comment on politics. They had a practical knowledge of men and affairs and of the Constitution and laws. This beat "black letter lore" in dealing with daily matters.[22] Too many idealists could make a hell out of heaven.[23]

The issue of ministers in politics was central to the Kansas issue from the Kansas-Nebraska debate forward. In March 1854 the *Richmond Christian Advocate* rebuked the political priesthood of New England. "This is a sad affair," its editor wrote then, "not for the country, but for Christianity, so shamefully outraged in the house of its friends." The religious opposition to the Nebraska bill, the journal thought, had "more of earth than of heaven, of time than eternity, in its elements and objects, and has a higher veneration for men's judgments than for God's."[24]

The awkward balancing of religion and politics became such a whipping boy as to generate jokes and mock narratives. One classic from August 1856 was entitled "Theology of Sharps Rifles," supposedly a sermon delivered by "Dr. Screecher." Screecher said, "[I] combatted the old-fashioned notion, and I think successfully, that the religion of the New Testament was to bring peace on earth and good-will to men. I showed the fallacy of all those teachings of the Apostles which speak of rendering unto Caesar the things which are Caesar's—of being subject to the higher powers, because they were ordained of God, &c. &c. I admitted that there was a time when these injunctions were imperative and binding; but I proved, and I think, clearly, that theology, like all other sciences is progressive, and that steam engines and Sharps rifles are now the true Evangels. In conformity with this position I assumed that the word translated 'preach,' should be rendered 'shoot,' so that the text, as in my version, would read:—'Go ye into all the world and shoot the Gospel (from Sharps rifles) at every creature.'" He concluded by saying that using the Bible for wadding in a Sharps rifle would allow the truth of Scripture to be "sent directly home to the hearts of the people, and be inwardly digested by them."[25]

One writer in a religious journal opined in 1857 that God himself had an interest in Kansas specifically. He would there cause the wrath of man to praise him and deliver the guilty United States from its abiding sin. "Kansas, located as she is appropriately in every way for the purpose, is to be the *fulcrum* on which the mighty lever is to rest which will uproot slavery from its foundation, and scatter its fragments to the winds."[26]

Many sermons employed this theme. One, delivered by Rev. John Holbrook at the Congregational church in Dubuque, Iowa, in the summer of 1856, said that the Kansas issue was a different kind of political issue, and one in which ministers must be involved. Earthly power alone could not stop slavery; heaven must be enlisted. A new element was to be brought into play: "The conscience and moral feelings of vast multitudes are enlisted as they have never been on mere points of political policy and economy heretofore."[27]

The origin of the "Beecher Bible" debate seems to have been a Kansas aid meeting held at North Church in New Haven in March 1855 for the purpose of equipping the Connecticut Kansas Colony, about to depart for the West. The New Haven gathering was the first of several meetings held there with similar players and purposes. Yale professor Benjamin Silliman organized the meeting, and Henry Ward Beecher addressed it. Not only was enough money raised to buy twenty-seven Sharps rifles, but also Beecher held forth on his ideas of the moral meaning of the firearms. In what his biographer has called "a fine web of Scripture and common sense to support the cause for Christian self-defense," Beecher presented his argument that "there was more moral power in one of these instruments, so far as the slaveholders of Kansas were concerned, than in a hundred Bibles." When a Mr. Killam rose to pledge money for a rifle, Beecher commented: "Killam, that's a significant name in connection with a Sharps rifle." The audience roared with laughter, but others around the country, including in some prominent centers of Christian opinion, were less amused.[28]

Reports of the meeting and of Beecher's continued unapologetic preaching on his crusading Sharps-rifle theme created a firestorm of national reaction. It peaked in the spring and summer of 1856 as events—the so-called Wakarusa war in Kansas, the raid on Lawrence, the Pottawatomie Creek massacre by John Brown and his followers, and the shooting of Douglas County sheriff Samuel Jones—highlighted the debate on violence and brought the free-state faction down off its nonviolent and above-the-fray philosophical perch.

For a minister to say at a public meeting that a rifle was a positive moral agent seemed bizarre to a great many. The *New York Observer & Chronicle* was willing to make allowances for eccentricities and idiosyncrasies of men, "but we cannot find in the peculiarities of genius or the infirmities of human temper, any adequate apology for such rampant appeals to the bloodiest passions of fighting men, by a preacher of the gospel of our Lord and Savior." The world was already too fond of arms. Surely Beecher would repent of his words.[29]

Beecher responded directly and confidently in his own religious paper, the *New York Independent*. Was self-defense wrong? Could someone being attacked by pirates on the sea rely on an appeal to their sense of justice, their respect for human rights, their consciences? Why should one expect to be able to do this in Kansas with respect to the border ruffians, "raked together from the purlieus of a frontier slave-State, drugged with whisky, and hounded by broken-down and desperate politicians?" Moral suasion was not enough, and never had been since the world began. Honesty was a good thing, but it was well to have legal penalties for lying to help it along. The Bible was a book of moral truths, preeminent in the sphere of moral truths. But the navigator at sea needed a compass more than a Bible. Christ healed the body before he preached truth. The founders of the American colonies had large, ugly swords and used them on the Indians. Beecher imagined one of his mild-mannered Christian critics "walking his rounds as a sentinel in Lawrence, armed with a folio, committing to memory over night, those texts which the next morning are to prove more potent with the rabble of drunken bandits than Sharps rifles!"[30] Beecher thought "we are hardly aware of what God is doing for us," and yet God led on even through the modern machinery of death.[31]

The editor at the *Observer* was shocked by such temerity and regretted that the inflated rhetoric should get such wide circulation in a community that badly needed calming. Beecher knew what he was saying, the editor continued, and knew very well how to say it, but he apparently valued fame above responsibility.[32] Horace Greeley at the *New York Daily Tribune* went right along with "the rifle preacher," as did hundreds of thousands of those fawning on every word of Beecher and other such opinion leaders.

Beecher did not back down. In an editorial entitled "How Peace Will Come," he used the imagery of a garden that had to be planted and defended against weeds and insects in order to grow the produce God had intended. Selfishness and pride grew easily and overtook the good plants, but justice, love, and goodness were "small in seed, slow in germination, tender in the blade, late in ripening, and beset by a thousand enemies." Truth had been so born in the cauldron of struggle that people had come to suspect anything that had not fought with evil and been subject to "rough usage." Godless men laughed and sneered and taunted the meek, asking, "Where is your God? What does he care for these little matters?"[33]

Beecher communicated that God *did* care in the way of the Old Testament's avenging Jehovah. "We think our own times afford eminent opportunities for coming sympathetically into the full meaning of the Psalms of David, and the majestic imprecations of the Prophets." He recommended particularly Psalms 37 and 73, about evildoers strutting around and "wearing pride as their necklace," getting their comeuppance. "Do not fret," went the Holy Writ, "for the wicked shall be cut off, / but those who wait for the LORD / Shall inherit the land."[34]

Sometimes theologians, when reading these and other "imprecatory psalms," asked how God could be so hateful. One scholar claimed in 1857 that these psalms, raining maledictions on the wicked, should not be considered part of inspired and inerrant scripture. Rather, they were utterances of private feeling designed for a Jewish system operating "on a low state of moral and spiritual culture." Beecher disagreed. Far from illustrating a defective morality, these indignant, cursing psalms showed the most intense form of holiness over against "abounding wickedness." God was a "consuming fire" to all iniquity, and anyone in sympathy with God must hate the wicked with a "perfect hatred" and act upon that hate.[35]

An obvious example was the Christian as Kansas pioneer. Let a godly man remove to that beleaguered territory with a view to establishing "the institutions of freedom and a pure Christianity," and he would soon confront a practical evil in the form of burning, robbing, and raping border ruffians. When he saw his dwelling, church, and village burned and his son shot, he needed "no theory to explain the Imprecatory Psalms."[36]

Gunja SenGupta's detailed study of evangelical entrepreneurs in Kansas Territory not only contains details on the lives of several ministers, but also documents the great interest and involvement of the American Missionary Association and the American Home Missionary Society. Rev. John Stewart, a pioneer Kansas minister, admitted, "We have come here to work, not to fight . . . to plant fields and build up towns, to erect schools and churches. . . . The proslavery party . . . mistook our quiet disposition for cowardice. How vividly they were mistaken, the history of our battles will prove." Beecher's description of Kansas as a battle between civilization and barbarism, SenGupta noted, "struck a deep chord in the culture of Victorian America with its concern for all-around human progress." In his sermons Beecher was "both molding and reflecting the sentiments of a significant segment of the Northern public." Yes, there were economic and political pressures, but there was also a "sincere ideological dimension" to the role of ministers in Kansas Territory. Although John Brown's brother-in-law, Rev. Samuel Adair, could not approve of Brown's identification with the violent avenging Jehovah in his murderous course, Adair did serve in the territorial legislature, and other ministers in Kansas served in military companies. Bleeding Kansas, SenGupta concluded, "forged a 'solemn and momentous' connection between politics and religion, prompting many antislavery clergymen to carry their campaign against the Slave Power outside the pulpit."[37]

Beecher claimed, "God has rolled discussion over the land like a flood."[38] Naturally, however, some Christians did not buy the package as that preacher presented it. Anti-Beecher opinion coalesced particularly in the pages of William Lloyd Garrison's abolitionist paper the *Liberator*. It concentrated on Beecher's doctrine not only as a generally aberrant reading of the Gospel, but as a particular offense to the nonviolence Jesus of Nazareth taught. Certainly, for years there had been those who tried to justify slavery from a reading of the Old Testament, and even from certain comments of Saint Paul. Brigham Young might justify polygamy in Utah in the same way. However, it was much more difficult to stretch the New Testament to include not only failure to love and forgive enemies, but a disposition to shoot them. Adherence to nonviolence when evil directly threatened loved ones, or when a good cause was at stake, was difficult, but the kingdom not of this world did seem to require it. Yes, the Puritans carried big swords. But Garrison thought it better to follow the pacific advice of William Penn than that of these blind guides.[39]

The advocates of violence abandoned principle for expediency, an occupational hazard of enthusiasts. When the free-state faction in Kansas Territory wanted the marauding Missourians kept away from their homes and from the polls, they favored intervention by the U.S. military, but when the military was to be used to disperse their illegal militias or to break up their extralegal Topeka legislature, their attitude toward force was entirely different. Did they not, asked Garrison, mock Christ? What did they expect? "They have predicted blood and fomented it,—and why should their labor be lost? Foolish men! They tell their dupes that the way to prevent bloodshed in

Kansas is to send plenty of Sharps rifles, and emigrants competent to use them. The way to prevent an explosion is to buy a keg of powder, light a match, and place it within an inch of the bung-hole!" Beecher might be qualified to use a rifle, Garrison thought, "but he is not yet competent to be a minister of the gospel of peace."[40] "We cannot serve our country in war, and serve God in peace. We cannot love our enemies and kill them."[41]

Not all the readers of the *Liberator* agreed with this position. Eugene Hutchinson of Milford, New Hampshire, wrote a letter to the editor in May 1856 taking sharp issue with the paper's position. Sin, right, and wrong, Hutchinson said, were relative, and there were no absolute and infallible guides to human action in all situations. Happiness for the greatest number was the best rule, and it was dangerous to lay aside the restraints of secular law and reason on behalf of an emotional sense of a higher law. Would a creed or dogma protect the settlers of Kansas? If they refused to defend themselves, would they not be their own murderers?[42]

Rev. Theodore Parker agreed. Among his many addresses concerning Kansas was one to a packed house at the New York Tabernacle in March 1856. There were three great religious sects in America, Parker said on that occasion: the Trinitarians, the Unitarians, and the Nothingarians. The last group worshipped God "as Nothing and Nobody and Nowhere." That sect gathered followers by the hour as pulpits were bottomed out on the almighty dollar and slavery as a new pope. Slavery, he said, to great laughter and applause, "was being translated out of the original tongues and appointed to be read in churches." In 150 years there would be 250 million slaves in the United States, and what then? "Shall 20,000,000 of men aid 300,000 wicked men to keep down 3,500,000 of poor bondsmen?" Surely freedom should and would triumph, "for it is the 19th century we live in, not the 9th." And when freedom won, America would become enormously rich and "will show the nations how divine a thing a people can be."[43]

Early in 1857 Parker saw the injured Charles Sumner, who had been beaten senseless by Preston Brooks in the Senate after an inflammatory speech, making his way haltingly around the winter streets of Boston, and it raised his ire. Yet some said that Sumner's feebleness was a sham and that he had had the beating coming. How could one react to such effrontery except with rage backed by practical means of correction and defense? The early Christians surely "spread the table of their Love-Feasts amid the fires which burnt their daughters and their sons." But must moderns react in a similarly passive way to the "battle all around," especially since they had the means to oppose their enemies? Twenty-five years earlier, Parker said, he had thought the battle over slavery would be a battle of the pen, but it now seemed otherwise. His slogan had become "The triumph of Freedom in America—Peaceably if we can, forcibly if we must."[44]

Even Garrison eventually drew back from his public stand on nonviolence. One biographer noted, concerning Garrison's role in the Kansas issue: "The more successful he became at persuading the society to take decisive action, the more it turned to modes that he rejected. His perfectionist vision would be overwhelmed by the weight of the republic's own history." Charles Stearns, a young Garrisonian who had served a jail term in Connecticut rather than serve in a militia, went to Kansas in the midst of the struggle and gave up on nonviolence while there.[45] Seeing the body of a murdered man, and seeing troops drawn up before Lawrence during the Wakarusa war there in late 1855, was "a fearful sight for a non-resistant." Stearns decided to pick up a gun. "I am sorry to deny the principles of Jesus Christ after contending for them for so long, but it is not for myself that I am going to fight. It is *for God* and *the slaves*."[46]

The same month that Stearns confessed a change of creed, a minister in Washington, D.C., preached on the text of James 2:17. That passage lies in the midst of a section that speaks of the pointlessness of faith without works and of the necessity as a Christian of acting in the world to relieve suffering. The title of the sermon was "First Pure, Then Peaceable."[47] A paper in Cincinnati noted that the ancient Hebrew priests never appeared before the Lord until they had washed themselves of every taint and blemish. Surely the church of the United States and its members must be sure that "their souls are arrayed in fine linen, clean and white, and fit to appear before so august a presence. And that meant ridding the body politic of slavery.[48] Even saints, the paper said, "were, in their day, persecutors; and burned each other in the full conviction that they were giving glory to God, and contributing to the happiness of mankind."[49]

The Kansas aid movement, unsuccessful financially up to that point, gained strength late in 1855 and early in 1856. It raised considerable money from clergymen in response to several direct appeals to them by Rev. Edward Everett Hale on behalf of the New England Emigrant Aid Company. One circular sent to clergymen proposed to raise $150,000 for Kansas aid. Nothing like that was forthcoming, but the Emigrant Aid Company did receive 400 contributions from clergymen in response to its first circular, totaling $1,557.78. One minister questioned whether the Aid Company was benevolent or for-profit, but another told the story of his entire congregation's contributing three cents each to the cause.[50]

Be that as it may, Garrison and those in his circle spoke strongly for a nonviolent solution in 1856. Perhaps most eloquent was Adin Ballou, who wrote a defense of nonviolence to the *Liberator* as events in Kansas reached a crisis in May of that year. There were still a few persons, he said, who regarded the world as their country and all people as their countrymen. There were a few who saw God as the supreme father and the whole human race as a brotherhood. Love of brothers and enemies was a great moral platform, Ballou thought, and the only possible objection to it was that it was too good for human nature at its current stage of development. He yearned for the freedom of the slaves but thought that defense of freedom in Kansas with Sharps rifles was wrong. The quality of that freedom was not so good, as people there were talking about banning free blacks from the new state, and the constitution drafted by the free-state rebel group would allow slavery there until 1857. Freedom in Kansas might be a fine thing for white people who loathed Negroes. "If unfortunately we should ever be deluded into the taking of arms to shed human blood in the cause of humanity, allow us at least to insist that it shall be a kind of humanity which does not outlaw men without crime, merely for a difference in the color of the skin."[51]

The "rifle rowdyism" issue went well beyond religious journals.[52] It was a prime lightning rod for opinion generally, filled with the polarizing emotion that made Kansas a sensation. It reached the Congress during the great Kansas debates of the spring of 1856. Lewis Cass highlighted the rifle-and-religion issue in the Senate. Cass, the inventor of the policy of popular sovereignty, saw fanaticism and its accompanying violence as the polluter of that pure spring. Passions were more easily excited than allayed, and before them "the guarantees of the Constitution may be prostrated as easily as the marks of the sand are obliterated by the incoming tide of the ocean." Oddly, he said, among the fomenters of unreasonable passions were men "professedly servants of the Most High, and ministering at his altar." In New Haven the house of prayer was made an armory for the collection of weapons to arm Americans against their countrymen. Clergymen were perhaps not exactly money changers in the temple, but they *were* gatherers of carnal instruments "to fight the battles of the flesh." Was it not enough for them to preach the Gospel of Jesus? Were they not, he asked, in canvassing for rifles, doing more harm to religion than had the writings of such skeptics as Voltaire and David Hume? What a literature the Kansas issue had generated! He compared the Kansas issue to the travels of Gulliver, too often drawing conclusions "from the dictates of a wild or false heart, or a disordered head," and said the dissemination of the Gospel was thus brought down to the level of political agitation. Instead of "instructing" human passions, these men were stimulating them—a dangerous occupation.[53]

The question of the appropriateness and religious significance of Sharps rifles in Kansas spread far and wide through the periodical and newspaper press and elicited many nuances of opinion. "Our political sermonizers," went an article in the *Boston Post*, "are now in full activity, and are figuring not only in their pulpits but in partisan indignation meetings. They often make queer work of it. . . . They show a good deal of the bitterness, though with less of the talent, of the political parson of the old federal times." Ministers were men and reflected their own times and the views of their parishioners. They were, therefore, "liable to be filled with all the malevolence, injustice, error, and prejudice that are afloat; and at such times they are fully as apt to preach and act themselves, as they are to preach and act the Christ they affect to serve."[54] The language of the political mountebanks, the *Post* thought, would amaze a stranger. Much of it was exaggerated, stereotyped "twaddle."[55] According to the *New York Observer & Chronicle*, the triumph of freedom would progress better by constitutional means than by violent rebellion. That journal predicted that soon the politicians and preachers counseling the sending of rifles to Kansas would be regarded as "seditious or deluded men."[56] To the writers at the *Detroit Daily Free Press*, Beecher stood "in the same relation to religion that PHINEAS T. BARNUM does to morals. Each is, in his peculiar line, a charlatan and a humbug."[57]

How could "rifles and ribaldry," asked the *Buffalo Commercial Advertiser*, substitute for the "gospel of peace?" Beecher was the center of attention. The *Advertiser* thought that his motivation was love of notoriety. "He loves to create a sensation by saying smart and startling things, and venturing to the very outermost verge of the region where innocent boldness ends, and blasphemy begins. . . . He goes into the pulpit of a Sunday, and preaches with a don't-care-a-damn style of oratory, because more popularity is to be gained by floating down stream with the current of unsanctified passions, than in stemming the tide. With him, the pulpit is an arena for the exhibition of profane and dazzling wit, and his chief pride is in mounting the leading hobby of the day."[58] The *New Bedford Mercury* agreed. In times of political excitement, it concluded, normally meek individuals grew warlike "and fulminate in their own thunder from their own Vatican, if it is no more than a garret . . . or an apple stall." The Kansas excitement had "proved rather fatal to many a well-poised brain" and had acted upon Beecher like "a draught of new and fiery wine." He gave orations "breathing bullets and gunpowder," and these "nitrous ebullitions" damaged the churches in which they were delivered. He was, sincerely perhaps, doing just what the border ruffians were doing in Kansas, although from opposite motives. A little less excitement, more regard to the established principles of government and the "sober voice of history," should teach Beecher "that to convert churches into market-houses . . . to assume that shooting each other is the only mode by which the American people can settle the organization of a Territory, must arise from a peculiarly excited condition of what doctors call, the cerebral function."[59]

The paper's local competitor, however, had just the opposite view. The editor at the *New Bedford Evening Standard* thought that Oliver Cromwell England was a fine model for Kansas, and that Beecher was his natural heir. The fanaticism of Cromwell's Roundheads was just what extracted British, and indirectly American, freedom from the clutches of the Cavalier aristocracy. Their spirit needed reviving, trusting in God and keeping the powder for Sharps rifles dry. "The facts call . . . for Sharps rifles—and we rejoice to say that Sharps rifles have responded."[60]

There were many who advocated that position. The *Chicago Daily Tribune,* for example, thought that defense of liberty required exchanging blows. "Despotism would walk over the earth did we falter here. . . . God and nature bid us strike ever, therefore, for home and its rights, and he is neither fit to live on Earth, or in Heaven, who will not do it." It was Sharps rifles that had saved Lawrence, Kansas, so far, the paper went on, and Beecher was wise to advocate them, however fashionable it was to denounce him in quarters where routine had become a virtue.[61] Yes, Beecher's statements had shocked some of the sensitive and "frightened a class of evangelical believers," but he was right. In the older states the tree of liberty had "under God . . . borne and shook down from its boughs all the fruits of an unparalleled prosperity." The newspaper quoted with approval C. B. Lines, the head of the Kansas colony going out from New Haven, who said, "These are times when self-defense is a religious duty. If that duty was ever imperative it is now, and in Kansas."[62]

Admittedly, avoiding war in Kansas was not going to be easy. It was a sport to speculate whether the random killings and militia actions there already amounted to civil war. But there were many who wondered whether those whooping it up for Sharps rifles really understood their effect. One act of hostility, said a writer in Lawrence, Massachusetts, always begets another, so the announcement of an armed company going out from Massachusetts would engender a similar company going out from Georgia. "Men, not braggarts or bullies are wanted in Kansas—MEN who can bear insults for a time."[63] The *Philadelphia Inquirer* thought events in Kansas proved humankind was savage. It was no longer amazed at the accounts of brutality that had passed down from history, given the "systematic ruffianism" reported in the daily news.[64]

Opinion in the South was amused and shocked. The pulpit shenanigans went beyond what even some of them considered typical fanatical Northern behavior. The treasury of Yale College, thought a writer for the *Charleston Mercury*, would have been better off had "Brother Beecher kept his puns and his rifles at home."[65] Abolitionism had itself become a faith. "It is a dogma for popular use and effect; a cry which catches the vulgar morbid ear," and a "powerful engine" of demagoguery. As a religious sentiment, abolitionism could not be crushed by legislation and required instead a countervailing faith to be advanced by the South against the "dark spirit, which invokes the storm."[66]

The *Richmond Enquirer* followed a similar line. Northern propaganda, it thought, was not to be underestimated, although it tended to "insubordination, anarchy and agrarianism." The United States was in the midst of the "mightiest intellectual, moral and social movement the world has ever known, whether we consider the ability of its leaders, the zeal and number of its proselytes, or the destructiveness of its purposes." The paper said that Gerrit Smith, William H. Seward, Theodore Parker, William Lloyd Garrison, and Henry Ward Beecher were secular preachers and political experts who promised "all the good things of this world, with the security and beatitude of the next" to come through what to a Southerner was a "monstrous" misinterpretation of traditional religion. It seemed that what was being preached was no less than a "proximate millennium" accomplished through political reform of the slave system. "They invoke a Deity to carry out their fiendish purposes. They incite the mob to upset all law and divide all property, but assure them, that in doing so, they are but acting as the instruments of God."[67]

The new scripture of this new faith, many Southerners claimed, was the *New York Daily Tribune*. The *Tribune* had referred to Sharps rifles as "true peacemakers" and therefore was perhaps capable of anything.[68] "It is a singular fact that every life that has been lost of late years in this country, in upholding the supremacy of the laws, has been at the hands of men who look to the *N.Y. Tribune* as the standard of their faith."[69] Some analysts blamed bankruptcies in New York, particularly among clerics, following upon the financial panic of 1857, on the influence of Greeley, the *Tribune*, and the new faith contained there. People had "exchanged the Bible for the *Tribune*, and took to study Greeley's free-love doctrines instead of the teachings of the Apostles and the Holy Fathers of the Church. . . . If the clergy return to the Gospel and cease preaching bleeding Kansas and Maine Liquor Laws . . . their morals will improve."[70]

Sometimes the spite was palpable. An editor in New Orleans wrote that Greeley was a fraud. "One would suppose that Mr. Greeley could find enough at home to make his newspaper readable and spicy, without always looking southward for a fresh item from Uncle Tom's Cabin. . . . Is New York without sin, that it should throw the first stone? . . . How long will whining hypocrisy thrive in our midst, and obtain 60,000 subscribers to its newspapers? How long will its unmeaning cant be mistaken for a new Evangel by the weak though well-meaning minds of the North?"[71]

That "wild and unreasoning" faith common in the North was not the faith the South held but was "not on that account the less a religion, a moral and political tenant to them."[72] Reasoning with these people, the *Mobile Register* commented, was like talking with madmen. "The hide of a rhinoceros is not more impervious to shot than the head of your Abolitionist is to reason. Starting with one idea, he loses sight of everything else."[73] The *New Orleans Daily Picayune* was reluctant to report on Sharps rifles, "blessed . . . for murder by Beecher and that crew." Its reporter was shocked that "such things are thought of in this day and generation."[74]

Sometimes the controversy seemed merely a matter of bad taste, shallow thinking, and disrespectful manners. A letter to the editor in the *Charleston Mercury* excoriated Professor Silliman for prostituting his talent and fame as a geologist to invade the purview of the "fanatical knaves" promoting Sharps rifles. "Philosophy, ay, the commonest discretion, should have saved you from this undressed exhibition of yourself, at once lamentable and ludicrous. . . . We are accustomed to think of you as a teacher of science and cultivator of letters, and so a softener and refiner of manners. Do you covet the honors of a pulpit brawler, or a sectional demagogue?" Silliman should think of the evil he would bring on his college and his city. "What spirit of misrule has tempted you to take a part in misleading the silly women and sillier men, who are giving their money, with you to buy SHARPs rifles? The simpletons are prone enough to self-satisfied self-sufficiency without your help."[75]

Congressmen commented regularly on the religious issue. J. F. Dowdell of Alabama, speaking on the floor of the House in July 1856, said he had little hope of being heeded "amid the noises and confusion which at present bewilder the public mind" but wanted to warn of the danger. It worried him that the conflict had entered the religious sphere; it reminded him of the Crusades. "Can we hope for a change of opinion in the northern mind, afflicted with this madness?"[76] However, one of his colleagues, J. H. Savage of Tennessee, was willing to play the religion card himself. God had not condemned slavery, he said, and it had been practiced through history. "The white man who fails or refuses to control the Negro who lives on the same soil with him violates the will of Heaven."[77]

The slavery issue split American congregations into Northern and Southern branches. There was not an issue in the church proper that was free of the politico-moral controversy gripping the nation. The *Richmond Enquirer* noted that a church in St. Joseph, Missouri, advertising for a minister, had to specify that it wanted one who was Southern in his feelings. For that the paper blamed the *New York Daily Tribune* and its followers. "It is to their unholy and incendiary teachings that we must look for the rise and progress of sectional Christianity. Had they taken St. Paul for their guide and exemplar in all things, the three thousand New England clergymen would never have departed from their proper sphere to sign a memorial on the subject of slavery." People should abide by the "plain word of God," rather than being drawn away by a "spurious, sectional Christianity, as unlike the Christianity of the Bible and the Apostles as hell is to heaven. It is a Christianity which tolerates such blasphemous monsters as Theodore Parker, when he stands in his pulpit, and curses a God and a Bible that approves of slavery; or sustains a hypocritical sheet like the *Tribune*, in its foul slanders of the Patriarchs, Prophets, Apostles, and Ministers of the present day. . . . Greeley's gospel is the curse of free society in this country."[78]

In 1857 the American Tract Society considered the recommendation of its publication committee that it publish a piece on slavery, not as a political issue but as a moral one. That distinction did not impress people in Georgia. The *Columbus Times & Sentinel* found the parsing of language by the Tract Society "deceitful" and thought there was no question but that its intent was to regard slavery as an evil in itself like drunkenness, war, and "popery." It recommended that churches of the South withdraw from the American Tract Society and form their own publication organization.[79]

The great evil of the era, the *Times & Sentinel* thought, was "a perverted spiritualism which steals the livery of heaven to serve the devil in." It was important to train youth to understand "the great principals of practical piety, and discounting a mere religion of feeling and sympathy by a sterner enforcement of the moral precepts taught by Jesus Christ." The Bible, conservatively interpreted, was the rule. The "wild ravings" of publicity seekers had "turned the world upside down, and cursed the country with a new set of Prophets and Prophetesses who mistake their own idle fancies for the divine afflatus. When," the paper asked, "will the world learn that violent emotions, prophetic visions and wild transports in prayer, are not religion?"[80] When a sawmill in Lawrence could be referred to seriously as a "temple of Liberty," religious perspective was out of adjustment.[81]

At the end of the period of great national focus on Kansas Territory, as the debate over the Lecompton Constitution and whether to admit the territory as a slave state made its way through Congress and a financial panic gripped the Union, the nation went through a remarkable religious revival. Some analysts then and now have questioned the spontaneity of the phenomenon, but none have doubted its sweep. The crowds at New York City's Burton Theater had never been greater for a dramatic performance than they were in the spring of 1858 to hear revival preaching or to attend the daily noon prayers. Merchants and clerks left their desks to be there, and ladies showed up in strong numbers.[82] At Jayne's Hall in Philadelphia, 4,000 to 6,000 people a day gathered for prayer meetings, and 2,000 people came to the "business men's" prayer meeting in Cincinnati.[83] Prayer meetings in Natchez, Mississippi, filled to overflowing. "The wild, enthusiastic chase after the almighty dollar seems to have been temporarily stayed," said an observer there. "The question which alone enlists the attention of all classes is . . . 'What must I do to be saved?'"[84] Whatever the reason for the revival, it provided another opportunity to comment on God's intentions in Kansas Territory.

In such a time, important principles of Christian significance were at stake in national affairs, said the *Christian Inquirer*. There was great fear of political dissolution, and maybe of the accompanying personal dissolution. "That gulf is full of darkness and threatenings; its lips are red with blood; and into its hateful jaws we see the industry, the education, the domestic comfort, the philanthropy and religion of the nation from either side, rushing down to a bottomless destruction. We cannot, we will not believe, that

God will permit that frightful chasm to open." But what was to be done? Could God teach Americans how to unite devotion to freedom with love of their political union? Would Americans be able to celebrate their national holidays together in the future, or would they celebrate as "different and hostile states?"[85]

There were two revivals, Beecher's *New York Independent* noted. One was a revival of religious sentiment, and the other, of agitation to re-create the slave trade. How could the latter happen in a civilized and religious country? Among the crowds packing the churches and meeting halls was circulated the news of barbarian usurpations of political rights in Kansas, all sorts of misrepresentations and "political fabrications," which sometimes found justification and cover in churches. "And so these two revivals are rushing side by side, if not hand in hand. It is a most extraordinary race."[86]

Theodore Parker saw two revivals also, but he divided them differently. There was a true return to religion and a false one. The false one, born of uncertainty and fear, predominated. Parker asked what was being revived as the newspapers hyped the stirring prayer and conversion events. It seemed to him that in revival preaching, the poorer the sermon, the more popular it was. People delighted in revealing the innermost secrets of their hearts to be published in the newspaper. Much of the hype was so tasteless it was driving the better-educated away from religion to more material pursuits, away even from the basic dictates of conscience. The churches, meanwhile, attracted what Parker called "cunning atheists." The false revival was all part of a culture of the inauthentic, which was blundering and stumbling toward disaster—sheep, Parker said, with no shepherd.[87] The revival was an "emotional contagion," without principle, the *Boston Liberator* commented, and an "imposition upon weak and unenlightened minds."[88]

North and South prayed to the same God, but, as with so many other things, interpreted his will for them on this earth differently. But all did pray, and all agreed about the importance of Providence to the unfolding destiny of the nation.

Beecher thought that the complaint about political preachers merely proved that the Kansas issue had deep moral and religious aspects. A minister could hardly read a passage of the Bible in the heated general atmosphere without being accused of attacking slavery or of taking sides in the sectional controversy.[89] In January 1856 the U.S. House of Representatives instituted regular prayer. The *Albany Argus* thought it was high time. "An assembly containing so many men so utterly lost to all sense of public duty, and sinking so fast into something too nearly akin to dementia, may well ask for divine guidance."[90]

As in politics and in constitutional scholarship, there was also a moderate middle in the religious approach to Kansas. Surely it was unfortunate, said Dudley Tyng, an Episcopal minister, in an 1856 sermon, when the "heated controversies of the day" were too mixed with "appropriate themes" in churches. But was there not an opposite extreme? Was silence from the pulpit right in the face of great principles? "May not the dread of offence be carried so far as to put the pulpit in bondage? And may not the refusal to take sides in great questions of public opinion, result in the gospel's being supposed to have nothing to do with the affairs of society?" Religion itself was often vitally affected by events in social and political life. Evil principles could gain strength there, which could come to damage the practical influence of religion over behavior. Tyng's text was 1 Corinthians 12:26: "And whether one member suffers, all the members suffer with it; or one member be honoured, all the members rejoice with it." He claimed the right, he said, as a Christian minister, "to declare what I believe to be important truth and to do my part, small as it may be, towards the settlement of the difficulties which encompass us."[91]

Hypocrisy was prominent. When the editor of the *Daily Cincinnati Commercial* came under attack in the summer of 1857 for his views of the Sabbath from one of the whited sepulchers in town, he took exception at length. There were people in the world, he said, whose piety was "more devilish than the wickedness of the ordinary reprobate." They practiced the forms of religion without understanding and "enter the church as they would a mutual insurance office," hoping for security while evading the payment. These hypocrites thought it their mission to criticize others, believing that the devil was loose, the present age was the worst in history, and that they personally were appointed to help bring down God's wrath on the wicked. Few people were more unpleasant to be around than these frauds, equipped as they were with a "shallow and inconsistent philosophy—a cold blooded and dyspeptic morality, and a repulsive and fanatical religion." The combination, the aggrieved editor thought, created "stupidly ferocious" Christians of whom authentic Christians were ashamed.[92]

On the matter of Christian ignorance, the same editor had more to say in a review of a pamphlet on slavery published by the Methodist Church and authored by Rev. Charles Elliott, D.D. He concluded that slavery was not authorized by God and should be dissolved with the least possible delay "in consistency with justice and humanity." The Cincinnati editor thought that phrase "capable of not a little latitude of construction." Slavery was an important topic, but the literature on it was shallow and ephemeral, as well as biased. Most of the pamphlets would die in less time than it took to produce them. What was needed was an approach not sectarian or partisan, but comprehensive and respectful of great complexities, historical, political, sociological, and psychological. These complexities could not be expressed in stereotypes, simplified into slogans, or reduced to an appeal for votes on the "slavery question." "Tortured" biblical exegesis tried to force out of scripture a clear answer to the political dilemma. Slavery needed to go, but "the Savior was content to plant the good seed and to leave it to do its work among men." This might take time, but some people tried to force the process. "In the place of gentle showers of persuasion," such people "[spout] upon the soil a huge and turbid flood of controversy; and the result is a harvest which even 'the enemy' might have been proud to produce."[93]

The Lewis Cass newspaper, the *Detroit Daily News*, agreed. It had wondered in 1855 what the rush was. Legislation fluctuated with changes of public opinion, and only a change in public opinion could change such an institution as slavery permanently. Abolitionism could be seen as delaying the process of the elimination of slavery. Meanwhile, "It is safe to leave Kansas to her natural destiny. Cannot those who profess to believe in the providence of God rest content that in regard to Kansas, as in regard to the economy of the whole Universe, 'he doeth all things well?'"[94]

No, said John Brown of Kansas. No, said many editors. No, said many historians over the years. But alternative scenarios continued to exist. A Bostonian asked, "Is Lachrymation the Remedy?" He accused the "moist-eyed Miss Nancys" of "quivering with an excess of solicitude." We should "remember that we are men," the editor said, "educated in common schools." Such men should not "hang their harps upon the willows, wring their hands, roll up their eyes, contort their visage, sit down by the waters of an imaginary Babylon, and weep for a Jerusalem not yet lost."[95]

There were those who went so far as to say that freedom itself, that great desideratum for which presumably everyone struggled, was, in the ultimate scheme of things, an illusion, a snare in the imperfect empire of this world. "There is no such thing as absolute freedom below the Almighty God," wrote a New York City editor in the spring of 1856. Human beings were all slaves to inexorable necessity, and yet were all free, no matter how shackled, if their hearts and consciences could contemplate their ultimate destiny. An actual slave might sleep more sweetly on a pallet of straw than did some of the "wretched nabobs" on their silk pillows in Gotham.[96] Of course, he continued, to render too much unto Caesar was to countenance nearly any form of tyranny on earth.

At the other extreme of religious thinking were those who thought that God cared about every election. During the presidential campaign of 1856, Beecher's publication, the *New York Independent*, editorialized that God had allowed the Kansas issue to emerge to try and prove his people. "It is not once in a thousand years that men are placed in circumstances where they are permitted and commanded to vote directly upon the life of an empire! . . . Every vote for Mr. Buchanan is an open . . . endorsement of the Kansas outrages." John Fremont would be the savior. "If you do not vote at all, your country suffers by neglect. If you vote wrong, you stab her. If you vote right, you raise her head and put the cup of salvation upon her lips!"[97] The *Boston Congregationalist* suggested in that election that to cast a Republican party ballot "breathes of broken chains, of tyrants thwarted, of danger overpast. . . . Cast that ballot, and the God of peace and purity shall smile upon you!"[98] It was fortunate that most opinion involving religion and politics in the 1850s fell between these poles.

Purifying and acting, doing the will of God on earth, seemed ever so desirable and yet ever so difficult. "What Shall I do?" as a Christian in the midst of systems "radically hostile to the Gospel of Christ" was not a question with a pat answer. But it was a question of fundamentally religious significance.[99]

Americans of the 1850s found they much resembled the Hebrews of an earlier time, with whom free-state pioneers in Kansas often identified themselves when they were not busy being modern-day Puritans. Newspapers of Southern sympathy in fact used the Hebrew parallel with negative connotations, calling the abolitionist propagandists "a Sanhedrin of puritans whose politics are better than all others because they are based on a purer morality; and they are sought to be enforced, reckless alike of consequences and of contemporary obligations." Propaganda came from a sure hand, "bigoted, self-willed, uncharitable, harsh, and tyrannical." It came from a faction that thought "its morality is purer, its men are wiser, its creed more orthodox, its ritual more devotional, its life more sanctimonious, its learning more complete, its government more Christian, and its promise of immortality exclusive!"[100]

Many people on both sides felt that praying was appropriate in the times. "Our hope for the Country is first in God," said a writer for the *Boston Congregationalist* during the trying year for Kansas matters of 1856. Among his purposes was "the preparation for freedom, and continual emancipation to its privileges of all the slaves of the South." But before that, there would be a struggle whose parameters and stakes would only be seen if somehow the "fogs of the political atmosphere" could be cleared away.[101] Of all the ways of framing freedom, the religious frames took in by far the broadest swatch of the universe and went deepest into the inner natures of the protagonists. What they discovered in the distance and up close was not altogether reassuring.

CHAPTER 5

MARTYROLOGY

———•◦•———

When considering Bleeding Kansas one must take account of blood. Indeed, considering the small number of people killed (about fifty-two between 1855 and 1858 by the latest estimates), historians and popular writers over the years have taken all too much account of that aspect of things.[1] Still, there is no denying that the up-close-and-personal killing, modest enough in scope that individual names could be attached to riveting stories, was a regular element of the Kansas Territory image the media promoted, and to some extent invented, in the middle 1850s. Often the terminology used was military, whether the events quite fitted or not. Houses where skirmishes took place or where arms were stored became "blockhouses," or even "forts," in the telling. Skirmishes among thugs, or even isolated criminal assaults and murders, were dignified by the name of "battle." And always there was talk of the events in Kansas constituting a war. Just as other wars had war stories, so did Kansas. As they had heroes and villains, so did Kansas. One could argue that the special religio-missionary nature of the conflict, as seen from the perspective of both sides, escalated the deaths in battle into something more significant than mere loss of life: They became martyrdoms, sacrifices for a great cause, and they were embellished as such in the telling.

To some people, the exaggeration was ludicrous, the expected but unfortunate violent fruit of irresponsible talk. A disgusted observer in New Orleans expressed a common view on Northern intransigence: "Preachers have exhorted in their favor, and begged from the pulpit for rifles, to be sent to them, to enable them to shoot down the officers of the law which they had determined to disobey; and grave Senators, the oracles of great parties, have lauded them as heroes in a cause all but holy, and invoked for them admiration and support."[2]

But the folks back home took their heroes seriously. "A cry of anguish reaches us," went a stanza of one of many bad poems written for the newspapers about Kansas,

From the far-distant West,
A tale of human suffering,
Of bloodshed and unrest;
Of widows weeping o'er the spot,
Where their protectors bled;
Of mothers, who, as one of old,
"Will not be comforted."[3]

Governor John Geary, arriving in Kansas in mid-September 1856, said he saw the bodies of twenty-six murdered men along the side of the road in the course of a day. According to the *Chicago Daily Tribune:* "Some of them had been shot or brained, and thrown out by the road-side to rot under the burning sun. Others had been scalped as the Indians scalp their victims. One was pinioned to a tree by a bowie-knife driven through his heart into the solid wood at his back."[4] Such scenes had an effect.

Not every incident of violence was escalated into a martyrdom story. Perhaps some lent themselves better to it than others, in their real or imagined details. Perhaps certain editors, with an interest in certain stories, were more skilled at spinning out of them more than they presented on the telegraphic surface. What would seem the premier martyr story of the era, the murder of proslavery settlers by John Brown and his associates in 1856, got relatively little contemporary attention, and the persecution of Brown's sons got almost none. The selection here, therefore, does not suggest that the incidents described were the most important in influencing events in Kansas, or the most significant in illuminating the stakes of the conflict from the perspective of later scholars. They were simply the ones that made the most national news, that became prototypes, icons, examples, or myths associated with the struggle. As with so many things, both the parts and the whole were to some extent creations.

More broadly, this chapter serves to collect the national concerns having to do with military actions generally in Kansas, particularly the action of factional militias against the territorial militia and potentially against U.S. dragoons. In a real sense, people felt that civilization and order were the greatest martyrs of all in the premises, and that thousands of Kansans, huddled in prairie homes, though they may not have died, nevertheless suffered—feared for their lives—every day in such an environment.

Military action has been the most discussed of all aspects of the Kansas struggle in books both academic and popular. But the perspective here is

different. The expanded story—the inflated characters seen from a distance
and from a certain political or social perspective—is the main subject here,
rather than strategic considerations in the field. The question was not so
much who would prevail in the military struggle, but whether there was any
alternative to violence. Both sides, when they emphasized what would now
be called "terrorist acts" committed by their political enemies, were expressing a hope as well as a fear. The hope was that the perpetuators of such
acts were "crazy" and nonrepresentative and that publicizing the atrocities
would so shock the sensible people of the nation that the military aspect of
the Kansas struggle would be replaced by a peaceful contest for dominance.
Almost never did a newspaper publish a glorification of a killing from the
perspective of the killer. Events were universally seen from the viewpoint of
the victim, a victim with whom the teller and the reader of the story deeply
identified.

In November 1856 newspapers in Pennsylvania followed a story of a relatively obscure Kansas event, which provided them with a model story of
martyrdom. J. W. H. Golden of Waynesburg, Pennsylvania, was attacked
along with two companions, Robert Roberts and Thomas Bishop, along the
road from Lawrence to Leavenworth. Supposedly, the three were not armed,
and their only offense was being of free-state sympathy politically. Golden
and Bishop were both shot and seriously wounded. Golden's jaw was broken
in two places, and he was unable to chew. Roberts died at the scene. He was
left lying on the road by his murderers and was buried the next day by U.S.
soldiers, using only bayonets to hollow out a shallow grave. When a correspondent for the *Cincinnati Gazette* passed by a few days later, one arm of the
deceased extended out of the ground, gnawed to the bone by wolves. The reporter visited Golden and Bishop in the hospital at Lawrence and then saw
Golden carried on board the steamer *Omaha*, bound for St. Louis. On the
boat, the story continued, he had a proslavery man for a roommate. Delirious with fear that he would be attacked, and haunted by hideous dreams, he
lost his mind and jumped overboard. There was little doubt, wrote a reporter
in Pittsburgh, that Golden had "drowned himself in a fit of insanity." In his
carpetbag were letters to his sister, showing the martyr to have been an intelligent and hard-working young man.[5]

Not all elements of this story panned out as reported. Golden turned up in
his hometown of Waynesburg in December. He had not committed suicide;
he had overheard a plot to murder him and so jumped overboard and hid in
the woods. He made his way to the railroad and thence to St. Louis and

home.[6] Even with this correction, however, the story did not lack the typical drama of the innocent Kansas settler set upon by ruffians, abused by those disrespectful of freedom and of American rights. The only elements missing in this case were the burned cabin and the grieving widow.

The lurid descriptions of violent confrontation, mutilation, and murder started early. "We have not yet learned," wrote a reporter in Kansas Territory in the spring of 1854, "whether the new settlers—those who would not hesitate to imbue their hands in their brothers' blood—emigrated from a Christian or barbarous land." But it was clear some were ready to fight with a "savage ferocity unknown to the aboriginal tribes."[7] Settlers from both North and South held "conventions" on the prairie and passed stirring resolutions. These were, quipped one Southern paper, "Monster meetings, high-spiced resolutions, harangues not always free from froth" and "boyish boasts."[8] Settlers were filled with enthusiasm for ideals. Wrote a Kansas settler back to his friends in Boston: "Tell the boys who want to have a hand in reclaiming the long-lost Garden of Eden, and in planting the tree of Liberty, whose leaves shall be the healing of the nations, the sooner they come on . . . the better."[9]

A gaggle of violent incidents in the spring of 1855 provided an opening for the genre of "outrage" and martyr reporting to get well underway. On April 14, a mob attacked the offices of the *Parkville (Mo.) Industrial Luminary* because the editor had questioned the honesty of the recent elections in Kansas. On April 30, in the proslavery town of Leavenworth, free-state partisans William Phillips and Cole McCrea heckled Malcolm Clarke as he was moderating a meeting. Harsh words ensued. Clarke attacked McCrea with a stick, and McCrea killed him with his pistol.[10] Later a crowd tarred and feathered Phillips, rode him on a rail, and mock-auctioned him for one dollar, employing a Negro auctioneer in front of a jeering crowd. In mid-August, a mob put the Reverend Pardee Butler, who had expressed free-state sentiments at Atchison, adrift on a raft in the Missouri River after the revelers subjected him to humiliation and stoning.[11]

The Northern press now had the opportunity to take the moral high ground, however mixed the actual motives. A Boston paper said that the mob attack in Parkville had done more damage to the Southern cause than the newspaper the mob destroyed ever would have. The action revealed "the link which connects . . . slavery with violence and lawlessness."[12] The London papers were shocked: "It is not easy to conceive of a people doing more than those Missourian citizens to bring themselves and their country into contempt."[13] An editor in Dayton was more generous, averring that the Parkville mob did not represent the respectable people of the South and that "sober second thought" would suppress the rowdies.[14]

There was a smugness in the reporting. Northerners did not respond to taunts, as Southerners would have done, wrote a reporter in Massachusetts: "We are not used to their ways. We do not stop our opponent's mouth with a bullet and parry his argument with the thrust of a dirk. We reason. . . . We forbear."[15] The editor of the *Luminary* went on a New England speaking tour, along with Samuel Pomeroy, the Lawrence agent of the New England Emigrant Aid Company. They talked about Phillips, saying that now was a time for patience but that when the time came, "a stroke will be given for God and liberty."[16]

Southerners too made some effort to keep the lid on. The *New Orleans Daily Picayune* reported Northern crusading in Kansas but said that the reports of violence were highly colored: "It is difficult to discriminate facts from the excited narratives of the actors in these altercations and encounters, since the passions which have been lashed into fury find their chief indulgence on each side in denouncing the motives and conduct of adversaries."[17] A journalist in Montgomery commented, "We will let the grasshopper sing his old song in the grass; noisy, but a harmless thing, 'twere a pity to crush him with our foot."[18]

Yet the moderates had little luck in capping rhetoric. Went a Boston headline in October 1855: "Murder rules in Kansas. The bloody plot thickens. . . . Blood flows. Freedom reels and staggers in a death-grapple with Slavery." The actual story that followed was an account of that month's Kansas Territory election.[19]

As the legislature of Kansas Territory met, first at the little town of Pawnee, shortly at Shawnee Mission, and eventually at Lecompton, the descriptive powers of reporters were beggared in trying to paint a primitive picture of frontier legislation and jurisprudence. One member of the Kansas House challenged a reporter from the *St. Louis Republican* to a duel after the reporter called him a "magnified tadpole."[20] Under the headline "The Kansas Saturnalia," a reporter in Albany commented, "Such a preposterous parody of law making the world never witnessed before. It is not simply foolish, but the acme of whiskyfield insanity. It knows but one offense, abolitionism, and but one penalty, death."[21]

Also ludicrous was a widely reported confrontation between territorial governor Andrew Reeder and proslavery partisan Benjamin Stringfellow.

Stringfellow came to the governor's office on June 27 and challenged him to a duel on the grounds that the governor had called him a "border ruffian." When Reeder refused the challenge, Stringfellow responded, "Then I will have to treat you as I would any other offensive animal." He knocked Reeder over in his chair and scratched him before the governor drew both his pistols.[22] On his way to Kansas, crowds on the levees had rudely insulted Governor Reeder. One bully reportedly told Reeder he would collect 10,000 men to come and hang the new governor.[23]

The North became, in these press pictures, an abused victim, and the official Kansas government was pictured as undignified, unworthy of respect—a comedy of knaves.[24] Appealing to the courts in Kansas, wrote one observer, was "a long and hopeless process."[25]

A Missouri convention issued an "Address to the People of the United States" in October 1855 that was not conciliatory in tone. Missouri had 100,000 slaves with a value of $50 million and was not about to see that investment threatened. To liberate the slaves would be "impractical and cruel," and to destroy the balance of power between North and South and "carry to their bitter end the mandates of ignorance, prejudice and bigotry" was a disaster. The South had not tried to colonize a state. It had sent "no armies to force slave labor upon those who preferred free labor." But the North was colonizing and forcing. The movement in Kansas would be "totally destructive of that fellowship and good feeling which should exist among citizens of confederated States."[26]

The South argued that it had no choice but to fight. Georgia created its own Emigrant Aid Society in the fall of 1855, and several Southern states carried out major fund-raising drives.[27] Jefferson Buford of Eufaula, Alabama, mounted a major expedition into Kansas. He recruited men from all over the South to arrive in the territory in the spring of 1856, and he invested $20,000 of his own money in the project. He brought males only, divided into military companies. They were instructed to take no baggage except six blankets, one gun, one knapsack, and a frying pan.[28]

"Kansas," Buford said, "is the great out-post and stand-point in the contest; a people who will not defend the out-posts have already succumbed to the invader. Do we fear to send one man, lest the North may send two?" The way to quell the fury of either an abolitionist or a wild beast, Buford wrote, was "to turn and look him in the eye, for else he will spring and rend you to pieces." Were Southerners prepared "to become the serfs of foreign intermeddlers and masters?"[29] Without Kansas as a slave state, he wrote, "free negrodom" would "soon crush out cattle, cotton, colleges, property and progress; drones will eat out the hive, railroads disappear, and wild beasts, briars and brambles overrun the land."[30]

Buford offered exactly the dystopian argument advanced by the North for the grim future business scenario if Kansas *did* become a slave state. But as when Alice passed through the looking glass in Lewis Carroll's nonsense tale, everything was reversed when looked at from another perspective. Of course, the Northern press described Buford's crew as a band of drunks, just as the Emigrant Aid Company's troops were a crowd of sissy hirelings to the Southern eye.[31]

In such a climate began what came to be known as the Wakarusa war. The Wakarusa was the name of a stream near Lawrence. Really the "war" was simply a point on a continuum of small-time murders. The incident that set it off was not one clearly related to the political struggle. There were no battles among organized or official armies. It was a war because the press wanted to make it a war. Newspapers talked about confrontation and called the agreement that temporarily ended the tension a "treaty," thus automatically, and by the application of language, elevating the matter to a dignity that was not intrinsic to it.

The initiating incident has been much discussed in histories of Kansas. On November 21, 1855, Frank Coleman killed Charles Dow in a dispute over a land claim. It happened that Dow was a free-state man and Coleman was of the proslavery persuasion. The Douglas County sheriff, Samuel Jones, arrested a man who had lived with Dow, Jacob Branson. A free-state group led by Samuel Wood subsequently "rescued" Branson. This resulted in recriminations about the Free State Party's tendency to ignore or defy the workings of the law in Kansas Territory. Jones complained to the new governor, Wilson Shannon. Shannon called out the territorial militia, and there was a threat of some sort of attack on Lawrence. Lawrence people, under the command of Mexican War–veteran James Lane, built fortifications. On December 6, roving militia headed by a U.S. Indian agent, George Clark, killed on the road an unassuming man, Thomas Barber, formerly of Shannon, Ohio. The scene with the body laid out in a hotel before a distraught wife was ready-made for the hagiographers in the eastern press.

Wrote Sara Robinson of Barber: "Words can never convey the mingling emotions which moved the crowd, or the heart-crushing agony of the young wife. There were no children in the household, and all the affections had twined around this one idol. All of life, all of happiness, were centered in

him; and to be bereaved thus was adding bitterness to the agony. It seems as
though her heart must break, and, in her distress and shrieks, the brave,
strong-hearted men mingled tears and muttered imprecations of vengeance
upon the murderers and upon him who had brought these murderers into
our midst."[32] Another woman at the scene, Hannah Ropes, described Barber's death in a similar way. She said the body, though pale from loss of
blood, had a "look of repose" that was "beautiful," just as one might expect of
the rest of a martyr and a saint. The wife, a "delicate, slight-built person,"
the perfect devoted companion, shrieked in pain at the disruption of civilization as it was supposed to be.[33] The domestic scene, the individual death,
the up-close detail were designed in every way to appeal to the sensibilities
of those of every gender, section, and persuasion.

The Wakarusa war came to what one historian calls "an inglorious and anticlimactic end" when Governor Shannon negotiated a vague agreement with
free-state leaders James Lane and Charles Robinson about being gentle in
their protest against the laws. He had proposed to disarm them but did not.
The cold rainy weather and the discomfort of the potential attackers in their
camp probably had something to do with his restraint.[34]

It can be argued that the events of the Wakarusa war, while dramatic,
were, in the context of other violence and lawlessness at the time around the
nation and the world, insignificant, even trivial. But its coverage in the national press was extensive, and the depth of the reaction through the United
States was substantial.

Robert Van Horn, editor of the *Kansas City Enterprise,* regretted that the
eastern press "seize upon everything looking like a difficulty in the Territory, to feed the morbid feelings of an excited public." Van Horn wrote that
the "infatuated men" of Lawrence were guilty of violent acts against innocent
proslavery settlers as much as the other way around. "There is nothing but
outlaws on one side and a civil posse on the other." It was terrible, he reported, "to witness in Republican America, lines of hostile citizens arrayed
against each other, waiting the order that is to witness the mutual murder of
men who are descendents of the heroes of Bunker Hill and Yorktown."[35]

The editor blamed the violence on people like Lane, who, he said, was
"broken down in fortunes" and "bankrupt in character" to the extent that he
had nothing to lose from any kind of recklessness. Lane did not know when
or where to stop. Van Horn could only hope that there were not many of this
type and that the Yankee pragmatic character would allow them to see that
their rebellion would not pay in the end.[36]

Naturally, papers in the South took that line. The people living in Lawrence, wrote the *New Orleans Daily Picayune*, had threatened to hang both Frank Coleman and Sheriff Jones. "They are drilling on the open prairie every day, and have . . . artillery."[37] The Southern press described the regular territorial militia, arrayed in opposition, as peopled by "men of character, hope, and enterprise," real settlers all.[38]

Former U.S. senator David Atchison wrote from the field that the Kansas code of laws would compare well with the legislation of any other state or territory and that there was no reason for the "Abolitionists" at Lawrence to repudiate it. The "paid reporters" of the Emigrant Aid Company had created a distorted image of the border ruffians, one so powerful in the mind's eye that Atchison himself often bragged that he was indeed a border ruffian. But the reality was not the image. Atchison wrote, "The border 'Ruffians,' I assert and believe, have shown a more amiable, Christian and forbearing spirit, than any other body of men would have shown under similar circumstances."[39] From Richmond came the assertion that many of the great heroes in American history, from John Smith of Jamestown forward, could be called border ruffians. Such men were impelled by love of adventure and excitement, but they planted civilization.[40]

Given the stereotyping and the state of the public mind, Atchison concluded by saying that he would not be astonished if the Wakarusa incidents laid the groundwork for a real, albeit guerrilla-type, war in Kansas.[41] That type of war, wrote a Charleston man, would favor the South. Sharps rifles were useful only when there were rules. In guerrilla conflict, Southern men would attack with double-barreled shotguns, Colt revolvers, and bowie knives at close quarters. "We are in the grand vortex, and can feel the danger."[42] Civil war might come, but worse was anarchy "in its direst form, when famine, fire and sword shall be upon us, and there shall be none to stand between the living and the dead to stay the plague."[43] Added the *Richmond Enquirer:* "Every impulse of pride, every instinct of interest, every calculation of policy, urges us to measures of prompt and effective aid to the slaveholders of Kansas. . . . We cannot flinch."[44]

Southern papers rejoiced when, in January, President Franklin Pierce set out the Kansas facts in what the papers called a "plain, clear and business-like manner," thus sending the Northern press into a "fury" and leading their editors to "fairly foam with rage." But, said a writer in Richmond, they could not continue to deny the facts, "and, like the guilty school boy when caught in a bad scrape . . . [they] stand up with flushed cheeks and brazen faces and exclaim, 'you lie!—you lie!—you lie!'" while all the while calling for more Sharps rifles and howitzers.[45]

Radical and elevated as these comments seem, the Southern press's reaction to the Wakarusa war did not compare to that of the North. Typically, the first telegraphic news was wildly exaggerated. There was at least one headline reading: "The border ruffians have burnt Lawrence! Ten men killed and fifty wounded!" The truth was more modest, but Charles Stearns, a nonpaid correspondent to the *Liberator*, did report that in December 1855 there were 1,000 well-armed men in Lawrence to face maybe 1,500 opposition men. On December 3, 600 settlers paraded in the streets of Lawrence, and they were, according to Stearns, "burning for the conflict."[46]

Greeley's *New York Daily Tribune* was its usual effusive self. A Christmas Day editorial headed "Kansas Delivered" credited the "courage and prudence" of the Lawrence people for avoiding a real battle. They had peaceably "rolled back the tide of barbarian invasion, and have secured for Freedom yet another breathing space."[47] The invaders had drawn arms from a U.S. arsenal, amid official claims that the federal government was not intervening in Kansas Territory. The body of Thomas Barber, "a martyr to the cause of Freedom," had lain in Lawrence throughout the negotiations with Governor Shannon. His blood, wrote the paper, "no less than the tears of his desolate widow cries aloud for legal interposition."[48]

The *Tribune* writers outdid themselves in setting an atmospheric scene. There was a long description of the night of December 8, when the negotiations took place, ending the war. It was a dark night, and the wind blew from the south all day. At evening came sleet and a hard wind. Patrols of horsemen among the militia passed back and forth through the camp "like shades in the gloom," while sentries shivered at their posts watching the lights of Lawrence. Men tried to sleep under wagon covers or to warm themselves around campfires piled high with logs, but "the wild gale swept the flames and sparks up through the gnarled limbs of the old oaks and walnuts in the Wakarusa bottom." Shots rang out in all directions, "the wild noise being suited to the taste of those Border crusaders." Atchison was there, but he was urging restraint. Shannon spoke standing at the door of a hotel, saying that he was not there to say whether the laws were valid are not, but that there was a "perfect understanding" between himself and the Lawrence Committee of Safety, as it was called. He would disband the posse, he said. The reporter noted that at the moment Shannon said that, a jackass brayed across the street. "Poor Governor Shannon," the reporter said. "He means as well as politicians can."[49]

The *Tribune*'s New York rival, the *Times*, was not far behind. A Kansas correspondent wrote, "I can only thank Providence that my feet have strayed to this chosen spot, and that I am permitted to show my fidelity to the Puritan faith in battling for the peace of our own firesides, and the free principles that constitute the gem of civilized society everywhere." The soil of Kansas, he added, had "drunk the blood of innocence," and "the martial drum beats the watchword over the plains to awaken the hundreds of brave hearts ever ready at the call to serve the right."[50] Later, he claimed that the "beasts of Ephesus were not more ferocious and unfeeling in olden times than those prowling leagues of darkness who threaten us without mercy."[51] With that introduction, one did not expect a neutral recital of the facts, or a balancing of claims and counterclaims.

On the subject of Atchison, whom the *Springfield Daily Republican* called the "actual governor of Kansas," and his forces, the *Times* was rabid. Atchison's letters to the Southern press, the paper said, were "exhortatory, imprecatory, inflammatory," and they appealed to the "meanest and vilest" of the Southern population. Yes, he was a hero and a martyr to his friends in the South, having resigned the presidency of the U.S. Senate to devote himself to the cause in Kansas, but to the North he was a "reckless, dram-drinking pettifogger." To the *Times* Atchison's every act was treason. "He breathes nothing but threatening, threatens nothing but slaughter. . . . Never was filibusterism half so audacious, half so dangerous."[52]

To the readers of the *Times*, the Wakarusa war became something monumental and fundamental. It was fearful, the paper wrote, to light the first fires of civil war, "to stand by your own farm-house and deliberately to shoot down a man of the same race and color and history." There was a conflict brewing, the editorials said, between slavery and freedom, and between the sections, which had an "utter difference of temperament and education and aversion to each other's habits." Thus came the grandeur of seemingly little things far away. "The Nation feels it; and the doings of a General of Militia and a cast-off politician in that obscure wilderness, are watched with a breathless interest, such as the campaigns on the Danube or the Black Sea have never aroused." There was, the paper continued, no neutrality and no quarter, and no one was exempt or could feel other than "solemn."[53]

As always, however, public opinion, as reflected in Northern newspapers, was more varied and complex than such accounts might suggest. It seemed more dominated by party than section. The Democratic dailies, no matter how far North their offices, took a dim view of the free-state activities in Kansas.

The *Providence Daily Post* was an example of this class. Under the headline "Unhappy Kansas," it applied a little early social psychology. The majority in Kansas seemed peaceable, but an aggressive minority was not. "Their lot seems to have been cast in the midst of turmoil and strife. They have been constantly expecting war and constantly realizing their expectations." It seemed there was a modicum of unhappiness among residents of Kansas. "Fear, revenge and bitterness have mingled with social life and distracted their common pursuits." The reason for the so-called war, the Rhode Island analysts said, was the propaganda promoted by the New England Emigrant Aid Company and the Northern press.[54] The region, the *Post* writers wrote, had become "a foot-ball," with its people living in constant apprehension and with the eyes of the country on their every move.[55] Was it any wonder they were jittery?

"A Settler," writing to the *Boston Post*, was as skeptical: "How it is the press of the country has so completely erred on almost every affair in Kansas is hard to conceive." A Settler claimed there was no rebellion or armed resistance at all there among the vast majority, who were cognizant of what their business was and were minding it. The difficulty was promoted by "mad-caps . . . political desperadoes . . . and men seeking preferment, who are not very scrupulous how it comes." There was no organized band of abolitionists with rifles; in fact, claimed the writer, there were not twenty genuine Garrisonian-style abolitionists in the entire territory. There was disputing and litigation about title to claims. There were angry words and sometimes blows. Many people did complain about the laws, as people around the North generally complained about the Fugitive Slave Act, but the complaints did not amount to revolution. Yes, they disliked the governors sent from Washington; they were not unique in that. As for the free-state movement, it had been wrong from the first, and would eventually wreck itself if left well enough alone.[56]

What do the Kansas agitators mean, asked an editorial in the *Post*, by "their unparalleled course of folly?"[57] What did the correspondents mean with their lies? William Phillips, the correspondent for the *New York Daily Tribune*, was, according to the *Post*, someone "whose moral integrity had but little advantage over his political honesty." It held the same low opinion of the *New York Herald*'s man on the scene.[58]

The *New York Herald* was officially cautious too. It wrote in April 1856, as the spring emigration from both sections arrived in Kansas, that "Kansas wrongs have been wept over long enough" and that the issue was at risk of becoming a bore. Lawrence people needed to get to farming and not just writing to newspapers. The crisis was a fraud. "Several little girls and one or two little boys were very much alarmed some time since, by the intelligence that the naughty people in Kansas had got cannon and pistols, and were going to do mischief with them; but the parents of these children have no doubt satisfied them by this time that there was too much barking in Kansas for much biting." Politicians had fed on the interest "and not a few of them have had greatness thrust upon them on its account."[59]

A case in point was a visit to Washington by James Lane in April to present a free-state memorial asking for immediate admission of Kansas as a state under the Topeka Constitution. While it is true enough that opinion varied along party lines, it is also true that the arguments could be compelling, and that some events created a near-universal positive or negative reaction. Lane's visit was bad universally for the free-state faction. He certainly played the martyr to the supposed tyrant in Washington, the insider Stephen Douglas, but it backfired. Lane had neither the youthful innocence of Thomas Barber nor a devoted wife to cry over wrongs done to him.

Lane was the right and the wrong person for the job. He was a former congressman from Indiana and one of the most powerful and popular leaders in Kansas. But he was outspoken to a fault, an inveterate quarreler, and a moral chameleon. He claimed to be a U.S. senator-elect under the new Topeka "state" constitution.

It turned out the document Lane presented had been modified, presumably by Lane himself, maybe with authority of a Topeka legislature whose own legitimacy was suspect, maybe not. The signatures on it were not authentic. Senator Douglas exposed it as a fraud and made some unkind comments on the floor of the Senate about the messenger. The Senate voted 32–2 against receiving the document. Lane took offense, sent a press release to all the media saying he had been betrayed and abused, and challenged Douglas to a duel.[60]

Even the *New York Daily Times* concluded that Lane had taken "a very injudicious and unwarrantable course in endeavoring to bring the wishes of the people of Kansas to the knowledge of the Senate."[61] A writer at the *Springfield Daily Republican* thought neither Lane nor Douglas showed well. They were two "bold, bad men," and "the fewer of such elements in our political life the better." It was bad for Kansas that it had sent Lane as its representative. Lane was an expert at insulting invective, but in the course of the debate in the Senate, when he was treated with contempt and indignity, no one dared defend him.[62] The *New York Herald* took the same line, calling the Lane memorial "a silly imposture." A few more such free-state experiments, the *Herald* wrote, "will open the eyes of many of our deluded people of the North to the desperate character of the leaders of this 'free state' business." What a "precious brotherhood . . . to be setting all the crazy abolition fanatics, and old women of the North to howling over the wrongs done to 'freedom in Kansas' by the atrocious 'border ruffians'. . . . Verily the fool killer has a vast amount of unfinished business on his books."[63]

Southern papers leaped enthusiastically at the opportunity Lane's shenanigans provided. The *Richmond Enquirer* commented, "The exposure of the fraud was complete; the conviction of guilt perfect." Lane had courage, but his press release was "vulgar." Douglas, the editor said, "has sounded the depths of their [the free-state group's] hypocrisy; has penetrated to their rotten core; has torn away the mask and exposed their hideous and revolting corruption."[64]

The confrontation did not stop Lane on his speaking tours. In June he was holding forth in Milwaukee in his usual style. The border ruffians, he said, should be "lashed naked." He had seen fourteen men tarred and feathered within ten miles of his home at Lawrence. Lane drew large crowds and raised money. "Admit Kansas, free," he would say, "and the agitation ceases."[65] Lane was a counter to Atchison. Simplification, charisma, and nerve were effective in each case.

The next developments in the Kansas story played better for the free-state cause. The basics are easily told and have been often told. Sheriff Jones, after several days of trying to make arrests in Lawrence, was shot in his tent outside town on April 23, 1856. The free-state forces denied responsibility, and Jones recovered from his wounds. However, on May 21 the "raid" on Lawrence occurred; it became almost as famous as the Quantrill raid of 1863, not only in the annals of Kansas but in the national memory.

But while 150 persons lost their lives in the Quantrill raid, only one died in the 1856 confrontation, hit by a falling cornice. There was no armed resistance and no battle. However, the militiamen destroyed the main hotel in town by a combination of cannonade and set charges. They burned Charles Robinson's house. There was some looting. Men entered the offices of the *Herald of Freedom* newspaper, upset the presses, and threw the type into the river. They said in justification that the hotel was a fort and that the newspaper was printing irresponsible material. A territorial court had declared both a nuisance. The raiders were simply abating that nuisance.

The rhetorical descriptions began right away. Atchison, who had led the militia, consisting largely of Buford's company of Southern emigrants, supposedly made an inflammatory speech before Lawrence. "Boys, this day I am a Kickapoo Ranger, by God!" he supposedly screamed. "We have entered this town, and taught the damned abolitionists a Southern lesson that they will remember until the day they die." If a woman took up a rifle, he is reputed to have ordered, "trample her under your feet as you would a snake." Atchison often later denied having said any such thing. Lane and Robinson took off on tours immediately after the raid, giving lurid descriptions of the event. An auditor of one of Lane's speeches in Chicago wrote, "They saw the contending factions in the Territory through his glasses. The Pro-Slavery party appeared like demons and assassins; the Free State party like heroes and martyrs."[66]

Another event, much more obscure at the time, much more famous later, was buried by news of the Lawrence raid. John Brown, upset that he had not been able to get to Lawrence to help mount a more vigorous defense and enraged by the news of the beating of Senator Sumner in Washington, D.C., carried out with a group of companions on the night of May 24–25 what became known as the Pottawatomie massacre. The Brown group took five men and boys from their homes and families and brutally murdered them with short swords, mutilating the bodies so badly that the initial explanation was that there must have been an Indian attack. Brown might argue that he was administering Old Testament justice against the slave drivers. However, nearly everyone agreed that the events on Pottawatomie Creek that night removed the free-state cause from any moral high ground it had occupied with regard to violence. Seventy-five percent of those killed in the Bleeding Kansas era were free-staters, and this massacre involved only five deaths. But it was sinister, smacking of random terrorism.[67] The free-staters no longer had the advantage in martyrs, though eventually they would make one of Brown himself.

The initial telegraphic reports of the attack on Lawrence were heavily exaggerated and included the standard story that Lawrence had been reduced to ashes, that hundreds had been killed, and that civil war was raging in the territory.[68] "War! War!," wrote a columnist in Milwaukee, "that monstrosity, the greatest of all evils in human society . . . is again threatened against us by the slave power."[69] However, even when the more modest facts became available, there was great concern that such a thing could happen in America.

National reaction came in two, somewhat contrasting, phases, first to the shooting of Jones, and second to the raid on Lawrence. Van Horn in Kansas City wrote after the Jones shooting that the Topeka rebels were indirectly to blame, even though they had offered a $500 reward for the apprehension of the attacker. "No special pleading, no sophistry, nor metaphysical morality," he said, could stave off the conclusion that these men were "moral murderers."[70] The *Boston Daily Atlas* took the positions that there was no such thing as freedom in Kansas and that Jones had been looking for trouble. "A fellow who undertakes to indulge in these amusements, in the midst of a free people and at the expense of an intelligent community, usually gets his quietus before all is over." The whole affair, it noted, could be chalked up to "mismanagement."[71]

Why should the Democratic papers make such a howl about Jones, the *Hartford Daily Courant* wondered, when they had been silent about the murders of Dow and others earlier?[72] After all, wrote the *New York Daily Times*, the shooter of Jones was just "some desperado, whose impulses were beyond control."[73] What did the Topeka resistance amount to, wondered editor Samuel Bowles in Springfield, Massachusetts? It was a "practical nullity," when people in Lawrence could be marched off to trial "simply for refusing to be the instrument in their own humiliation, for declining to assist in the arrest of their fellow-citizens for technical offenses under the bogus government of Missouri."[74] Certainly, added a New York observer, something had to be done in Kansas by the federal government, and soon, "unless Kansas is to be abandoned to anarchy and disorder."[75]

A Richmond paper thought that even with the passage of time there would still be a "maze of local and personal prejudices" through which any news would have to filter. And the editor admitted his own prejudice, that there was a difference between "the attempt to perpetuate and the attempt to defeat a wrong." The former in his view was what the "violence of the Massachusetts Emigrant Aid Societies" was about, and the latter was characteristic of the "calm resolution of Virginia gentlemen not to be despoiled of their property." There was a difference between the "treasonous designs" of Greeley and the "patriotic purpose" of Atchison. At least, however, the

Lawrence events provided a "palpable issue" around which discussions could revolve, and a "visible and tangible advantage" for which the South could organize and fight.[76]

Of course, the picture given in the Southern press of Atchison, Jones, and other players in Kansas was in contrast to what Northern newspapers communicated. To the press in the South, Jones was an innocent public official trying to carry out his duties of maintaining law and order, a real martyr to the cause. Editors in the South quoted the words that Jones purportedly uttered as he fell: "They have got me at last! I would not have believed it! But I die in the vindication of my country's laws; and will they not avenge me?" It fit the attempt to transform a forward, hard-headed, narrow young man into a saint with a vision.

What hypocrisy, wrote a correspondent in St. Louis, that Robinson washed his hands of the Jones matter. The "supreme Judases" of the free-state faction made it their business "to deprecate and lament these bloody measures, and say that it is through the sweet influences of humanity and religion that they wish to triumph." Not likely.[77] A Richmond newspaper thought that Lawrence people were not less disposed toward violence for being hypocritical in talking about it. The town, it said, was filled with "a set of hired assassins."[78] Two St. Louis dailies, usually at odds, agreed that Jones was a hero: "A braver man never lived."[79]

The *New York Daily Times* teased about it: Was it not amazing that Jones was "resurrected" in time to lead the troops in the raid on Lawrence, but was it not appropriate? "Jones was already sainted in the calendar of the Border devotion; Jones already figured among the acts and monuments of martyrdom. Suddenly, as if by miraculous touch, or diabolical enchantment, the dying man resumes his health, and youth and strength . . . and plays out his ferocious part." Had he ever been shot at all, the paper wondered?[80]

Many observers agreed that the Jones incident was not so important. The *New York Herald* said the accounts of it were mostly "Black Republican balderdash." A sheriff could not serve a writ without an outcry from the national press. "An abolitionist cannot lose his baggage without a groan . . . that the entire North is being despoiled." Such statements needed to be taken with a grain of salt. "We entreat respectable men, who allow their nerves to be shaken by this rodomontade, to understand that it is all mere gabble."[81] Democratic and moderate papers, North and South, took the position that Jones was merely doing his job in a system that was still the American way.

The *New York Daily Tribune* compared President Pierce to Emperor Louis Napoleon in France, a despot who "with his minions with gun and bayonet, coerces into bitter obedience to the legislation of fraud the free people of Kansas."[82] The free-staters were often likened to the participants in the American Revolution. A Chicago newspaper asked a litany of questions: Who stood at Thermopylae? Who caused the Reformation? Who made Bunker Hill sacred? Was it not a handful bound together by conscience, as the Free State men were?[83] The residents of Lawrence en masse had become the ultimate martyrs.

Many people thought that was going too far. "It is the merest folly," said a columnist at the *Boston Post*, "a downright insult to American intelligence, to compare President Pierce, executing the laws of the Congress of these United States—laws made by the people—with George III, executing edicts in which the people had no voice."[84] The reaction to the attack on Lawrence was different. U.S. dragoons did not directly participate, but that seemed a technical distinction, since the territorial militia was a "creature" of the governor appointed by Washington. In another controversial legal development almost buried in the military excitement, "Governor" Robinson, head of the Topeka government faction, was taken off the steamship *Star of the West* on May 10 and imprisoned for treason. He was detained for four months.[85]

There had been plenty of warning that an attack was to come, as troops massed outside Lawrence. Still, the event, when it came, was "startling," an account to be read with "intense and melancholy interest."[86] There was speculation about the true cause of the attack. Maybe it was to disrupt the proceedings of the Howard Commission.[87] Perhaps it was just an attempt to enforce official authority.

But the most common analysis was that the crisis arose in the newspaper press because of the polarizing way the issue in Kansas had been framed and escalated by a "depraved journalism," which ministered to the "bad passions of bad men."[88] Then the newspapers proceeded, in criticizing irresponsibility, to indulge in the same thing all over again. The language became purple. Pierce, wrote one enthusiast at the *New York Daily Tribune*, would present himself for election in 1856 "sprinkled from head to foot with the blood of the Free State men of Kansas, and his whole person illuminated and lighted with the blaze of their burning houses."[89] "Are eighty years the limit of Freedom's life?" asked a columnist in Hartford. "Is it reserved for us who have been the nerve to all the world—the hope to the millions enslaved—the beacon star to light the nations to a haven of rest—is it reserved to us to dash out that beacon, when it should shine the clearest, and to give the lie to the immortal declaration which proclaimed us free? . . . Slavery rides unchecked in Kansas."[90] Maybe Preston Brooks, the caner of Senator Sumner, should go to Kansas. "If he can only catch the Kansas commissioners singly and unarmed, he would soon put the troublesome fellows out of the way, and thus give 'repose' to Kansas and the Democratic party."[91]

Thomas Gladstone from England, whose reminiscences were later published in book form, wrote back to his newspaper in lurid prose about the Lawrence attack. He would, he said, "never forget the appearances of the lawless mob that poured into the place, inflamed with drink, glutted with the indulgence of the vilest passions, displaying, with loud boasts, the 'plunder' they had taken from the inhabitants." They were men of large frame, he wrote, wearing red flannel shirts and big boots, "their faces unwashed and unshaven, still reeking with the dust and smoke and bloodshed of Lawrence, wearing the most savage looks, and giving utterance to the most horrible imprecations and blasphemies."[92]

The technical term for such language is hyperbole, but that is the mildest description of it. The *Detroit Daily Free Press* commented on speeches in their city by former governor Reeder and others; Reeder described the attack on Lawrence in a way the reviewers found "pathetic." He spoke of the "ruthless butchery" of men, women, and children, while other speakers described "smoking ruins" and "desolate wastes." It reminded one, the Detroit newspapermen thought, of the boy who said he had seen 1,000 cats. Told that this was a great many, he reduced the number to 500. The number went down with each question until he finally concluded that he had seen one, and if it was not a cat it was something black at least.[93]

The journalists at the *New York Herald* said of the language of their peers that if the country were actually in civil war there would be no place further to go with the language of war than had already been reached by the press in covering Kansas. The *Times* had written of "savages" and "slaughter" in Lawrence.[94] The *Tribune* had commented that the Lawrence raid was "one of the most execrable crimes recorded in history," a "gigantic wickedness." It had called the raid "the first act in the great tragedy of enslaving Kansas." It had described a "pyramid of fire that shot up from the devoted City of Freedom."[95] It was, wrote a columnist in Albany, a "raw-head and bloody-bones" rhetoric that was "flinging its banners of death-head and cross-bones too early to the breeze."[96]

The Pottawatomie massacre, which one would think would be a public relations bonanza for the South, was surprisingly little commented upon in contemporary newspapers. John Brown became famous nationally only with the Harpers Ferry raid and his hanging for it in 1859. A correspondent for the *St. Louis Daily Missouri Republican* mentioned the 1856 Pottawatomie killings without any lurid comment and expressed the hope that it might not be the commencement of a series of such vengeance killings.[97] The *New York Daily Tribune* called it only a claim dispute.[98] The *Springfield Daily Republican* wrote that the idea that a group of proslavery men would be taken out of their houses and killed and mutilated so brutally was so incredible as to provide ipso facto evidence that it was not true.[99] The *Milwaukee Daily Sentinel* reported the event the same way: "The account is its own refutation. Besides the greater reliability of the Free State reports, the transaction is in no wise characteristic of the men of the party."[100] Some Northern papers reported the Brown incident as a case of self-defense, saying the Brown party had come across the five they killed about to hang some free-staters. That, said a St. Louis paper, was as ridiculous as the claim that Robinson was held by a mob or that Jones had never been shot, or that the streets of Lawrence were lined with dead bodies.[101] Leverett Spring, who composed one of the first scholarly histories of Kansas in 1885, wrote, "John Brown is a parenthesis in the history of Kansas. The immense vibration of his career upon the nation had its source in the Virginia campaign and its ill-fated but heroic sequel, rather than in contributions to the territorial struggle."[102] That seems exactly accurate.

Following the Brown incident, there was a period of small-time guerrilla action by irregular party militias, which lasted until the arrival of Governor John Geary in September.[103] Numerous fights occurred—Black Jack, Palmyra, Fort Titus, Hickory Point, Osawatomie—and newspapers reported on each, but reactions tended to be predictable and repetitive, with estimates of numbers involved and numbers killed varying wildly depending upon the political stance of the reporting newspaper. There was "something like civil war," the *New Orleans Daily Picayune* reported, but the reports were "conflicting and contradictory as to the specific facts, vague in consequence of our remoteness from the scene of conflict, and colored by the medium through which they are brought."[104]

All observers agreed, however, on a dangerous insecurity in Kansas. A writer in Springfield, Massachusetts, commented that an American citizen could not travel in Kansas during those months without danger to life and limb. The militias there had taken on "all the remorseless characteristics of

Italian brigands."[105] The *New York Herald* made similar comments. "What a picture," a writer there said. "We are reduced to the conclusion that the general repugnance of mankind to pirates and highway robbers, to burglars and midnight assassins, is but a mockery and a delusion—that the securities which the laws of the land and the usages of civilized society throw around us and over us, like a strong shield, are subject, like Kansas, to the law of ruffianism and the chances of the hour—that man, after all, is but a savage cannibal, and that his social, political, moral and religious elevation is but a humbug and a cheat."[106] A Kansas resident reported in July: "We go armed to our work; we worship God with our hands on our revolvers. There is no safety. We need help. God defend us!"[107] Wrote Mrs. Mary Livermore in rhyme:

> Hunted like the prairie bison.
> Slaughtered like the prairie deer.
> With the crack of gun and rifle
> Ringing sharply in their ear;
> With their homes a blaze behind them,
> And their children on before,
> See the hosts of Freedom fleeing
> From a country theirs no more![108]

In what age are we living, asked a religious newspaper? "In what country? Under what government?"[109] The situation was, said Senator John Bell of Tennessee, "a mad, preposterous, and reckless game, in which the party that wins must eventually lose more than it gains." Bell was willing to see Kansas a free state rather than win it for slavery by such means. "Let it become another Dead Sea, rather than continue the pestilent source of mortal disease to our system."[110]

Representative of the coverage of these small-time but disturbing military actions in Kansas was that of the movements of James Lane. Lane was a politician and a field commander at the same time. A writer from Kansas to a Chicago newspaper estimated in October 1856 that Lane's militia had robbed seventy-five stores and 200 private dwellings and had stolen 5,000 items, "from a horse, to a chicken, from a bed quilt to a pocket handkerchief," worth an estimated $1 million.[111] "Lane's voice," wrote a Cincinnati reporter, "has been given continuously for war."[112]

Particularly galling was the report that Lane on his fund-raising trips was raising money to equip an army of 5,000, which he intended to take into

Kansas from the North along a new route that avoided the blockade established by the proslavery faction on the Missouri River. Lane reportedly
bragged from a camp in Nebraska that he had enough men and artillery to
batter down any town that tried to stop him.[113] Late in August 1856, he attacked Franklin, near Lawrence.[114] There were reports that he had burned
Lecompton.[115] A Michigan writer thought Lane's men were the "scum of the
earth" and that "not any earthly power save the army of the United States"
could prevent their actions from escalating into civil war.[116] A Missouri man
claimed that for the first time in the history of the United States, a political
party had arisen "upon a money and military basis" proposing the destruction of the Union.[117]

Martyrology was in full cry. When Lane's group attacked the house, or as
Lane called it, the "fort," of Henry Titus near Lecompton on August 16, a
free-state soldier named Henry Shombre died.[118] His reputed last words,
about his willingness to die for freedom in Kansas, made their way to his
home in Indiana, where one newspaper said that although Shombre had
been a little erratic, he had been "a noble specimen of mankind." It was not
a time to dwell on his weaknesses, the paper continued. "He has fallen,
fighting in as good a cause as Heaven ever smiled upon and he bequeathed to
his country the rich example of a brave man dying for the rights of man."[119]

The *St. Louis Daily Missouri Democrat,* reporting these eulogies, thought
that Shombre may have been a clever man, but its estimate of the justice of
the cause in which he died was different.[120] To Southern papers, Titus, who
was badly wounded in the affray, became a kind of martyr also. Titus became
head of the official Kansas Territory militia in time and eventually joined
William Walker's filibustering expedition to Nicaragua.[121] One eyewitness of
the Titus attack noted that the free-state crew took the wardrobe of Mrs. Titus for its own use, robbed stores, and carried away loot in loaded wagons,
threatening to kill anyone who interfered with them. Titus later complained
that they took an oil painting of his wife's mother out of his house while he
writhed in pain from a wound in the hand. Somehow, this activity did not
seem appropriate to defensive action in a high-minded cause. David Atchison argued that although he differed with Governor Geary, he, Atchison, was
willing to disband his militia in accordance with the governor's wishes. It
was Lane who remained defiant.[122] A newspaper in Ohio reported on Lane
with tongue in cheek: "What choice instruments the Republicans must feel
who have idolized this hero of Freedom. What happy text the life of this
Kansas martyr has furnished the pulpits of our political clergy."[123]

Lane did once threaten an attack on Lecompton and was diverted only by the appearance of federal troops.[124] Dressed in a slouch hat, open shirt, blue woolen overshirt, and coarse tweed trousers tucked in his boots, Lane demanded and got unquestioning loyalty from his troops. He claimed, "We will drive those fiends to burning hell before we get through with them."[125] Had not the federal government begun to intervene more strongly, a writer at Kansas City observed late in September, Kansas would have become a charnel house.[126]

As it was, the fights at Grasshopper Falls on September 12 and Hickory Point on September 13, 1856, were the last major engagements before Geary and his dragoons, partly by arresting members of Lane's militia, regained some semblance of military control.[127] Neither battle was decisive, but both provided descriptions of heroics for presses in Boston and in Savannah.[128]

From Fremont County, Iowa, where he had fled to avoid arrest, Lane wrote on September 22 denying that his soldiers had committed any disorderly acts. He suggested that the question of slavery in Kansas be decided by a duel between 100 picked men from each side, with twelve U.S. senators and twelve U.S. representatives as referees.[129] The *New York Daily Tribune* thought the suggestion was an attempt at humor, a spoof of Southern ideas of chivalry. But Lane would probably have loved to try it.[130] An Ohio editor called Lane a "degraded libertine," cast out of decent society, who would be glad to have somebody kill him.[131] Lane responded in kind, calling his enemies "wolves" and lacing his speeches with a litany of proslavery atrocities.[132]

More unusual than the standard responses to the battles was the reaction of the national press to the stance and actions of the federal government in these months. The government's crackdown, which began with the dispersal of the Topeka legislature by dragoons on July 4, escalated quickly. Of particular interest were various bills in Congress to "pacify" Kansas, attempts to even out the administration of justice in Kansas for "ordinary" crimes, the detention and trial of persons in Kansas suspected of fomenting or sustaining the violence, and a remarkable debate on the annual army appropriations bill. In each case it was clear that events in Kansas dominated discussion in Washington and that federal Kansas policy had a large impact on the political future of those creating and executing it.

An editorial in the *London Times* late in October 1856 took the view that "the United States Government is ruling things with a high hand in Kansas." However, observers in England thought that the "magnificent language of authority" in regard to the "insurgents" there was artificial. One would suppose from the dispatches issued by the Department of War that the U.S. government was based on passive obedience and was "supported by the traditions of ages, and the smell of sacred parchments and medieval rolls." Reality was otherwise. There was no consistency in federal action. It seemed moved first in one direction and then the other by pressure from the influences that could be brought to bear on both sides of the Kansas question. If the Free State Party instigators were to be tried or shot as rebels and insurgents, as advertised, why was former governor Reeder allowed to speak on their behalf at high-toned dinners in New York City? An "insurgent" met government officials every day on the street. "At every dinner party, at every railway, half the guests and half the travelers are insurgents; half, more than half, of the American people are engaged in an open conspiracy, carried on by advertisements and subscription lists, against the Government at Washington." Why did the federal government not suppress this? "Simply for this reason—that, just as treason, which is successful is never called treason, rebellion which is universal can never be rebellion."[133] John Brown made that argument at his trial several years later. If he was mad, he said, half the world was mad with him.

There were extensive congressional debates in 1856 over bills to deal with the Kansas question by setting aside either the worst laws of the territorial legislature or the legislature itself, and allowing Kansas Territory to start over with a new election supervised either directly by Congress or by a commission appointed by Congress.[134] These bills all violated the principles of popular sovereignty and congressional nonintervention established in 1854. And they all engendered debate along strictly partisan lines and ended up being defeated in the conservative Senate. The rhetoric in Congress and in the national press concerning these debates turned not on strictly military events in Kansas but on the broader questions of the nature of the Union and its constitutional guarantees, and on the proper orientation of the federal government toward the institution of slavery.

More germane to the question of the bleeding martyrs of Kansas was the controversy, which arose in August 1856, over the annual army appropriations bill. A group in the House of Representatives proposed an amendment to that bill requiring as a condition of passage that President Pierce not use the U.S. military to enforce the territorial laws of Kansas. In other words, they asked that federal troops not be used against the free-state insurgents. There was enough support for this that the first session of the Thirty-fourth

Congress adjourned without passing the $12 million military appropriations bill. This left the country defenseless not only in Kansas but against uprisings among the Indians and the Mormons, not to mention against potential foreign threats.[135] The bill passed only after the president called a special session of Congress to discuss that issue alone.[136]

The *Congressional Globe* was filled with accounts of the barbarities in Kansas instigated by both sides and of the malfeasances of officers there. Senator William Seward of New York said that the appropriations bill was a device for defending Kansas against slavery and that he would not be a party to "emasculating" it as it came from the House. "Sir, I could never forgive myself hereafter, when reviewing the course of my public life, if I had assented to inflict upon even the present settlers of Kansas, few and poor, and scattered through its forests and prairies as they are, what I deem the mischiefs and evils of a system of compulsory labor, excluding, as we know by experience that it always does, the intelligent labor of free men. . . . Policy forbids me to do it. Justice forbids me to do it. Humanity forbids me to do it."[137]

Many newspapers in the North thought holding up the appropriations bill was reasonable. The *New York Herald* wrote an editorial saying that the House had done nothing more than to insist on the safety of the settlers of Kansas.[138] The *Chicago Daily Tribune* found it fine, too: "Better that the army should have been disbanded years ago . . . than that such crimes as have been committed in Kansas, in the name of law and order, should be repeated."[139] As usual, the *New York Daily Tribune* was the most extreme: "Better that confusion should ensue—better that discord should reign in the national councils—better that Congress should break up in wild disorder—nay, better the Capitol itself should blaze by the torch of the incendiary, or fall and bury its inmates beneath its crumbling ruins, than that this perfidy [passage of an appropriations bill without restrictions] should be finally accomplished."[140] Other papers were not so sure. An Albany editor thought attaching conditions to appropriations was a "violation of the public honor and good faith—and the discredit of the United States in the eyes of the civilized world."[141]

Newspapers in the South saw in this strategy the writing on the wall. What a Hobson's choice it was to be offered the options of, on the one hand, abolitionizing Kansas by forbidding the federal government to enforce the laws or, on the other, leaving the U.S. defenseless. The *Charleston Mercury* thought that it was a "one-sided game" and that it might be well to withdraw federal troops from Kansas completely and let the militias have it out. It thought that the federal military, far from advancing Southern interest as the free-state faction claimed, had patched up temporary peace at the expense of the South, "nipped in the bud the Southern predominance in that Territory, and sheltered the Abolitionists from the storm they had invited and provoked."[142] The *New Orleans Daily Picayune* wrote that the army bill debate was "another step in the march of disorder."[143] How long would it be, asked a reporter in Louisville, "before the spirit that has taken this first step toward dissolution will make another?" The right arm of the government had been paralyzed, the reporter thought, and "the councils of the nation" had been "disfigured and disgraced by . . . hair-brains and hot-spurs, whose only chance of notoriety consisted in goading and snarling at their superiors from opposite sections of the North." In another aspect of the "tilt of words," both sides were guilty of wielding them irresponsibly.[144]

Just as the debate on the army bill began, a delegation from the National Kansas Committee visited President Pierce at the White House. Pierce had been complaining that federal troops were prevented from maintaining order in Kansas by the activities of aid societies. Pierce thought "the sufferings of the settlers there are . . . of their own seeking, and the legitimate fruit of that gunpowder-bible preaching which they . . . have advocated." The committee arrived to set him straight. It blamed Pierce for not doing more to stop the disorders and said the germ of the evil was in the territorial laws. The president responded, "This question I do not propose to discuss at the present time." The committee averred that there had been "disorders that would shame the worst despotisms of the worst ages" and asked if there would be any change of policy. Pierce replied in anger, "No, Sirs! There will be none!"[145] The confrontation in Congress followed.

Closely related to the question of maintaining order in Kansas Territory was the question of the administration of justice there. The territorial courts were the responsibility of the federal government. It was widely charged that their judges were partisan and venal. This issue came up in the national press whenever a free-state partisan was murdered and the miscreant killer went free or was let out on bail. Judges Samuel Lecompte and S. G. Cato were among the most excoriated of territorial officials. The concern over justice reached a fever pitch in reporting on the draconian measures Governor Geary took to try to quell the violence in Kansas and on the horrific conditions under which free-state prisoners were kept in the prisons of Lecompton.

Geary was shocked when he arrived in Kansas at the state of the justice system. In one incident, Charles Fugit purportedly murdered a man named Hopps on a wager. Fugit bet, for a six-dollar pair of boots, that he could kill an abolitionist before the sun set. He scalped his victim and displayed the trophy proudly over drinks that evening. The court, under Judge Lecompte, acquitted Fugit.[146] The Reverend Ephraim Nute, a well-known resident of Lawrence and Hopps's brother-in-law, was upset, he said, at how some of the Democratic papers, even in the North, laughed at the incident. "You may imagine," he wrote, "the feeling with which I read the cold-blooded sneers, the diabolical sport, which is made of our sufferings in the Boston Post." Had all feelings of humanity been subsumed by political interest?[147] Nute wrote to Theodore Parker, who preached on the subject at the Music Hall in Boston, where he collected $280 for Kansas aid.[148]

A second victim, named David Hoyt, was a Mexican War veteran from Deerfield, Massachusetts, who was hacked to pieces while on a peaceful information mission from Lawrence to the proslavery militia. A memorial came from his fellow townsmen in Deerfield to President Pierce. It argued that Hoyt had been murdered under circumstances of particular cruelty and atrocity, that he had been guilty of nothing, that the U.S. military was complicit in allowing outlaws to run loose, and that the U.S. government was "on the side of the past, shoring up the tottering walls of old oppression." It went on to say that the civil officers in Kansas, appointed by Pierce, were corrupt. The memorial admitted to perhaps seeming disrespectful to the office of president but said that democracy should be a name of honor, and that if Pierce had not approved these things personally, he should get rid of the advisers who had. Hoyt's disfigured body appeared at the camp of John Brown, whose natural rage was enhanced by the spectacle.[149]

Geary was especially upset to be eyewitness to an example of the random, but presumably politically motivated, violence. After a meeting with Southern militia in which Geary asked them to disband, one of the militiamen, on the way home, shot and killed David Buffum, reportedly because he would not part with his horse. He called Buffum a "damned Abolitionist," grabbed him by the collar and shot him in the stomach. The new governor arrived at the scene a few minutes after the event to watch Buffum bleed to death, holding the governor's hand and saying he was innocent.[150] Geary offered a $500 reward for Buffum's murderer, but Northern newspapers thought that even if the man were captured, no jury in the territory would convict him.[151] When a Missourian named Charles Hays was arrested for the crime, after a search that Geary said cost him $700 of his own money, Judge Lecompte freed him on $1,000 bail. Geary ordered that Hays be arrested again, but his anger seemed impotent. "Poor, unfortunate man," wrote a Missouri correspondent. "He can't govern Lecompton, to say nothing of the rest of the world."[152]

More dramatic yet was the situation of detainees and prisoners. Two incidents were particularly effective material for propaganda. The first was the arrest and brief detention at the opening of the Geary regime of a company of free-state emigrants coming into Kansas along the Iowa route. The second was a series of revelations about the treatment of free-state prisoners, particularly a group captured for attacking Hickory Point after the governor, in a September 11 proclamation, had ordered the partisan militias to cease and desist.[153]

The emigrant party incident took place early in October. Federal dragoons intercepted more than 200 people—families from Ohio, Illinois, and Wisconsin.[154] The soldiers searched their baggage, which included rifles and pistols, but also farm implements. Then the whole group was arrested. Edward Daniels, one of the party, wrote back to his local newspaper that he thought they would be released and their arms returned, but the experience was humiliating and a violation of their constitutional rights.[155] The soldiers broke open trunks and valises, threw beds out into the rain, and treated ladies rudely.[156] It was, wrote a reporter at the *New York Daily Tribune*, "a stylish piece of official felony."[157] In Hartford, the newspaper reaction was "horror and indignation." The prison to which these farmers and families were hurried, the *Courant* explained, was "not the hacienda of a petty Mexican tyrant—It belonged to this free republic." What laws, it wanted to know, had been broken?[158]

Several well-known people were with the train: James Redpath was a journalist who later wrote a biography of John Brown. The Reverend Thomas Higginson, who was the organizer and conductor of the train, was a well-known New England author. Higginson wrote about his experience in Kansas in a pamphlet entitled *A Ride through Kansas*, published within a year of the events. He described both the dragoons and Governor Geary as arrogant. "When you see that a man makes an effort to be dignified and commanding, it is all over with him. The new Governor's eyes look at you . . . 'with a very intensified nothing in them.'" He wrote from Lawrence on October 4: "I have been looking for *men*. I have found them in Kansas. The virtue of courage . . . has not died out for the Anglo-Saxon race." The Anti-Slavery

Society of New York City paid for the printing of Higginson's pamphlet and distributed it free.[159]

The Southern view was different. The *Montgomery Advertiser & State Gazette* expressed a popular view of the events by praising Governor Geary for a straightforward enforcement of the law in the "once wild and savage territory of Kansas." Col. W. J. Preston of Virginia, a U.S. marshal in Kansas Territory, had been with the arresting party, and the *Advertiser* thought that arresting the emigrants had been a necessary precaution. Geary released them the day after they arrived at Lecompton. They did have extra arms. Among their stores were sixty dragoon saddles and sixty sabers without a single horse to put them on. Perhaps, thought the *Advertiser*, they intended to steal horses and form a military company.[160]

As always, the closer one got to an unvarnished account, the more ambiguous reality became. John Gihon, a physician who was Governor Geary's private secretary, had every reason to know the details of the governor's handling of the emigrant arrest question, and he published his account of it in 1857, while memories were fresh. According to his account, representatives of the train met with Geary on October 1. They denied they had anything to do with Lane or had anything but peaceful purposes, and Geary then said they would be welcome. However, there was a proviso: They were to enter unarmed, and they were to notify the governor of their arrival so he could give them an escort. The next thing the governor heard was an October 10 dispatch from Phillip St. George Crook, commanding dragoons at the Nebraska border, that he had arrested and disarmed a large body of *professed* immigrants, drawn up in military order, and equipped with munitions of war hardly well adapted to hunting rabbits on the farm. The train was not delayed but, rather, escorted on its way by the troops, but not before the group was lectured on the dangers of armed invasion of the territory and the inappropriateness of their vindictive attitude when accosted. They had not gotten proper permission and were therefore technically in violation of the governor's proclamation preventing armed military companies from entering Kansas Territory.[161] One can easily speculate how many eager readers this pedestrian account, which was printed in book form by an obscure Philadelphia publisher, had in comparison to the screaming headlines of the *New York Daily Tribune*.

There were, absenting the emigrant train, trials and prisoners enough. Through the fall and early winter of 1856, trials were held for people indicted for treason, as was the case with "Governor" Robinson, or for participation in illegal militia activity, as was the case with a free-state group arrested for attacking Hickory Point. Eighty-eight men were indicted for murder in connection with that raid. A few were convicted of manslaughter and were sentenced to five years hard labor with ball and chain. Some escaped. Most were acquitted.[162] The charge against Robinson was reduced from treason to the violation of a law preventing exercising an office without a "lawful appointment or deputation." Some members of the Topeka legislature went to prison on the same charge, but the charges did not stick.[163]

Robinson's four-month imprisonment, while stressful, was under light security and decent conditions, notwithstanding the complaint of Sara Robinson that, being near Lecompton, the prisoners could "smell the brimstone and see the smoke" from that hellhole.[164] The same could not be said for the militiamen from the Hickory Point attack. Their situation was the very stuff of martyr stories, the kind at which the national press had by this time become expert.

The prisoners made up a memorial, which went out to the national press. They were, they said, held under horrible conditions. A few of their guards were kind, but most were "drunken, brawling demons, too vile and wicked for portrayal," who threatened to shoot or stab their wards. They heaped insults on the prisoners every day. The prisoners were poorly clad and had no bedding. The prison was filthy and crawling with vermin. More and more became sick as time passed, and at least one died.[165] Governor Geary visited them but seemed unable to ameliorate their condition.[166]

Reporters, who described the appearance of Lecompton generally at the time, did not think conditions in the rest of the town much better. The courtroom on a rainy day had inches of mud on the floor. The streets were packed with people who called themselves deputy U.S. marshals and drew salaries for arresting people. "They might be termed a kind of gubernatorial excrescence," wrote a St. Louis visitor, "but I cannot blame them for wanting to live, and unless they can make money where a Cape Cod Yankee would starve to death, they certainly would be forced to leave Lecompton."[167] Trials were regular, and convictions carried draconian sentences. "All the time," a reporter wrote, "the Governor paced his office floor with hurried steps, exclaiming every now and then, in sentences denouncing the acts of the officials, and telling what he was resolved upon doing about it."[168] The prisoners, wrote a reporter in Massachusetts, would be tried "if they do not previously die in Titus' black hole."[169] The Lecompton prisoners were held "like the caged beasts of a menagerie," readers of the *New York Daily Tribune* learned.[170]

Some Southern papers tried correctives. A St. Louis paper said that the prisoners were not working on public works during the day dragging ball and chain but had been hired out at high wages to public parties.[171] But the prevailing impression of newspaper readers around the country was of the unjustified sufferings of innocent men. Wrote one prisoner home: "I have not done the first act since I came to Kansas in relation to the difficulties here that I am sorry for, or that would cause a friend to blush for me." He told of a friend who had been arrested and imprisoned with no charge being made. This man could not get bail to attend the funeral of his wife. The writer of the letter was too sick to sit up, and he had lost his home in a ruffian raid. "Still," he concluded, "remember me at that Throne of Grace we have so often approached together."[172] Fund-raisers in the East solicited books for a library for the free-state prisoners. "All kinds of moral and religious books will be acceptable."[173]

All the while, there were memorials and speaking tours, often beginning with a litany of the military horrors and a list of the martyrs who had suffered physically in Kansas. The South had some speakers and it had its list of victims, but the technique was far more developed in the North.

Former governor Reeder was an effective speaker on tour. During the Buchanan-Fremont presidential election campaign of 1856, he gave an address in New Haven, Connecticut, that contained many of the elements that made free-state propaganda work. He started by saying that the events in Kansas were the most important thing to happen to the United States since the War of Independence. The conflict, he said, was not as much a matter of slavery and freedom as of an appropriate way to administer self-government. In Reeder's view, it was not the Law and Order Party but the Free State Party that truly stood for order and justice as well as right. "If the problem of self-government is only to be solved in the result of anarchy and bloodshed, in the lawless rule of the strong over the weak, and the devastation of the social structure and the domestic hearth at the pleasure of the lawless ruffian, while the Government looks idly and smilingly on, and the residue of the people (so long as their own localities are exempt from the curse) in heartless selfishness refuse to recognize their obligation to interfere, then indeed had the problem better have remained forever unsolved in the brain of visionary philanthropy, and the blood of the Revolution have been better unshed." Self-government, he claimed, was distorted in the South, where labor was degraded and freedom of speech denied. It was distorted in Mormon Utah, where the separation between church and state was relaxed. In Kansas there was the irony that the very officers of the law were robbers and pirates; the very arrangers of elections were the manipulators of elections. People who were accustomed to the "restraints, protection, and refinements of society" could not well imagine the situation as it was in Kansas, where the position of the majority was "less tolerable than that of the serfs of Russia." A proslavery plot went well beyond the region: "The scheme to force Slavery upon us is . . . seated upon our necks, beyond all remedy but revolution."

That said, Reeder followed with the usual litany of atrocities, the list of martyrs, and the embroidering of the details of their passing. He cited "ridiculous indictments" being handed down against heroes and said the press was throttled. A Lawrence hotel, he reported, had been battered down with cannon in an attack on the accoutrements as well as the substance of civilization itself. "Its walls were battered with cannon, its floors exploded by kegs of powder, and its splendid furniture cut into piles of kindling." Looters broke open trunks and stole money, watches, and clothing, "even down to the last quarter-eagle of a poor mechanic taken from his pocket on the street." Books and papers were burned. Property the ruffians did not need was cast into the street. "But," he said, "I must forbear details, or my task is endless." He would say only that these attacks reduced the settlers to a "disorganized mass of subjects," who could not even send a messenger under a flag of truce without being murdered. If this valiant "pioneer band" were allowed to fail, he noted, something basic in the country would fail also.[174] Applause and money followed upon Reeder's every word, as it did with Lane and with another less frequent but effective speaker, John Brown.

On February 18, 1857, Brown spoke at the State House chambers in Massachusetts. The occasion was a meeting of a legislative committee considering an appropriation from the state of Massachusetts to aid Kansas. Franklin Sanborn, who was to write extensively about Brown after his death, introduced the Kansas hero by saying that they were not asking for money just to clothe the naked and feed the hungry, but to prevent the encroachments of the slave power on the "domain of the Freemen of the Nation." He then introduced "glorious Old Brown of Osawatomie," who, though only in his late fifties, had the look of a 600-year-old patriarch of the book of Genesis about him. Brown talked about his sons, who were among the abused prisoners at Lecompton. He talked about the battles in which he had been personally in-

volved. He talked about his personal witness to the bodies of martyred men
and the bravery of their families. He did so in graphic and gripping detail,
down to the work of the flies on stinking corpses.[175] It was through such public appearances as this, and private meetings with the rich and famous, that
Brown came to be thought of, not as a primitive and courageous fighter only,
but as an eloquent spokesperson for a cause and for the higher law.[176]

Not only were there live speeches, but many printed pamphlets were also
circulated. A masterpiece of the martyrology type was "An Address to the
People of the United States and Kansas Territory, by the Free State Topeka
Convention." The convention took place on March 10, 1857. The proslavery
group had branded Lane, Robinson, Reeder, and "a host of other good men
and true" as mere hired emissaries involved in a filibuster. It was necessary
to "unmask the hypocrisy" and "expose the falsehoods" of such literature.
All that was necessary to do so, the pamphlet continued, was to talk about the
martyrs. The oppressions of the free-staters were "written in characters of
blood, and burned into the memory of every honest citizen of our country."
Subterfuge and deceit, circulated to the newspapers, would avail nothing,
"for the great truths, in the gigantic wrongs of Kansas history, have been
seen and known and pondered of all men, and will stand, like the Egyptian
pyramids, to the surprise and wonder of coming generations." Free-staters
had violated no law, "for what is not just is not law." There followed an account of every meeting, every battle, every death, every supposed deception
and betrayal. Who could blame them, the pamphlet asked, for finally taking
up arms? "Inspired by a cause as pure and holy as that for which Washington
fought . . . they rallied under a common banner, and went forth . . . to defend those rights which are intuitive in the manly breast." They did it, they
had to do it, to preserve their self-respect.[177]

There was more guerrilla war to come, particularly the jayhawker campaigns in southeast Kansas during 1858. But the victims of those events were
not written about as individual martyrs the way Dow, Barber, Hoyt, and
Hopps had been. The proslavery and free-state leaders of that guerrilla action, Charles Hamilton and James Montgomery, were not praised or excoriated in the manner of Atchison, Jones, Lane, or Brown. There was a turn in
1857 from violence to politics, and from blood and rhetoric about blood to
constitutions and rhetoric about constitutions. As the Lecompton government moved toward creating an "official" constitution and applying seriously for admission under it, and as territorial governors exercised better
control of the private militias, as well as pursuing a more evenhanded and

effective policy in promising and delivering more fair elections, both Northern and Southern sectional advocates found that military action was impossible. As the military phase ended, dramatizing the sufferings of martyrs became ineffective. No longer could propagandists repeat the tale of the sack of Lawrence or the burning of Osawatomie or the massacre on Pottawatomie Creek and be sure that it would move opinion their way. Instead, they had to turn their attention to the broad question of whether and how the Union would survive as a "House Divided." Instead of denying that the Kansas fight was about slavery in order to concentrate on the details of local elections or guerrilla fights, all the while demonizing individual enemies, they increasingly were forced to confront the giants in the shadows.

John Brown spoke of the "Serpent at the Heart" of the Union that was the institution of slavery, and he believed it would be necessary to purge the country with blood, even risking the destruction of the Union itself, in order to be rid of that dark, corrupting influence that made a mockery of every decent initiative. In hindsight, that may seem a prescient view, but to moderates on both sides in the 1850s it represented a fearful prospect, but one that they could not entirely dismiss. When fighting temporarily calmed in Kansas in 1857 and the fortifications at Lawrence came down, Lane left the state. Supposedly, he said, "D—n Kansas, she may go to h—l for me; I never shall return to her again." A letter writer to a St. Louis paper, however, had no doubt that the "grim chieftain," Lane, still worked for the cause. He would, the writer said, "hasten to the arms of GREELEY, BEECHER & Co. and they will receive him in a warm embrace, and shriek louder than ever over the wrongs of Kansas."[178]

News from and about the "far-famed" Kansas Territory overwhelmed 1850s newspaper readers.

New York Daily Tribune building, 1850s.

Ten-cylinder Hoe newspaper press of the type that churned out Kansas editorials in the metropolitan dailies.

Plymouth Church, Brooklyn, New York, where Henry Ward Beecher advocated pursuing freedom in Kansas with the aid of Sharps rifles.

A SPEECH ON THE KANSAS QUESTION

Many 1850s readers recognized that the debate on Kansas was hardly among the calmest of philosophical discussion.

Constitutional Convention, Topeka, 1855.
Kansas became expert at creating unsuccessful constitutions.

Free-state prisoners near Lecompton.
Their fate became a national cause célèbre in 1856.

Colonel Fremont's Last Grand Exploring Expedition in 1856. Note Horace Greeley,
the New York Daily Tribune editor, pulling along a four-legged John Fremont, the 1856 Republican
presidential candidate. Henry Ward Beecher, carrying guns and trailing behind, is saying,
"Be heavenly minded my brethren all. But if you fall out at trifles, Settle the matter with powder
and ball and I will furnish the rifles." Lithograph by N. Currier, Library of Congress.

A Kansas fund-raising meeting in St. Louis, a scene that was repeated innumerable times across the nation.

Structure in Lecompton that was laughingly called "the Governor's Mansion."

During the Lecompton debate in 1858, decorum in the U.S. House of Representatives declined.

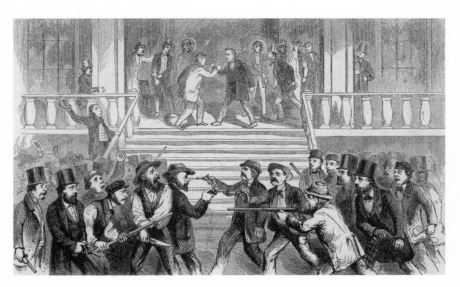

A Kansas confrontation, Fort Scott, 1858.
The tempest may have been in a teapot, but it was a teapot closely watched.

CHAPTER 6
A SERPENT AT THE HEART

In September 1855 the *Louisville Daily Journal* was trying out the new type and the double-cylinder power press that it needed to keep up its increasing circulation.[1] It ran an editorial on the subject of the American Union. The paper had been accused of being secessionist. But the editor was uncomfortable with giving space to a "theme so abhorrent and revolting to every patriotic instinct in our bosoms as that of a cool reckoning of the value of the Union." The desire to preserve the Union, it said, came not from a business calculation but from deep psychological feeling. Calculating its value would be like estimating the value of life itself. "The subject is too shocking and repulsive for a moment's contemplation." The "paramount and transcendent" value of the Union was a matter of faith, not understanding—a conviction "enveloped in a world of hallowed associations rather than a naked judgment—a vital instinct rather than a deliberate persuasion." So it should remain. Discussing the survival of the Union in connection with the Kansas debate would "weaken the spell of that grand and profound nationality which holds the Union serenely beneath its sway." Such discussion was leaving the masses prone to fanatics by serving "to disenchant and denationalize the whole people." The value of the Union should be "as unquestioned as it is unquestionable." Yes, there would be turbulent congressional sessions with Kansas on the table, but, no, that should not threaten the sacred Union.[2]

The *Journal* was not the only Southern paper expressing shock at the situation vis-à-vis the Union. The *New Orleans Daily Picayune*, also benefiting from the prosperity of political stability enough to buy itself a four-cylinder, 10,000-impression-an-hour newspaper press, expressed the same sentiments.[3] "The flippancy with which some demagogues speak and write of the probability, nay more, the desirableness of a dissolution of the Union," wrote a journalist there in the fall of 1856, "is one of the worst signs of the times. It is evidence of a sad decay of true American feeling."[4]

Such talk also seemed an outrage to common sense. The United States had grown under its Constitution from a population of 3 million to one of 30 million prosperous folks. That growth was because its citizens had once agreed "to form a more perfect Union, establish justice, insure domestic tranquility, provide for the common defense, promote the general welfare, and secure the blessings of liberty to ourselves and our posterity." And, the *Picayune* asked, had it not worked? "The wilderness has been subdued. The country had advanced in every way, and the people of Louisiana, are as true to the Union as a needle to the pole." The federal Union was the "heritage of the people," nothing less.[5]

But however nostalgic some Southern newspapers were about the Union, there was no question among them that it had to be a Union with slavery in it. Eliminating that institution—suddenly or gradually, violently or peaceably— seemed to be a thought as unthinkable as dissolving the Union. A Virginia man, writing to the *New York Daily Times* during the Kansas-Nebraska bill debate, wrote, "You Northern people don't understand the difficulties of our case. . . . It is the difficulty of *getting rid of the negroes,* if we were disposed to set them free, and to make them as well off as they are now."[6] Freedom for slaves was a complex matter, others said, and the arguments for it were hackneyed. A Baltimore paper expressed the view that while it was no friend of slavery in the abstract, "involved in this question of slavery are other questions of quite as vital importance, not to the South alone, but to the whole Confederacy, as freedom to the negro."[7] A writer in Mobile, Alabama, thought antislavery was just another Northern folly, which threatened, by a moral earthquake, to crack the foundations of society.[8]

A Charleston newspaper was of the opinion that a subtle question had been framed as an either-or polarity. The truth of history demanded continuance of "our settled and almost traditional policy." Property was important. It could not be "dust in the balance" of a debate on morality.[9] "I know no Abolitionist," wrote a journalist in Charleston, "that is not a socialist, and prepared to modify or destroy the right of property." Slavery relieved labor of the greatest of evils, "the heartless, grinding, and exacting despotism of Capital."[10] Order was important. The *Washington Union* emphasized that the liberation of the black race would enslave the white race, partly by raising the prices of commodities produced in the South and partly by releasing on society a group of "idle savages."[11] It was often said that slavery kept the South orderly, the relation between master and slave regulating society as no central government could or would. Aristotle had seen the slave as an essential part of the family, and the family as the regulator of society.[12]

Slavery must expand in order to survive. If the "free and normal process" of the expansion of slavery were arrested, a writer for the *South* in Richmond said, it would stagnate in corruption and disease and infect the social system "with hideous and fatal maladies." The possession of Kansas, not so important per se, would give the North new moral as well as physical power and thus endanger the institution of slavery as a whole.[13] Kansas, if it became a free state, would not be just another free state but "an outpost of Abolitionism, garrisoned by the most restless, adventurous and fearless spirits."[14]

Could the North not simply leave the South alone? If the South were so "imbecile," how had it cooked up so powerful a conspiracy as that with which the North charged it? Nature and commerce were fighting the South's battles, Southern newspapers said, as were reason, humanity, and religion. All that was needed was a level playing field.[15]

The prognosis became increasingly grim. The *Charleston Mercury* in the summer of 1857 thought that Kansas might well be lost.[16] The South loved the Union, said a writer in Montgomery, "but when it departs from its principles for the mere sake of power and influence, when it forgets its ancient prestige, when it bows the knee to Baal, then . . . it is no longer worthy [of] a patriot's support, and we will turn from it, to seek refuge in another ark of safety."[17]

Northern papers often hooted at such talk of disunion. In an April 1858 editorial entitled "The Bugbear of Disunion," the *Chicago Daily Tribune* contended that the threat of disunion was like the deus ex machina in classical drama, which appeared to solve some knotty problem amid stage thunder. "It is a *monstrum horrendum,* which is kept especially for crises in Congress and Presidential elections." Was the North supposed to shiver in terror? "The Union is not an African *fetish,* to be superstitiously worshipped, whether it subserves or contradicts the objects of its framers: and if the South cannot remain in the confederacy except on condition that its whole legislation shall be controlled for her especial benefit, the sooner we dissolve co-partnership the better."[18]

It was impossible to ignore the slavery question in the interest of the preservation of the Union, or for any other reason. It was, said a writer in Louisville, fast becoming the "master element" of politics. It "divides and distracts State Legislatures and city councils, and enters intimately into every theme of deliberation and every measure of policy that arises in the halls of Congress. It is the baneful atmosphere that envelops all other questions in its destructive folds and threatens to dissolve the Union and extinguish liberty itself."[19]

Thomas Higginson thought to talk of the Union at all was idle, since "mere talking is so insignificant in comparison with the vast processes, that, beneath God's laws, are going on." He wrote in 1857 that there were already two countries within the United States, and that they hated each other. When Higginson visited Kansas in 1856, nothing impressed him so much as "the general, deep, vague, but unquestionable, absolute, total alienation between every man in Kansas who came from a free State, and every man who came from a slave State. It was an actual inevitable thing." The animosity was not a question of the Constitution, "not the severing of a parchment, but the severing of two hostile races."[20]

Public opinion on the slavery question flowed against the South. A "perilous agitation" had begun, wrote a Georgia newspaperman in the spring of 1854. "The bonds of our Union have wonderful tenacity and can stand, as they have done, many a rude shock, but can they bear the silent and insidious rust of a progressing perverted and corrupt public opinion, such as we know has been manufactured with more than Jesuitical zeal and perseverance for a quarter of a century."[21] The *Washington Union* noticed the same trend. While the press was looked on as a "palladium," it was "prolific of mischief to a vast extent if vicious minds wield its influence."[22] If any class deserved to be treated with contempt, said a congressman, it was the correspondents in Washington—"that poor miserable class who hang round . . . in the shape of demented fragments of humanity, for the purpose of gathering up every whisper and word and circulating it through the land."[23] The editor of the *Washington Union* thought the air was "impregnated with sophism and falsehood" on the subject of obedience to authority. "Men can almost walk through the States on sheets of paper filled with inflammatory articles."[24] The whole literature of the North was, the *New Orleans Daily Picayune* thought, "tainted" with abolitionism. "The trail of the serpent is over them all."[25]

Leonard Richards has written about the slave conspiracy theory in his book *The Slave Power: The Free North and Southern Domination, 1780–1860* (2000). While historians once dismissed the nineteenth-century idea that there was a slave power dominating American politics, feeling that the idea was purely a creation of the newspapers of the time, Richards found fire behind the smoke. That some members of a lunatic fringe used the argument regularly did not mean it had no actual substance. It was true, Richards argued, that Lincoln, Seward, and others had a distorted view of the world, focusing on some facts and ignoring others. "They minimized divisions in the plantation South. They exaggerated differences between North and South. They often failed to see the whole picture, often failed to put events into a large context, often failed to see the world about them as later generations of historians would see it. They were, in short, no different than scores of other groups historians have studied." The difference was that they carried so many other antebellum Americans with them, and the slave power thesis became conventional wisdom in Republican circles. This was due to newspapers. These newspapers were irresponsible sometimes, certainly, but the men who ran the *New York Daily Times* hardly belonged to the lunatic fringe, and their readers knew it.[26]

The slave power argument gained credibility and currency and slowly became a basis for thought and then for action. There was considerable skepticism about the press, but it was indeed the instrument through which random information formed into patterns and became beliefs to be acted on.

The rhetoric in the most radical Northern press was indeed earnest. The Kansas-Nebraska bill, wrote journalists at the *New York Daily Tribune*, was the end of compromises on the subject. "Let the Baptist's bloody head welter in the charger. . . . Human liberty has been beheaded to gratify the dainty courtesan, Slavery. . . . We are despised for it all over the planet."[27] Harriet Beecher Stowe's *Uncle Tom's Cabin* had sold well. In the spring of 1854, one could see a stage version of it in three New York City theaters. "We seriously doubt," wrote one New Yorker, "if the famine in Ireland ever caused so many tears as have Uncle Tom's sorrows."[28]

Why pay so much attention to blacks, people discussing the Kansas struggle often asked, when the prosperity and happiness of whites and the existence of the Union was at stake? Why worry about the few blacks actually in Kansas when the issue there was not race but self-government? That argument, wrote the *Washington National Era*, was a ruse. Slavery was behind it all: all the euphemisms, all the sophisms, and all the devices. "Whatever may be said in excuse of a State for tolerating the evil institution on the ground that it took root in a dark age, when the subject was little understood, and grew insidiously until it had so interlaced itself with the whole social system that its sudden extirpation would prove dangerous—what possible excuse could be set up for the People of Kansas, now, if, at this age of the world, with their eyes wide open to the wickedness and baleful workings of the system, they should establish it in their new State?"[29]

There were a few moderate voices, but these were loudly criticized. The writers at the *New York Daily Tribune* laughed at the commercial conservatism of the *New York Journal of Commerce*, which advised going slow in the wake of the supposed frauds in the Kansas elections of 1855 and the shipping of Sharps rifles to the state. What cowards! "Had the *Journal of Commerce* been published in the year 1773 we very much fear it would have strenuously advocated the patriots of those times to pay the tax, drink the tea, and wait for Parliament to repeal the law."[30] Was the United States really a free country, asked a Detroit newspaper? Its answer was no. The Declaration of Independence had been a "veil thrown over great National errors and wrongs." Slavery could not be left alone. It would "infuse its virus" into government and poison everything. "It wars upon freedom everywhere, and until this Nation is purified of its accursed influence, it will know no peace."[31]

A complication was that not only in the South but also in the North and in Kansas, African Americans were generally considered an inferior race. There were admitted to be outstanding exceptions to the rule, and there were powerful arguments that, even given the inferiority, slavery was an abomination and the country should grant equal political opportunity to blacks, if not full social acceptance.[32] But still, there was an underlying indifference. The *Daily Alta California* in San Francisco claimed there were no abolitionists or secessionists there. Why force the slavery issue by framing it in a certain way, thus opening "old and irritating subjects?"[33]

It is a shock to read in a Detroit newspaper, "The Democratic Party does not hold nigger freedom to be paramount to white freedom." Whites, the writer said, had "the right to self-government, without regard to niggers."[34] The "n word" was ubiquitous. The *Detroit Daily Free Press* quoted with approval in 1856 the statement of the *New York Herald:* "Niggers—nothing but niggers—the beginning or the end, it is niggers."[35] According to the *Free Press*, it was questionable whether blacks were capable of a degree of civilization that would ever bring them above brutes.[36]

U.S. Senator Henry Wilson of Massachusetts, the *New York Herald* wrote in 1855, wanted to repeal the Fugitive Slave Act, to abolish slavery in the District of Columbia, to organize the North against the admission of Kansas as a slave state, and to abolish all laws making distinctions between individuals on account of race. That, said the paper, made Wilson more dangerous than Theodore Parker or William Lloyd Garrison. Those men just talked absurdity, but here was a program for the federal government to do something specific. To talk of free blacks living together with whites was idle because "freedom to the black man is a myth and a mockery." The real condition of the freeman in New York City was worse than that of the slave in Georgia.[37] Industrial progress required freedom, but freedom for whites. The germs of progress were with the Anglo-Saxons and not other races and cultures. The Asiatic and the African were inferior, it continued, and created inferior civilizations.[38]

Senator G. W. Jones of Iowa brought the inferiority argument to the Senate floor during debates on Kansas admission bills in April 1856. In his "limited" reading, he said, he had failed to find any fact to sustain the belief that blacks were equal to whites in powers of mind. The Negro race, he went on, was cursed by the Almighty and destined "to be the servants of servants forever." Africans, the Iowan claimed, had no poets, no history. "The black tribes have given nothing useful nor brilliant from the mental mind—and to this day they are the same stupid idolaters that they were found to be when first visited by the Christian missionary; worshipping leaks, onions, snakes, and filthy insects." It was against the law of Iowa for a free Negro to enter that state, and Jones saw nothing wrong with its being against the law of a proposed state of Kansas. The idea of social equality of blacks and whites was one he found "shocking—loathsome."[39]

During the same debate, Senator G. E. Pugh of Ohio argued that slavery needed to expand to keep blacks spread out lest there be, instead of prosperous communities, polities such as Haiti or Jamaica, "quenched by the blackness of darkness forever." He asked what an integrated society would really be like. "Would you suffer some brawny knave, half brute and half savage, to sit in this Hall as a Senator? No sir, you would not!" The Caucasians of the North, he said, "would never associate on terms of such equality with the base and incapable negro." Pugh claimed he was neither an enemy of the Negro race nor a friend of slavery, and he wished them liberty at a time and under such circumstances as would not debase the white man or overthrow the safeguards of American liberty. That time, he said, was not 1856 and the circumstances were not the admission of Kansas.[40]

Sometimes Southerners tried to veil the racism in their arguments. Senator Robert Hunter of Virginia argued, for example, during the Kansas-Nebraska debates of 1854 that the bill did not directly concern the expansion of slavery but was only an example of American free enterprise and laissez-faire government policy.[41] Preston Brooks of South Carolina thought it was as impossible for a Northerner to judge about slavery as for a blind man about color. Prejudices had "been fostered through life by association, misrepresentation, and remoteness."[42]

But others were more blunt. G. S. Brown of Mississippi said he had no fellowship "with that sickly sentimentality that speaks of slavery as a great moral evil." Who, he asked, favored real equality for African Americans? "Would any man take his boot-black, would any lady take her chambermaid into companionship?"[43] T. L. Clingman of North Carolina argued that scientific knowledge had shown the inferiority of black people, and it was common sense anyway: "Why, Mr. Chairman, if all the literary men on the earth were to argue that the rays of the sun were the cause of darkness and cold, they could never convince people who walk in this glorious sunshine that their theory was correct."[44]

Most direct and philosophical was Alexander Stephens of Georgia. "Graduation," Stephens said, "is stamped upon everything animate, as well as inanimate. . . . A scale, from the lowest degree of inferiority to the highest degree of superiority, runs through all animal life. We see it in the insect tribes—we see it in the fishes of the sea, the fowls of the air, in the beasts of the earth and we see it in the races of men." Even the stars differed in magnitude. "Do what you will, a negro is a negro, and he will remain a negro still."[45]

The *Washington Daily Union* was a quasi-official administration paper, but it was a Southern paper withal. The model of the abolitionists, wrote its editorial staff in the fall of 1855, was the man who would feel stimulated by drink at a tavern and then put the lash to his horse, thinking he must feel stimulated too. Abolitionists "have a keen perception and high appreciation of 'liberty' themselves, and, mistaking the negro for a white man, think, of course, that he is animated by the same sentiments, while all this time he is indifferent—indeed is as utterly incapable of this feeling as the wearied and worn-down horses were of the driver's when stimulated by brandy." Liberty was as impossible to the Negro as straight hair or rosy cheeks. "The negro *is* a negro, and is not a white man. The external attributes of black skin and woolly hair, and beardless face, &c., which every one sees plain enough, vary no more from those of the white man than do all those things not seen." African Americans, the paper thought, were not just inferior to whites, but vastly so, "the furthest removed from us of all the races." Not an atom of a black man's body or an instinct of his mind was in common with a white man's. Blacks were perpetual children, whom the South dominated easily.[46]

Beyond the disagreements about the nature of the black and white races and about the possible results of emancipation, newspapers in the South thought that the Kansas struggle was being waged to humiliate their section. "I contribute to your support gentlemen," went a letter from an Alabaman published in the *New York Daily Times* in March 1854, "while you are threatening my throat. You took me into the family of the Union—a sort of bastard perhaps—but I'm in, for all that, and I don't exactly like the way of being starved out on very short allowance!"[47]

No one in the North was more idealistic or more consistent in antislavery sentiment than the *Boston Liberator*. Charles Stearns, residing in Lawrence, wrote to that paper that he could not accept the 1855 Big Springs platform of the free-state faction in Kansas because of its many compromises on the issue of the status of free blacks in the future state. At least Southerners were honest. The peace of the free-state faction, Stearns thought, was the peace of "moral death." Did he come to Kansas, he asked, "to turn tyrant, and to close my door against the poor manacled slave, who begs me, for Heaven's sake, to shelter him for a single night?"[48]

Illustrative of the working of all these tensions in the specific Kansas issue was the fate of and national reaction to a series of proposals for solving the Kansas imbroglio that made their way through Congress in 1856. The *Charleston Mercury* in February 1856 held forth little hope that rational and law-limited procedure would work any longer in the national capital. After all, at the beginning of the session there had been weeks of wrangling just trying to select a speaker of the House. "The government vibrates between revolution and anarchy. Apathetic despair seems to have seized the members—they meet and adjourn without even balloting, as though such forms were obsolete." The fate of the Republic, the paper said, depended upon public opinion, but what now, it asked, when "vile passions canker at its heart"?[49]

No one doubted which issue would dominate the first session of the Thirty-fourth Congress: It would be Kansas. The *St. Louis Daily Missouri Democrat* spoke that February, under the headline "The Calumet of Peace for Kansas," of a "stormy conflict of minds." The parties in Kansas were temporarily quiet, but watchful. "With an avidity scarcely paralleled in regard to the great events of the Crimean war, every item of intelligences, every floating rumor, every reported affray in the far off territory is sought after by the news-gatherers, and made to flash along the telegraphic wires from Independence to Boston." Kansas had begun to affect the national credit and was a "watchword" in the South, "embodying their power, their wealth, their social position, their very existence as dominant race." Propaganda was everywhere. In Congress "a heavy swell is caused by every ripple in Kansas."[50] The history of Kansas was told and retold.

The slavery issue in Kansas and in Congress now, wrote the *New Orleans Daily Picayune*, was a "grave" matter, "full of danger and ominous of evil."[51] A writer in Richmond quoted Thomas Carlyle that republican institutions were "anarchy, plus a street constable" and predicted that if Kansas were admitted in 1856, that statement would prove true, as Kansas had only an organized anarchy. Why, the writer asked, not admit the Indians too as a state? Why not the Mormon polygamists? Why not a colony of free Negroes under the lead of abolitionists? These could organize as good a state government as had the Topeka rebels.[52]

Both sections had conspiracy theories. An editorial in the *Mobile Daily Tribune* in the fall of 1855 cited the various public meetings in the North, its organized societies, "the intolerant arrogance of their ecclesiastical bodies . . . the sleepless espionage they exercise over the most private domestic concerns, through the agency of hired emissaries, who sit at our tables, share our firesides, and mingle in our daily intercourse, unsuspected." There was a "secret but systematic" effort to entice slaves away from their masters and an "open assault" in Congress on slavery.[53] There was equivalent paranoia in the North, where conspiratorial imagery was a staple of political rhetoric. "They lay their mesmeric hands upon the moral pulse of the nation," said George Julian of the supposed Southern conspirators, "and it ceases to beat. Nothing that is earthly can stand before the dread authority of these men." At first serving as mere defensive rhetoric, conspiracy theory hardened into conviction, which required the entire reassessment of American history in the interest of sectional power. It was a Circe's spell in whose thrall the country could not advance.[54]

The Kansas debate of 1856 opened with President Franklin Pierce's message to Congress late in January. He expressed his dismay at the disturbances in Kansas. They were part, he thought, of a long and pernicious "agitation on the subject of the condition of the colored persons held to service in some of the States, which has so long disturbed the repose of our country, and excited individuals, otherwise patriotic and law-abiding, to toil with misdirected zeal in the attempt to propagate their social theories, by the perversions and abuse of the powers of Congress." The "path of duty" was plain: to enforce the laws of the territories and the United States in Kansas and everywhere else. "Our system affords no justification of revolutionary acts, providing as it did for reform in a constitutional mode."[55]

The *New York Daily Times* called the message "inane." It ignored public opinion and assumed "that the only streams of information are monopolized by Government, and that it may safely dilute or drug the article at pleasure." The world was too well posted for that. The *Times* had correspondents in Kansas. To say at this date that Kansas should submit to the bogus legislature there was to presuppose public ignorance.[56] Words had become mere tools, commented a paper in Albany, New York. "Which side President Pierce espouses in the war of dictionaries we know not."[57] Pierce, the *Chicago Daily Tribune* wrote, "leaps into the pro-slavery current as if it were his native element," hoping to swim in it into office again. "He sees nothing, hears nothing, considers nothing, evidently which does not look to this end, as he madly puts aside the land marks of the Fathers, and struggles to build up a class interest and a class power."[58]

Two of the issues that arose during that summer's debate, the contested election for congressional delegate between Whitfield and Reeder and the attempted amendment of the army appropriations bill, have been addressed. Much of the remaining time was taken up with proposals for settling the Kansas issue through intervention by Congress to reorganize the territory and thus to soften the impact of its initial badly flawed electoral and legislative history. Such proposals flew in the face of the popular sovereignty and nonintervention ideals of the Kansas-Nebraska Act, but at this juncture even the author of that act, Senator Stephen Douglas, sponsored a bill that was an admission that the squatter sovereignty machine had not worked.

Senator Henry Wilson of Massachusetts started the fireworks in Washington early with an emotional speech on February 18. He claimed that the resistors in Kansas were not trying to cause trouble but were steadfast in a cause. "The sons of the free States—of Puritan New England, of the great central states, and of the Northwest—men who call no man master, and who wish to make no man a slave, were invited to plant upon the soil of Kansas those institutions that have blessed, beautified, and adorned the homes of their childhood." They stood in stark contrast to the sons of the South, who hailed from regions "once teeming with the rich fruits of fields, now blasted, blighted, and withered, by the sweat of untutored and unrewarded toil."[59]

On March 5 appeared the report of the House Committee on Elections on the case of the two delegates from Kansas. On March 12, Douglas presented the report of the Senate Committee on Territories, which he chaired, on the

Kansas issue. The *New York Daily Tribune* claimed that it was too "immensely extended" to print, and besides, it asked, what would be the point? "The fact that this gentleman finds it necessary at this present stage of the Kansas question to write a book explanatory of the case, shows of itself plainly enough in what complications, in what difficulties, what embarrassments the pernicious Kansas Nebraska Act has involved the question of slavery in the Territories." Douglas only wanted to extricate himself and his party "from the load under which they stagger" amid a "wilderness of words."[60] On March 17, Douglas introduced his bill to organize a government for Kansas under congressional supervision. On March 19 came the authorization of the Howard Commission, whose investigations were interrupted by the militia raid on Lawrence. On April 7 came James Lane's petition for admission under the Topeka Constitution and Douglas's scornful rejection of it. However, the idea of admitting Kansas under the Topeka Constitution directly was a live proposal, which had majority support in the House of Representatives.[61] A bill to do that, sponsored by G. A. Grow of Pennsylvania, passed the House early in July, only to be rejected by the Senate. The Douglas bill, on the other hand, succeeded in the Senate but failed in the House.[62]

Douglas was a powerful, savvy, and eloquent proponent for some type of compromise. He enjoyed support in both sections. And his voluminous report must have attracted some interest, as nearly 100,000 copies of it were printed. He blamed the emigrant aid societies of the North for distorting the intent of the Kansas-Nebraska Act. Yes, people were free to go where they wanted, "but it is a very different thing where a State creates a vast moneyed corporation for the purpose of controlling the domestic institutions of a distinct political community." It was never right to force a blessing, however great it was in one's own eyes, onto one's neighbor, Douglas noted.

Senator Douglas proceeded, as had so many before him, to set out what he said was an accurate history of Kansas Territory since 1854. His account was in contradistinction to what he called the "gross misrepresentations" and "inflammatory appeals" that had passed for history in so many publications. He listed things people believed about Kansas and its legislature that were demonstrably untrue, including the widely held idea that it was illegal to discuss slavery in the territory. The territorial law did say it was a penal offense to deny the right of a person to hold slaves there or to advise the slaves to rebel, but the scope and import of that law were much exaggerated. Douglas and many of his colleagues disapproved of some of the laws of Kansas, but that was true of the laws of any territory. "The remedy for such evils is to be found in public opinion, to which, sooner or later, in a government like ours, all laws must conform."[63]

An equally straightforward minority report for the Senate Committee on Territories reflected the views on Kansas of the new Republican Party. The nation, Senator Jacob Collamer of Vermont wrote in that report, was caught up in "temporary palliatives," while the real cause of the troubles lay uncorrected. That cause—the thing that made Kansas different from all territories before it—was slavery. Congress had the power to dictate on this during the territorial stage, yet a competition had been invited in Kansas. "Was it to be expected that this great proclamation for the political tournament would be listened to with indifference and apathy? Was it prepared and presented in that spirit? Did it relate to a subject on which the people were cool or indifferent?" The compromises of 1820 and 1850 went out the window, and public opinion, fueled by the penny press, came to the fore. "This subject, then, which Congress has been unable to settle in such a way as the slave states will sustain, is now turned over to those who have or shall become inhabitants of Kansas to arrange; and all men are invited to participate in the experiment, regardless of their character, political or religious views, or place of nativity." Violence, said Collamer, was the inevitable result of a mistaken law, and so was propaganda. It was wrong to characterize the Topeka government as rebellious or unlawful, he wrote. "Are they to be dragooned into submission? Is that an experiment pleasant to execute on our own free people?" It would be better to repeal the Kansas-Nebraska Act instead.[64]

The Republicans warmed up with the speech of Senator William Seward of New York on April 9, immediately following the Lawrence raid and the Pottawatomie massacre. "Mr. President," he opened, "to obtain empire is easy and common; to govern it well is difficult and rare indeed." President Pierce seemed to think the free-staters in Kansas were men of narrow views and sectional purposes, as well as impractical visionaries. He had gone so far as to call them "mad men." Seward denied it. Abolitionism was no visionary crusade, he said, but rather "a slow, but irresistible uprising of principles of natural justice and humanity." It was right that Kansas had become a public issue, debated in every morning paper and on every village street corner. "It belongs to other than statesmen, charged with the care of present interests, to conduct the social reformation of mankind in its broadest bearings." The Kansas issue was nothing less than that. It was time to go back to the Declaration of Independence and its statement of the equality of all men.[65]

Southern newspapers were disturbed by this tone and by the "definite shape" the Kansas controversy had assumed that spring in Congress, just as it seemed that the military was getting some control in the field outside Lawrence. It appeared that there was a fusion of antislavery forces in the wake of the decline of the old Whig Party. These fusionists had united on the Kansas issue, and their proposal to admit Kansas at once as a free state under the Topeka Constitution became a test of political loyalty and moral soundness. Seward's speech had announced the new campaign, lending his "mighty influence" to the cause, framing the exclusive choices, and marshaling the simple battle between good and evil with all his eloquence. His speech, wrote the *New Orleans Daily Picayune*, was an "authoritative enunciation" that would lead to a line of conduct. The mantra was that there could be no cure for the disorders in Kansas except a summary abrogation of the territorial authorities and all their acts and the immediate acceptance of a constitution supposedly approved by the sovereign people of Kansas, although at a party election unjustified by any regular law. It was an "ingenious" plan, the newspaper said, in that it did not directly raise the issue of the existence or extension of slavery, but simply said that the will of the people in Kansas Territory was already known and should be respected.

Moderate newspapers saw that the wave of language, and of the organization of mass thought, was against them. A Charleston editor wrote that the science of statesmanship was not well understood. "Like the shifting sands of the desert waste, it is moved, and assumes new phrases and forms, with the breath of every wind." One could study conventions, political statements, debates, party tactics, and newspapers but come only to the conclusion that there was something in the form of the words themselves that belied their supposed substance. "Its vocabulary, its language, is the *linqua non scripta*, the unwritten verbosity of jingling echoes and clap-trap rejoinders, its *argumentum ad hominem*, the soiled and well-thumbed scrap books of party hacks." Too often the leaders were merely the masters of quick phrases.[66] Kansas was a powerful motivator for the masses.[67] When it came to armed conflict, perhaps the North would flinch and perhaps not, but now was the time to know.

The highlight of the session was the enormous address of Senator Charles Sumner on May 19–20, which was widely distributed in pamphlet form under the title "The Crime against Kansas." It was this speech that led to Sumner's beating by Preston Brooks of South Carolina. The speech is justifiably famous, although it is often unjustifiably isolated and quoted as typical. It was not typical but somewhat on the radical wing at the time. It contained brutal language. In fact, its very extremism was what made it popular, given the sensationalist tendencies of the newspaper press, which had prepared its otherwise bored readers to expect just this sort of extravaganza even in the halls of Congress.

Rare-book dealers of the twenty-first century usually demand high prices for pamphlets of the middle 1850s concerning the Kansas issue. Five hundred dollars is not an uncommon asking price. However, the most famous of them all, Sumner's "Crime," sells for around $50. The reason, according to Stephen Finer Rare Books of Greenfield, Massachusetts, is that within a few weeks of the delivery of Sumner's speech, millions of copies were sold. There were at least three editions with different imprints in addition to the standard Buell & Blanchard Washington imprint typical of these pieces. One large edition went out from the offices of the *New York Daily Tribune*, another from Boston, a third from Concord, Massachusetts.[68] The speech was a public phenomenon.

Sumner's address, filled with classical allusion, was obviously intended for the history books, but it also struck the nerve of the times. Kansas, Sumner said, was geographically at the center of the nation and was also at the heart of its identity, "worthy to be a central pivot of American institutions." The slave power was trying to control public opinion through a "prostituted" press. The enemy was before the people, "heartless, grasping and tyrannical." In charging that Northerners were fanatics, Sumner said, the South "cast contumely upon the noble army of martyrs, from the earliest day down to this hour, upon the great tribunes of human rights, by whom life, liberty, and happiness on earth have been secured."[69]

Sumner gave his own history of Kansas, where, he claimed, "private griefs mingle their poignancy with public wrongs." He described the bitter plains winter during which the families of Lawrence were constrained to sleep under arms "with sentinels treading their constant watch against surprise." Was this age not as cruel as any? "Murder has stalked—assassination has skulked in the tall grass of the prairie, and the vindictiveness of man has assumed unwonted forms."

Metaphorical images and visualizations were Sumner's specialty. He went on, "Thus was the crime consummated. Slavery now stands erect, clanking its chains on the Territory of Kansas, surrounded by the code of death." It was a ship with a pirate crew, and "even now the black flag of the land pirates from Missouri waves at the mast head; in their laws you hear the pirate yell, and see the flash of the pirate knife." By contrast there were the real, honest, antislave "people" of Kansas, "bone of your bone, and flesh of your flesh, with the education of freemen and the rights of American citizens" standing at the door. "Will you send them away or bid them enter?" Public opinion was building in the right way. And in the cause of freedom in Kansas was "angelic power." Unseen by men, "the great spirits of History combat by the side of the people of Kansas, breathing a divine courage." Could hearers not see the ghostly figure of George Washington marching beside Lane's militia?

The speech was too much for some observers. The *Philadelphia Daily Enquirer* commented that some of this was ludicrous. To compare the people of Lawrence to Roman heroes was a laugh. "It is fortunate for the world that, unlike the siege of Troy, that of Lawrence will have more than a score of Homers to hand down the renown of its heroes and heroines."[70] A writer in New Orleans said that Sumner's speech was a "sanctimonious laudation" of himself and his friends "in this crusade of hatred, as God's chosen instruments, to whom the earth is given, as saints, with a commission to go forth in the name of Heaven, to kill, take, and occupy."[71] The editor there hoped that this was the "madness of the hour, for which there must be a healing reaction in public sentiment, or else the whole history of our Government is an error and a delusion."[72]

The speech was much criticized by Sumner's colleagues. Lewis Cass said that it was the most "un-American and unpatriotic" that he had ever heard in the Senate. Douglas attacked it for its lurid classical allusions, even though couched in the original Latin, in the presence of ladies, and for the "depth of malignity" in every sentence.[73] However, it played well in the press and in the world of emotional pamphlets. A man who had heard Sumner personally wrote to the *Daily Cleveland Herald* that it was "the speech, so far, of the session."[74] And its notoriety was helped by the fact that Sumner himself became a physical martyr over it. A New Orleans paper claimed that Sumner deserved a beating and that his speech was "overbearing, dogmatical, self-righteous, and intolerant."[75]

The *London Times* saw trends clearly from a distance. The slavery question, it observed, was the "great difficulty" of the United States, and with the Kansas debates a chronic disease had festered into a terrible sore. The United States was growing in wealth, but not in peace and harmony. Citizens could not agree to differ on slavery. "People are too serious about it and too much in earnest to be able to treat it as a neutral question. It excites their enthusiasm, and you cannot put down genuine natural enthusiasm." Perhaps

Kansas was "a useful vent, and a convenient blister to draw off the noxious passions now diffused over the whole of American society to a distant and local scene of action."[76]

Southerners did respond to the likes of Seward and Sumner in Congress with their own brand of oratory about Kansas. People said there had been troubles since the Kansas-Nebraska Act, said Senator Alexander Stephens of Georgia. What troubles? The country was prosperous and peaceful. The troubles grew out of "nothing but that exuberance of liberty and multitude of blessings, which seem to be driving us on to licentiousness." A "class of restless malcontents" had invented the Kansas issue. How far would this minority be allowed to go, he asked, "until checked by a sound reactive public sentiment?" How many deaths had there really been in Kansas? How many of them were really politically motivated? Was it any worse there than in any new territory? And what about freedom? Was it not an abused and misunderstood term? Constitutional liberty was the desirable thing. "None of your Socialism liberty. None of your Fourierism liberty. . . . [We want a] 'law and order' abiding liberty."[77]

One speech followed another. One night in July there was a continuous session of twenty hours. The speeches were about Kansas, but they were also about many other things folded into the Kansas issue. Kansas, the *New York Herald* reported in July, had been "the standing dish" of Congress since the December prior. The Kansas speeches would go on until the middle of August. The *Herald* listed the proposals put forward in the Senate alone during that period: Seward's for admitting Kansas directly under the free-state Topeka Constitution; Douglas's for supervised elections when the Kansas Territory population reached 93,000; John Clayton's for abolishing all existing laws and tests in Kansas and appointing commissioners to take a new census and appoint a new legislature; Robert Toombs's for admission under federal supervision, but immediately and without regard to population; H. S. Geyer's for the election of a new territorial legislature under supervision; John Crittenden's for sending Gen. Winfield Scott to Kansas to reduce the belligerents to good behavior and maintain law and order. The House had fewer schemes, but it was then poring over the Howard Commission report "full of vouchers, of lawless outrages, illegal legislators, and unconstitutional pains and penalties." But no matter how many proposals came from what the newspaper called "the tinkers of Washington," the problem was the political makeup of the Congress. "All experiments . . . for the relief of the

Territory . . . will most likely fall between the two wings of the Capitol, the House being too decidedly no-slavery and the Senate too pro-slavery for any half-way compromise."[78]

The *Herald* liked the idea of sending troops to Kansas best. There needed to be order, its writers thought, in consideration of a decent respect for the opinions of mankind. But it doubted that the "hacks," busy as they were with "their patchwork and plastering schemes for the purpose of an armistice on this Kansas difficulty," were likely to succeed. The "peddling politicians" could not understand the momentum of the public. The paper accused James Buchanan, the Democratic candidate for president, of sitting at his home, Wheatland, and smoking a cigar, thinking the trouble would be over in six weeks. Wrong, said the *Herald*. It might continue for 60 or even 600 years.[79]

Some analysts hoped for scholarship and reason. Samuel Bowles at the *Springfield Daily Republican* felt that the Howard report should get wide distribution. "Inflammatory appeal, specious argument, conventions, flags, banners, gunpowder, and hurrahs," he wrote, "are all of secondary consideration." What mattered were the plain and attested facts. The danger was that these would be repressed, and thus "elevate the claptrap which dazzles the senses into supreme agency." Maybe the Kansas clubs, which had raised money for aid, should use some of it to distribute a summary of the Howard report on the Kansas election frauds. Such a thing could be printed as a pamphlet for $2.50 per 100 or $20 per 1,000 copies. "The contest is mainly that of Intelligence against Ignorance. See that Ignorance is made intelligent, and the battle is won."[80]

But the contest was driven more by framing than by intelligence. In a speech in the House late in July, James Stewart of Maryland created a contrast between the Topeka government and the way things should be that was a study in exaggerated contrast and clever polarities. Why should a handful of rebels in Kansas alarm the whole country? Good men were amazed by the boldness of the demonstration. "All our recognized authorities are utterly disregarded. Upon the President down to the most obscure official, one unbroken torrent of insane abuse is poured." The outrage was the Topeka government, not the border ruffians. "For ought that appears, they are men in buckram—in Kansas to-day, gone to-morrow; and if you inaugurate their government, will not you have to issue a search warrant to find them?" Did they not sit on stumps in the open air at their so-called constitutional convention? "May heaven forever defend us from such miserable trumpery and hoy-de-doy buffoonery!"[81]

Once a robber was brought before Alexander the Great, Stewart related. The man claimed he was no different from Alexander and was only called a thief because he robbed on a smaller scale. Stewart thought the Topeka faction was like that. They said they were high-souled patriots in order to "bewilder by their audacity," but they were really only small-fry disturbers of the peace. Behind them was a "motley assortment of the most discordant elements, bearing aloft on the standard the black flag of anarchy and disunion, fanaticism, agrarianism, higher-lawism, and other abominable monstrosities that no sensible man can define." Stewart added that it was "wisdom and common sense" to know that both blacks and women were created to do the drudgery of white men.[82]

As the first session of the Thirty-fourth Congress wound down in August, the *Charleston Mercury* despaired of any congressional solution. The slavery issue, its columnist wrote, had "deranged the whole harmony of the Government." A law just to the South would disappoint the North and make it more aggressive, while a law propitiating that section would swell its power and insolence further. There was no possibility of reconciliation, as "the same poison which infected Congressional legislation, would infect also popular sovereignty." Intervention or nonintervention, abolition, in some shape, would fasten itself on the politics of the country through the Kansas debate "to the destruction of its peace, and the peril of the South." The Kansas-Nebraska idea of untrammeled popular sovereignty had not worked, the columnist said, and the return of congressional intervention was not going to work, and the abolition sentiment had a life longer than either. There would have to be an uncompromising struggle by the South for life. "All other methods failing, this is left."[83]

Indeed, what was framed, what was intimated by all the language, was battle—a war, in which to yield was to lose in ignominy to an enemy who was the quintessence of evil. "Shame on us," wrote a Georgia editor, "for a mean, stingy, craven hearted people, if we desert our banners at this stage of the conflict, and leave our vanguard in Kansas to the tender mercies of a pitiless foe."[84] A lifeless abstraction, wrote a Washington reporter, had in Kansas been magnified into a national feud.[85] All the while, the conflict in Kansas seemed like a drama, a play, but one with deadly consequence. Wrote a Missouri newspaperman: "Kansas has been the scene of a great act in our political drama, the battle-field of parties, the arena in which hostile ideas and institutions have encountered in prolonged and deadly strife. Upon its organization it was placed under a regime of a novel and fantastic principle, the essence of which was identical with that of trial by combat." Congress, like the ancient kings, had summoned hostile clans to combat, prepared the list, and acted as judge. Whichever triumphed would be right and would be allowed to write the history of the struggle. "Everything was left to force, to accident and chance. Wisdom, policy and justice were banished from the tribunal." It was "insane," but real.[86]

There was the usual extreme rhetoric leading up to the November 1856 presidential election, especially among the Democrats, as to what would happen if the Republican, John Fremont, were elected. But few expected a real revolutionary change in the administration of the staid Democrat James Buchanan. A president, any president, could only do so much, even the *New York Daily Tribune* admitted. What was to become of Kansas was "gloriously uncertain," and it was best not to "go too far nor too fast in any direction upon this grave and complicated question."[87]

Abstractions were the warriors. "The fire, once opened," wrote a Washington newspaper, "in too many instances judgment, common sense, facts, appeals, and arguments have been lost sight of in the din and confusion occasioned by this uncalled-for and scandalous waste of saltpeter; and in the heat and strife of the battle the guns have been as often pointed at real friends as imaginary foes. . . . They deal the fiercest blows against traitors they cannot see or feel, and push and thrust at airy phantoms."[88] Possibly before the Lecompton Constitution was ever submitted to Congress, the South and slavery had lost Kansas. But that did not diminish the smoke and noise.

Perhaps there would be civil war. The *Hartford Daily Courant* thought so early in 1858. Maybe war would be in the interest of the North as well as of the South. Perhaps it would relieve the tension and make the conflict a real one with a definite end one way or another. That, the paper's writers believed, would be the "the proud day of Kansas." For the government had gone wrong. "No Government in God's world can withstand the destructive power of such corruption and villainy as ours has been guilty of in the past few years. And no people in the world can endorse such corruption and submit to such villainy, as the persistent policy of a Government, without becoming so debased, so mean, so spiritless, as to deserve to be swept out of existence."[89]

There was a serpent at the heart of the nation. It involved more than the institution of slavery, and it stung and benumbed its host with increasing regularity.

CHAPTER 7
THE GRAVEYARD OF GOVERNORS

On Monday May 24, 1857, Kansas Territory welcomed Robert J. Walker, then fifty-six years old. Walker was the fourth regular governor of Kansas Territory (not to mention two acting governors and one unofficial Topeka-faction governor) in three years. He was the most experienced and distinguished man ever sent there. He had been secretary of the Treasury in the Polk administration, had been a principle in several grandiose railroad schemes, and had been considered for the post of ambassador to China before being dispatched to Kansas, going as a personal favor to President Buchanan. His predecessor in the office had heralded Walker as "not only the greatest man alive, but the greatest man who could live."[1]

He arrived at the Leavenworth dock aboard the Missouri River steamer *New Lucy*. Kansans sighted the boat at a distance "walking the current of the turbid Missouri as a thing of life, with banners flying and crowded with passengers." Decorated with gay colors and moving at speed, "she presented a lovely spectacle" to the thousands of spectators gathered to meet the dignitary. There was music from a brass band, and a man remarked that things had changed since the previous year, when ruffians had stopped these steamers to take off Emigrant Aid Company passengers and their guns.

James Lane of the free-state faction was there to meet Governor Walker. Lane gave an impromptu address, minimizing the famed Kansas troubles. His faction, he said, merely wanted to be able to travel its own road. It was a contest in Kansas, a footrace, and it could be run without violence.

The governor, surrounded by the "anxious and curious," went by carriage to a champagne reception at the Planter's House, the finest hotel in the largest city in Kansas.[2] Walker made the usual casual promises to the crowds about how he intended to enforce the laws and be neutral as to party and faction. "Everybody is more or less excited," wrote the *Chicago Daily Tribune* correspondent, "especially the flunkeys and toadies who palaver and blarney about Walker, as though he were Jehovah. I am sick of such gammon." There was a dinner for seventy and a dress ball. Shortly, Walker attended a meeting at the Unitarian church in Lawrence, and there he received the history of Kansas from the free-state perspective.[3] He then repaired to his office at Lecompton. Soon he delivered his inaugural address, which created a furor in the national press.

The new man, a reporter wrote, was "small in stature, mind and soul, incapable, from his very organization, of entertaining a liberal and generous sentiment, and hostile, from association and subserviency, to the glorious principles upon which our government was organized."[4] He was trying to impress on Kansans "that they have in him been favored with the presence of a statesmen of gigantic caliber."[5]

Kansas governors faced a negative tide from the outset, cynical as the nation was about the abilities of contemporary political leadership generally and of appointed bureaucrats in particular. Also, there had developed a considerable awareness of the complexity and intensity of the Kansas issue and a deep doubt as to whether the glib bromides, the speaking out of both sides of the mouth to paper over the abyss between the factions, could accomplish anything but provoke a horselaugh. What was a territorial governor anyway, asked the *Richmond South*? "Is he a sort of a Satrap, with absolute power over his province, except insofar as he may be responsible to some supreme despot?"[6] Walker had talent, but "he has never yet been suspected of the least particle of personal honesty. A bankrupt with a splendid income, a millionaire at the expense of widows and orphans, a speculator in fictitious stocks, and a jobber upon other people's money."[7] He had been a "political and pecuniary adventurer," and it was as certain that he would obey his own "venal ambition" as that "a vulture is governed by the instinct for carrion."[8]

The occasion of the arrival of this governor was an opportunity for the press to comment upon the likely fate of all Kansas territorial governors. It appeared, wrote a reporter in Georgia, that Kansas was a place for politicians to make "noodles" of themselves in a short time.[9] Andrew Reeder was "notorious," wrote the *Washington Union*.[10] He had had to escape Kansas in disguise, and he then showed up as a Free State delegate to Congress and as a speaker for hire to comment on the failures of his successors.[11] Wilson Shannon was known for his "imbecility and utter unfitness for the position."[12] He had fled from Kansas hidden in a government wagon.[13] "Has he no sense," Sara Robinson had written, "or has his brain become so muddled in the bad whiskey in which he floats, as to dull all his perception of justice and right?"[14] John Geary was called "an immeasurable ass, and an abolitionist to boot."[15] He came in "with a flourish of trumpets" and went out to "derisive sneers."[16]

The *New York Daily Tribune* speculated about "What Drives Kansas Governors Mad?" It might seem, the reporter thought, "as if there were something in the air or water of Kansas, or, perhaps among its vegetable production, some 'insane root,' which seriously disagrees with the brains if not the stomachs of her Territorial Governors, and drives them to the extremity of making a public exhibition of their folly, and that not merely in the sight of the people of Kansas, but in the eyes of the whole country." Since the passage of the Kansas-Nebraska Act and the arrival of Reeder in 1854, each governor in turn had become a victim of "delusions." Walker was the latest, and as the summer of 1857 arrived, the observers at the *Tribune* thought that he too began to show "evidence of being affected with that epidemic insanity which had proved fatal to all his predecessors. He does not foam at the mouth . . . but still he gives unequivocal symptoms of the Kansas disorder."[17] There were only two opinions of Walker by August 1857 according to a correspondent in St. Louis: First, that he was a drunk, and second, that he was crazy.[18]

Kansas, a Missouri reporter concluded, was "a political cemetery"—the "graveyard of governors"—where it was dangerous for political celebrities to travel.[19] "They go out," a reporter in Pittsburgh wrote, "as the captains with their hundreds did to seize the prophet, and one after another they are consumed by the fire. They go to conquer a peace, they return vanquished by fraud and rascality." The best they could hope for was fame as "magnificent blunderers."[20] An observer in Providence, Rhode Island, wrote at the end of 1857: "Kansas is certainly enchanted ground. Nobody but rabid people can live there. Border Ruffians of the hot-blooded species, and red-hot abolitionists, thrive like stalled oxen. But men deemed fit to be Governors—having something of the moderation supposed to be essential to official life, a fair modicum of common sense, and a tolerable acquaintance with administrative duties—die certainly and suddenly."[21]

And why was there such an "epidemic for suicide" among governors of Kansas? The *Washington National Era* thought that it was because they were required to enter a system founded in fraud and force, in a place where the inanities of the legislature had alienated most of the population. Walker, or anyone else, would fail in such a situation. "It is an attempt to reconcile right and wrong. It is a miserable endeavor to cross-marry eternal right to miserable expediency. It was never done—it cannot be done." The governors were "pets" of a corrupt administration, and could never escape that connection.[22]

The *Washington Union* had another idea. There was a vast gulf between theory and practice and between what the president in Washington might wish to happen in Kansas and what a governor in the field was able to accomplish. Walker had fine theories about fairness and sovereignty. "But fine theories, eloquently developed, poorly suit the rough-and-tumble exigencies of the Kansas imbroglio. They would furnish a beautiful chapter in the Utopia of New Atlantis, but they are as little adapted to the case of Kansas as the constitution ex-cogitated in his study by Locke suited the homely requirements of the incipient Carolinas." Walker's theories were impractical, and therefore his attempt to apply them was impertinent. Everyone agreed about the sovereignty of the people. "But as a practical question, it is beset by a thousand embarrassments." Who were the people? Could they be found by a "pell-mell count of noses?" What was the role of Congress? Could sovereignty be delegated? To whom? When?[23]

The Kansas governor tried to mediate between factions in Kansas and between those factions and the sections and the authorities in Washington. Sometimes, it seemed like a game of "Simon says": "Simon first told R. J. Walker to twirl his thumbs," said a journalist in Georgia. "Walker first obeyed and then refused, and forthwith becomes a 'Judas,' and a 'traitor.'"[24] It was hard to please anyone for long under such circumstances. "It is perfectly astonishing," wrote a Connecticut columnist, "how this Kansas iniquity eats up the moral sense and integrity of men, hitherto deemed honest. They close their eyes and shut their ears."[25]

The list of men whose ruin might be assigned to Kansas Territory is lengthy, given its short history. It can be argued that Kansas Territory ruined the reputations of two presidents—Franklin Pierce and James Buchanan—and ten governors or acting governors over a period of seven years. Of these, governors Hugh Walsh, Samuel Medary, and George Beebe fall outside the scope of this study, and James Denver barely figures. That leaves Andrew Reeder, Daniel Woodson (acting), Wilson Shannon, John Geary, Frederick Stanton (acting), and Robert Walker.[26] These men not only failed, but failed spectacularly, to tremendous national publicity. They were made scapegoats, creeping home in disgrace with a load of guilt that no person was designed to bear.

It has become an academic gospel that history must no longer be mere political history and that the older histories' easy organization according to men and administrations is certainly passé among the new social historians with their broader sensibilities. However, such a political progression can hardly be ignored, nor can the influence of personality and biography among people in elite positions of leadership be wholly ignored in favor of analyzing the inchoate direction of the masses. Some of the debate in America over Kansas was constitutional, some of it was religious, but some of it was personal. Whether the political leaders as portrayed in the press were the real men is easy to answer: They were not. But those portrayals were created from elements of the real people, and the real leaders had to lead or fail to lead according to the way they were created by or communicated through the media. The governors of Kansas, particularly, were natural and efficient foci of opinion about the crisis into which they found themselves thrust. When the national press wanted to talk about Kansas, it often started and often ended by talking about the personality and policy of the current governor of Kansas. To love the governors or to hate them was a way of refining, developing, and expressing opinion and emotion about issues more complex than they or their supporters and critics could well imagine.

Reeder was first. He was slow to arrive in Kansas, understandably dallying at his home in Easton, Pennsylvania. For this he was criticized later.[27] When he did arrive in October 1854, a platform went up in Lawrence, and Samuel Pomeroy, the agent of the Emigrant Aid Company, welcomed Governor Reeder. "Our treasures, as you see," Pomeroy said, "are little else than our *true hearts* and *free hands*. Yet with these . . . we welcome you to our frugal board and tented homes." The Northern emigrants, Pomeroy went on, had already dedicated the prairie, "but yesterday awakened from the slumber of ages" to industrial enterprise, Yankee style, and to literature, science, justice, and religion. Reeder responded that he would enjoy seeing the wilderness blossom and that he would stand together with them in making the territory "what God intended it to be." Pomeroy and Reeder went up the hill behind Lawrence and looked out over the open plains, where, a reporter from Kansas City wrote, "earth and heaven seem blent."[28]

Reeder gave a speech right away, attended by people from miles around. He was, he said, in a "position of high and solemn responsibility in a strange land." He was sensible of the difficulties that might beset him, and he relied on friendship, tolerance, and kindly feeling as well as indulgence from the population. Kansas was the "very heart of the Republic" and on the highway of trade, and it must be, first and foremost, an orderly and law-abiding place. "No man must be allowed to cast contempt upon the law—to unsettle the foundations of society, to mar our future destinies—to cause us to be shunned and avoided by good citizens—and to turn us upon the retrograde path toward barbarism, by substituting his own unbridled passions for the administration of justice, and by redressing his real and imaginary wrongs by the red and cowardly hand of assassination and ruffianism of the outlaw." Reeder would, he said, crush this or sacrifice himself in the effort. Sacrifice himself it was to be.[29]

The infamous early elections in Kansas for delegate and legislature put Reeder in a dilemma. If he complained about fraud and about an invasion of Missourians at the polls, which he did, he received criticism from the South. If he generally granted election certificates and failed to go behind the returns, as he also did (citing limits in his powers), he was criticized by the North. As early as February 1855, a California newspaper noted that Reeder was turning out to be something other than a pliant tool of the Pierce administration and the slaveocracy. It seemed Reeder was determined "that he would not disgrace himself, and render his name a hissing byword to posterity."[30]

Reeder did two things that provided easy justification for his dismissal. First, he refused to recognize the decision of the territorial legislature to move the capital of Kansas from the primitive town of Pawnee, near Fort Riley, to Shawnee Mission, much nearer the "fleshpots" of Missouri. Second, and relatedly, he was involved in land speculation. Some of the land was part of the town site of Pawnee, leading to what a modern attorney would call a conflict of interest. Also, some was purchased from Indians, which led Reeder into a conflict with Indian Commissioner George Manypenny over whether such transactions were appropriate.[31]

The press had a field day with the idea that public officials were trying to make speculative gains out of the emigration to Kansas and at the expense of "poor and simple half-breed Indians."[32] Who, asked a writer at the *Boston Liberator*, was the governor of Kansas? "Who made him? Why was he made? Does he stand for anything? . . . Or is he a man of straw, a thing tricked out in official garb, with but a broomstick for a backbone and chaff for brains?"[33] The altercation with Benjamin Stringfellow in the governor's office did not help Reeder's reputation for dignity.

Reeder claimed that the land speculation charge was a ruse, and that the real reason for his dismissal was that he questioned the honesty of the legislative election. When he went to Washington to defend himself, a reporter there wrote, "It is satisfactory to observe the contrast between his quiet and manly deportment and the violent expressions unjustly charged to him by his enemies."[34] However, Pierce characterized Reeder's explanation to him as "unsatisfactory and evasive."[35]

Reeder's defense was that he and a group of friends had made contingent contracts with Indians for the purchase of their lands, which were to become valid only when confirmed by the Indian Office in Washington. When they were not confirmed, that should have been the end of it. Manypenny, however, took the issue to the press, asserting that such transactions had "a demoralizing tendency upon the inhabitants of the Territory, both Indians and whites," and represented a "systematic plan to purchase Indian reserves at artificially low prices."[36] The sellers were mixed-blood Kanza women, whose power to dispose of these tracts was in question and whose white husbands did the dealing with Reeder and associates.[37]

In the end, Pierce dismissed Reeder.[38] A Missouri reporter commented, "It seems to have been the Governor's study to do nothing to gratify the people, and to do every thing that they deprecated and disapproved. He has been the most contrary and obstinate man that ever held office, and no lessons nor experiences seem to improve him."[39] The *New York Herald* called him a "foolish, ill-tempered man."[40] The *Daily Cleveland Herald* called him a "miserable *critter*," and said he was just smart enough to hang himself if he got sufficient rope.[41] The *Albany Atlas & Argus* compared Reeder to Satan. "Kansas was cursed at its birth with a pettifogger; and the Evil Genius of Chicanery had no sooner set his seal on her destiny, than the Father of Lies and all his legions of evil spirits seemed to follow her." A simply bad man in government, the paper went on, might work evil by his example. A covetous man might do wrong to others by unjust exactions. A tyrant or a fool might lay the seeds of future misgovernment. But a pettifogger was the worst of all. By substituting trickery for statesmanship, by basing state policy on "systematic duplicity," Reeder not only had ruined himself but had extinguished respect for his office.[42]

It might be said that such hateful expressions coming from all sides was evidence that Reeder was trying to pursue a neutral course. But there was no disposition to give him the benefit of that doubt.

After John Dawson of Pennsylvania had turned down the job of Kansas governor, the next appointee was Wilson Shannon, who had been governor of Ohio and member of Congress from that state.[43] Between Reeder's firing on July 28, 1855, and Shannon's taking up the office on September 7, the territorial secretary, Daniel Woodson, handled matters at the governor's office.[44] By the time Shannon arrived, the capital of Kansas was at Lecompton.

Shannon was disrespected by all elements of the national press almost from the beginning. A correspondent for the *Boston Liberator* described a speech Shannon gave in Missouri on the way to Kansas as "a long and dreary rehash of the thousand times adduced arguments, which were originally intended to prove that slavery is a divine, profitable and advantageous institution." His enunciation, the reporter said, was that of a serpent, and he read his lecture in a dry nasal tone.[45] His policy, wrote the *New York Herald*, was to do as little as possible "and to be a perfect Know Nothing on the negro question."[46] An Albany writer was more mean-spirited still. Pierce, he concluded, had picked in Shannon "an unscrupulous and pig-headed toady." The minute Shannon opened his mouth in Kansas, "he emitted such a torrent of blatant stupidities, arrant nonsense and cringing servilities, that we wonder the barbarians of Missouri had a stomach for it."[47]

The commentary was patently unfair, but it was typical of the reception new governors of Kansas received. Shannon had a drinking problem and a temper, but he was no lackey, nor was he inarticulate. In an early speech, for instance, he spoke of the varied backgrounds of Kansans and of the difficulty of pleasing them all. "By respecting the opinions and even the prejudices of each other," he said, "and cultivating a social feeling, we will soon harmonize, and learn to act together for the benefit and advancement of our highly favored country."[48] A newspaper writer in Springfield, Massachusetts, granted that perhaps Shannon was "not so obstinate a jackass" as to fail to see the obvious.[49]

Shannon, however, got into deep difficulty during the Wakarusa war and the subsequent raid on Lawrence. He did not show much sensitivity to free-state grievances, mouthing, as did all the territory's governors, that he was there to enforce the law. But he did make the "treaty" with Lane and Robinson that delayed a confrontation and limited the violence in the spring of 1856. Mediating between Charles Robinson and David Atchison was no mean task. The *New York Daily Times* correspondent in Kansas interviewed Shannon regularly in 1855 and 1856 and said, "I am disposed to give him credit for greater intentions than most do."[50]

Shannon spoke regularly on the theme of press exaggeration. In replying to a memorial from the Topeka group in June 1856, he spoke of the way things had been colored and concluded that there were men in Kansas who were "desirous to complicate the present difficulties in this Territory" and who would not be upset should civil war occur. Law-abiding citizens should react with caution "and not . . . lend a too willing ear to all the reports that are floating around the country."[51] Much of the exaggeration concerned him.

A Milwaukee letter spoke of "petticoat" Shannon, helpless with fear and seeing nothing "but the ghosts of murdered men."[52]

Shannon had to go. He sent in his letter of resignation on August 18, 1856; it crossed in the mail the notice of his removal wending its way west from Washington. John Geary, a Mexican War veteran and former mayor of San Francisco, took his place.[53] "Poor Shannon!" wrote a journalist at the *New York Daily Tribune*. "I am almost sorry for him. . . . Having 'put his hand to the Border Ruffian's plow, he looked back,' and now stands like another pillar of salt, on this plain of Sodom."[54]

Geary, with his military experience, turned his attention to disbanding the roving factional militias and had some success at calming the violence in Kansas, at least long enough for the 1856 presidential election.[55] The *St. Louis Daily Missouri Democrat* commented that his inaugural address was "not without a certain amount of rodomontade and threadbare denunciation; yet on the whole the temper is good."[56] His theme was that the laws should be faithfully executed.[57]

That did not satisfy everyone in the North. Yes, wrote the *New York Daily Tribune*, Geary had restored peace, but that peace was a "delusive fantasy." It was the peace of a military dictatorship; Geary had simply converted the private militias of the proslavery faction into the official militia, with the notorious Henry Titus at its head. Dragoons were watching the Northern emigration routes, while the border ruffians blockaded the Missouri River. Geary was not a "respectable tyrant, nor yet an imbecile," the *Tribune* concluded. He was only a politician.[58]

Geary, however, proved a less easy target for the national press than Shannon, and a number of newspapers gave him grudging respect. He doubtless prevented another attack on Lawrence, which was in the offing at his arrival. He manned his militia with soldiers from both sides, and he rid the territory for a time of private armies. He spent a great deal of his own money, in the absence of sufficient federal appropriations, to, among other things, sort out the flawed justice system in Kansas Territory. He took an extensive tour of the territory on horseback, speaking to all factions in all places. He used his veto regularly with the territorial legislature. And he spoke with a certain force about maintaining an evenhanded stance.[59] He was, a writer in Hartford thought, "one of the most important men in the nation," and his message to the territorial legislature "one of the most important public documents of the age." His style, while "expansively verbose," was sensible. The main problem, from the perspective of the North, was that he recognized the legality of the territorial legislature. "The pious remarks of the Governor . . . are all very proper, but directed as they are to the attention of that bogus Legislature, they seem like asking grace over a meal gotten by rapine."[60]

For Geary, the end was due not so much to pressure from Washington as to his own dissatisfaction at the lack of support by the administration and his frustration at the insecure, even dangerous, atmosphere in which he worked.

One dramatic incident captured the flavor best. In February 1857, Geary refused to commission William Sherrard as Samuel Jones's replacement as sheriff of Douglas County. Douglas County, where Lawrence was located, was a sensitive venue, and Sherrard, the recommendation of the legislature for the post, was more of a loud bully than Jones had been. He was a heavy drinker and brawler, among other disqualifications. Geary ignored it when Sherrard met him on the street and spat in the governor's face. But in a confrontation at a protest meeting organized by Geary's friends in the legislative chambers on February 18, Sherrard fired four times at his critics, wounding some of them, and was in turned killed by one of them with a shot through the head.[61] The "sanguinary affair," wrote the *New York Daily Tribune*, was "a pretty kettle of fish wherewith to furnish Mr. Buchanan's inauguration table."[62] On March 4, Geary, fearing assassination, resigned.[63]

Both sections excoriated him as a tool of the other. The *Charleston Mercury* said Geary resigned because of "a collision with the whole force of public sentiment" and predicted he would never be heard of again. He muddled all questions in order to keep the peace, expecting "that out of these dirty waters there may possibly come some bubble upon which politicians may safely ride."[64]

A few defended him with faint praise, noting that things could be worse. "The lovers of quiet and prophesiers of smooth things," said the *New York Daily Tribune*, "have rested on Geary as the corner-stone of their hopes." Given the "fatal position" of his party, he had done his best. He was at least not willing to be "dragged behind the chariot wheels" of the extensive fraud going on in Kansas. In his place would doubtless come a more reliable proslavery partisan. "Thus closes another act in the fearful drama of 'crushing our Freedom in Kansas'; what, O oracles of Cotton! shall be the next, and the next?"[65] The *New York Daily Times* was disappointed that Geary had abandoned his duty out of personal fear and political frustration.[66] Still, as the

New Orleans Daily Delta put it, Kansas governors "have not gone to a bed of roses or a castle of indolence in that distracted Territory."[67]

Geary's farewell address expressed all that, as well as his pride in having dealt fairly effectively with an intractable situation. He had found Kansas a desolate ruin and restored to it some order and security. He had expected vituperation, but he was tired of it. He had given Kansas a chance, but it was up to Kansans now to unite and preserve the peace. He left them in the care "of that Great Being who holds in his hand the destinies of men and of nations."[68]

Robert Walker of Mississippi was next. The *New York Herald* crowed that Walker's appointment was "immeasurably" the most important act of the new presidential administration and that it would "test to the uttermost the political fitness, the moral firmness, the intellectual resources, and even the physical capabilities of Mr. Walker, as they have never been tried in the whole course of his life. He will find that the care of the Treasury Department during a foreign war, and the financiering required of a half dozen Pacific railroads, will stand as light amusements compared to the rough work of law and order in Kansas, and the solution there of the tremendous issue of African slavery." Kansas had destroyed the Pierce administration, said the paper, and it bode well to do the same to Buchanan and his ward Walker.[69] After a dinner at the Astor House in New York with his friends, Walker boarded the railroad for his eventual arrival aboard the *New Lucy* at Leavenworth, and his destiny.

There was, however, a twist at the outset. Things happened slowly in the 1850s. Therefore, before Walker arrived late in May, his new secretary, Frederick Stanton, who arrived in Kansas early in April, took charge as acting governor. Stanton was not satisfied to remain passive. Some journalists in the South hoped that with the election of Buchanan over the Republican Fremont and with the Supreme Court's Dred Scott decision upholding the idea that slave property could be carried into free states, the Kansas controversy might calm and the free-state faction would give up its rebellion.[70] But it was not to be. Geary was thinking of publishing his diary; Reeder was on the speaking circuit; and Stanton did not wait for Walker.[71]

Stanton started out with a strong speech and a manifesto. He would enforce the laws of the legislature, and the Free State Party needed to participate in the June elections for delegates to the constitutional convention or forever abandon its pretensions to power.[72] The reaction of the *Kansas City Enterprise*'s editor Robert Van Horn was that he hoped officials in Kansas would stop making speeches. Speeches did not pay in Kansas. Only action did, or "masterly inaction." Speeches aggravated the soreheads, giving them consequence in their own estimation and allowing them to "play their pranks and exhibit their antics." Governors should "stand by the bone and sinew," and affairs would regulate themselves.[73] The *Chicago Daily Tribune* noted that either Stanton was a fool or he thought the people of Kansas were fools. However, there was "no statute against persons biting off their own noses."[74]

Stanton's pretentious inaugural address was followed an awkward confrontation with the free-state leadership at Lawrence. Charles Robinson submitted some conditions under which his faction would participate in the upcoming election. Stanton dismissed them and had the temerity to speak at the Cincinnati House in Lawrence before a crowd of about 1,000. He started out humbly, stating that he was just the secretary and acting governor, not the real governor. That governor, Walker, was a man of "gigantic ability," admired all over the world. He probably should have stopped there. But he went on for nearly an hour. He said he would enforce the federal laws. That was fine with the audience. And he said he would enforce the territorial laws. Cries went up of "Never! Never!" Stanton stopped and faced the hecklers. "Then you and I are at war upon this point; but I shall spill every drop of blood in my body but what the laws shall be enforced." Voices from the crowd said they would like to see him try. Stanton responded that at least they understood each other, and it would be war to the knife. At that point, an old man drew a knife and said, "Come on then, if you want to try that game." It was not a dignified occasion. The acting governor had, it seemed, "fulfilled his mission in stirring up the animals." Wrote the correspondent JUNIUS to his paper in Chicago: "Stanton stock is way below par, and no power on earth can raise it."[75]

Walker started his tenure with an elaborate inaugural address on May 27. He began with the usual disclaimer that he did not want the job (who did?) and that he was doing it as a favor to the president and out of patriotism. The territory was about to elect delegates to a constitutional convention, and this, he stated, was a great watershed, and it was important that all participate and have an official voice, rather than, as heretofore, carping from the sidelines. He spoke of railroads and of the possible future prosperity of a state of Kansas. Slavery issues, he continued, should be decided in the territory, as the Kansas-Nebraska Act had specified, and not by Congress.

So far, so good. But he then did two controversial things. First, he went out on a limb by saying that any constitution created by the upcoming convention would have to be ratified by a vote of the people of Kansas before being submitted to Congress. In that, he thought he had the support of President Buchanan, but it turned out he did not. Second, as a subtext of his slavery comments, Walker spent a few minutes talking about a pet theory of his, and the words he used were to haunt him through the rest of his administration. There was, he said, a law of nature that would prevent slavery from ever establishing itself in Kansas, and therefore the political argument about it was moot. He spoke of the climatic law of "isothermal lines," which dictated cultures and economies. This argument was a standard of the literature of the times, but Walker's using it in this context offended nearly everyone.[76]

One group offended was the abolitionist ideologues. The geographical destiny argument seemed to them to make light of a serious moral question and to divert attention from an ideological crusade. Slavery was "intrinsically absurd and unjust," and its extension to the territories was "an outrage upon common sense and Republican principles."[77] It was "not climate, but conscience" that really mattered.[78]

Another criticism was that the address was silly, pandering to a popular audience rather than being, as it should have been, a "severe State paper."[79] The part about isothermal lines, wrote a Chicago commentator, was "bald humbug."[80] There was substance in the inaugural, a writer in Louisville thought, but it hid amid irrelevancies "like kernels . . . in a huge pile of chaff." The address, that analyst believed, showed power of expression but lacked thought. It was "unbecoming, impertinent, crude, rambling, confused, and incorrect."[81] There seemed to be a gap between Walker's promise and performance, and he seemed to have an excess of ego. "Nominally there is no better Governor in Christendom than Robert J. Walker of Kansas. Practically, however, the affairs of the world are no nearer settlement than when Mr. Walker was debating which hemisphere stood most in need of him. The man who carries off any glory as Territorial Governor of Kansas is yet to be heard from."[82]

Walker's next error was tactical. On June 9, he gave a conciliatory address to the Topeka Free State legislature. His motive was clear. He wanted to bring the factions together and to get everyone to participate in the upcoming election for a constitutional convention. But his appearance in Topeka and his kind words were poison to the South, which regarded the Topeka group as acting a "desperately false and silly part." The "refractory spirit," which the Topeka rebels represented, must, according to Southern journalists, be subdued. "It cannot rage longer without overthrowing law in Kansas, and degrading the nation everywhere."[83] If anything were needed to show that Walker, despite his administration credentials, was a traitor to the South, this was it. Instead of going to Topeka with a sword to disperse the rebels, as he should, a Georgia journalist wrote, Walker "met them with honeyed words of friendship and entreaty."[84]

Walker did not succeed in convincing the free-state faction to vote in the June convention elections, and his appearance before them, so damaging to his reputation, was in vain. However, given the problems that nonparticipation created for the ratification of the resulting Lecompton Constitution, no one in hindsight could fault him for trying. And his words at Topeka were not so very kind. He did guarantee a vote on whatever constitution was formed, but he said that in the meantime he would execute the law. There were cries of "No! No!" at that. Walker said he had nothing to do with the people of either Massachusetts or Missouri, but if the Topeka faction wanted war, all it had to do was set up a state government against the government approved by the president and Congress. There may have been problems in the past, Walker said. He had no control of the past, but he could and would control the future.[85]

Southerners were upset not so much by what Governor Walker said at Topeka as by his appearing there at all. The *Jackson Mississippian* commented, "These traitors, headed by Lane, Robinson, and other noted characters, were fresh from the orgies of a so-called Convention, which characterized as invalid and illegal the acts of the regular and proper Legislature of the Territory, and announced their purpose to persist in their disorganizing and lawless course." Why, the paper asked, should the governor give a "harangue" before this "lawless conclave"? His talk, the reporter wrote, "elicited the wildest and most extravagant laudation from the vile crew of rabid fanatics and unscrupulous demagogues and agitators to whom it was addressed. If Jim Lane, the noted outlaw, and Robinson, the bogus Governor, approved and applauded it, patriotic and law-abiding citizens will know at once that it is not such an emanation as they can endorse. . . . You cannot travel the same road with Lane, Robinson and their co-traitors in Kansas."[86]

In addition, Walker's insistence that any Lecompton constitution would not be valid without a vote in Kansas ratifying it, in addition to the election by which its delegates were appointed, enraged the South. Southern newspapers called for his impeachment. "We have not asked him to be on our side," wrote a columnist in the *New Orleans Daily Picayune*, but his trying to dictate a process that had already been set by law was going too far.[87]

If a Mississippi native and lifelong Democrat like Walker could not gain the support of the South in Kansas, who could? The answer was, increasingly, no one. The peace of Kansas, wrote the *New York Daily Tribune*, did not depend on its governor. "None of these are or have been anything more than mere corks bobbing on the surface, mere indicators of the way the wind is blowing."[88]

The governors, however, had done some things. The *Charleston Mercury* thought Reeder had played the free-state game too strongly. Shannon did little for the South, but he did have Col. Edwin Sumner break up the Free State legislature, and he had Robinson and others indicted. Geary broke the militias, which may or may not have been an advantage to the South, depending on how one estimated relative military strength at the time.

But it was too little. Geary tried to veto a few legislative actions, then resigned "baffled and exposed." Walker came in with "notorious" opinions and, according to the *Mercury*, "played the part of Abolition emissary in Kansas." Walker's tenure was just another manifestation of the "grand drama of Southern discomfiture and humiliation," this time through federal misrule in Kansas.[89]

Walker, perhaps smarting under the criticism from the South about his Topeka address, followed it with a military adventure that, however reasonable and well intentioned, made him a laughingstock. The town of Lawrence, which refused to recognize or operate under the charter issued it by the territorial legislature, created in July 1857 a municipal charter of its own. Walker objected, and when he was rebuffed, he challenged the town of Lawrence with seven companies of U.S. infantry at his back.[90] Yes, Lawrence's snub was an act of rebellion, but what was new? Why pick this relatively trivial ground upon which to stage an elaborate demonstration?

Walker's ego got in the way, his rhetoric became inflated, and he overstepped himself. "Let me adjure you," he wrote in a proclamation to Lawrence, "once more to abandon these proceedings before you involve yourselves in the crime of treason, and subject the people of Lawrence to all the horrors and calamity of insurrection and civil war." All the powers of the federal government would be used, Walker said, to keep Lawrence from operating under its municipal code.[91]

The confrontation was portrayed as a tempest in a teapot. Reporting on Walker's appearance before Lawrence with his troops, the *New York Daily Tribune* chuckled, "We trust he does not mean to hurt anybody." It was no doubt, the New York reporters thought, intended as a moot demonstration to influence elections in the South, and the governor did not intend to push things. However, it was dangerous to feint.[92]

It was comedy. What an end for Walker's promise! "His serene Highness," wrote a Cincinnati reporter, "a little higher than usual in consequence of the inspiring qualities of the juice of corn, if rumor is accurate, passed through that awful den of conspirators, the town of Lawrence, while his sensitive soul was smarting under the severity of the tone toward him of the Southern press." In Lawrence, the reporter went on, he saw an ordinance establishing the new town government. "His Highness snuffed treason in the tainted air" and brought troops to bear before the "doomed city." There he sweltered in the ninety-degree heat, while "he made a fool of himself."[93] The *New York Daily Tribune* published a mock edict signed "Robertus J. Wakerus," which threatened Lawrence with destruction for removing a dead horse from the street.[94] The *Chicago Daily Tribune* hooted at the governor's attempt to confiscate a water cart as contraband of war. "The folly of the movement seemed indigenous in the man, so impromptu and original was its luxuriance. Its absurdity was so *naïve*—its nonsense so pastoral. There was a freshness of blunder—a felicity of *faux pas* in it worthy of a political Malaprop." Walker was wound up in words and in ego, and in technicalities, the newspaper thought, and had become a buffoon. "His worst enemy could not make him more ridiculous than he persists in making himself."[95] The demonstration before Lawrence was, wrote RANDOLPH for the *St. Louis Daily Missouri Democrat*, an "unwarrantable aggression" and a mistake that would doom Walker for life. "Why, there is not a schoolboy in Lawrence but has too much sagacity to bring an army of four hundred upon a thriving town and people in time of peace."[96]

The criticism was independent of section. The *Boston Liberator* ran an editorial declaring that Walker's proclamation against Lawrence was "in the spirit and style of Austria or the Russian Autocrat when admonishing the subjugated but restless masses." It would be a subject for ridicule "on the score of its egotism, bombast, towering indignation, and terrible threatening, were it not that the struggle in Kansas is no child's play." Walker, the writers in Boston said, was a "blustering miscreant" and "base dissembler" who ought to be dismissed forthwith.[97]

Reporters competed with each other for color in covering this story. JACO-
BIUS from the *St. Louis Daily Missouri Democrat* went to Walker's sweltering
tent for an interview. "Like Jonah the governor came here to warn the city of
its impending destruction unless it turned from the error of its ways. But,
unlike Nineveh, Lawrence has not repented." The correspondent asked
Walker if he had come to collect territorial taxes from Lawrence. Walker sat
down and looked the journalist in the eye. The reporter stared back into blue
eyes and thought of the mythical basilisk, whose glance was destruction.
Walker said the tax question was impertinent and he would not answer it.
Newspaper correspondents, he said, had spread a thousand lies about him,
and he was not going to give them any more ammunition. Lawrence pretended its new government was merely about cleaning up dead dogs in the
street, the governor said, but it had greater significance than that. People in
Lawrence were in a state of insurrection against the laws. His tone made the
reporter believe that Walker, as was said of him, had once been a slave
trader. "I presume he thought I should be intimidated by his grandeur. But I
had seen too many governors of Kansas and of other states—seen what they
were made of and how they were manufactured—to feel any awe when in the
presence of such a man." The reporter thought that Walker, "an impulsive
little man," had made a mistake in attacking Lawrence, but might still, with
wiser council, make a decent governor.[98]

A correspondent of the moderate *Richmond Daily Enquirer* shared that
opinion. He was "mortified" at the outcry against Walker. "Is there nothing
in bearing such a character as Robert J. Walker, to cause men to hesitate one
moment before they almost *lynch* him, morally and politically?" Apparently
there was not.

Walker, with his troops, shortly withdrew from Lawrence, with the excuse
that there was an Indian uprising elsewhere. One Missouri reporter called
him then a "poor, infatuated old ninny."[99] The "Isothermal War" was over,
wrote a columnist in Cincinnati. "The Dragoons joined the Lawrencites in
laughing at ye great Isothermal Governor." It was hot, the columnist explained, elections in the Southern states were over, and liquor and food were
growing short. So the expedition folded its tents and crept away.[100]

Walker was gone in November. And Governor James Denver came and
went, a flash in the pan, while the Kansas issue was still prominent in the nation. However, that last piece of territorial gubernatorial history is best
viewed through the lens and in the context of the grand debate over the
Lecompton Constitution, an event as extensive and controversial as the

Kansas-Nebraska debate. In that cataclysmic confrontation, there coalesced all the issues, all the arguments, all the mean epithets that had been developed by the newspaper press and the printers of scurrilous pamphlets over the years. And then, as suddenly and as surprisingly as it had come before the people of the United States, the Kansas issue disappeared from the stage almost entirely.

Governor Shannon once commented, "Govern Kansas . . . ! You might as well attempt to govern the devil in hell."[101] Indeed, it is probable that the fault was in fact in the stars and not in themselves, that the Kansas governors were such failures. The situation was quite impossible, and whatever they did or said, whatever conciliatory actions they took, the highly partisan press turned it against them. They were set up to be villains from the start, and the tendency of both sides to excoriate them is probably testimony to their basic fairness. A twentieth-century Wichita local official once said, off the record, that the city commission was the "pissing post" of the community. In a sense, the Kansas territorial governors were lightning rods, symbols, convenient scapegoats for all that ailed society, and targets for its quarreling factions. Some of them, admittedly, were underpowered, but men like Geary, Walker, and Denver were certainly people who had proved elsewhere that they had leadership skills and persuasive powers. But as the leadership in Kansas improved, the opportunity for the exercise of leadership diminished—the fundamental trust or deference among the population necessary for a leader to lead had much diminished. There was no more savvy politician or articulate persuader than Abraham Lincoln. But even he proved unable to deal effectively with the Kansas situation and its immediate aftermath. It was too much to expect from an Andrew Reeder. Words from Kansas governors did not flow into a neutral space where they were objectively examined in context. Instead, they were chopped and diced, one by one and in detail, by a mature propaganda machine, spinning out of control. Walker could not say the single word "isothermal" without generating mountains of national press and having it attached to him as an unfortunate "handle," which he could never shake. Shannon made some intemperate remarks that were repeated over and over again, while his wiser statements disappeared on the back pages.

Governor Denver wrote his wife in February 1858 that he thought the newspapers thus far had been fair to him, "but whether it will hold out much longer is doubtful." He had to stand up to people on both sides, and they were all getting "sore" at him. He wondered whether his talent mattered, as "one man of ordinary sense [would] do as well here now as another"—that is, not very well at all. "I don't know whether I can succeed," he wrote, "but there is nothing like trying."[102] Trying, however, was a frustrating activity, and, it sometimes seems, productive as much of further bitterness as of peace. One voice of reason, whether in the political forum, or in the press— even a dozen or a hundred such voices—could not be effectively heard amid the cacophony of noise Kansas was generating.

CHAPTER 8
LECOMPTON

To review, the Lecompton struggle began with the Kansas elections for delegate to a constitutional convention, held June 15, 1857. The Free State Party boycotted the election, and the proslavery faction dominated it by default. The constitutional convention began meeting in September and produced in mid-November a constitution unremarkable except for its inclusion of slavery. In spite of Governor Walker's pledges to the contrary, the convention provided not for a vote on the entire constitution but only for one on the slavery clause. The free-state faction boycotted that election, held December 21, and therefore the "with slavery" version easily prevailed. On October 5, however, at the legislative elections in Kansas, the free-state faction did participate and won a majority in the new legislature. Stanton, again serving as acting governor, called that legislature into a special session. President Buchanan removed Stanton from office for this. James Denver became governor in December. The new legislature created a militia under the leadership of Lane, repealed some actions of the former legislature, and scheduled an election for January 4, 1858, the same day there was to be voting on potential state officers under the Lecompton Constitution. At that election the people of Kansas voted on whether they wanted the Lecompton Constitution at all in any form.

The members of the free-state faction voted in both sections of the January 4 election. Voting on state officers allowed their enemies to say that the free-staters recognized the legitimacy of the constitutional convention and therefore of the Lecompton Constitution and the territorial legislature that had authorized it. However, in the second part of the January 4 election, voters overwhelmingly rejected the Lecompton Constitution itself. Both votes went to Congress, along with the Lecompton Constitution itself.

A massive debate followed, with no straightforward resolution. The Democratic Party split. President Buchanan supported admission under the Lecompton Constitution. Senator Douglas and others did not. Governor

Walker resigned over the issue. To complicate things further, the free-state faction replaced its Topeka Constitution with another, far more liberal, one created in Leavenworth. After many attempts to amend the Lecompton Constitution, a conference committee finally passed the English Compromise, which allowed a vote in Kansas, not on the Lecompton Constitution proper but on an accompanying schedule providing for land grants. This allowed Southern Democrats to say that there was no interference by Congress and that Congress had not set the precedent of requiring a further vote on the Lecompton Constitution. The Republicans could say that in effect this vote on the accompanying schedule was a vote on the Lecompton Constitution.

At any rate, when voters in Kansas rejected the English provisions, the Lecompton Constitution itself became a dead letter. National attention turned to the Lincoln-Douglas debates. Kansas, languishing in the publicity shadows, became a state in 1861. It was admitted under the Wyandotte Constitution, an entirely new document created by people who had become practiced at the making of constitutions.[1]

Historian Kenneth Stampp called his chapter on the Lecompton Constitution "Politics as Farce."[2] Contemporary observers recognized the farce, and they knew also that the farcical part hid the profound part. To this contest came many preexisting facts, the major one being that of the "two irreconcilable elements of civilization and barbarism," but observers of the time held different perspectives on which policies and which sections and which opinions represented civilization, and which barbarism. "Compromises may evade and party drill postpone the hour of crisis; but it must come." And compromise was deeply important, for all the joking. "This popular tumult— this disorganizing of parties—this confusion of the appliances intended to restore harmony, does not result so much from a desire on the part of statesmen, North or South, to foment agitation and increase sectional strife, as it does from the conflict of two great interests, of which they are the visible representatives and agents. Their folly may exasperate the strife, and their ambition precipitate the contest," but the main problem was that founding landmarks and temporizing devices had been removed and the race was open.[3] The ugly center of the disagreement was thoroughly unmasked during the Lecompton debates, and it lay there open in all its ghastly and threatening horror for everyone to contemplate. And the contemplators were too tired to do anything about it but shovel in a wheelbarrow full of dirt and hope the murdered thing would stay buried.

Obviously, the scene was set for complications and bitter recrimination.

It was set, too, for epic myth, exaggeration, emotion, and falsification. The national newspaper press was, by long habit and practice, well prepared for that. Lecompton, with its multiple threats, inflated rhetoric, and egregious misunderstandings, represented the apotheosis of the Kansas issue from a sensationalist journalist's point of view.

Four elections had turned on the Lecompton Constitution question: on June 15, October 5, and December 21, 1857, and January 4, 1858. But they seemed to resolve nothing. "There is no end to a Kansas election," commented a man in Providence, Rhode Island. "It has as many lives as a cat, and as many forms as there are fashions for whiskers. In nine cases out of ten, the developments of a few months knock all our guesswork into the regions of absurdity, and we are left to quit the field in despair or guess again."[4] There was early hope that since "everybody has turned attention to getting rich," and "railroads and Indian lands are all the rage now," the politics of Kansas might go on a back burner.[5] That did not happen.

Much of the news early in 1857 emphasized the necessity for some change by illustrating the foolish behavior both of the regular territorial legislature and of its free-state rump equivalent. The regular legislature seemed obsessed with charters and land deals. Most of the roads laid out were "of too wild a character for any rational hope to be based on them" and represented "local whims." There were dream railroad charters. Five railroads received charters by March 1857. One of them, to be called the Kansas, Nebraska, and Gulf, was projected to connect Kansas with port cities.[6] The *New York Daily Tribune* thought the convention held by the proslavery faction at Lecompton was a comedy. "Whatever its devotees may think of 'law,' they have a rather confused idea of 'order.' It is not an unusual thing for half a dozen to be talking at a time. A respectable number of delegates keep their hats on, while smoking, chewing and squirting tobacco juice on the floor."[7]

Free-staters' activities did not fare better in the press. Former governor Reeder, still trying for recognition as a Free State congressional delegate, applied early in 1857 to the federal government for a mileage allowance and a per diem, leading some newspapers to speculate that this was another way of funding "Kansas loafers" to hang around Washington.[8] There were charges that the Free State legislature had used aid money for the Kansas settlers to back scrip it issued for party and partisan purposes.[9] Robinson temporarily resigned his post as Free State governor, some said to pursue town-site speculation at Quindaro. Robinson denied it and said the newspapers were persecuting him. "Not one despises their picayune quarrels more than I do, and

I shall feel that the millennium has certainly dawned should I be allowed to visit the East once without hearing in my rear howls of hungry prairie wolves that feast upon human character."[10] Still, he told a meeting of his peers in April that he did not blame them for criticizing him. "I may have erred in judgment—I probably have; I am fallible as all men are—I am very fallible."[11] A Missouri man thought worse of Robinson than that. He wrote, "The assuming of office, in a time of peace, is a crime of which the Government can take no more cognizance, officially, than of an act of burglary or murder."[12]

The free-staters' continued refusal to vote annoyed many observers. The free-staters, one noted, were filled with flimsy pretext, and their position was "an idle, hollow falsehood, unworthy even of the most barefaced disorganizer."[13] There was a Free State victory in April in the municipal elections at the former proslavery stronghold of Leavenworth.[14] Every train West brought emigrants of free-soil sentiment.[15] Even if free-state voting failed to win the elections, it would give a grounds for legitimate protest, would retain and increase the Free State Party moral power, and would lay a foundation for future success. "But," a Washington paper asked, "if we retire from the contest, crying out fraud! fraud!, for heaven's sake, tell us, how we are going to gain anything?"[16] The idea that the administration was trying to force slavery on Kansas was, wrote the *Providence Daily Post*, a "worn-out humbug."[17]

Nonetheless, through the June election the Free State Party stuck to its nonvoting policy and vowed to shun any delegate who had been elected to the constitutional convention, as well as to ignore any constitution that was written by that group. Jim Lane aroused free-state crowds with such rhetoric, even saying that free-staters should not listen to anything further that Governor Walker had to say to them. The crowd shouted: "Lane forever!" "Go to it Lane."[18] Robinson told a Free State legislative meeting immediately after the delegate election that the territorial legislature and the new constitutional convention were merely the "inanimate framework."

A job printer produced 5,000 copies of Robinson's speech in English and 1,000 in German.[19] Nor were the correspondents any less active than ever. On a hot day in July, one of them said he could not help thinking "that there is a streak of the supernatural in the industry which collects, digests and writes two columns and a half a day when the thermometer is ranging from nine to ten thousand degrees Fahrenheit."[20]

The new president, Buchanan, was undoubtedly in a bind. There was tension between Buchanan and Walker, but to many observers they both seemed out of touch, "as if one was the Man in the Moon and the other a missionary to the Celestial Empire."[21] The South was tremendously disaffected by Walker, particularly because of his insistence that the Lecompton Constitution would have to be voted upon by the Kansas population after it was framed by the convention. "We were not aware," said a Southern observer, "that he [Walker] had become a law-maker after the manner of the Shaw of Persia."[22]

Southern papers did realize that in the Kansas situation the nation was on the "verge of a vortex."[23] Many Southerners had given up the idea that Kansas would ever become a slave state but insisted on defense of constitutional principles and procedures there. A writer in the *Charleston Mercury* noted that it was worse to rob through love than through fear, and in Kansas the South's love of the Democratic Party was being used "to injure, and degrade us still further." It was a matter of no great consequence, that newspaper thought, whether Kansas became slave or free, but it was "a matter of the first importance that the rules for the admission of States into the Union should be uniform and inflexible—that a free State should not be rushed into the Union against all law and all precedent, while a slave State is kept out by new-sprung preposterous conditions, that were never heard of before."[24] Would it not be a miscarriage of justice, another writer in the paper asked, for Governor Walker to interfere in what the duly elected Lecompton constitutional convention had produced?[25] Laurence Keitt of South Carolina, defending the Kansas constitutional convention as representative of the sovereignty of the people, said that anything else was "of French Republican growth."[26]

There was much evidence that the split was deep. "The action of the Lecompton Convention," wrote a correspondent from Chicago, "is of just as much consequence to the people of the Territory as the decisions of the Supreme Court of Hahoo to the movement of the Asteroids."[27] On the contrary, said the *Richmond South.* Respect for the forms was vital, and to lose them in Kansas and to lose Kansas and its possible proslavery constitution, as a result, would be a fatal blow. "It will completely arrest our march in the only direction in which it is possible for us to advance."[28]

Late in August 1857 a small but revealing incident received much more national publicity than it was worth. In the wake of Governor Walker's ignominious demonstration against Lawrence, Professor Benjamin Silliman of Yale College and a group of ministers sent President Buchanan a letter protesting the use of troops in Kansas to support Walker. This aroused some anti-intellectual sentiment to the detriment of the free-state cause. "The public are curious to know," said a writer in Washington, "upon what grounds a college professor has undertaken to impart to the President of the United States lessons in regard to his constitutional duties and obligations."[29] Silliman had been involved in the publicity surrounding the Beecher's Bibles a year earlier, which had similarly left him open to the charge of stirring in matters where eggheads and preachers should leave well enough alone.

Buchanan responded to the Silliman letter and seemed to many people to have had the advantage in the exchange. The main criticism of Buchanan was from those who thought the dignity of his office should have freed him from having to reply at all.[30] The *New York Herald* thought, "We do not believe the country contains a more foolish or more mischievous body of men than the New England clergy. . . . Their standpoint in life is bad; their standards are false; their logic is incorrect; their aims are puerile or mean; their instruments unworthy."[31] It was a discredit, said *Boston Post*, "to northern intellect and common sense."[32] Silliman, one paper said, was well named—a "silly man."[33]

The intellectuals' counterargument did not play well with the press. George William Curtis was no Theodore Parker or Henry Ward Beecher, so his 1856 oration "The Duty of the American Scholar to Politics and the Times" had not the currency of those ministers' pleas for the baptism of rifles and the involvement of clerics in the Kansas issue. Curtis made a similar point, however. He wrote that the scholar had a duty to apply what he had learned to social change, rather than sticking to the conjugation of Latin verbs. "Because we are scholars of to-day, shall we shrink from touching the interests of to-day? . . . Of what use are your books?" He wrote, "While we read history, we should be making history." So Curtis summoned academics to the fight for freedom in Kansas.[34]

The October 1857 legislative election in Kansas occurred in the midst of a national financial panic (or "revulsion," as it was then called), but that did not prevent it from receiving much attention outside Kansas itself. Walker had promised a fair election, and for the most part he delivered.[35] There were, however, notable exceptions, most prominently in the Oxford precinct in Johnson County, where 1,600 proslavery votes were returned from a border area that had 100 residents and half a dozen houses.[36] The names on the ballots had been copied from a Cincinnati street directory, and the fraud was so palpable that Governor Walker rejected those returns, giving the Free State Party an overall victory.[37] Although Walker was criticized for disallowing the Oxford precinct votes and for allowing soldiers to vote in the territory, many people observed the conditions for voting had improved.[38]

The *Philadelphia Press* commented editorially that Walker's handling of the situation was "masterful." To him would belong the credit "not only of pointing out to Kansas the safest, most practicable mode of getting rid of her troubles, but of inducing a people, smarting with outrage and defeat, inflamed by demagogues, ready for revenge, and rebellious at heart, to adopt his counsel; and thus . . . to destroy all cause of further complaint."[39] As far as the *Press*'s editor John Forney was concerned, it was time for the nation to accept the possible and to give up on the ideal of "schoolmen" like Silliman. The Kansas government, bogus or not, had operated. It had chartered railroads and towns and had granted divorces, even handling a divorce petition from James Lane, leader of the opposition. Yes, it was imperfect, but, the paper asked, "Is life to be recognized only in full health?" It seemed some were too idealistic, pursuing an "unapproachable mirage of excellence, rather than accepting the bad with the good."[40]

That was all well and good as far as it went. However, there were idealists on both sides. Walker resigned under pressure. The South complained about the governor's going beyond his authority in laying aside the election returns, however obvious the fraud might appear. Also, Walker still insisted on a vote of the general population on the Lecompton Constitution, while Buchanan was willing to compromise there. Buchanan had directed Walker to refer all questions of election fraud to the territorial legislature.[41] In violating that order, commented a correspondent in Chicago, Walker had "brought down the vengeance of the strabismus-eyed President and his cabinet upon his head."[42] Secretary of State Lewis Cass reminded Walker that the governor of Kansas had to represent the establishment and law and order. Cass objected to Walker's letter of resignation, highly critical of the president, which Walker released to the press. "If every officer of the government who feels himself constrained to refuse obedience to the instructions of the President should pursue this unusual course . . . no person knows better than yourself to what consequences this might lead."[43] But the Buchanan administration was already beyond a simple show of unity, though it was not without resources to try to enforce one.

On his way home aboard the steamer *Oglesby*, Walker expressed his frustration with the old legislature and the Lecompton Convention in an "excited" and "horribly profane" manner.[44] For all the efforts of the new legislature to stop it, the Lecompton convention proceeded. Went an editorial from Rhode Island: "The men in Kansas who have advocated this snarling, factious, miserable, dog-in-the-manger course, have achieved no triumph in this October election. . . . The very idea that a few or a great many addlebrained politicians in Kansas, who have been fattening on the peoples' miseries, can rub out laws or constitutions as they would rub out pencil marks on a slate . . . may as well be forever abandoned."[45]

By November, when the text of the Lecompton Constitution became available, the debate was joined, first in the press and shortly thereafter in the halls of Congress. "A commercial crisis has just swept over the business world," commented the *New York Daily Tribune*. "We stand on the threshold of a political crisis in Kansas." Using a strikingly modern-sounding phrase, the paper wrote that the proposed December 21 vote for the constitution with slavery or without slavery was a "heads I win, tails you lose proposition." It expressed the view that became Northern orthodoxy in the case, that voting for the Lecompton Constitution without slavery would not stop slavery in Kansas since that constitution recognized slave property currently in Kansas and contained provisions forbidding constitutional amendment until 1864.[46] "Nothing is hazarded. The people are mocked and insulted, where they thought they had a peaceable triumph. . . . The offspring of the Territorial Legislature, while hardly out of the swaddling clothes of its political birth, turns round like a hungry ogre to devour its parent." In the interim before acceptance or rejection of the Lecompton Constitution, power was to go to John Calhoun, forty-eight, surveyor general of Kansas and as such the most senior official in Kansas at the time. Calhoun, though a New England native who had come to Kansas from Illinois, was portrayed in the Northern press as a representative of slaveocracy evil and as trickery incarnate.[47]

The *New York Daily Times* added that the proceedings of the Lecompton Convention read "more like the delirious motions of madmen, than the deliberate conduct of rational conspirators."[48] Few would deny, said a journalist in Cincinnati, "that this style of submitting the Constitution to the people is no submission at all. . . . There is no outlet from the iron web of iniquities woven all over them, but to rend the prison bars by the strong arm of revolutionary violence."[49] The *New York Herald*, no friend of the free-state group, explained that the Calhoun "regency" and the new Lecompton Constitution, along with the procedures for ratifying it, were sillier as a "political pretension" than even the Topeka government.[50] The *Detroit Daily Free Press* said that the convention had "disgraced itself in the eyes of decent men" and that there had "never been anything like this in the history of this country."[51]

Journalists abroad were amazed. *Le Constitutionnel* in France observed, "The Democracy of America often startles us by its feats of characteristic audacity." The illustration was Kansas, where both the Topeka Constitution of 1856 and the Lecompton Constitution of 1857 had been created by means even the French considered irregular and individualistic to an extreme. "How will they make their escape from this labyrinth?"[52]

Nor was the amazement much less in the United States. A Chicago journalist wrote that some of the provisions of the Lecompton Constitution were "merely ridiculous," while others "would disgrace a despotism." It was a "satire upon representative bodies" and deserved nothing but contempt.[53] "Governors' proclamations are as numerous in Kansas as bogus writs were in the days of Sheriff Jones," wrote a St. Louis reporter. "The triumvirate of Robinson, Denver, and Calhoun, has flooded Kansas with this kind of literature. It is not an uncommon occurrence in this part of God's moral vineyard, to have three or four proclamations issued on the same day antagonistical to each other—from different governments—and all recommending and urging a different line of policy to be adopted by the settlers of Kansas."[54] The more things changed, wrote a Cincinnati editor, the more they remained the same. The federal government was still oppressing the free-state majority in Kansas. "It has dropped the profession of garrotter and assumed that of the thimble-rigger. Bravoes, bludgeons and bowie-knives have gone out, and in their place have come in the isothermal wizard with his patent safe."[55]

Lines were drawn. Douglas, as has been mentioned, split with Buchanan over whether a vote on the entire constitution was necessary. So did Forney. Perhaps the Lecompton Constitution was fine, Forney wrote. Perhaps the slavery clause was the only controversial thing about it. But that was for the voters to decide. Not having a vote on the whole instrument was fatal. Calhoun, the president of the convention, seemed to be in charge of the December 21 election. No wonder, Forney continued, the free-state faction would not vote.[56] The question, thought Forney, could not be settled by bluster on either side. If Kansas could not be a slave state by fair means, "a resort to foul would deluge it in blood."[57]

Surprisingly, there was some support in the South for the idea that the entire Lecompton Constitution should go to a vote, on the grounds that it was better to lose in an honorable vote according to real principles of popular sovereignty than to win under a pall. "A Kentucky Subscriber" wrote to the *New York Daily Times* in November, "It were infinitely better for the

South to lose a dozen such States as Kansas than to allow even a suspicion that she had countenanced any fraud or juggling for her benefit."[58]

Predictably, however, the majority opinion in that section was clear: A duly constituted body had created the Lecompton Constitution. Sovereignty could be delegated from the people to an administrative body, and it was therefore not necessary legally to take any more action to give its decisions full legitimacy.[59]

Typical was the statement of the *Charleston Mercury* that even if the free-state faction did vote in the December election, the proslavery faction might win. If the free-state group did not vote, the game was up, although the *Mercury* expected a fight in Washington "which will rock the Capitol to its foundations."[60] Under the Dred Scott doctrine, the *St. Louis Daily Missouri Democrat* emphasized, slavery existed where it was not abolished by positive law, and so it would be in Kansas. The prohibition against changing the Lecompton Constitution for eight years was wise, as it needed time to "extend and solidify."[61] The *Richmond Enquirer* also stood on principles of conservatism. The Kansas question had gone on too long, the paper thought, and it was time to settle it, however imperfect the instrument of doing so might be. "When a noble packet ship has been struggling against a terrible and protracted storm which still threatens to engulf her; the men almost exhausted with fatigue, and the officers worn down with uninterrupted vigilance, and anxiety for the safety of the vessel and the precious cargo she contains, the signs of the skies are often scanned." Fair weather gladdened the heart, and this new Lecompton Constitution promised the clearing of the clouds.[62]

The Richmond paper felt it unlikely that Kansas would ever be a slave state but insisted upon the "great principle of equality." Admittedly, this voting had not been simple. "From its inception until now, this question, seemingly and really so easy of solution and of settlement upon its own inherent merits, has presented itself, or rather it has been presented, in such a variety of phrases and in so complicated a character, as to have rendered it one of the most difficult and dangerous problems that have ever been presented to the American Congress."[63]

The opinion of the *Macon Georgia Telegraph* was similar, that the waters of what should have been a simple question had been muddied by Northern conspirators and lying correspondents. The path of peace lay in the shortest road to state government, and that was in adopting the Lecompton Constitution. "As soon as this controversy becomes what it should be—a mere question of a constitution for Kansas, it will be settled at once and peaceably. But from the very beginning the Topekaites have been mere tools and strikers of Seward, Greeley & Co." Admit Kansas as a state, the paper said, and that game was at an end.[64]

The Eufaula, Alabama, paper regretted that even so much as the slavery clause of the constitution was going to a vote. Kansas, the editor of the *Eufaula Spirit of the South* wrote, had ceased to be a territory when her people voted in June to form a constitutional convention. Sovereignty at that moment passed from the people to the convention. Congress had the power to admit states, and under the Lecompton Constitution Kansas was already a sovereign state, and it would be an independent sovereign state under that constitution even if Congress had the temerity to reject its application for admission to the Union. "Majestic in the possession of every element of physical greatness and interesting in proportion to the magnitude of the results which await her movements, she stands, for the present, outside the Union, clad in the panoply of her own sovereignty and exercising its undoubted rights, while the world watches with anxiety."[65]

That was an extreme position. But no fire-eater of the South consumed a hotter mixture than did James Lane of Kansas. At a mass meeting in Leavenworth on November 27, Lane commented upon the recently promulgated Lecompton Constitution: "We have come to the last move on the chessboard of Kansas politics! . . . It stirs up all our blood, and we hardly know what to do in this trying time." The constitution itself, he said, was "awful, disgraceful, and damnable in all its forms." Kansas was a slave state today and forever unless the process stopped. The Lecompton Constitution was no honest document, he said, but a device concocted by the "bloodhounds" at Lecompton, "outlaws," than whom a "blacker set you cannot find outside of hell." Lane averred that the framers were "d—d sons of b—s" and that he could not live on the same soil with such "black-hearted fiends." Someone should inscribe "Felon! Felon! Felon!" on the tombstone of John Calhoun (a statement that drew loud and prolonged cheers from Lane's audience). The Lecompton Convention, he said, had separated itself from honor, and the people in it no longer knew what truth was. Lane had told one of them that the Free State Party would head them or behead them. He did not advocate war, exactly. But, he said, "we have now got the goats so separated from the sheep, that we can easily kill them without committing a crime! . . . For I truly believe that if God should show his special providence here to-night,

we should see in these starry heavens his hand, commanding us to *extermi-
nate these damned villains!*" As Lane went on to talk about hanging the mis-
creants, his audience interrupted with stamping and applause. "You may
say," the speaker cried, "'LANE, you are excited.' I say ought we not to be excited? Have we not suffered enough to excite every nerve in our body?" He
himself saw no way to get rid of the Lecompton Constitution but by force. He
had a list of the men who had voted for it and said they should be tried and
put to death.[66] The newspapers called Lane irresponsible, the "Prince of
Ragamuffin," a "pretentious scoundrel," and worse.[67] But he was extreme,
frightening, exciting, spectacular, and therefore irresistible to the popular
press. He was quoted verbatim and in extenso everywhere.

Just at the time Lane was holding forth, guerrilla warfare broke out
around Fort Scott in the southeastern part of Kansas Territory. Through the
next months, as the Lecompton Constitution was debated in Congress,
bands of so-called jayhawkers under Lane, Charles Jennison, and James
Montgomery clashed with groups of proslavery partisans in small battles
reminiscent of the summer of 1856. It seemed again that negotiations for a
peaceful settlement were taking place against the backdrop of real potential
for civil war.[68] The people of Missouri, wrote a St. Louis reporter, would pay
little attention to the "silly vaporings" of orators like Lane, but if he and his
mob thought they could ride into Missouri, they would find Missourians
ready for them.[69] As usual, the telegraph was hot with spectacular exaggeration. Passengers and officers of the steamboats coming into St. Louis, said a
reporter there, "appear to be greatly amazed and somewhat amused at the
tales of blood and slaughter—the terrible battle between the chivalrous Lane
and the dragoons of the United States . . . inasmuch as they had never heard
of any such marvelous events while in the Territory."[70]

The elections of December 21, 1857, and January 4, 1858, confused more
than clarified the issue. Both sides claimed a mandate. There was no consistency. It seemed, wrote a columnist in the *Cincinnati Enquirer*, that the Free
State Party in Kansas became "sensible by fits and starts." And they had a
nerve: "These are men who, after having trifled with their own political interests and the peace of this country, expect, in return, that they can trifle
with the President, Congress, and the people of the states."[71] There were the
usual charges of fraud. Supposedly on December 21 James Buchanan cast a
vote in Kansas for the constitution with slavery, as did William H. Seward,
John Fremont, Horace Greeley, and Thomas H. Benton.[72] There were splits
in the Free State Party about voting on January 4, particularly in the election

for state officers under the Lecompton Constitution, and some of the free-staters did not vote. "If the Free State partisans were acting under instructions from JEFFERSON DAVIS and the Charleston *Mercury*," went a New York editorial, "they could not play into their hands more directly, or promote more effectually the ends at which they aim."[73]

Such mixed signals led many conservative Democratic papers, in the North as well as the South, to push for rapid admission under Lecompton. "No matter what is right or what is wrong that has been done or left undone," wrote the *Boston Post*, it was time to end the tension. Even the Free State Party should recognize that President Buchanan could bring much power to bear on behalf of Lecompton and that he was determined to do so. If that constitution failed, it might be years before Kansas could be admitted as a state and before the free-state majority there could gain offices and send senators and representatives to Washington. The proviso against amending the Lecompton Constitution surely would not meet a legal test, and therefore passing the constitution would make Kansas a slave state only temporarily. To resist Lecompton was, therefore, "perversity," advanced by "insane" men.[74]

But insane they did seem to be. The new Kansas legislature passed a bill making it a felony punishable by death to set up a government under the Lecompton Constitution, whatever Congress might decree. There was but one way, the *Boston Post* thought, to deal with such "wrongheadedness," and that was to create a state under the Lecompton Constitution. "Admit Kansas at once as a State, no matter with what Constitution, or even if without any Constitution. . . . Make her a State, and instead of this vague, shadowy, undefined 'squatter sovereignty' clothe her with the real sovereignty of the people to make or unmake Constitutions which is the sovereignty in government that belongs only to a State."[75]

Just following the January 4, 1858, elections, Congress reassembled, and the great Kansas question once again found its way to Washington. A Chicago reporter, taking his place in the galleries for the duration, watched the Lecompton advocates filibuster, piling "motions on motions," while the newspapermen took notes and rushed for the telegraph. On February 6, at 1 AM, he wrote, "The House presents a strange and impressive appearance under the mysterious looking yellow light, that descends from the pictured ceiling from the ruddy and golden interior of the hall. The members, worn and sleepy, are stretched in various attitudes upon their chairs and desks, a few fortunate ones having secured the sofas. At the sides of the chamber they are unusually quiet, and answer languidly to their names as the everlasting call of the roll goes on."[76] Fights had broken out, and there was a refusal to adjourn at 4 AM.[77]

John Calhoun appeared in Washington with election results showing passage of the Lecompton Constitution with slavery on December 21, defeat of the entire constitution on January 4, and, at the same time, election of officers under it. Excitement, conflict, and confusion were inevitable, Calhoun said, when government was organized for a frontier community "brought together from all parts of the world, and actuated by different objects, motives and prejudices." Good men had sought a peaceful solution to the Kansas impasse at the ballot box, but could not prevent violation of rights when too many had been "governed by no scruples as to public or private action." He received pressure from both sides concerning his report of the returns.[78]

Frederick Stanton, who had served twice as acting governor of Kansas, gave a three-hour speech in February 1858 at the Chinese Assembly Rooms in New York City. He expressed the opinion that if Kansas were admitted under the Lecompton Constitution, there would be civil war in the entire United States.[79] Some papers in the South threatened the same civil war directly if Lecompton were rejected. "When the Union becomes a mere name," an editor in Georgia wrote, "—a song which is piped for one section at the expense of the other—a mere instrument of partial legislation, and is made to pander to the views and ends of hypocritical demagogues, we must confess our love for it ceases."[80]

Such talk, wrote the moderates at the *Providence Daily Post*, was irresponsible. The Free State Party was in control and would retain control peaceably. "Must the government—must Congress—yield to the demand of a mob? Must this or that line of policy be adopted, merely because its advocates appear to us with torches, bludgeons, revolvers, rifles and bowie knives in their hands?"[81]

The nation had learned cynicism concerning Kansas. Many newspaper writers noted the "chasm" of opinion in the press on the questions involved. Yes, wrote historian George Bancroft, Lecompton was probably a small wrong, and the whole affair seemed of little consequence. But, he wrote, "there is in political justice no such thing as a small wrong. A small wrong contains within itself the seeds of all evil." The policy of forcing the Lecompton Constitution on an unwilling population was, thought Bancroft, "neither wise, nor expedient, nor possible."[82] A writer in Chicago felt, "The pent up volcano will belch forth fire and smoke and pour out rivers of molten lava."

It would have been better not to "ring that horrid bell" that sounded out when Lecompton reached the capital city.[83]

President Buchanan set the tone on February 2, 1858, with a special message to Congress on Kansas. The message was intransigent and aggressive. The president said that he had received the Lecompton Constitution from Calhoun and that he intended to support admission under it. "A great delusion seems to pervade the public mind in relation to the condition of parties in Kansas." He characterized the free-staters as rebellious, even treasonous. They had a military leader (Lane) who was of a "most turbulent and dangerous character." Even when provided with the opportunity to vote, on December 21, the Free State Party had refused but had threatened to disrupt the election, which had to be carried out under the eye of federal troops. As far as Buchanan was concerned, submitting the slavery clause to a vote was sufficient recognition of popular sovereignty as imagined under the Kansas-Nebraska Act. The portion of the January 4 election that rejected Lecompton had no validity. Kansas was, Buchanan said, at that moment as much a slave state as South Carolina or Georgia. Every patriot should hope that Kansas would be admitted under this constitution and that its admission would not only close the Kansas question but the slavery question, which had "convulsed" the country for twenty years. The Kansas cause was "trifling." It could change its constitution anytime. The issue should not be allowed to threaten the Union.[84]

The *Philadelphia Public Ledger & Daily Transcript* thought the message "clear and calm."[85] The *New York Daily Tribune* felt otherwise and called the message a "monstrous . . . compendium of fallacies and misstatements—of suppression and misrepresentation." The newspaper claimed it had "neither time nor space to expose this atrocious document in detail" and to show its "toilsome sophistry."[86] But, responded the *Washington Union*, was it not the *Tribune* that had lost its senses? "Our philosopher raves, fumes, gnashes, swears."[87]

Other papers joined the fray directly and with gusto. Opinions were equally divided, always strong, and often boisterously expressed.[88] There were questions of procedure, questions of substance, questions of party, questions of principle, and questions of morality, with many subtle gradations.[89] The *Bangor Union* supported admission under Lecompton because the Democratic Party, which supported that solution, was the "last bond of the American Union; every other bond, political and religious, is severed."[90] So did the *Richmond South*, arguing that Buchanan's message was "but an emanation from, and an embodiment of, the Higher Law."[91] The *Columbus Times & Sentinel Tri-Weekly* followed Buchanan in arguing that the election on January 4 was a "solemn farce" and said that by then the Lecompton Constitution was already the "suprema lex" of Kansas.[92] Better disunion than to lose honor and equality, it concluded: "Rome falls, but we are innocent."[93]

On the other hand, a Southern paper in Louisville argued that Buchanan had contradicted himself in trying to deny "what . . . no living man is hardy or silly enough to deny"—that the majority in Kansas was against the Lecompton Constitution. In making in his message the legalistic argument that this majority, if it existed, had not expressed itself in the established forms, he only ensured that "the villainous document cuts its own throat." The "wretched minority" that was pushing Lecompton had "nothing to recommend it but the shadow of formality."[94] The *Milwaukee Daily Sentinel* believed Buchanan's message was "one tissue of unfounded statements, intemperate and undignified accusations, and lame arguments. It is false in its history, false in its logic, and false in its law."[95] A writer to the *New York Independent* used a threatening tone: "As the Lord lives, you may rest assured that if that Constitution is forced upon us, no earthly power can prevent an outburst of popular resistance which will tear it to tatters, and drive all its framers and abettors from the territory."[96]

Former governor Walker was at the Willard Hotel in Washington, ready to play his part in the Lecompton struggle.[97] Thousands of others, at every distance and of every persuasion, girded their loins as well.

Representative Henry Phillips of Pennsylvania spoke early in the debate. He wished, he said, he did not have to talk about Kansas any more. Kansas had been a "theater of strife and tumult." Phillips thought that admitting Kansas under the Lecompton Constitution would stop the strife, and that was the great necessity of the hour.[98]

Some of the cynicism abroad in the nation existed in Congress too. It was time to act, many members said. At a long discussion at the outset of the debate about the rules, they expressed frustration that the same arguments—technical, legal, and moral—were to be brought out again. Had they not been through that in 1854 and 1856? Was Congress to endure all-night sessions and two-day addresses again? Senator George Pugh of Ohio said, with an edge in his voice, that he disclaimed the right "to stand here and talk against time, day after day and week after week in order that my speeches may be taken down by that gentleman and distributed throughout the country. If gentlemen want to talk, let them talk to their own constituents, and at their own expense." And if they talked, he continued, they should stick to the point. "We cannot have a question of the present condition of the bill for the admission of Kansas brought up but we must have gentlemen go back to the ordinance of 1787, to the Dred Scott case, to the old black-letter English law, and spread out over any number of hours; and if not allowed to do it, then a great outrage is perpetrated."[99]

The Democrats managed to quash a number of proposals to investigate matters in Kansas further and to publish another thick report.[100] But they could not limit debate. The Republicans saw haste as an administration device for ramming Lecompton through. Henry Wilson of Massachusetts spoke the party line: "Senators, know that this is a question which interests every man, woman, and child in the Republic. No such domestic question has been presented to the Senate of the United States during this century. It is not only of itself one of transcendent magnitude and importance, in which the people are deeply interested, but it towers above all other questions."[101] To pass Lecompton, said Senator Daniel Clark of New Hampshire, would not bring peace; rather, it would "give the people of Kansas the torch of civil war and tell them to go and light it."[102] And so they talked, all day and often most of the night, almost exclusively about Kansas, for more than a month.

As feared, there was little new, and the arguments were along party lines, most of them long since sorted out and pushed to the point of tedium in the popular press. The speeches, however, were delivered with a passion that suggested compromise would be difficult. Lecompton was not a sectional question, said Senator Robert Toombs of Georgia, but a fundamental constitutional one. The North was determined there should be no more slave states, and that was the "living, breathing spirit that animates the opposition to the admission of Kansas into the Union under the Lecompton Constitution." The "universal, popular feeling" understood the debate as a battle between "mighty elements" for the future.[103]

How they talked! They talked about whether there was to be intervention or nonintervention, whether the votes in Kansas were legal or not, what the true intention of the Kansas-Nebraska Act was, what the springs and consequences of public opinion were, how the Kansas census had been taken and its districts apportioned, what version of Kansas history was accurate, whether the Kansas governors had had any talent, whether the free-state faction had committed treason, whether sovereignty was indivisible, what the relative status was of form and substance, which Kansas election had recorded the most votes, how bad the violence in Kansas was, when Kansas could amend its constitution, what the comparative number of schools and libraries were in the North and in the South, what the president's motives were, and what the teachings of the Bible were. Kansas was only the occasion for all this talk, the proverbial Pandora's box, the famous straw that compromised the dromedary.

Any pairing of speeches might as well illustrate the rhetorical chasm that divided equal and opposite defenses of versions of order, piety, and civilization in the Lecompton debate. But those of Senator Henry Wilson of Massachusetts and Representative Miles Taylor of Louisiana will do. Using very similar language, and seemingly similar assumptions, they came to diametrically opposed conclusions.

Wilson said the Republicans had nearly given up hope when the president delivered his annual message. "Hardly a ray of hope illumined our pathway. We heard the imperious voice of that gigantic power which sways the national Government, demanding the consummation of this crime against the people of Kansas. We saw the Chief Magistrate of the Republic holding in one hand honors and patronage to seduce and corrupt, and in the other power to smite down him who would not yield to his glittering blandishments." But, he continued, hope was strong that Lecompton, and with it the slave power and a corrupt executive, would be "consigned to that grave which knows no resurrection." Slavery perverted morality, and the Lecompton trickery proved it, all the way from Lecompton itself to Washington. "In this age, and in this land, where the lights of Christian civilization are flashing upon our pathway, that moral nature must be tainted, that heart must form false estimates of virtue and vice, and that reason must be perverted, before any citizen of America could be impelled to enact such crimes as have been enacted in Kansas, or uphold, defend, or apologize for them."[104]

Indeed, roared Taylor, civilization and Christian morality were threatened, but not by the Democrats or the administration, or Lecompton, but by the Black Republicans and the abolitionists. Kansas was a "mere incident" in a broader struggle. There was a conspiracy in the North to break the bonds of the Union by an "unhallowed enterprise" and an "unholy purpose." Wealth, which the North was gaining, was not everything. Look at the evils of industrial, free civilization worldwide! Not only would the North close the American West to slavery, he declared, but it would also open it to emigration from abroad, even from Asia. Christianity would be replaced in the West by Buddhism. The "ministers of the meek and lowly Jesus would give place to the bronzes, and to the varied tribes of ignorant and besotted priests, who bow down before the misshapen and monstrous images of their gods; and the civilization, refinement, and elevated philosophy of the white races of Europe and America who now people those shores, would be trodden out by the pagan barbarianism of the yellow races of Asia."[105]

Clearly, the early attempts of the moderates and of the administration lackeys to limit either the length or the focus of the debate had failed. The oratory soared through a firmament most wide, and so did editorial comment upon it. Buchanan had spoken of "delusion," but he had had no idea. Representative John Gilmer of North Carolina was expressing the weary depression of many people when he noted that the Kansas question had taken up the entire attention of Congress for a good part of four years. "We have been figuring about it until, I believe, not only the country but the Government itself is upon the verge of bankruptcy." It appeared, Gilmer said, that the prescription for relieving the pain of someone choking on a turnip was to get him to swallow a pumpkin.[106]

Senator Pugh, a Democrat from Ohio who supported Lecompton with provisos, had nearly the last words in the debate, and he pointed out the irony in the whole situation: The United States had risen from a few "feeble colonies" to become the "mightiest empire in the history of time." All the while, its constitutional government had protected and blessed it. Would that be sacrificed to a "Kansas game of foot-ball" every four years for partisan purposes? Would the interests of the rest of America be sacrificed to the "miserable disputes and quarrels" of those in Kansas who could not learn from experience? He hoped not.[107]

The atmosphere was so charged that it was almost visible to the reporters covering the night sessions of Congress. TYPHIA wrote to the *Charleston Mercury* on March 23 that the day before, the Senate had met from 10 AM until midnight. By eight in the morning the ladies' gallery was full, and by ten every space in the galleries and corridors was packed. Charles Stuart of Michigan had taken the floor, "a very unprepossessing man, with a mean, repulsive countenance, which, with his narrow, illiberal feelings, more befits him for a petty constable than a Senator." Then came James Bayard of Delaware. Douglas showed up and took his seat. The Senate recessed at four. "As soon as the galleries were cleared, the immense crowd that had been waiting outside, now rushed in, and a tremendous compression of hoops and crinoline, squeezing, pushing and crowding, took place, amid all sorts of ejaculations from the fair as well as the rougher sex." Every niche and recess in the windows was filled, as were the anteroom and vestibule of the Senate.

On reassembly at seven, William Gwin of California moved to admit the ladies to the floor, and the motion carried. Douglas spoke, apologizing for a weakness due to illness. Then Robert Toombs of Georgia replied, with a "withering, crushing speech."[108]

The next day the debate continued. Charles Sumner appeared, still limping from his beating, and for only the second time in the session, to vote against the Lecompton Constitution. Through the lens of the Southern observer he was described in less than neutral tones: "This masterdon of hypocrisy, cowardice and infamy, as he passed out of the Senate into the Rotunda, with his hang-dog look, excited the ridicule and contempt of the spectators, as they looked upon his gross, beefy carcass, which he would have his nigger-worshipping friends believe was still laboring under the affliction of great feebleness and debility." President Buchanan hosted a party that night, at which the chief executive appeared in high spirits and jovial, despite the challenges facing his Kansas program.[109]

Every day the national newspaper press covered and commented on these proceedings, and pundits maneuvered for position. The *New York Herald* analyzed the stakes early in an editorial entitled "The Impending Political Convulsion on the Slavery Question." For all the talk about popular sovereignty, the difficulty arose in two questions: What would the North lose by consenting to the admission of Kansas as a slave state, and what reparation could the South expect for the refusal to admit Kansas with its proslavery constitution? Yes, the paper noted, it was a moot point in a way. Kansas would soon change the Lecompton Constitution, even if admitted under it. But the rejection of Lecompton would be "a Congressional edict against the South of the most decisive character; for, from that moment the organic law of the South will be the law of submission—absolute submission—to the will of an overwhelming Northern majority." The law of the strong arm would supersede the old policy of fraternal obligation. Therefore, the South could not retreat on the Lecompton issue. "We have passed through many convulsions and revulsions, political and financial, during the last half century; but the sharp and salient point to which this Kansas squabble has been reduced threatens the most perilous of all our sectional agitations."[110]

There were many surprises. Governor Henry Wise of Virginia caused "astonishment and mortification" in the South and "exultation" in the North when he announced that he favored a vote in Kansas on the full Lecompton Constitution before Congress should accept it. The *Richmond Whig* chalked his statement up to ambition for the 1860 presidential nomination. "May heaven snatch the country from the deadly embrace of ambitious dema-gogues." The *New York Daily Times* thought Wise's announcement a "perfect bombshell."[111]

Similarly surprising were the strong statements of former Kansas gover-nor Robert Walker. In Hoboken, New Jersey, in March, Walker came out strongly against admitting Kansas with the Lecompton Constitution. "We are now in the midst of the battle," he said, "the bugle notes are sounding the advances of the approaching columns; the principles of our Revolutionary Fathers are now endangered. . . . No miserable quibbles . . . Shall we drag Kansas from the camp and prison-house of Lecompton, as a chained and collared convict, into the Union?" If that happened, he said, he feared "the whole fabric of popular liberty will tumble into ruins."[112] Former acting gov-ernor Frederick Stanton gave a similarly strong anti-Lecompton speech, completing the negative sweep of those who had seen the process of consti-tution making up close from an official perspective.[113]

There were four proposals for moving Lecompton along: Buchanan's, to admit Kansas directly under Lecompton; Douglas's, to have Congress inter-fere and call a new constitutional convention; Pugh's, to admit under Lecompton conditionally, with a new vote on the slavery clause; and Wise's, to send Lecompton back to Kansas for a full vote.[114] A number of observers distrusted everyone's motives. A writer at the *New Orleans Daily Delta* thought the time had come when people would say almost anything to get at-tention, and say it in the most irresponsible manner. "What cared the brawlers of the night, the hungry expectant of place and the subsidized or-gan-grinder, whether the laudation showered upon the men . . . elevated to power was a cunningly devised fable, or truth as invincible and immaculate as the principles of the divine Nazarene when he sat among his disciples upon the Mount? What matter it to a servile and venal press, whose liberties would be battered down, whose sacred rights invaded . . . so that the game of public plunder was played out to the last political trick?"[115] It was difficult, said a New York sheet, to "light the way through the labyrinth" when "agita-tion, wrath, vengeance and war are the order of the day on both sides." If a hundred or so of the "leading vagabonds" on each side with Kansas as their stock in trade were killed off, the paper felt, it would be a good thing for the moral health of the state.[116]

The coalitions on Lecompton were uncertain and shifting. Of fifty Demo-cratic newspapers in the West, the *Columbus Daily Ohio Statesman* claimed that only six supported the straight passage of the Lecompton Constitution.[117] "We do not know how to reason with a man who is in favor of forcing the Lecompton Constitution upon Kansas," wrote the Democratic *Detroit Daily Free Press.* "The proposition is the most extraordinary ever made since the adoption of the Federal Constitution. . . . All our honest impulses revolt against it. . . . It promises good to nobody, but injury to everybody." Kansas would not in the end be a slave state. The South would dishonor itself by trying to force that result, and the Democratic Party would become as sectional as the Republican.[118]

The *Charleston Mercury* turned on John Calhoun. Calhoun went to Washington with election results certifying that the Free State Party had won in October 1857 and again in January 1858. Perhaps, the *Mercury* suggested, in the "reeking atmosphere" of Washington, Calhoun had become an abolitionist.[119] Calhoun's new behavior did not, however, change the opinion of the *Chicago Daily Tribune,* which called him a "rotten" figure: "Were not his pimpled and burnished hide tanned with the whiskey that he has for years been pouring down his open gullet, he would fall to pieces on the street."[120] Southern papers also attacked John Crittenden of Kentucky for proposing a compromise that passed the House. That action gave comfort to the enemy, a Georgia newspaper wrote, and showed that not everyone who wore a hood was a monk.[121]

Much of the reporting illustrated a sad spectacle. The only reason for the administration's forcing acceptance of the Lecompton Constitution, thought the *New York Daily Times,* was the "eagerness of disgust" to get rid of the Kansas issue.[122] What passed for argument in Congress, the *Times* thought, was nothing more than "stereotyped casuistry."[123] Other than a few "personal scrimmages," the proceedings were dull. The members were speaking not to the issue but to the public "in forms to be printed at the public expense. They are making essays and pamphlets and books, not speeches."[124] Exhausted by "perpetual meetings, and with the ceaseless clamor of journalists and politicians, the public mind . . . now finds the very name of Kansas insupportable."[125]

The *New York Herald* expressed the opinion that no American could read the congressional proceedings on Lecompton "without a thrill of indignation and shame." It was hard to find a parallel for it in the "lowest groggery, in the vilest hell which is to be met with in our metropolitan news." What was one to think, it asked, of people who carried into the councils of the nation "the habits of the bully and prize fighter"? If leaders conducted themselves like savages, and Congress was reduced to a gladiatorial arena, the nation should expect to pay the penalty.[126] Reading the debates in Washington, the *Herald* editor wrote, "one is more and more startled by the marked inappropriateness of the speeches made on the question at issue, and alarmed by the tendency of the school of oratory of which they must be regarded as symptoms." One might expect a cool, businesslike, statistical debate that at least stuck to the subject of Kansas. But there was no such thing. The debate was about section and slavery and philosophy and law, with many of the speakers taking "no more notice of Kansas than of Canada." And the speeches were all vituperation and spite and playing for effect. "And what good can come of those loose, idle diatribes against this or that section of the country by the people of either?"[127] The country was going to ruin, the paper said, and the masses "have become sick and disgusted with this senseless Kansas fuss, froth and fury among the politicians."[128]

The *Washington Union*, which supported the president and the Lecompton Constitution, had to agree about the dreariness and lack of focus of the debate. Late in March, it was appalled to report that there were yet forty speeches to be made in the House alone on the subject of Kansas. They were limited to one hour by the House rules, but would be "harangues." Forty hours of such speeches was "worse than forty years in the desert, or forty days of fasting in Lent, or the horrors endured by the forty thieves in their forty jars when the oil was poured upon their frying bodies and souls." An hour of Milton or Homer might be unpleasant enough, "but an hour of Smith, or Jones . . . bored into you in the middle of the day, in business hours, is murder by inches." These speeches went forth to an enervated or even sleeping audience and then found "a fitting receptacle in that mausoleum of prose, the *Congressional Globe*." Sometimes the speakers had their talks ghostwritten. "Thus are our modern orators manufactured—by the hour rule and by the official reporter. It is one of the most splendid triumphs of modern machinery—that clever orators may be made even out of downright blockheads." Like so much else about Lecompton, it said, the speeches themselves were shams.[129]

Other Southern papers were not kind either. Washington and Franklin, according to the editor at the *New Orleans Daily Delta*, seldom spoke more than fifteen minutes, and Patrick Henry never unless he had something to say. Not so with the Lecompton debate, which illustrated "the prevailing mania of Congress." Every member considered that he had the ear of the country, and he "fires away as if he were an especial representative of the present generation, and the dimly seen but inevitable posterity. Wrapped in

the impenetrable mail of egotism—and egotism, too often resting upon sublime mediocrity—the self-satisfied possessor of this ridiculous quality
imagines that the peace and permanency of the Union depend upon the utterance of his badly digested views." The session was prolonged, the treasury
was taxed. "The practical affairs of the country are lost in the whirlpool of
Congressional speech-making."[130]

There was disgust enough, too, in the hinterlands. The *Daily Cincinnati
Commercial* expressed disappointment about its representatives, as they
groveled and waited to be begged to join shifting alliances on the Lecompton
bill. "From what we know of the characters of the men, we certainly never
looked for anything like shining wisdom, consummate statesmanship, high
courage, or strong humanity in their conduct." Even so, their behavior was
now disappointing. "Destitute of knowledge of politics as the science of human conduct, ignorant of men, and wanting in that peculiar talent known as
political sagacity, they belong to that order of persons who, the moment they
step out of the sphere for which they were designed, and to which they are
accustomed, become incapable of self guidance, and grasp instinctively at
whatever of power and organization there is, upon which to throw a responsibility that alone they feel themselves unable to endure." The editor could
only comment on the "inconsistent and unstable course" of the Ohio representatives and on their "Protean rascality."[131]

That Congress was doing nothing was disturbing in the extreme. War had
broken out again in Kansas. Charles Robinson circulated a letter to the press
stating that although the free-state faction thought that some version of the
Lecompton Constitution would pass, they would not stand for its ever being
implemented in Kansas. Their enemies underestimated them, he said.
"They doubtless think that wearied out, poor and oppressed as we are, we
shall submit, or if not, that we can be crushed like a worm. I need not tell you
that we shall not submit. If we did, we should deserve to be yoked with the
negro slaves that they seek to impose upon us, and driven forth in chains
from the glorious land that we were too base and too cowardly to defend. . . .
I know that the people are religiously resolved upon resistance."[132]

And so came the amendments, the speeches, and the votes, one by one,
hour by hour, day by day. The House, on April Fools' Day, passed the
Lecompton Constitution measure with what was called the Crittenden/
Montgomery Amendment, providing for a resubmission election and a new
constitutional convention if Kansas voted it down. The *Washington Union*
called the measure "a Pandora's box full of the caged elements of explosion

and strife."[133] The *New Orleans Daily Delta* thought it was "a frightful enormity . . . without a precedent, and without a parallel."[134] The Senate rejected the amended measure, preferring to back Lecompton in its straight and original form. The House would not agree to the Senate version. The whole issue, therefore, by a tie vote of 108–108 in the House, broken by the speaker's vote, went to a Conference Committee, where there was a last chance to make some extraordinary salvage deal. That deal became the infamous English Compromise.[135]

As proposal after proposal fell, and as the rhetoric in Congress and the press escalated, there was more talk about the instability of the Union. "Those of us who have been in the habit of regarding the American Union as a tolerably substantial reality," went an article in the *New York Daily Times*, "founded upon the good sense, the justice, the patriotism, and the common interest of the States which compose it, have something left to learn."[136] There would doubtless be, said the *Charleston Mercury*, great efforts "by shuffling and evasion, to patch up a hollow truce between the sections." But the hour was late.[137]

There was a sense of perplexed and anxious confusion. A writer in New Orleans commented that whatever light there had been in the Lecompton measure had flickered out, "leaving the battlefield as dark as Egypt, as disordered as Chaos, and as sweltering with death and putrefaction as Gehenna."[138] The *Washington Union* used a different image: The car was off the track; the train had been delayed. "Nobody has been benefited; our engineers and brakemen were unfaithful."[139] The result was none the worse for being a kind of accident resulting from ignorance. Leaders in press and politics were simply out of their league. What was needed, said the *New Orleans Daily Delta*, and what was not achieved, was the doing of something that was not worse than nothing.[140] "In the affairs of government," said the *Charleston Mercury*, "weakness or ignorance is often worse than crime. One-half the evils of life are unintentional."[141]

The Lecompton debate was at the same time the climax and the anticlimax of the Kansas affair. In some ways it seemed repetitive. Most of the issues, most of the arguments, had already been raised in 1854 during the great Kansas-Nebraska spectacle. But the tone was entirely different, reflecting as it did a long and tiring struggle that had made a mockery of the promise of popular sovereignty and had moved the nation further away than ever from a peaceful resolution of the question of the expansion of slavery into the territories. Many people were bored, and those that were not bored were frightened. Such solutions as were proposed were characterized by enormous cynicism, clothed in the garb of "practicality" or "expedience." Unbelievably, in the middle of the nineteenth century, there were people in positions of leadership who said that truth no longer mattered at all and that the American attempt to make themselves and the world better had best come to an end. Why, they asked, not accept the status quo? Why not recognize the de facto situation, whatever it was, and move toward the possible rather than the even minimally desirable? Who, after all, could muster up concern for the condition of black slaves, when doing anything about it had turned out to be so much trouble? Best let the ravaged economy recover, and leave all that alone, they concluded.

Politics had become vicious because everything was reduced to politics—to the mathematics of the exercise of raw power. There was no good will or consensus or understanding behind it, no assurance that a minority's rights would be respected or that past agreements or understandings within government would be honored when a new majority might appear after an election. The election of an Abraham Lincoln, or his Whig equivalent, might not have been the occasion for the splitting of the Union in 1850. It was in 1860. What had intervened? Notably and prominently, the Kansas debate.

Yet there were idealists remaining, ensuring that such a solution would not sit well for long. The contrast between the historian George Bancroft and President Buchanan is instructive. Buchanan was saying that the Kansas issue was trivial, a series of legal technicalities, which politicians, particularly with patronage at their backs, should be able to take care of without much fuss. It was a disastrous error, leaving his presidency disrespected then and by later history. More insightful, and with a longer view, was Bancroft. Yes, he said, freedom was frustrating. Parliamentary procedure could be messy and boring. But it was at base a seeking after justice, equal justice for all, through debate, however amateur, among the representatives of the population of a republic. "A small wrong," he emphasized, contained "the seeds of all evil." There was a point in the career of practicality and compromise, in the art of the possible, where everything that might be desirable was lost. The Lecompton controversy was reaching very close to that point.

CONCLUSION: THE FIRES GO OUT

———————

Early in 1858, as the Lecompton Constitution was arriving at Congress for debate, the *Leviathan*, the largest steamship yet built, was finally, after enormous effort and innovation, dragged sideways into the Thames and set afloat. The ship was the project of an engineering genius named Isambard Kingdom Brunel, who had irretrievably damaged his health building it and died soon after it was launched. It was 700 feet long, 89 feet broad, and 60 feet tall. It cost over 250,000 pounds sterling and could carry 5,000 passengers and 17,500 tons of cargo at twenty miles per hour across the Atlantic. The writers at the *New Orleans Daily Delta* were impressed and encouraged. "The mammoth steamer—perhaps the most stupendous combination of skill, enterprise and capital of an age replete with wonders—is at last afloat on the element over which it is destined to reign supreme until eclipsed by some more daring conception of scientific and constructive genius." The floating palace, the paper thought, would travel on the wings of the wind and aid the South by carrying bulky freight at reduced prices straight to Southern deepwater ports, which were among the few capable of handling it. "Our commercial bondage and our political subjugation will ever go hand in hand," the *Delta* opined. "Unless we can destroy by direct trade, or by severing political bonds, the moneyed monopoly seated at New York, which remorselessly exacts from us like Shylock its 'pound of flesh,' the South now bound hand and foot, will gradually sink into such abject servility and degradation as we never witness even in the most despotic countries."[1] While the ship project, according to the *Daily Richmond Enquirer*, "bewilders the mind," it just might work.[2]

In the end, the *Leviathan* turned out not to be the South's savior. Renamed *Great Eastern*, the ship had the distinction of helping lay the Atlantic cable, but it was never profitable for its various owners and was never fully employed in the tasks that its original owners and builders had imagined for it. The cost overruns in its construction, launching, and operation were extreme. Its promoters staked everything on it, they pursued it with determination and intelligence, and it ruined them.[3]

The Kansas issue seemed analogous to the building of that great ship. "Kansas, like the *Leviathan*," wrote the *Richmond South* early in 1858, "has approached her future element by slow and painful process. The political machinery relied on to put her afloat has proved insufficient, and she has repeatedly been on the eve of settling down in the mud, as a monument of futile endeavor or mistaken calculation. At last, the welcome cry 'She moves!' is heard, and she gradually floats into the halls of legislation."[4] The Kansas matter, wrote the *Washington Union* two months later, "moves more slowly than did the great *Leviathan* before she was launched. The Atlantic Telegraph gets along as bravely. It is a slow coach, foundering in the mud, hub-deep. It is a long land, however, that has no turn; and we live in hopeful expectation. Israel in the wilderness at last found a fortuitous way into Canaan."[5] But, like *Leviathan*, the Kansas solution would prove unwieldy, a cobbled-together design, enormous and impressive but ultimately unsuited to the purpose at hand.

The form in which the Lecompton Constitution came out of Congress, the so-called English Compromise, seemed to many the ultimate hulking cobbled-together *Leviathan*, as difficult to float well as to launch at all. More than one historian has characterized Buchanan's backing of this device and of the Lecompton Constitution itself as the ultimate blunder of the blundering generation, and "the most important single decision of the 1850s."[6] Wrote Buchanan's biographer Jean Baker: "The explanation of why Buchanan failed so miserably remains a worthwhile historical consideration."[7]

The English Compromise was a perfect example of what contemporary slang would have called a "pettifogging device." As was true of the "popular sovereignty" language of the Kansas-Nebraska Act, it was framed in such a way as to be capable of deceiving all who wished to be deceived and none who did not. But unlike the Kansas-Nebraska Act, it made no pretension of high purpose. "Lecompton, Jr." as one paper jokingly called the English Compromise, was the "down and dirty" politics of accommodation from stem to stern.[8]

The bill had several obvious flaws in the area of straightforwardness. Only the schedule for granting lands in connection with the Lecompton Constitution was to be submitted for a vote in Kansas. The land grant was not unusual, but some people saw it, and the promise of immediate public offices, as a bribe. Such an evasive vote was unusual, and it was widely considered deceitful. If Kansas accepted the schedule, and therefore by implication the constitution, Congress would admit it as a state right away. Otherwise, it had to await a growth in population. William English's bill was modified from day to day so that the ark might contain all the diverse political wildlife that needed to travel in it.[9]

The press was not pleased, regardless of section and party. "This bill is a complete evasion of the issue," wrote the *Louisville Daily Journal.* "It is a cunningly devised amalgam of bribery and menace to produce the . . . acceptance of the Lecompton Constitution by the people of Kansas in order to give the Lecompton party in Congress an empty victory, or at least to save them from the mortification of an unqualified defeat."[10] It was, wrote the *Chicago Daily Tribune,* a showing of the "cloven foot" that had been there all along.[11] A Cincinnati headline called it "Another Twist of the Kansas Snarl."[12]

If anyone doubted the degeneracy of national politics, wrote editor Samuel Bowles in Springfield, let him look at English's Kansas bill. "It is a mere trick, and not a very cute one at that."[13] The *New York Daily Times* referred to it as a "sneaking, undignified, and disgraceful specimen of the worst kind of legislative legerdemain." The bill was the kind of thing one would expect from politicians who conducted their business on principles "which are despised on the race-course."[14] The *New York Daily Tribune* noticed that a topic under much discussion was whether "the pea Submission really is or is not under the English thimble." The *Tribune* thought the bill would bring about the virtual submission of the Lecompton Constitution, "though in a blind, confused, juggling, equivocal fashion."[15] It seemed a sort of Sphinx, asking unanswerable riddles and threatening doom.[16] It mystified its friends as much as it did its enemies.[17] It was, said a writer in Dayton, "the last act of the tedious Kansas drama."[18]

Nevertheless, some people thought the vote in Kansas on this proposition might be favorable. The territory was poor, and its leaders were eager for office. They were more certain than before that the elections there were fair and that therefore the free-state faction could maintain control of any state legislature. And the English package might be better than continued uncertainty. "Let us not blame them too severely," said a writer in Hartford, "if they should choose the alternative so artfully presented them."[19] It did offer a certain release of tension. Wrote the *New York Daily Times:* "The country can breathe again."[20]

That last was a common sentiment. The Kansas issue had been for four years an excitement, but also a fear. There were few who would not be relieved to have it disappear into the background, whether well resolved or merely festering more quietly. "What is Kansas that she should have caused all this turmoil and confusion throughout the land for the past four years," wrote the *Columbus (Ga.) Times & Sentinel Tri-Weekly*. It was time, the paper said, to act not like visionary fanatics, but like practical men. "Let well enough alone, and leave the solution of this matter to time and Providence."[21]

It was true that after the passage of the English Compromise, the national press coverage of Kansas, which had been increasing since 1854, dropped off precipitously, surprisingly, noticeably. There was some "little breeze of excitement" over the guerrilla troubles around Fort Scott and about the Marais des Cygnes massacre of a group of free-state settlers there, and some coverage of the murder trial of James Lane for killing a fellow free-state settler over the use of a well.[22] But it was nothing compared with that of the summer of 1856.

Press opinion was that the "Kansas bubble has burst."[23] "Who talks about Kansas now?" asked a writer in Detroit in July. "Whose sleep is disturbed by visions of bleeding, mangled freedmen there? What has become of BEECHER? . . . Why is GREELEY dumb?—Where are the Kansas aid societies and the Kansas State and national committees?"[24]

The great drama was over. The *Washington Union* ran an editorial called "The Fires Going Out," saying, "Perhaps the minds of people having been whetted to the point of constant alarm and expectation, find the events of real life in Kansas, as they actually transpire, too uninteresting and stolid for their morbid appetites. . . . Kansas, like a poor play, well advertised and shockingly performed, is cursed by nine-tenths of the community, and voted a *bore*. Of course, everybody knew, who had sense enough to comprehend the distinction between real and representative life, that it would be so."[25]

There was one more election, anticlimactic in the extreme. Kansans on August 2, 1858, overwhelmingly rejected the English schedule and therefore, by implication, the Lecompton Constitution. They then began their long wait, lasting until 1861, for statehood by some more regular process. During that period the nation was more interested in the Atlantic telegraph, the Lincoln-Douglas debates, or, if Kansas had to be mentioned at all, the gold rush on its western boundary. Went a lonely Kansas editorial in October: "No political movements outside her own borders can materially affect her future condition. . . . As a political issue, therefore, the Kansas question belongs to the past. In its nature it was temporary. Time and events have settled it."[26]

In the immediate sense of being a media obsession, it was true that Kansas was over in the summer of 1858. But the issues it had raised would not stay down. The failure to "solve" the Kansas issue in a meaningful way was diagnostic of a national political failure. With the Kansas debate, the newspaper readership of the country got a front-row seat into the smoke-filled back rooms of American republican machinery, and the performance they saw was not impressive. There was too much emotion, too much ambition, too little tolerance and moderation. "We are too much inclined," wrote a New Orleans journalist, "to think it our right and duty to cudgel all the world out of its own garments to put on a uniform of our making. And all this is contrary to the complex but beautiful idea at the bottom of the confederation of sovereign states, that is, diversity in unity."[27] It seemed that freedom and democracy, however well they sounded, did not work of themselves and were not even so easily talked about without violent misunderstanding among people whose fundamental cultures differed.

Michael Davis, in ruminating recently on the benefits of liberal education, has noted that a difficulty with democracy is that the majority must respect the minority, and vice versa. "And this means that you are not to take your principles—your god—too seriously. You must separate the holy from the just, for if you do not, the resulting unbending adherence to the holy will ultimately lead to civil war."[28] That concept was emotionally distant from the writers and readers of the American 1850s. To them, the principle or absolute truth was fundamental.

The spawn of Kansas was deep cynicism and profound disaffection, often expressed with a black, sardonic humor. The political remnants left over after Kansas, a writer at the *Washington Union* said in 1858, must be sold. "They are out of size and out of pattern—out of favor and out of fashion. . . . Nobody thinks of preserving them. They are used for patchwork, to eke out an old dress and give it the appearance of a new one." National politics, the writer went on, was made of materials "left over after half a dozen auction sales and as many private bargains, that carried off nearly all that was available." All that remained were some implements for the manufacture of burglar's tools.[29]

Newspapers and magazines in the South wrote of hopelessness as Kansas faded from the headlines, as though the debate over Kansas had been the last chance for the American confederation as that section saw it. Now the South was at the mercy of its enemies, huge as they were in numbers and in industrial might. The Kansas debate was a forewarning of what the North intended for the South, namely, that its dreams of territorial expansion should be thwarted not only in the American West and Southwest but in the Caribbean and Central America, too. Slavery would be contained and soon eliminated by a North "insolent in its strength," and with the bland certainty it had shown in the Kansas controversy. The Panic of 1857 was only a temporary setback for the rise of manufacturing over the trade on which the South depended. The next president of the United States was likely to be a Black Republican, thus denying the executive office to the South, which had already lost legislative power.

And what of good will? Southerners had observed how that worked. "We are hugging a most allusive hope to our bosom, if we imagine that we are secure a moment longer than the abolitionists have the power to ruin us."[30] The rejection of the Lecompton Constitution might not be itself a cause for the final disruption of the Union. But it was an occasion for thinking seriously about it.[31]

The North, looking to the future, could see nothing more cheerful. "That gulf is full of darkness and theatenings," said a writer for the *New York Christian Inquirer,* "its lips are red with blood; and into its hateful jaws we see the industry, the education, the domestic comfort, the philanthropy and religion of the nation from either side, rushing down to bottomless destruction."[32] A. C. Monk, a representative in the Massachusetts legislature, in a debate there over the Kansas issue in 1857, said, "I am ready to stake the issue in Kansas; let us do what we can to save her to freedom; and if she is lost, let Massachusetts call home her Representatives from the Congress of the nation, and save herself from the black pall of slavery that is now spreading darkness over the whole land."[33]

There were only two sources of hope: God, who seemed especially distant, and public opinion, which seemed remarkably corrupt. This book has been about the latter. To enlighten the public mind, wrote a New Hampshire man, "would be regarded as beyond the province of those who move in the humbler walks of life, whose business is to guide the plow, or swing the hammer, but we hold that it is the mass, the common people, who check the wrong and enforce the right, who interpose the 'sober second thought,' who give tone, character, and destiny to a nation or a people."[34] These ploughmen and carpenters were reading newspapers, and the newspapers were filled with epithets, stereotypes, and invective. They were influenced by penny papers and pulp pamphlets. And they derived from these their views concerning not only what the answers were, but also what the questions were.

The manufacturing of opinion was key: to the understanding of the Kansas-Nebraska Act, to voting, to the impression of martyrs, to the reputation of governors, to the image of the Union, to the impact of religion, and to the fate of the Lecompton Constitution. These were all realities, but they were also constructions. The true events were far less vivid and compelling, and also less emotional and polarizing, than the media-filtered version. Reality was more complex, more ambiguous, more amendable to the scholar in his study than was the Manichaean morality play that appeared before the newspaper reader. Had a more nuanced version prevailed somehow, the reaction to the "enemy" might have been closer to pity than anger. Like Dr. Frankenstein, the popular press created a creature out of actual body parts, and like Dr. Frankenstein's, the result was not a real man but, rather, a monster, a similitude built of false pride and distorted dreams.

The net result was a kind of protective ennui. George Steiner, in his masterful account of the nature of culture, *In Bluebeard's Castle*, wrote that boredom was a symptom of romanticism as well as of modernism and that the pressures and ambiguities of modern life could lead, in the romantic soul, to a death wish, a "nostalgia for disaster." The outlet was in violence, in an escape from freedom and civilization and their discontents back to the simple and primitive calculus of violence and force. Romantics were utopians, Steiner wrote, hoping for "faery lands forlorn" and feeling impotent "in the face of political reaction and philistine rule." They therefore had a "hunger for new shapes, new possibilities of nervous discovery, to set against the morose proprieties of bourgeois and Victorian modes." Romantic ideals and the "cultivation of the pathological" could, people thought, "restore personal existence to a full pitch of reality, and somehow negate the gray world of middle-class fact."[35] Whatever else it was, the Civil War was sensational. It replaced with slaughter and flags some mighty tedious talk, the tiring panoply of words, words, words.

Many people recognized what was happening and hoped for something better. Commenting on Kansas, a writer in Albany in 1855 said, "It will be well for the public mind, and, indeed, for the public morals, if something more of sense and less of spirit can be introduced into our public discussions. We want a good fight, not for feeling but for facts. The great question of the day requires solemn discussion. . . . Between the fanaticism, which bellows for bread and butter, and the solemnity, which pulls a long face for the same farinaceous and lubricious purpose, we see little to choose. Both are a holy sham, to which people are continually selling themselves. Certainly the South would have accomplished more long ago, if the action had but kept pace with its prattle. Certainly, the North will never recover the rights which it has lost until with the coolness of a public notary, it shall make its demand, and then protesting in form against the swindle, go to the Courts and to Congress for redress."[36]

Instead, there was "sensation." That led, the *London Times* concluded, to "the uncontrolled supremacy of mere will, and the indisposition to submit it to law and order," which it saw as typical of the United States in the 1850s. Rather than appealing to compromise and conciliation, parties framed issues as battles to be won or lost in blood. They were, said the *Times*, thus sharpening a sword for civil strife, "careless of the serious injury they are doing to the interests and reputation of their country."[37] American politics was like the boiling vortex between Scylla and Charybdis, with the air on all sides "rent with screams and howls, and strange, uncouth names."[38]

There were dissenting voices in this storm, but they did not prevail. Perhaps, thought some 1850s journalists, Americans should study history more deeply. At least it could provide a longer horizon. "Whatever diverts the attention of our town populations from the engrossing pursuit of wealth, or the agitation of petty contests or the ignoble bickerings of sectarianism, to the exercise of study and reflection, is so much gained to their moral health and dignity. And no study is so well calculated to raise their thoughts and improve their civil condition as that of history." Citizens of a free country could not afford to ignore the recorded teachings of past times. "Thoughtful and reflective, and apt to turn meditation to a practical end, they are not likely to be seduced by false lights, or to be lost in the maze of false inductions." History could bring amusement and instruction more lasting than the "excitement of trashy fiction or rabid local politics." History was no perfect science, but it could teach lessons "traced in strong and living" and, above all, *real* characters in time.[39]

Men were much the same now as ever, wrote a newspaperman in Boston. Modern progress in steam technology did not apply to human behavior. The writer quoted a memorial of certain Baptists to Charles II, written in 1657: "Time, the great discoverer of all things, has at length unmasked the disguised designs of this mysterious age, and made that obvious to the dull sense of fools, which was before visible enough to the quick-witted prudence of wise men—that *liberty, religion and reformation,* the wanted engines of politicians, are but deceitful baits, by which the easily-deluded multitude are tempted to a greedy pursuit of their own ruin."[40]

Did anyone study the rhetoric seriously, asked a Charleston newspaper writer in 1856? And was anything more important? Language, the writer said, was in a period of rapid change in the 1850s. "Like the shifting sands of the desert waste, it has moved, and assumes new phrases and forms, with the breath of every wind." People should study its vocabulary, its "jingling echoes and clap-trap rejoinders," for the serious impact they had. The public was responsible for the impact it had in that the public was not educating itself to see through deceptions and to know when someone was talking nonsense.[41]

Thought, the *Daily Richmond Enquirer* claimed, was being centralized as much as were commerce, publishing, and manufacturing. The control of that thought was primarily coming from the newspaper empires and the propaganda machine of the North. Thought, like fashion, was manufactured and marketed. Opinions came and went, but they caused damage before they were gone. Nothing, said the Richmond writer, was safe from these "absorbing maelstroms" of public opinion, which begat imitations and clamped down a single, repeated, and too-simple set of ideas.[42]

The moderates pleaded not for surrender of principle but for moderation in discussion, for a decent respect for law and order, and for an appreciation for the dangers of edged tools. There were efforts, wrote the *Washington Union,* to educate the public mind in a dangerous independence. It had been the duty of moralists to "teach men to keep their plighted faith," but now the public mind was "filled with sophisms," which might lead it to "stab the fair form of constitutional freedom in the 'house of its friends.'" What, the *Union* asked, were obligations compared with passion; what was law compared with charisma? Was not every man a law into himself? Who worried any longer about "bad faith"?[43]

Yes, surely, Southern pleas for moderation were at that moment in the middle 1850s part of the defense of slavery. But there was a broader application. And the North was not insensitive to the same concerns. What, asked a newspaperman in Philadelphia in 1857, had been learned in the preceding ten years? Money had been lavished on "brown-stone houses, marble banks, granite blocks, and churches frescoed and carved." But the development of the inner man had lagged behind the increase in railway mileage. The art of "intelligent intercourse" was much neglected.[44] There was indeed a discipline to democracy, and it was being neglected.

I found three major surprises at the interpretive level in the research for this book. The first was the extraordinary volume of journalism directed at Kansas in the period 1854–1858. There was a tendency to channel various and complex public concerns into a single and highly symbolic issue and then to concentrate on that single issue to such an extent that it risked being run into the ground. A second surprise was the extraordinary variety in the mix of positions the newspapers took even within sections or parties. These positions were driven by the interaction among events and the sensibilities of editors and audiences. And they showed the most flexibility at the extremes. Northern free-soil newspapers criticized the New England Emigrant Aid Company and the Topeka Constitution, and prominent newspapers in the South criticized the pushing of the Lecompton Constitution through without a further vote of the people. The third revelation was the extent of moderate thought. There was evidence of an evolution of thought, evidence that positions were not so ideologically fixed or predetermined as to be not amenable to change. Amid the hype and hyperbole, the stereotyping and the propaganda, there was a good deal of thoughtful, well-expressed journalism that showed deep awareness of the nature and dangers of manipulation by words. Editors with this moderate approach appeared in all parties and in all sections, and their comments were as insightful as any analysis by a modern communications scholar. By contrast to the image of struggle among extremes that one gets through the traditional approach to Bleeding Kansas—comparing the editorials in the *Herald of Freedom* and the *Squatter Sovereign*, both Kansas party sheets of questionable quality—the scenario that emerges from a broader reading of the national press is both more subtle and more hopeful. Neither newspaper writers nor their readers were universally vapid, ignorant, or silly. The daily newspapers contained not only decent intellectual content but vivid imagery of real literary worth. A criticism of what was said and how it was said must ultimately be a value judgment about selection and impact, not about style. Who, reading the editorials written in the midst of a titanic struggle of unknown issue, can fail to be moved? Who, regarding the prose as dangerous or irresponsible, can regard it as simply silly? This gives the story of the failure to resolve national differences peaceably an aura of tragedy rather than of farce.

The more moderate interpretations did not compete well in currency or mass quotability. It is a current popular myth that nineteenth-century newspapers, being pre-Watergate and therefore supposedly in an innocent time before investigative reporting, were boosters and cheerleaders for party, section, or nation. News-gathering was more primitive, indeed. But then, as now, it was tempting, even mandatory, to pillory public figures, to muckrake after scandal, and to denigrate the workings of public institutions from a snide "behind the scenes" perspective. Such activity often went beyond responsible criticism and into circulation-building invective. It was, as Southern editors loved to notice, an abuse of the freedom so valued by the press. Centralization of media in urban centers was already strongly present. The pull of "isms" was at work, the faddish manias with their vocabulary of cant and chant and the concentration on the personal and self-centered, so familiar to the twenty-first century. There was, too, the ubiquitous, persistent nature of the Kansas news. "Let a man only tell his story every morning and evening," wrote Edmund Burke, "and at the end of twelvemonth he will become your master."[45]

One point, made early, should be reemphasized. This study may well be useful in documenting the impact of national press exchanges in the coming of the Civil War. It offers insights on the nature of the voting franchise, on the role of religion, on the vagaries of leadership, on race, on the role of law, on the proper balance of freedom and authority in a republic, on legitimate bases for revolution or "holy war," on the definition of treason, and even on the way issues are treated generally in many times and places by a free press in a democracy. However, its narrowest purpose is its most important contribution. That is, the deepest significance here is in increased understanding of how the nation dealt with the issue of the admission of Kansas, a topic of great importance all by itself. It should be clear to the reader of this book that Kansas was not only a national issue but, for a period of four years, *the* national issue. If there was one last chance to avoid civil war, and the great majority of Americans in the middle 1850s thought there was, working things out in Kansas was it.

Did publicists and the manipulators of opinion really believe the propaganda they were creating? Did their readers actually swallow it whole?

The evidence here strongly indicates that many looked askance at more radical statements, characterizing them as fanaticism and suggesting that those views were promulgated by people who took themselves and their influence all too seriously. There was a deep cynicism, even among newspaper editors ostensibly playing the game themselves, about political leaders and initiatives of all stripes and about the impartiality of any report, investigation, or debate in which opinions came down so predictably along lines of party or economic interest.

However, there was a strong countervailing trend toward acceptance, even gullibility. It should have been obvious that newspapers were businesses, and businesses whose fortunes were often closely tied to the direction and strength of the political wind. Untruths and distortions sold as many papers, usually more, than did sober analysis. However, editors loved to pretend that they had a higher calling than mere industrialists, preachers, or party hacks, and that they were not really in it for the money. They cultivated an impression of themselves as hardheaded, practical, and unsentimental, but not money-grubbing or venal. In their own minds, they were disinterested seekers of the truth and instruments of effective democracy in leading and reflecting public opinion responsibly.

They were, they thought, the right people for the job. The take on scholars and ministers from the business rooms of the daily newspaper was bemused. The *Boston Post* thought George Curtis's "Duty of the American Scholar" an "ingenious but pretentious prelude to a regular freesoil speech upon Kansas and slavery." The speech itself was a clear statement of noble principles, the newspaper writer thought, "cunningly applied to matters and things with which they have no real concern." Curtis's work was on "Liberty" in the abstract, and according to the lights of the author, "The whole is an exaggerated and illogical production, eloquently written. With a flourish about Leonidas and his three hundred, Kansas is grandiloquently termed the American Thermopylae."

There was no problem talking about slavery in a general way. No doubt it was an evil. But the real question, the typical editor thought, was the application of what Kansas editor William Allen White later called "practical idealism." It was a question of "how to treat the matter at present" without destroying the basis of self-government in the United States. It was a matter of being practical without drifting into relativism; of being judiciously hopeful without being maudlin, sickly, or just plain irrelevant; of taking into account the complexities of the affairs of humanity without becoming paralyzed by the contemplation of them. "For an experienced and eloquent man it is much easier to pen an elegantly written discourse, based on one idea, and running that idea into the ground, than to produce an essay which shall be full of rounded and complete wisdom, shall be large and liberal in its views, shall have regard for the facts of human nature and the various interests, probabilities, and possibilities of the subject under discussion." To write a responsible editorial, urging reasonable action on a complex issue, was much harder than to learn Greek and Latin and "to write amusing books and flippant lectures." Curtis was, the writer thought, "a fluent and learned quack, believing, probably, in his own nostrums, but not the less to be shunned on that account."[46]

So, for all their protests about fanaticism, editors were in danger of losing proper perspective upon themselves and invoking the no-compromise higher law right along with the abolitionists and fire-eaters. Yes, they came to believe much of their own rhetoric, and to act on it along with a tide of others. And, as much scholarship has shown, there was more than a grain of truth in much of what they believed. It was a patchwork pattern of irresponsible application, but it was made of real cloth. And the alternative to committing to action, to purposive behavior based upon some species of simplification and aimed at reform and improvement, was something most nineteenth-century Americans were not prepared to contemplate.

The idealism present in every nuance of public opinion and every kind of propaganda on the Kansas issue is easy to criticize as simple-minded, or even to excoriate as "bungling." In retrospect, though, however tragic the form of the debate was for the stability of the Union in the short term, it was not an unattractive characteristic for the long term. G. K. Chesterton noted that most progress comes from what some would call naive hayseeds rather than from the cynical and wordly-wise, who know that worthwhile change is impossible and that the status quo is forever. The editors and readers of the 1850s rejected the nihilism, the sad pragmatism of the Kansas English Compromise. They would rather fight for their manufactured truths, believing that there was some real truth incorporated therein, than acquiesce to the future that giving up on absolutes portended. And therefore they did remain true believers and optimists, trusting that individual life and society could be improved and would be improved on their own ground, however much activists disagreed about the what and the how of it. Americans had been and remained people of action, who were willing to make commitments and decisions under conditions of great uncertainty. Newspaper reading helped them consider. It was no game, leading as it ultimately did to action for which each individual was responsible, perhaps even to death.

Editors often claimed that the public had been "trained" and that the evil in a sense grew by what it fed on. Indeed, there was a complex dance, a drama involving a back-and-forth interaction between communicators and audiences. The cold confidence with which the public eventually greeted the war evolved in an endless loop: The public responded to its own reflection, distorted by ever-so-tiny steps, and that response was fed back to it for further response, so that it was unclear sometimes who was the manipulator and who the manipulated. The image, so often used in the press of the 1850s, of a beast, an "intellectual cannibal," feeding on sensation, hungry for change, and riding a wave it sees as modern progress, was a powerful and accurate analogy. But ultimately, everyone was looking for solutions that were not hopeless. They believed, believed even the unbelievable, because they had a will to believe. They accepted distorted certainties because they were weary of the complex ambiguities of events as they actually unfolded among flawed humankind. They desperately wanted meaning. In 1858 Charles Darwin's *Origin of Species* was still a year away, but already the atmosphere was building of the shocks, precipitated by the carnage of the Civil War itself, that were to come to tradition and to historical continuity in America. Clearly, the new "Puritans" of Massachusetts and the new "Cavaliers" of Virginia were hardly of the same type as prevailed among their God-fearing, traditionalist, and ill-informed ancestors. Still, Lincoln in the middle of the war was able to give a kind of Periclean funeral oration, harking back to classical values. The old kind of certainty was no longer to be had, but the desire for some form of it was still present.

Thus, both the "bungling generation" school and the "irrepressible conflict" school of interpreters of the Civil War have uncovered a piece of the core. The public did become weary of the rhetoric and cynical about the results politicians or publicists were able to deliver in Kansas. Many people recognized that the "blatherskite" of public discourse about the issue was not ultimately satisfying, or normative. The weariness and frustration with the "bunglers" was definitely a factor in the move toward the Civil War, particularly for bringing on the war when and how it happened. As logicians would say, the bungling and the name-calling were a sufficient cause of the Civil War. But they were not a necessary one. Behind that smoke there were smoldering fires, which would have smoldered nonetheless. The rhetoric created the tension because it reached emotions, which were being driven by causes beyond the mere expression of opinion. As has been emphasized, many editors, politicians, and members of the public thought they could fling mean epithets, thus boosting their fame and their circulation, with impunity. They thought that whatever deep-seated values the states' rights and antislavery positions represented, in the end they were mostly posturing, that love of the Union was stronger, and that breaking the Union was unthinkable. In that they were deadly wrong.

Where the "bungling generation" school erred was in going beyond saying that the rhetoric was the proximate and effective cause of the war, and averring that the war itself was unnecessary and avoidable, that it would never have happened had leadership been stronger. Thus, intellectual historian Rush Welter concluded, "The roads the Americans took led to civil war. . . . A generation that had very little sense of where it was going and virtually no prior intention of carrying out the measures it finally adopted entered into a war that few men believed was desirable for ends that were only vaguely defined."[47]

The Kansas story belies that thesis by revealing that, along with and underneath the awkward talk, there lay intractable moral issues on which fundamentally idealistic, even romantic, people came more and more to take inflexible stands. In that sense the war was unavoidable, whether leaders talked about the issues responsibly or not. Kansas proved the inadequacy of the stumbling new political and rhetorical directions, if it needed proving. But no modern student has been as glib as debunking scholars once were in saying that the Civil War, or at least some sort of cataclysmic and painful change, was unnecessary, or that, horrible as it was, the nation did not emerge from the bloody cauldron of the arguments and fights of the 1850s and 1860s tempered and, by fits and starts, stronger and better.

Kansas was a political unit where there had not been one before. It had boundaries and institutions. But what really constituted a state? A journalist in 1858 wrote that a true state of the United States had to be a community of "homogeneous people" and an aggregation of families. A "mere expanse" of land could not develop those by magic, nor did one make a real state by putting down a few thousand "straggling, interloping speculators from every point of the compass."[48] Perhaps the creation of Kansas was too precocious and too rapid.

Yet circumstances were the leaders of thought, the stimulators of the fictions by which people lived. "Men are subdued to that which they work in," said a writer in New Orleans. "In political and governmental matters they are, to a great extent, the slaves of the machinery they use. Circumstances but too often mould their policy and fashion their legislation into concrete results, in which the essence of pure right and justice may be scarcely discernable."[49] Kansas framed the debate over freedom in the United States in the 1850s, and that debate was a watershed one for the nation, leading to the most momentous results imaginable.

James Russell Lowell, looking back on the events in Kansas in 1861, as civil war broke out, was disappointed that that had been the way of things. He thought the country had been "cheated with plays on words." The United States was a nation, not a mass meeting. The people had become too accustomed to "the Buncombe style of oratory." Eloquence had become a "chronic disease."[50] Where, asked Walt Whitman, commenting on Bleeding Kansas, was the real America?[51]

Whether the intellectuals then or now liked it or not, the real America was precisely where it seemed to be, in all that Buncombe and wordplay, all that straining for superlative and for sensation that covered newspaper pages reporting on far-away Kansas every day to an anxious people. "Between the center at Washington and the border of Kansas," wrote Denton Snider in 1906 of Bleeding Kansas, "lay the listening nation."[52] R. G. Elliot, in his *Footnotes on Kansas History*, published in 1906, said the story of Bleeding Kansas was an epic in which "the players were a composite of the chosen representatives of, and in electric contact with, an indignant people . . . surcharged with destructive voltage."[53] Indeed it was. The drama of the Kansas debate was in its reality as much as its artificiality.

Kansas, wrote *Philadelphia Press* editor Forney in 1858, was "consigned to an endless sleep," as far as national publicity was concerned, but the matter did not end there. "The American heart has been stirred to its profoundest depths by the Kansas issue. If it had involved nothing but a mere question of expediency it might have soon been forgotten. But it strikes deeper than that. It reaches the very groundwork of Government." America, he continued, had created Kansas, and Kansas was, in many ways, creating a new America. The United States had succeeded because it had started with the right principles and had adhered to them. No people who became indifferent to those matters could remain free. Kansas and the national debate over Kansas, with its excess of ink and shortage of thoughtful reflection, were object lessons and warnings. It was time to go back to first principles and "returning like a Prodigal Son from the forbidden paths where it has strayed, and where naught but wretched disgrace and poverty awaits it, re-assume its habiliments of Popular Sovereignty, and be re-baptized in the sacred waters of self-government."[54]

The great Kansas debate of 1854–1858 had shown the necessity for such a rededication, such a new baptism, such a redefinition and rebirth of freedom. It had also demonstrated how difficult it was going to be.

NOTES

---•◆•---

PREFACE

1. *Transactions of the Kansas State Historical Society: First and Second Biennial Reports*, vols. 1 and 2 (Topeka: George W. Martin, Kansas Publishing House, 1881), 36–37.

2. An extensive survey of Southern newspapers, but for the year 1860 only, is Donald Reynolds, *Editors Make War: Southern Newspapers in the Secession Crisis* (Nashville, Tenn.: Vanderbilt University Press, 1970). Reynolds read close to 200 Southern newspapers, and I have benefited from his insights about the nature of the press in the South in the period. For the Civil War, see Harry Maihafer, *War of Words: Abraham Lincoln and the Civil War Press* (Washington, D.C.: Brassey's, 2001); Brayton Harris, *Blue and Gray in Black and White: Newspapers in the Civil War* (Washington, D.C.: Brassey's, 1999); and David Sachsman, S. Kittrell Rushing, and Debra Reddin van Tuyll, eds. *The Civil War and the Press* (New Brunswick, N.J.: Transaction, 2000).

3. Sachsman, Rushing, and van Tuyll, *Civil War and the Press*, xi, 5–6, 12.

4. Reynolds, *Editors Make War*, 217.

5. *Bellows Falls, Vermont, Chronicle*, Nov. 20, 1829.

6. Reynolds, *Editors Make War*, 3–5.

7. Augustine's discussion is in book 10 of the *Confessions*. For Pocock, see "Working on Ideas in Time," in *The Historian's Workshop*, ed. L. P. Curtis (New York: Alfred A. Knopf, 1970), 155–166.

8. Craig Miner, "Stereotyping and the Pacific Railroad Issue," *Canadian Review of American Studies* 6, no. 1 (Spring 1975): 59–73.

9. David Nord, *Communities of Journalism: A History of American Newspapers and Their Readers* (Urbana and Chicago: University of Illinois Press, 2001), 6, 246; Carey quoted on page 6.

INTRODUCTION

1. C. Stearns, in *Boston Liberator*, Jan. 12, 1855.

2. *Louisville (Ky.) Democrat*, quoted in *Detroit Daily Free Press*, Dec. 31, 1857.

3. Denton Snider, *The American Ten Years' War: 1855–1865* (St. Louis, Mo.: Sigma, 1906); Craig Miner, *Kansas: The History of the Sunflower State* (Lawrence: University Press of Kansas, 2002), x.

4. Edward Ayers, *What Caused the Civil War? Reflections on the South and Southern History* (New York: W. W. Norton, 2005), 140.

5. Walter Lippmann, *Public Opinion* (New York: Harcourt, Brace, 1922), 4–5; Stephen Harnett, *Democratic Dissent and the Cultural Fictions of Antebellum America* (Urbana and Chicago: University of Illinois Press, 2002), 88, 173.

6. Paul Starr, *The Creation of the Media: Political Origins of Modern Communications* (New York: Basic Books, 2004), 2.

7. *Charleston (S.C.) Mercury*, May 1, 1855.

8. *Daily Richmond (Va.) Enquirer*, Nov. 1, 1855.

9. *Chicago Daily Tribune*, Sept. 3, 1857.

10. Ayers, *What Caused the Civil War?* 140.

11. Michael Shapiro, ed., *Language and Politics* (New York: New York University Press, 1984), 2, 125–126.

12. Stephen Poole, *Unspeak: How Words Become Weapons, How Weapons Become a Message, and How That Message Becomes Reality* (New York: Grove Press, 2006), 3–4.

13. Henry Nash Smith, *Virgin Land: The American West as Symbol and Myth* (Cambridge, Mass.: Harvard University Press, 1950); R. W. B. Lewis, *The American Adam: Innocence, Tragedy, and Tradition in the Nineteenth Century* (Chicago: University of Chicago Press, 1955); Leo Marx, *The Machine in the Garden: Technology and the Pastoral Ideal in America* (New York: Oxford University Press, 1964); and John Stilgoe, *Metropolitan Corridor: Railroads and the American Scene* (New Haven, Conn.: Yale University Press, 1983).

14. Aaron Wildavsky and Richard Ellis, "A Cultural Analysis of the Role of Abolitionists in the Coming of the Civil War," in Aaron Wildavsky, *Cultural Analysis: Politics, Public Law, and Administration* (New Brunswick, N.J.: Transaction, 2006), xi, 10, 37, 39, 47.

15. David Davis, *The Slave Power Conspiracy and the Paranoid Style* (Baton Rouge: Louisiana State University Press,

1969), 3, 6–7, 25, 74. See also Leonard Richards, *The Slave Power: The Free North and Southern Domination, 1780–1860* (Baton Rouge: Louisiana State University Press, 2000).

16. Harnett, *Democratic Dissent and the Cultural Fictions*, 1, 2–3, 18, 30, 88, 182.

17. Gunja SenGupta, *For God and Mammon: Evangelicals and Entrepreneurs, Masters and Slaves in Territorial Kansas, 1854–1860* (Athens and London: University of Georgia Press, 1996), 2, 5, 157.

18. Gunja SenGupta, "Bleeding Kansas: Review Essay Series," *Kansas History* 24, no. 4 (Winter 2001–2002): 321, 332, 341.

19. There is a good summary in Nicole Etcheson, *Bleeding Kansas: Contested Liberty in the Civil War Era* (Lawrence: University Press of Kansas, 2004), 1–8.

20. Allan Nevins, *The Emergence of Lincoln*, vol. 1, *Douglas, Buchanan, and Party Chaos, 1857–1859* (New York: Charles Scribner's Sons, 1950), 148.

21. David Potter, *The Impending Crisis, 1848–1861* (New York: Harper & Row, 1976), 43, 217.

22. James Malin, *The Nebraska Question, 1852–1854* (Lawrence, Kans.: Privately printed, 1953), 15.

23. Roy Nichols, *The Disruption of American Democracy* (New York: Macmillan, 1948), 5.

24. Wildavsky and Ellis, "A Cultural Analysis," 34–35.

25. See Paul Gates, *Fifty Million Acres: Conflicts over Kansas Land Policy, 1854–1890* (Ithaca, N.Y.: Cornell University Press, 1954), vi, 1–4.

26. William Freehling, *The Road to Disunion*, vol. 2, *Secessionists Trium-*

phant, 1854–1861 (New York: Oxford University Press, 2007), xii–xiv, 80–82. For a rhetorical analysis of Sumner, see Michael Pierson, "'All South Society Is Assailed by the Foulest Charges': Charles Sumner's 'The Crime against Kansas' and the Escalation of Republican Anti-Slavery Rhetoric," *New England Quarterly* 43 (December 1995): 531, 546.

27. Louis Menand, *The Metaphysical Club: A Story of Ideas in America* (New York: Farrar, Straus & Giroux, 2001), 4, 14, 22, 64–65.

28. Jeremy Waldron, "What Would Hannah Say?" *New York Review of Books*, Mar. 15, 2007, 10, 12.

29. *Washington (D.C.) National Era*, Feb. 25, 1858.

30. *Boston Daily Advertiser*, Aug. 18, 1856, in Thomas W. Webb scrapbooks, New England Emigrant Aid Company collection, Kansas State Historical Society, Topeka, Kansas, 16:75.

31. The exhibit was described in *American Railway Times*, Apr. 9, 1857.

32. Databases of historic newspapers show, for example, that the *New York Herald* published 279 articles on Kansas in 1854, 627 in 1855, and 2,651 in 1856.

33. Useful recent studies of Bleeding Kansas are Etcheson, *Bleeding Kansas*; Thomas Goodrich, *War to the Knife: Bleeding Kansas, 1854–1861* (Mechanicsburg, Pa.: Stackpole Books, 1998); and Virgil Dean, ed., *Kansas Territorial Reader* (Topeka: Kansas State Historical Society, 2005). Among older overviews still useful are Alice Nichols, *Bleeding Kansas* (New York: Oxford University Press, 1954), and Samuel Johnson, *The Battle Cry of Freedom: The New England Emigrant Aid Company in the Kansas Crusade* (Lawrence: University Press of Kansas,

1954). Among eyewitness accounts, the least biased and most complete were written at a little distance from the events and include prominently Charles Robinson, *The Kansas Conflict* (New York: Harper & Brothers, 1892), and Eli Thayer, *The Kansas Crusade* (New York: Harper & Brothers, 1889).

34. *St. Louis Daily Missouri Republican*, Feb. 7, 1858.

CHAPTER ONE

1. A powerful editorial on this theme appeared in the *Daily Richmond (Va.) Enquirer*, Oct. 3, 1856. But the opinion was commonly expressed by the press nationwide.

2. The early ideas for a motto and seal were discussed in the *Hartford (Conn.) Daily Courant*, Oct. 2, 1854.

3. *Columbus (Ga.) Times & Sentinel Tri-Weekly*, Mar. 7, 1857.

4. These statistics come from a search of the electronic version of the *New York Herald*. The *Charleston (S.C.) Mercury* for the period contained 1,380 Kansas articles; the *Washington (D.C.) National Era*, 2,022; the *Boston Liberator*, 1,466; the *Boston Independent*, 908; the *New York Daily Times*, 5,214; the *Hartford Daily Courant*, 3,391; the *Chicago Daily Tribune*, 1,947; and the *Columbus Daily Ohio Statesman*, 1,844.

5. *New York Daily Times*, Nov. 13, 1856.

6. *Daily Albany (N.Y.) Argus*, quoted in *Concord New Hampshire Patriot & State Gazette*, Jan. 20, 1858.

7. A typical "resurrection" story appeared in the *Pittsfield (Mass.) Sun*, Jan. 21, 1858.

8. *Dayton (Ohio) Daily Empire*, Mar. 25, 1858.

9. One of many such reports about Lane appeared in the *Macon Georgia Telegraph*, Jan. 26, 1858.

10. *New York Herald*, May 2, 1858.

11. One example of a survivor account appeared in the *Hartford Daily Courant*, July 3, 1858.

12. *Chicago Daily Tribune*, May 20, 1856.

13. Ibid., Jan. 2, 1858.

14. *Richmond (Va.) South*, Apr. 7, 1857.

15. Quoted in *Columbus Times & Sentinel Tri-Weekly*, May 11, 1858.

16. Quoted in *Concord New Hampshire Patriot & State Gazette*, Dec. 23, 1857.

17. *Providence (R.I.) Daily Post*, Jan. 11, Mar. 13, 1858.

18. *Concord New Hampshire Patriot & State Gazette*, Sept. 23, 1857.

19. SEA SHORE in ibid., Sept. 2, 1857.

20. *Washington (D.C.) Union*, May 6, 1858.

21. *New York Daily Tribune*, Oct. 4, 1856.

22. *Columbus Times & Sentinel Tri-Weekly*, Jan. 18, 1855.

23. Ibid., Feb. 22, 1856.

24. *Montgomery Mail*, quoted in *Columbus (Ga.) Enquirer Tri-Weekly*, Jan. 8, 1857.

25. *Daily Cincinnati Commercial*, Apr. 24, 1857.

26. Speech of L. S. Foster, June 25, 1856, in *Congressional Globe*, 34th Cong., 1st sess., appendix, 683.

27. Samuel S. Cox, *Three Decades of Federal Legislation, 1855 to 1885* (Providence, R.I.: J. A. & R. A. Reid, 1894), 56.

28. David Reynolds, *John Brown, Abolitionist: The Man Who Killed Slavery, Sparked the Civil War, and Seeded Civil Rights* (New York: Alfred A. Knopf, 2005), 174–178. Reynolds cited a con-temporary editorial comment on the affair in *DeBow's New Orleans Review*. Indeed, this article, published in August 1856, goes into some detail on the horror of these events. The editor noted that the massacre was not the extravagance of a few demented individuals but was the "legitimate fruit" of abolition party measures and a natural result of their "public teachings, advice, and counsel of their chief men." The wonder is that more journals and newspapers, North and South, did not do the same. See *DeBow's New Orleans Review* 1 (Aug. 1856): 189–190.

29. Here one might consult the insight on Brown of Merrill Peterson, *John Brown: The Legend Revisited* (Charlottesville: University of Virginia Press, 2002), 82.

30. Speech of H. M. Phillips, March 9, 1858, in *Congressional Globe*, 35th Cong., 1st sess., appendix.

31. *Columbus Enquirer Tri-Weekly*, Feb. 26, 1857.

32. *Daily Cincinnati Commercial*, July 21, 1855.

33. Paul Starr, *The Creation of the Media: Political Origins of Modern Communications* (New York: Basic Books, 2004), 131. Circulation figures for the *Herald* are from *New York Herald*, Oct. 16, 1857, and from Douglas Fermer, *James Gordon Bennett and the "New York Herald": A Study of Editorial Opinion in the Civil War Era, 1854–1857* (New York: St. Martin's Press, 1986), 323.

34. *New York Herald*, Dec. 11, 1857.

35. Ibid., Jan. 25, 1854.

36. Quoted in *New York Daily Tribune*, Nov. 14, 1855.

37. *New York Herald*, May 8, 1855.

38. Henry Ward Beecher, in *New York Independent*, quoted in *Chicago Daily*

Tribune, Feb. 20, 1856. A readable recent biography of Beecher is Debby Applegate, *The Most Famous Man in America* (New York: Doubleday, 2006).

39. *Chicago Daily Tribune*, Feb. 27, 1856.

40. *Charleston Mercury*, Dec. 28, 1857.

41. *St. Louis Daily Missouri Republican*, Apr. 30, 1856.

42. *Richmond South*, Apr. 14, 1857.

43. *Columbus Enquirer Tri-Weekly*, May 19, 1857.

44. *Muscogee (Ala.) Herald*, quoted in *Hartford Daily Courant*, Oct. 28, 1856.

45. *New Orleans Daily Delta*, May 19, 1855.

46. Ibid., Jan. 7, 1856.

47. Ibid., May 17, 1854.

48. Ibid., June 8, 1855.

49. *Daily Richmond Enquirer*, June 7, 1854.

50. Ibid., Aug. 5, 1855.

51. Ibid., Aug. 18, 1855.

52. Ibid., Mar. 19, 1856; Nov. 21, 1855.

53. Ibid., June 11, 1856.

54. Ibid., June 11, 1856; Jan. 5, 1857. For the *Herald's* original success, which came in its reporting of the murder of prostitute Helen Jewett in April 1836, see Starr, *Creation of the Media*, 133.

55. *Daily Richmond Enquirer*, Mar. 21, 1857.

56. Ibid., Aug. 26, 1856.

57. Ibid., Feb. 27, 1854, for the phrase "dragon of abolition."

58. Ibid., June 9, 1855.

59. Ibid., June 16, 1855.

60. Ibid., Aug. 3, 1855.

61. Ibid., Oct. 11, 1856.

62. Ibid., Apr. 15, 1856.

63. Ibid., Dec. 28, 1855.

64. *New Orleans Daily Picayune*, Mar. 18, 1858.

65. Ibid., Dec. 18, 1855; July 3, 1857.

66. The term "stereotyped slang" comes from the *Concord New Hampshire Patriot & State Gazette*, Nov. 18, 1857.

67. *New York Daily Times*, quoted in *New York Christian Inquirer*, Sept. 22, 1855.

68. *Louisville (Ky.) Daily Journal*, June 27, 1855.

69. *Charleston Mercury*, July 25, 1857.

70. *Washington Union*, Apr. 20, 1858.

71. *St. Louis Daily Missouri Democrat*, Feb. 20, 1856.

72. "Unscrupulous and pig-headed toady" is from the *Boston Daily Atlas*, quoted in *Liberator*, Sept. 28, 1855. The other characterizations were common.

73. *St. Louis Daily Missouri Democrat*, Feb. 8, 1856.

74. Ibid., Apr. 12, 1856.

75. Ibid., Jan. 31, Aug. 23, 1856.

76. Ibid., Feb. 7, 1856.

77. *Philadelphia Public Ledger & Daily Transcript*, Nov. 27, 1856.

78. Ibid., Sept. 22, 1856.

79. *Putnam's Monthly Magazine of American Literature, Science & Art* 6 (Oct. 1855): 425.

80. *Detroit Daily Advertiser*, July 21, 1856, quoted in Thomas W. Webb scrapbooks, New England Emigrant Aid Company collection, Kansas State Historical Society, 15:60.

81. *St. Louis Daily Missouri Republican*, Apr. 30, 1856.

82. Menahem Blondheim, *News over the Wires: The Telegraph and the Flow of Public Information in America, 1844–1897* (Cambridge, Mass.: Harvard University Press, 1994), 3, 6, 38.

83. RANDOLPH, in *Chicago Daily Tribune*, May 22, 1857.

84. Charles Stearns, in *Boston Liberator*, Mar. 16, Apr. 27, 1855.

85. *New York Daily Tribune,* June 13, 1856.

86. Erik Schmeller has identified the *Times* correspondent LITERAL as James Winchell and RANDOLPH as William Hutchinson. Erik Schmeller, "Propagandists for a Free-State Kansas: *New York Times'* Correspondents and Bleeding Kansas, 1856," *Heritage of the Great Plains* 23, no. 3 (Summer 1990): 8.

87. *Concord New Hampshire Patriot & State Gazette,* Jan. 27, 1857.

88. *Washington National Era,* Feb. 18, 1858.

89. *Western Argus,* quoted in *Boston Post,* July 19, 1858.

90. *Washington National Era,* Jan. 21, 1858.

91. *Indianapolis State Journal,* Feb. 14, 1856.

92. Douglas Brewerton, *The War in Kansas: A Rough Trip to the Border among New Homes and a Strange People* (New York: Derby & Jackson, 1856), 255, 258, 284, 384; quotation on 284.

93. *Boston Post,* Jan. 18, 1856.

94. *Theodore Parker: An Anthology,* ed. Henry Steel Commager (Boston: Beacon Press, 1960), 176–181; quotation on 180–181.

95. *New Orleans Daily Picayune,* Jan. 9, 1858.

96. *Pittsburg Daily Dispatch,* Aug. 27, 1855.

97. *Daily Cincinnati Commercial,* Oct. 24, Nov. 13, Nov. 15, 1854.

98. *Philadelphia Public Ledger & Daily Transcript,* Aug. 12, 1856.

99. *Washington Union,* Mar. 31, 1858.

100. *Louisville Daily Journal,* Aug. 26, 1854.

101. *Natchez (Miss.) Daily Courier,* Jan. 29, 1858.

102. *Charleston Mercury,* July 11, 1857.

103. *New York Herald,* Jan. 11, 1857.

104. *Philadelphia Public Ledger & Daily Transcript,* June 13, 1854; Dec. 21, 1853.

105. *Springfield (Mass.) Daily Republican,* Mar. 8, 1854.

106. *Washington (D.C.) Daily Union,* Apr. 30, 1854.

107. *Daily Cincinnati Commercial,* Nov. 10, 1856; Sept. 3, 1855.

108. *New York Herald,* May 19, 1854.

109. *New York Daily Times,* May 31, 1854.

110. James Malin, *The Nebraska Question* (Lawrence, Kans.: Privately printed, 1953), 327, 404, 412.

111. Lewis Cass, speech in U.S. Senate, May 12, 1856, in *Congressional Globe,* 34th Cong., 1st sess., appendix, 521.

112. *Washington Union,* Dec. 5, 1857.

113. Gordon S. Wood, "The Rise of American Democracy: A Constant Struggle," review of *The Rise of American Democracy: Jefferson to Lincoln,* by Sean Wilentz, *New York Times Book Review,* Nov. 13, 2005, 11.

114. A fine summary of the thought of Hobbes and other philosophers on politics is Bryan Garsten, *Saving Persuasion: A Defense of Rhetoric and Judgment* (Cambridge, Mass.: Harvard University Press, 2006). See especially for Hobbes, 5–54.

115. See Nicole Etcheson, *Bleeding Kansas: Contested Liberty in the Civil War Era* (Lawrence: University Press of Kansas, 2004), 7, 187–188.

116. The best-known study of this phenomenon is Eric Fromm, *Escape from Freedom* (New York: Reinhart, 1941).

117. Henry Ward Beecher, in the *New York Independent,* quoted in *Chicago Daily Tribune,* Feb. 20, 1856.

118. *New York Christian Inquirer,* Apr. 7, 1855.

119. *Daily Cincinnati Commercial*, July 8, 1854.

120. *Columbus Daily Ohio Statesman*, Feb. 2, 1858.

121. *New Orleans Daily Picayune*, Mar. 18, 1858.

122. Ibid.

123. *Daily Cincinnati Commercial*, July 7, 1855.

124. *Commercial Advertiser*, quoted in *Macon Georgia Telegraph*, Feb. 16, 1858.

125. *Washington Union*, Apr. 1, 1857.

126. Ibid., Apr. 20, 1858.

127. "Earnestness vs. Enthusiasm," *Albany (N.Y.) Atlas & Argus*, in Webb scrapbooks, 4:183.

128. The articles appeared in the *Washington National Era*, Sept. 6, Sept. 13, 1855.

CHAPTER TWO

1. Orman Ray, *The Repeal of the Missouri Compromise* (Cleveland, Ohio: Arthur H. Clark, 1909), 15.

2. Speech of Charles Hughes, Apr. 27, 1854, in *Congressional Globe*, 33rd Cong., 1st sess., appendix, 535.

3. *Iowa Miner's Express*, quoted in *Washington (D.C.) Daily Union*, Feb. 15, 1854.

4. *New York Herald*, Jan. 10, 1854.

5. Speech of Charles Sumner, Feb. 24, 1854, in *Congressional Globe*, 33rd Cong., 1st sess., appendix, 262, 269.

6. Speech of Israel Washburn, Apr. 7, 1854, in ibid., 499.

7. Speech of Laurence Keitt, Mar. 30, 1854, in ibid., 464–467.

8. Ibid.

9. Speech of Gerrit Smith, Apr. 6, 1854, in ibid., 519–530.

10. Ibid.

11. James C. Malin, *The Nebraska Question, 1852–1854* (Lawrence, Kans.: Privately printed, 1953), 100, 288, 327.

12. For the politics, see especially Michael Holt, *The Rise and Fall of the American Whig Party: Jacksonian Politics and the Onset of the Civil War* (New York: Oxford University Press, 1999), 804–835. Throughout, for those needing reinforcement of their survey understanding of American history for this period, Sean Wilentz's *The Rise of American Democracy* (New York: W. W. Norton, 2007) is clear, modern, and sophisticated.

13. *New York Herald*, Feb. 3, 1854.

14. Allan Nevins, *Ordeal of the Union*, vol. 2, *A House Dividing, 1852–1857* (New York: Charles Scribner's Sons, 1947), 106–110.

15. *Charleston (S.C.) Mercury*, Feb. 8, 1854.

16. David Potter, *The Impending Crisis, 1848–1861* (New York: Harper & Row, 1976), 201.

17. *New York Herald*, Jan. 29, 1854.

18. Speech of Richard Yates, Mar. 28, 1854, in *Congressional Globe*, 33rd Cong., 1st sess., appendix, 443.

19. *Charleston Mercury*, Jan. 20, 1854.

20. *Washington Daily Union*, Jan. 24, 1854.

21. Ibid., Jan. 26, 1854.

22. *Charleston Mercury*, Jan. 10, 1854.

23. *Washington Daily Union*, Feb. 11, 1854.

24. *New York Herald*, Jan. 25, 1854.

25. *Washington Daily Union*, Jan. 27, 1854.

26. *Richmond (Va.) Enquirer* (semi-weekly), Feb. 3, 1854.

27. *New York Herald*, Jan. 27, 1854.

28. *Springfield (Mass.) Daily Republican*, Feb. 8, 1854.

29. *Amherst (N.H.) Farmer's Cabinet,* Feb. 9, 1854.

30. *Milwaukee Daily Sentinel,* Feb. 15, 1854.

31. *Chicago Daily Tribune,* Feb. 10, 1854.

32. *Daily Cincinnati Commercial,* Mar. 1, 1854.

33. *Milwaukee Daily Sentinel,* June 9, 1854.

34. *Daily Cincinnati Commercial,* May 24, 1854.

35. *New York Daily Tribune,* Mar. 21, 1854.

36. Ibid., Mar. 28, 1854.

37. *San Francisco Daily Alta California,* Apr. 6, 1854.

38. *Daily Richmond (Va.) Enquirer,* Feb. 16, 1854.

39. *New Orleans Daily Delta,* June 5, 1854.

40. *New Orleans Daily Picayune,* Mar. 19, 1854.

41. *St. Louis Daily Missouri Democrat,* Feb. 20, 1854.

42. *Boston Post,* May 30, 31, 1854.

43. A. P. Butler, quoted in *Charleston Mercury,* Mar. 3, 1854.

44. *New York Daily Tribune,* Feb. 1, 1854.

45. *Washington Daily Union,* Feb. 3, 1854.

46. *St. Louis Daily Missouri Republican,* Feb. 7, 1854.

47. *St. Louis Daily Missouri Democrat,* Feb. 8, 1854.

48. *Washington (D.C.) National Era,* Mar. 2, 1854.

49. *Detroit Daily Free Press,* Mar. 4, 1854.

50. Ibid., Mar. 16, 1854.

51. *Daily Albany (N.Y.) Argus,* Aug. 1, 1854.

52. *Chicago Daily Tribune,* Mar. 8, 1854.

53. *Richmond Enquirer* (semi-weekly), May 2, 1854.

54. *Philadelphia Public Ledger & Daily Transcript,* May 11, 1854.

55. *Springfield Daily Republican,* Feb. 24, 1854.

56. *Providence (R.I.) Daily Post,* Jan. 19, 1854.

57. *New York Daily Tribune,* Feb. 2, 1854.

58. Quoted by C. K. W., in *Boston Liberator,* Feb. 17, 1854.

59. Quoted in *New York Daily Times,* Feb. 23, 1854.

60. Ibid., Feb. 22, 1854.

61. *Springfield Daily Republican,* Mar. 7, 1854.

62. *Tuskegee (Ala.) South-Western Baptist,* Mar. 16, 1854.

63. *Richmond (Va.) Christian Advocate,* quoted in *Daily Richmond Enquirer,* Mar. 23, 1854.

64. *Macon Georgia Telegraph,* Apr. 4, 1854.

65. *Milwaukee Daily Sentinel,* Apr. 6, 1854.

66. *Boston Christian Watchman & Reflector,* Apr. 6, 1854.

67. *New York Daily Times,* Apr. 13, 1854.

68. *Richmond Enquirer* (semi-weekly), May 26, 1854; *Boston Post,* June 10, 1854.

69. *Washington Daily Union,* Apr. 26, 1854.

70. See Paul Gates, *Fifty Million Acres: Conflicts over Kansas Land Policy, 1854–1890* (Ithaca, N.Y.: Cornell University Press, 1954), 3. See also Craig Miner and William Unrau, *The End of Indian Kansas: A Study of Cultural Revo-*

lution, *1854–1871* (Lawrence: Regents
Press of Kansas, 1978), particularly the
chapter entitled "Territorial Kansas and
the Indian," 1–24.

71. These arguments are found in the
Detroit Daily Free Press, Jan. 26, 1854.

72. *Austin Texas State Gazette*, Feb. 28,
1854.

73. *Louisville (Ky.) Daily Journal*, Aug.
25, 1854.

74. *Pittsfield (Mass.) Sun*, Mar. 23,
1854.

75. *Hartford (Conn.) Daily Courant*,
Mar. 30, 1854.

76. Ibid., June 23, 1854.

77. *Louisville Daily Journal*, Aug. 25,
1854.

78. *New Orleans Daily Picayune*, Aug.
31, 1854.

79. *Hartford Daily Courant*, Mar. 1,
1854.

80. *Boston Post*, May 27, 1854.

81. *Chicago Daily Tribune*, Nov. 17,
1853.

82. *Louisville Daily Journal*, Jan. 26,
1854.

83. *New York Herald*, Feb. 9, 1854.

84. *Chicago Daily Tribune*, Mar. 3,
1854.

85. *New York Daily Tribune*, quoted in
Daily Richmond Enquirer, Mar. 11, 1854.

86. *New York Daily Tribune*, May 10,
1854.

87. *Louisville Daily Journal*, May 31,
1854.

88. Ibid., June 12, 1854.

89. *Daily Richmond Enquirer*, June 7,
1854.

90. *Austin Texas State Gazette*, Apr.
29, 1854.

91. *Daily Albany Argus*, May 19, 1854.

92. *Louisville Daily Journal*, July 17,
1854.

93. *Washington National Era*, June 29,
1854.

94. *New York Daily Tribune*, Jan. 10,
1854.

95. *St. Louis Daily Missouri Democrat*,
Jan. 13, 1854.

96. *Springfield Daily Republican*, Feb.
7, 1854.

97. *Chicago Daily Tribune*, Feb. 10,
1854.

98. *New Orleans Daily Delta*, Feb. 15,
1854; *St. Louis Daily Missouri Republican*,
Feb. 16, 1854; *Detroit Daily Free Press*,
Feb. 21, 1854.

99. *New York Herald*, Jan. 21, 1854.

100. *St. Louis Daily Missouri Republican*, Feb. 16, 1854.

101. *New York Herald*, Feb. 14, 1854.

102. An example of this kind of rhetoric appears in the *Detroit Daily Free Press*, Feb. 15, 1854.

103. *Springfield Daily Republican*, May
22, 1854.

104. *Louisville Daily Journal*, Apr. 12,
1854.

105. *Natchez (Miss.) Daily Courier*,
Oct. 6, 1854.

106. *New York Evangelist*, May 25, 1854.

107. Speech of S. P. Chase, Feb. 4,
1854, in *Congressional Globe*, 33rd Cong.,
1st sess., appendix, 133.

108. *Springfield Daily Republican*,
Mar. 8, 1854.

109. ARISTIDES, in *Daily Richmond Enquirer*, May 17, 1854; *Daily Richmond Enquirer*, May 15, 1854.

110. Speech of A. Dixon, Feb. 4,
1854, in *Congressional Globe*, 33rd Cong.,
1st sess., appendix, 145.

111. Speech of G. E. Badger, Feb. 16,
1854, in ibid., 149.

112. Speech of A. H. Stephens, Feb.
17, 1854, in ibid., 197.

113. Speech of J. Weller, Feb. 13, 1854, in ibid., 200.

114. Speech of A. P. Butler, Feb. 24, 1854, in ibid., 240.

115. Speech of Lewis Cass, Feb. 20, 1854, in ibid., 277.

116. Speech of W. Seward, Feb. 8, 1854, in ibid., 155.

117. Speech of R. Hunter, Feb. 24, 1854, in ibid., 226.

118. Speech of C. Sumner, Feb. 24, 1854, in ibid., 269.

119. Speech of J. Millison, Mar. 23, 1854, in ibid., 426.

120. Speech of R. Yates, Mar. 28, 1854, in ibid., 445.

121. *New York Herald*, May 24, 1854.

122. Speech of W. Sapp, Apr. 28, 1854, in *Congressional Globe*, 33rd Cong., 1st sess., appendix, 562.

123. Speech of T. Benton, Apr. 25, 1854, in ibid., 560.

124. Speech of C. Hughes, Apr. 27, 1854, in ibid., 536.

125. Speech of P. Ewing, Feb. 20, 1854, in ibid., 251.

126. *New York Daily Tribune*, Mar. 3, 1854.

127. *St. Louis Daily Missouri Democrat*, Mar. 10, 1854.

128. *Charleston Mercury*, Aug. 5, 1854.

129. *Washington National Era*, July 27, 1854.

130. *Washington Daily Union*, Mar. 10, 1854.

131. *New York Daily Times*, May 2, 1854.

132. *Detroit Daily Free Press*, May 13, 1854.

133. *Charleston Mercury*, June 21, 1854.

134. *New York Daily Times*, Mar. 25, 1854.

CHAPTER THREE

1. *New Haven Palladium Whig* and *Albany Register*, quoted in *New York Daily Sun*, May 29, 1854, in Thomas W. Webb scrapbooks, New England Emigrant Aid Company collection, Kansas State Historical Society, Topeka, Kansas, 1:18.

2. *Charleston (S.C.) Mercury*, Oct. 9, 1854.

3. *Natchez (Miss.) Daily Courier*, Dec. 5, 1854.

4. *Columbus (Ga.) Times & Sentinel Tri-Weekly*, Apr. 6, 1855.

5. *Hartford (Conn.) Daily Courant*, Aug. 31, 1854.

6. The most complete history of the company is Samuel Johnson, *The Battle Cry of Freedom: The New England Emigrant Aid Company in the Kansas Crusade* (Lawrence: University Press of Kansas, 1954).

7. *New York Herald*, June 16, 1854.

8. Ibid., Oct. 5, 1854.

9. Ibid., June 30, 1854.

10. Johnson, *Battle Cry of Freedom*, 17, 21, 95.

11. *Richmond (Va.) Enquirer* (semiweekly), Dec. 21, 1855.

12. *Daily Richmond (Va.) Enquirer*, June 24, 1854.

13. "Address to the People of the United States," from a convention at Lexington, Missouri, quoted in *Washington (D.C.) Daily Union*, Oct. 3, 1855.

14. *Washington Sentinel*, Dec. 23, 1854, in Webb scrapbooks, 2:97.

15. *New York Journal of Commerce*, Jan. 5, 1855, in Webb scrapbooks, 2:183–194.

16. Undated clipping from the *Boston Commonwealth*, in Webb scrapbooks, 1:46.

17. *Boston Christian Register*, May 20, 1854, in Webb scrapbooks, 1:6.

18. *New York Daily Tribune,* May 20, 1854.

19. *Boston Journal,* July 31, 1854, in Webb scrapbooks, 1:71.

20. Eli Thayer, *The Kansas Crusade* (New York: Harper & Brothers, 1889), 16, 24, 31.

21. Ibid., 31.

22. Robert Williams, *Horace Greeley: Champion of American Freedom* (New York: New York University Press, 2006), 316, 1, 166, 188.

23. *New York Daily Tribune,* Aug. 21, 1854.

24. *Amherst (N.H.) Farmer's Cabinet,* Aug. 28, 1856.

25. *New York Daily Tribune,* May 24, 1854, two editorials.

26. Ibid., June 19, 1854.

27. Ibid., June 17, 1854.

28. E. D. L., in *Milwaukee Daily Sentinel,* Oct. 19, 1854.

29. A. K. Moulton Lowell, in *Dover (N.H.) Morning Star,* in Webb scrapbooks, 2:19.

30. A good primary picture of the early town may be had in Richard Cordley, *A History of Lawrence, Kansas, from the First Settlement to the Close of the Rebellion* (Lawrence, Kans.: Lawrence Journal Press, 1895).

31. DESCANDUM [Amasa Soule], in *Telegraphy & Pioneer,* n.p., Dec. 15, 1854, in Webb scrapbooks, 2:61.

32. A. O. Carpenter, letter to *Brattleboro (Vt.) Eagle,* Dec. 29, 1854, in Webb scrapbooks, 2:124–125.

33. Udolpho Wolfe Jr., in *St. Louis Daily Missouri Republican,* Dec. 30, 1854, in Webb scrapbooks, 2:127.

34. J. R., in *St. Louis Daily Missouri Democrat,* Oct. 23, 1855.

35. Clarina Nichols, in *Springfield (Vt.) Daily Republican,* Jan. 8, 1855, in Webb scrapbooks, 2:128. An excellent recent biography of Nichols is Diane Eickhoff, *Revolutionary Heart: The Life of Clarina Nichols and the Pioneering Crusade for Women's Rights* (Kansas City, Kans.: Quindaro Press, 2006).

36. Charles Robinson, *The Kansas Conflict* (New York: Harper & Brothers, 1892), 21–22.

37. *Boston Daily Advertiser,* July 31, 1854, in Webb scrapbooks, 1:74.

38. RANDOLPH, in *New York Daily Times,* Feb. 25, 1856.

39. Gerrit Smith, quoted in *New York Daily Times,* Mar. 17, 1856.

40. *New York Weekly Tribune,* July 26, 1854, in Webb scrapbooks, 1:69.

41. *St. Louis Daily Missouri Democrat,* Sept. 15, 1855.

42. KANSAS, in *Boston Daily Atlas,* Aug. 2, 1854.

43. *New York Daily Times,* Mar. 25, 1856.

44. *New York Christian Inquirer,* May 16, 1857.

45. *New York Daily Times,* Feb. 5, 1856.

46. Ibid., Sept. 10, 1855.

47. Ibid., Feb. 4, 1856.

48. *Detroit Daily Free Press,* Nov. 11, 1855.

49. *New York Herald,* May 27, 1856.

50. *Chicago Daily Tribune,* Sept. 23, 1857.

51. Correspondent's letter, Nov. 13, 1857, in *Chicago Daily Tribune,* Dec. 2, 1857.

52. *Milwaukee Daily Sentinel,* June 4, 1856.

53. *Providence (R.I.) Daily Post,* Oct. 19, 1855.

54. See, for example, JACOBIUS, in

Boston Traveler, reprinted in *Macon Georgia Telegraph*, Sept. 29, 1857.

55. *St. Louis Daily Missouri Republican*, Oct. 10, 1855.

56. *Conneantville (Pa.) Courier*, Aug. 16, 1854, in Webb scrapbooks, 1:93.

57. *St. Louis Daily Missouri Democrat*, Dec. 31, 1855.

58. *New Orleans Daily Picayune*, May 21, 1854.

59. *New Orleans Daily Delta*, June 8, 1855.

60. Ibid., Sept. 11, 1856.

61. *Washington Union*, Apr. 16, 1858.

62. *St. Louis Daily Missouri Republican*, June 6, 1856.

63. *New Orleans Daily Delta*, Nov. 7, 1856; *St. Louis Daily Missouri Democrat*, Nov. 26, 1856.

64. *Charleston Mercury*, July 5, 1858.

65. *Providence Daily Post*, Dec. 25, 1855.

66. *New York Daily Tribune*, June 1, 1854.

67. B. F. Stringfellow, in ibid., Jan. 27, 1855.

68. *St. Louis Daily Missouri Democrat*, Apr. 12, 1856.

69. *Daily Richmond Enquirer*, May 16, 1856.

70. T., in *St. Louis Daily Missouri Republican*, Mar. 24, 1855.

71. *Macon Georgia Telegraph*, Dec. 2, 1856.

72. Ibid., Dec. 25, 1855.

73. T, in *St. Louis Daily Missouri Republican*, May 3, 1855.

74. Ibid., May 23, 1855.

75. Quoted in *New York Daily Tribune*, Nov. 30, 1855.

76. *Springfield Daily Republican*, n.d. [c. Nov. 1855], in Webb scrapbooks, 7:31.

77. Speech of H. Bennett, Mar. 14, 1856, in *Congressional Globe*, 34th Cong., 1st sess., appendix, 279.

78. Speech of M. Trafton, Mar. 12, 1856, in ibid., 149.

79. *Columbus Times & Sentinel Tri-Weekly*, Oct. 1, 1856.

80. *Cincinnati Times*, Dec. 8, 1855, in Webb scrapbooks, 7:116; *New Orleans Daily Delta*, Apr. 7, 1856.

81. *New Orleans Daily Delta*, Jan. 7, 1856.

82. *St. Louis Daily Missouri Republican*, Sept. 19, 1854.

83. *Columbus Daily Ohio Statesman*, Jan. 23, 1856.

84. *New Orleans Daily Delta*, Apr. 2, 1855.

85. *Philadelphia Public Ledger & Daily Transcript*, Sept. 22, 1856.

86. *Boston Liberator*, Oct. 16, 1857.

87. *St. Louis Daily Missouri Democrat*, May 2, 1856; *Pittsfield (Mass.) Sun*, Sept. 13, 1855.

88. Paul Gates, *Fifty Million Acres: Conflicts over Kansas Land Policy, 1854–1890* (Ithaca, N.Y.: Cornell University Press, 1954), 6–7. A list of the Kansas land cession and removal treaties of 1854–1855 is on 17.

89. Ibid., 18–19.

90. *Philadelphia Public Ledger & Daily Transcript*, Feb. 15, 1854.

91. *New York Daily Times*, Aug. 30, 1854.

92. *Washington (D.C.) Daily Union*, July 13, 1855.

93. *Kansas City (Mo.) Enterprise*, Nov. 10, 1855.

94. *Milwaukee Daily Sentinel*, Oct. 15, 1855.

95. An example on the Delaware land sales appears in the *St. Louis Daily Missouri Democrat*, Nov. 20, 1856.

96. Sigma, in *New York Daily Times,*
Jan. 3, 1857.

97. A. B., in *Montgomery (Ala.) Advertiser & State Gazette,* Dec. 6, 1854.

98. *Philadelphia Press,* Aug. 5, 1857.

99. The story may be followed in
Craig Miner and William Unrau, *The
End of Indian Kansas: A Study of Cultural
Revolution, 1854–1871* (Lawrence: Re-
gents Press of Kansas, 1978).

100. *New York Daily Tribune,* Dec. 4,
1854. A detailed timeline is found in
Daniel Wilder, *The Annals of Kansas,
1541–1885* (Topeka: T. Dwight Thacher,
Kansas Publishing House, 1886).

101. *New York Daily Tribune,* Dec. 12,
1854.

102. *Detroit Daily Free Press,* Dec. 19,
1854; *New York Daily Tribune,* Dec. 22,
1854. A good example of recent historical analysis is Nicole Etcheson, *Bleeding
Kansas: Contested Liberty in the Civil War
Era* (Lawrence: University Press of
Kansas, 2004), 54–55.

103. Ignatius, in *Charleston News,* in
Webb scrapbooks, 2:70.

104. *Springfield Daily Republican,* n.d.
[January 1855], in ibid., 2:170.

105. B. F. Stringfellow, in *New York
Daily Tribune,* Jan. 27, 1855.

106. One such was M. F. Conway,
who accompanied his resignation with a
protest that became nationally circulated; *Keene New Hampshire Sentinel,*
Aug. 3, 1855.

107. *Charleston Mercury,* Apr. 4, 1855.

108. The Howard report is U.S. Congress, House, *Report of the Special Committee Appointed to Investigate the Troubles
in Kansas . . . ,* HR 200, 34th Cong., 1st
sess. (Washington, D.C.: Cornelius Wendell, Printer, 1856). While the report
concluded that Missourians had fraudu-

lently voted in the election, the investigation was a highly politicized affair. The
one Democrat on the committee, Congressman Mordecai Oliver from Missouri, submitted a minority report coming to exactly the opposite conclusion.

109. *New York Daily Tribune,* Apr. 18,
1855.

110. *Bangor (Maine) Daily Whig &
Courier,* Apr. 19, 1855.

111. *Washington (D.C.) National Era,*
Apr. 19, 1855.

112. *Montgomery Advertiser & State
Gazette,* Apr. 18, 1855.

113. *Charleston Mercury,* Apr. 18, 1855.

114. *Columbia Daily South Carolinian,*
May 3, 1855.

115. *Daily Cincinnati Commercial,*
Apr. 23, 1855.

116. *Chicago Daily Tribune,* May 4,
1855.

117. *Dayton (Ohio) Daily Empire,* May
23, 1855.

118. *New York Daily Times,* May 24,
1855.

119. *Daily Albany (N.Y.) Argus,* June
15, 1855.

120. *Buffalo (N.Y.) Evening Bulletin,*
May 4, 1855.

121. *New York Daily Tribune,* June 11,
1855.

122. A. B., in *Montgomery Advertiser &
State Gazette,* June 20, 1855.

123. *New Orleans Daily Picayune,* June
30, 1855.

124. *St. Louis Daily Missouri Republican,* Aug. 28, 1855.

125. Speech of James Stewart of
Maryland, July 23, 1856, *Congressional
Globe,* 34th Cong., 1st sess., appendix,
989.

126. *Cleveland Leader,* quoted in *Milwaukee Daily Sentinel,* Oct. 15, 1855.

127. *St. Louis Daily Missouri Republican*, Oct. 23, 1855.

128. The debate may be followed in *Congressional Globe*, 34th Cong., 1st sess., appendix.

129. *New York Daily Times*, Nov. 21, 1855.

130. *St. Louis Daily Missouri Republican*, Nov. 30, 1855.

131. H. G., in *New York Daily Tribune*, Dec. 11, 1855.

132. *Dayton Daily Empire*, Jan. 7, 1856.

133. Ibid., Jan. 8, 1856.

134. *Charleston Mercury*, Feb. 4, 18, 1856; *New York Herald*, Feb. 18, 1856.

135. *Columbus Times & Sentinel Tri-Weekly*, Feb. 22, 1856.

136. Speech of Alexander Stephens, Mar. 11, 1856, *Congressional Globe*, 34th Cong., 1st sess., appendix, 182.

137. *New Orleans Daily Picayune*, Mar. 23, 1856.

138. RANDOLPH, in *Chicago Daily Tribune*, Mar. 28, 1856.

139. *New Orleans Daily Delta*, Apr. 7, 1856. See *Charleston Mercury*, Apr. 9, 12, 1856, for detailed accounts of Kansas meetings there.

140. D, in *Chicago Daily Tribune*, Apr. 18, 1856.

141. *New York Daily Times*, May 20, 1856.

142. *Louisville (Ky.) Daily Journal*, Mar. 26, 1856.

143. LITERAL, in *New York Daily Times*, May 12, 1856; *St. Louis Daily Missouri Democrat*, Apr. 28, 1856.

144. *New Orleans Daily Picayune*, May 15, 1856.

145. *Chicago Daily Tribune*, Apr. 23, 1856.

146. *Dayton Daily Empire*, Apr. 25, 1856.

147. *Kansas City Enterprise*, May 21, 1856.

148. *St. Louis Daily Missouri Republican*, July 10, 1856.

149. L., in *Milwaukee Daily Sentinel*, June 18, 1856.

150. Smith, in *Buffalo Commercial Advertiser*, July 23, 1856, in Webb scrapbooks, 15:92–93.

151. *New Orleans Daily Delta*, Aug. 38, 1856.

152. *Dayton Daily Empire*, May 29, 1856.

153. *Milwaukee Daily Sentinel*, June 3, 1856.

154. E. P. C., in *New York Daily Tribune*, June 5, 1856.

155. Quoted in Craig Miner, *Kansas: The History of the Sunflower State* (Lawrence: University Press of Kansas, 2002), 72.

156. A fine description of one party is that by J. W. Wells, in *Milwaukee Daily Sentinel*, Sept. 4, 1856.

157. LITERAL, in *New York Daily Times*, Oct. 17, 1856.

158. *Louisville Daily Journal*, Nov. 10, 1856.

159. *New York Daily Tribune*, Nov. 22, 1856.

160. *Chicago Weekly Times*, Apr. 9, 1857.

161. *Washington National Era*, Apr. 9, 1857.

162. Ibid., Apr. 23, 1857.

163. Ibid., Apr. 22, 1857.

164. *New York Daily Times*, June 30, 1857.

165. *Washington National Era*, Apr. 23, 1857.

166. *St. Louis Daily Missouri Republican*, June 27, 1857.

167. Orville Vernon Burton, *The Age*

of Lincoln (New York: Hill & Wang, 2007), 5, 9, 11.

168. Richard Cawardine, *Lincoln: A Life of Purpose and Power* (New York: Alfred A. Knopf, 2006), 48, 66, 150, 202.

169. *New Orleans Daily Picayune*, Aug. 1, 1857.

170. *Washington Union*, June 24, 1857.

171. *Louisville Daily Journal*, June 20, 1857.

172. *New Orleans Daily Picayune*, Apr. 9, 1857. On Dred Scott and its effect, see Don Fehrenbacher, *The Dred Scott Case: Its Significance in American Law and Politics* (New York: Oxford University Press, 1978).

173. *St. Louis Daily Missouri Democrat*, June 17, 1857.

174. *Washington National Era*, May 7, 1857.

175. *Chicago Daily Tribune*, May 8, 1857.

176. *Daily Cincinnati Commercial*, May 19, 1857.

177. *New York Daily Tribune*, Sept. 7, 1857.

178. JACOBIUS, in *St. Louis Daily Missouri Democrat*, Sept. 2, 1857.

179. *New York Daily Times*, Oct. 13, 1857. For further summary of the election results, see X, in *St. Louis Daily Missouri Republican*, Oct. 26, 1857.

180. Burton, *Age of Lincoln*, 54.

181. *Buffalo Commercial Advertiser*, quoted in *Chicago Weekly Times*, Nov. 26, 1857.

182. *Washington National Era*, Oct. 22, 1857.

183. *New York Daily Tribune*, Oct. 21, 1857.

184. *Detroit Daily Free Press*, Jan. 3, 1858.

185. *Washington Union*, Apr. 22, 1858.

186. *Boston Daily Advertiser*, Aug. 18, 1856, in Webb scrapbooks, 16:75–78.

187. *St. Louis Intelligencer*, Feb. 26, 1855, in ibid., 3:17.

CHAPTER FOUR

1. Thomas Goodrich, *War to the Knife: Bleeding Kansas, 1854–1861* (Mechanicsburg, Pa.: Stackpole Books, 1998), 83.

2. *St. Louis Daily Missouri Democrat*, Dec. 13, 1855.

3. *New York Journal of Commerce*, quoted in *Charleston (S.C.) Mercury*, Sept. 1, 1856.

4. *Hartford (Conn.) Daily Courant*, Feb. 26, 1856.

5. *Charleston Mercury*, Sept. 19, 1856.

6. *Chicago Daily Tribune*, Apr. 7, 1856.

7. *Louisville (Ky.) Christian Observer*, Dec. 23, 1854.

8. *Middlesex (Conn.) Argus*, quoted in *Fayetteville (N.C.) Observer*, Mar. 31, 1856.

9. A typical report appears in the *New York Observer & Chronicle*, Jan. 31, 1856.

10. [Henry Ward Beecher], *Defense of Kansas by Henry Ward Beecher* (Washington, D.C.: Buell & Blanchard, Printers, 1856), 1, 3–4, 7.

11. *Cleveland Plain Dealer*, quoted in *Columbus Daily Ohio Statesman*, Aug. 7, 1856.

12. *Detroit Daily Free Press*, Mar. 27, 1856.

13. *St. Louis Daily Missouri Republican*, June 6, 1856.

14. BRUTUS, in *Charleston Mercury*, Apr. 7, 1856.

15. *Dallas Herald* (weekly), Aug. 2, 1856.

16. *Washington (D.C.) Union*, Apr. 16, 1857.

17. *Indianapolis State Sentinel* (weekly), Dec. 13, 1855.

18. Ibid., Oct. 2, 1856.

19. *Concord New Hampshire Patriot & State Gazette*, Sept. 2, 1857.

20. *Boston Post*, Aug. 12, 1856, in Thomas W. Webb scrapbooks, New England Emigrant Aid Company collection, Kansas State Historical Society, Topeka, Kansas, 16:12.

21. A fine summary of these trends is Paul Conkin, *American Originals: Homemade Varieties of Christianity* (Chapel Hill: University of North Carolina Press, 1997), 57, 69–87.

22. *New York Herald*, Jan. 24, 1855.

23. *Boston Atlas*, in *New York Weekly Tribune*, Jan. 3, 1855, in Webb scrapbooks, 2:134.

24. *Richmond Christian Advocate*, quoted in *Daily Richmond (Va.) Enquirer*, Mar. 23, 1854.

25. *Louisville Christian Observer*, Aug. 28, 1856.

26. C. B. L., in *New York Independent*, Oct. 29, 1857.

27. [John Holbrook], *Our Country's Crisis: A Discourse Delivered in Dubuque, Iowa, on Sabbath Evening, July 6, 1856, by Rev. John C. Holbrook, Pastor of the Congregational Church* (n.p., n.d.). Published as part of Gale Group microfiche antislavery pamphlets (Louisville, Ky.: Lost Cause Press, 1962).

28. Debby Applegate, *The Most Famous Man in America* (New York: Doubleday, 2006), 280–282.

29. *New York Observer & Chronicle*, Jan. 31, 1856.

30. *New York Independent*, Feb. 7, 1856.

31. *Chicago Daily Tribune*, Mar. 26, 1856.

32. *New York Observer & Chronicle*, Feb. 14, 1856.

33. *New York Independent*, Mar. 26, 1857.

34. Psalms 73:6 and 37:8–9, quoted in ibid.

35. *New York Independent*, July 9, 1857.

36. Ibid.

37. Gunja SenGupta, *For God and Mammon: Evangelicals and Entrepreneurs, Masters and Slaves in Territorial Kansas, 1854–1860* (Athens and London: University of Georgia Press, 1996), 1, 79, 97, 101, 112.

38. *New York Independent*, Mar. 27, 1856.

39. *Boston Liberator*, Feb. 29, 1856.

40. Ibid.

41. Ibid., Mar. 14, 1856.

42. Eugene Hutchinson, in ibid., May 9, 1856.

43. Theodore Parker, in ibid., Mar. 14, 1856.

44. Theodore Parker, in ibid., Jan. 9, 1857.

45. Henry Mayer, *All on Fire: William Lloyd Garrison and the Abolition of Slavery* (New York: St. Martins Press, 1998), 448, 450, 554.

46. C. Stearns, in *Boston Liberator*, Jan. 4, 1856.

47. Unidentified clipping, Jan. 26, 1856, in Webb scrapbooks, 9:242.

48. *Daily Cincinnati Commercial*, Apr. 13, 1858.

49. Ibid., Nov. 20, 1857.

50. Ralph Harlow, "The Rise and Fall of the Kansas Aid Movement," *American Historical Review* 41, no. 1 (October 1935): 1, 5–6, 8.

51. Adin Ballou, in *Boston Liberator*, May 2, 1856.

52. The phrase is from the *Detroit Daily Free Press*, June 6, 1856.

53. Speech of Lewis Cass, May 12, 13,

1856, *Congressional Globe*, 34th Cong., 1st sess., appendix, 513, 521–522.

54. *Boston Post*, June 13, 1856.

55. Ibid., Aug. 12, 1856.

56. *New York Observer & Chronicle*, Mar. 6, 1856.

57. *Detroit Daily Free Press*, Mar. 27, 1856.

58. *Buffalo Commercial Advertiser*, Mar. 28, 1856, in Webb scrapbooks, 10:202–203.

59. *New Bedford (Mass.) Mercury*, Mar. 29, 1856, in Webb scrapbooks, 10:213.

60. *New Bedford (Mass.) Evening Standard*, Mar. 27, 1856, in Webb scrapbooks, 10:198.

61. *Chicago Daily Tribune*, Apr. 2, 1856.

62. Ibid., Apr. 7, 1856.

63. *Lawrence (Mass.) Courier*, July 3, 1856, in Webb scrapbooks, 14:33.

64. *Philadelphia Inquirer*, July 3, 1856, in Webb scrapbooks, 14:41–42.

65. *Charleston Mercury*, Aug. 11, 1856.

66. Brutus, in *Charleston Mercury*, Apr. 7, 1856.

67. *Richmond (Va.) Enquirer* (semiweekly), Aug. 26, 1856.

68. *New York Daily Tribune*, Dec. 12, 1855.

69. *Charleston Mercury*, quoted in *Pittsfield (Mass.) Sun*, Aug. 7, 1856.

70. *Concord New Hampshire Patriot & State Gazette*, Sept. 23, 1857.

71. *New Orleans Daily Delta*, May 17, 1854.

72. Brutus, in *Charleston Mercury*, Apr. 9, 1856.

73. *Mobile (Ala.) Register*, quoted in *Charleston Mercury*, Aug. 29, 1855.

74. *New Orleans Daily Picayune*, Aug. 31, 1856.

75. John Brown, in *Charleston Mercury*, Apr. 3, 1856.

76. Speech of J. F. Dowdell, July 28, 1856, in *Congressional Globe*, 34th Cong., 1st sess., appendix, 1057–1058.

77. Speech of J. H. Savage, July 31, 1856, in ibid., 1035.

78. *Daily Richmond Enquirer*, July 28, 1855.

79. *Columbus (Ga.) Times & Sentinel Tri-Weekly*, June 5, 1857.

80. Ibid., Jan. 9, 1856.

81. *New York Daily Times*, May 24, 1855.

82. *Columbus Times & Sentinel Tri-Weekly*, Mar. 25, 1858.

83. *Daily Cincinnati Commercial*, Mar. 27, 1858.

84. *Natchez (Miss.) Daily Courier*, May 5, 1858.

85. *New York Christian Inquirer*, Feb. 27, 1858.

86. *New York Independent*, Mar. 4, 1858.

87. Theodore Parker, "A False and True Revival of Religion," in *Boston Liberator*, Apr. 16, 1858.

88. *Boston Liberator*, Apr. 30, 1858.

89. *New York Independent*, Oct. 16, 1856.

90. *Daily Albany (N.Y.) Argus*, Jan. 24, 1856, in Webb scrapbooks, 8:195.

91. Clipping, no place or paper listed, June 29, 1856, in Webb scrapbooks, 14:43.

92. *Daily Cincinnati Commercial*, July 22, 1857.

93. Ibid., July 25, 1857.

94. *Detroit Daily Free Press*, May 5, 1855.

95. *Boston Atlas*, quoted in *Keene New Hampshire Sentinel*, Aug. 17, 1855.

96. *New York City Evening Mirror*, Mar. 1, 1856.

97. *New York Independent*, Oct. 2, 1856.

98. *Boston Congregationalist*, Oct. 31, 1856.

99. *New York Independent*, Oct. 2, 1856.

100. *Washington Union*, Apr. 20, 1858.

101. *Boston Congregationalist*, Sept. 12, 1856.

CHAPTER FIVE

1. The estimates are from David Reynolds, *John Brown, Abolitionist: The Man Who Killed Slavery, Sparked the Civil War, and Seeded Civil Rights* (New York: Alfred A. Knopf, 2005), 163.

2. *New Orleans Daily Picayune*, May 15, 1856.

3. Poem by Mrs. E. M. Bruce, in *Boston Liberator*, Oct. 25, 1856.

4. *Chicago Daily Tribune*, quoted in *Boston Liberator*, May 15, 1857.

5. *Pittsburg Daily Dispatch*, Nov. 10, 1856.

6. Ibid., Dec. 16, 1856.

7. *Independence Messenger* [June 1854], in Thomas W. Webb scrapbooks, New England Emigrant Aid Company collection, Kansas State Historical Society, Topeka, Kansas, 1:48a, 49.

8. *Daily Richmond (Va.) Enquirer*, July 11, 1854.

9. *Boston Atlas*, quoted in *New York Weekly Tribune*, Jan. 3, 1855.

10. Thomas Goodrich, *War to the Knife: Bleeding Kansas, 1854–1861* (Mechanicsburg, Pa.: Stackpole Books, 1998), 43–46. This source and Daniel Wilder, *Annals of Kansas, 1541–1885* (Topeka: T. Dwight Thacher, Kansas Publishing House, 1886), are good places to follow the details of these incidents. Another rich repository of detail is the first history of Kansas, J. N. Hol-

loway, *History of Kansas from the First Exploration of the Mississippi Valley to Its Admission into the Union. . . .* (Lafayette, Ind.: James, Emmons, 1868).

11. George Martin, *The First Two Years of Kansas. . . . An Address* (Topeka, Kans.: State Printing Office, 1907), 14–15. These incidents are legion, and it is not my purpose to be definitive here in detailing them.

12. *Boston Journal*, Apr. 30, 1855, in Webb scrapbooks, 3:197.

13. *London Morning Advertiser*, May 30, 1855, in ibid., 4:112.

14. *Dayton (Ohio) Daily Empire*, May 23, 1855.

15. *Springfield (Mass.) Daily Republican*, May 28, 1855.

16. Ibid., June 4, 1855.

17. *New Orleans Daily Picayune*, June 30, 1855.

18. *Montgomery (Ala.) Advertiser & State Gazette* (weekly), July 11, 1855.

19. *Boston Liberator*, Oct. 19, 1855.

20. Quoted in *Springfield Daily Republican*, Aug. 29, 1855.

21. *Daily Albany (N.Y.) Argus*, Sept. 1, 1855.

22. T, in *St. Louis Daily Missouri Republican*, July 3, 1855; Nicole Etcheson, *Bleeding Kansas: Contested Liberty in the Civil War Era* (Lawrence: University Press of Kansas, 2004), 67; Wilder, *Annals of Kansas*, 66; *Daily Albany (N.Y.) Argus*, July 10, 1855.

23. *Springfield Daily Republican*, July 18, 1855.

24. Ibid., Aug. 29, 1855.

25. Ibid., Sept. 14, 1855.

26. "Address to the People of the United States," in *Daily Richmond Enquirer*, Oct. 3, 1855.

27. *Columbus (Ga.) Times & Sentinel Tri-Weekly*, Oct. 6, 1855.

28. Ibid., Dec. 19, 1855.

29. *Charleston (S.C.) Mercury*, Feb. 4, 1856.

30. *New York Herald*, Feb. 18, 1856.

31. An example is RANDOLPH, in *New York Daily Times*, May 23, 1856.

32. Sara Robinson, *Kansas: Its Exterior and Interior Life. . . .* (Boston: Crosby, Nichols, 1856), 145–146.

33. [Hannah Ropes], *Six Months in Kansas. By a Lady* (Boston: John P. Jewett, 1856), 136–137.

34. Goodrich, *War to the Knife*, 73–86; quotation on 86. Many sources cover this event.

35. *Kansas City (Mo.) Enterprise*, Dec. 1, 1855.

36. Ibid., Dec. 8, 1855.

37. *New Orleans Daily Picayune*, Dec. 7, 1855.

38. *Charleston Mercury*, Mar. 7, 1856.

39. Atchison remarks and letter, in *Charleston Mercury*, Jan. 12, 1856.

40. *Richmond (Va.) Enquirer* (semi-weekly), Apr. 15, 1856.

41. Atchison remarks and letter, in *Charleston Mercury*, Jan. 12, 1856.

42. Ibid., Apr. 8, 1856.

43. *Columbus Times & Sentinel Tri-Weekly*, Jan. 18, 1856.

44. *Daily Richmond Enquirer*, Apr. 14, 1856.

45. *Richmond Enquirer* (semi-weekly), Jan. 29, 1856.

46. Charles Stearns, in *Boston Liberator*, Dec. 21, 1855.

47. *New York Daily Tribune*, Dec. 25, 1855.

48. Ibid., Dec. 29, 1855.

49. Ibid.

50. *New York Daily Times*, Dec. 11, 1855.

51. Ibid., Feb. 9, 1856.

52. *Springfield Daily Republican*, Dec. 14, 1855; *New York Daily Times*, Feb. 4, 1856.

53. *New York Daily Times*, Feb. 6, 1856.

54. *Providence (R.I.) Daily Post*, Dec. 25, 1855; Feb. 4, 1856.

55. Ibid., Dec. 29, 1855.

56. "Things in Kansas," in *Boston Post*, Jan. 18, 1856.

57. Ibid., Feb. 21, 1856.

58. Ibid., Mar. 19, 1856.

59. *New York Herald*, Apr. 10, 1856.

60. *New York Daily Times*, Apr. 25, 1856.

61. Ibid., Apr. 27, 1856; Apr. 28, 1856.

62. *Springfield Daily Republican*, Apr. 29, 1856.

63. *New York Herald*, Apr. 12, 1856.

64. *Daily Richmond Enquirer*, Apr. 29, 1856.

65. *Milwaukee Daily Sentinel*, June 3, 1856.

66. Goodrich, *War to the Knife*, 109–119; Wilder, *Annals of Kansas*, 116; *Albany (N.Y.) Atlas & Argus*, June 10, 1856. The *St. Louis Daily Missouri Republican* and the *St. Louis Daily Missouri Democrat* contained particularly detailed accounts of the events, from which the basic facts used by most other newspapers were derived.

67. Reynolds, *John Brown*, 154–167.

68. Examples are *New York Daily Times*, May 26, 1856, and *St. Louis Daily Missouri Democrat*, May 23, 1856.

69. *Milwaukee Daily Sentinel*, Apr. 30, 1856.

70. *Kansas City Enterprise*, May 2, 1856.

71. *Boston Daily Atlas*, May 5, 1856.

72. *Hartford (Conn.) Daily Courant*, May 7, 1856.

73. *New York Daily Times*, May 8, 1856.

74. *Springfield Daily Republican*, May 7, 1856.

75. *New York Daily Times*, May 8, 1856.

76. *Daily Richmond Enquirer*, May 8, 1856.

77. T, in *St. Louis Daily Missouri Republican*, May 9, 1856.

78. *Daily Richmond Enquirer*, May 16, 1856.

79. *St. Louis Daily Missouri Democrat*, May 10, 1856.

80. *New York Daily Times*, May 30, 1856.

81. *New York Herald*, May 14, 1856.

82. *New York Daily Tribune*, May 15, 1856.

83. *Chicago Daily Tribune*, May 20, 1856.

84. *Boston Post*, May 14, 1856.

85. *Springfield Daily Republican*, May 14, 1856; *St. Louis Daily Missouri Republican*, May 16, 1856; Wilder, *Annals of Kansas*, 118.

86. *New York Daily Tribune*, May 26, 1856.

87. *Milwaukee Daily Sentinel*, June 4, 1856.

88. *St. Louis Daily Missouri Democrat*, May 23, 1856.

89. *New York Daily Tribune*, May 26, 1856.

90. *Hartford Daily Courant*, May 29, 1856.

91. *Springfield Daily Republican*, May 29, 1856.

92. Thomas Gladstone, to the *London Times*, quoted in *Boston Liberator*, Nov. 7, 1856. Gladstone's book was *Kansas; or, Squatter Life and Border Warfare in the Far West* (London: G. Routledge, 1857). Modern reprintings are titled *An Englishman in Kansas*.

93. *Detroit Daily Free Press*, June 3, 1856.

94. *New York Daily Times*, quoted in *New York Herald*, May 27, 1856.

95. *New York Daily Tribune*, May 27 and 29, 1856.

96. *Albany Atlas & Argus*, May 31, 1856.

97. M, in *St. Louis Daily Missouri Republican*, May 30, 1856.

98. *New York Daily Tribune*, June 3, 1856.

99. *Springfield Daily Republican*, June 4, 1856. The paper later did come to believe the story; see ibid., June 28, 1856.

100. *Milwaukee Daily Sentinel*, June 6, 1856.

101. *St. Louis Daily Missouri Republican*, June 17, 1856.

102. Leverett Spring, *Kansas: The Prelude to the War for the Union* (Boston: Houghton, Mifflin, 1885), 137.

103. A good guide to changing governors and their biographies is Homer Socolofsky, *Kansas Governors* (Lawrence: University Press of Kansas, 1990). The section on Geary begins on page 49. The role of the governors will be treated more extensively in chapter 7.

104. *New Orleans Daily Picayune*, June 18, 1856.

105. *Springfield Daily Republican*, July 1, 1856.

106. *New York Herald*, July 3, 1856.

107. Quoted in *Springfield Daily Republican*, July 8, 1856.

108. Quoted in *Detroit Daily Tribune*, July 26, 1856, in Webb scrapbooks, 15:132.

109. *New York Independent*, Sept. 11, 1856.

110. Speech of John Bell, July 2, 1856, in *Congressional Globe*, 34th Cong., 1st sess., appendix, 788.

111. A KANSAS CITIZEN, in *Chicago Weekly Times*, Oct. 30, 1856.

112. *Daily Cincinnati Commercial*, July 16, 1856.

113. T, in *St. Louis Daily Missouri Republican*, Aug. 12, 1856.

114. *St. Louis Daily Missouri Republican*, Aug. 21, 1856; *Detroit Daily Free Press*, Aug. 27, 1856.

115. *St. Louis Daily Missouri Republican*, Aug. 22, 1856.

116. *Detroit Daily Free Press*, Aug. 23, 1856.

117. Quoted in *St. Louis Daily Missouri Republican*, Aug. 23, 1856.

118. For an account, see Goodrich, *War to the Knife*, 150–155.

119. Quoted in *St. Louis Daily Missouri Democrat*, Sept. 3, 1856.

120. Ibid.

121. *Montgomery Advertiser & State Gazette* (weekly), Oct. 15, 1856.

122. Benj. Castleman, in *St. Louis Daily Missouri Republican*, Sept. 14, 1856; H. C. P., in *St. Louis Daily Missouri Republican*, Sept. 25, 1856.

123. *Wayne County Democrat*, quoted in *Daily Columbus Ohio Statesman*, Sept. 13, 1856.

124. *New York Daily Tribune*, Sept. 17, 1856.

125. C. C. H., in ibid., Sept. 17, 1856.

126. *Kansas City Enterprise*, Sept. 20, 1856.

127. Wilder, *Annals of Kansas*, 137; Goodrich, *War to the Knife*, 174–179.

128. See, for example, coverage in *Savannah Daily Georgian*, Oct. 2, 1856.

129. Wilder, *Annals of Kansas*, 139.

130. *New York Daily Tribune*, Oct. 4, 1856.

131. *Columbus Daily Ohio Statesman*, Oct. 8, 1856.

132. Letter of James Lane to A. W. Doniphan and A. G. Boone, Sept. 22, 1856, in *New York Daily Tribune*, Oct. 4, 1856.

133. *London Times*, quoted in *Boston Daily Atlas*, Oct. 20, 1856.

134. One may follow these well in Etcheson, *Bleeding Kansas*. I will return to this debate in more detail in chapter 8.

135. *Albany Atlas & Argus*, Aug. 23, 1856.

136. *Chicago Daily Tribune*, Aug. 26, 1856; *Philadelphia Public Ledger & Daily Transcript*, Sept. 1, 1856.

137. Speech of William Seward, Aug. 7, 1856, in *Congressional Globe*, 34th Cong., 1st sess., appendix, 1110.

138. *New York Herald*, Aug. 23, 1856.

139. *Chicago Daily Tribune*, Aug. 26, 1856.

140. *New York Daily Tribune*, quoted in *St. Louis Daily Missouri Republican*, Sept. 4, 1856.

141. *Albany Atlas & Argus*, Aug. 23, 1856.

142. *Charleston Mercury*, Aug. 5, 1856.

143. *New Orleans Daily Picayune*, Aug. 5, 1856.

144. *Louisville (Ky.) Daily Journal*, Aug. 20, 1856.

145. *Springfield Daily Republican*, Sept. 6, 1856; *St. Louis Daily Missouri Republican*, Sept. 7, 1856.

146. *Hartford Daily Courant*, Sept. 27, 1856; *New York Daily Tribune*, June 27, 1857.

147. *Springfield Daily Republican*, Sept. 2, 1856.

148. Ibid., Sept. 30, 1856.

149. *New York Daily Tribune*, Oct. 4, 1856, Feb. 21, 1857; *Boston Liberator*, Oct. 10, 1856; *Springfield Daily Republican*, Sept. 3, 16, 1856.

150. *St. Louis Daily Missouri Democrat,* Mar. 17, Apr. 28, 1857. A firsthand account by Geary's secretary is John Gihon, *Geary and Kansas . . .* (Philadelphia: Chas. C. Rhodes, 1857), 166–173.

151. *Springfield Daily Republican,* Oct. 28, 1856.

152. *St. Louis Daily Missouri Democrat,* Nov. 18, 1856.

153. See *New York Daily Tribune,* Dec. 13, 1856, for the proclamation.

154. *Springfield Daily Republican,* Oct. 14, 1856; *Milwaukee Daily Sentinel,* Nov. 3, 1856.

155. *Milwaukee Daily Sentinel,* Oct. 20, 1856.

156. *Springfield Daily Republican,* Oct. 24, 1856.

157. *New York Daily Tribune,* Oct. 25, 1856.

158. *Hartford Daily Courant,* Oct. 22, 1856.

159. Thomas Higginson, *A Ride through Kansas* (New York: Anti-Slavery Society, 1856), 6, 8, 14.

160. J. S. R., in *Montgomery Advertiser & State Gazette* (weekly), Nov. 12, 1856.

161. Gihon, *Geary and Kansas,* 187–191.

162. *New York Daily Tribune,* Dec. 13, 1856.

163. *St. Louis Daily Missouri Republican,* Jan. 17, May 8, 1857; *St. Louis Daily Missouri Democrat,* Aug. 24, 1857; *Springfield Daily Republican,* Mar. 5, 1857; Etcheson, *Bleeding Kansas,* 125–126. A good summary of Geary's attempt to make the justice system work in Kansas is Spring, *Kansas,* 202–204.

164. Sara Robinson, *Kansas,* 307. Charles himself wrote briefly of his arrest in *The Kansas Conflict* (New York: Harper & Brothers, 1892), 236–239.

165. Memorial, quoted in Gladstone, *Kansas,* 291–292. See *New York Daily Tribune,* Oct. 31, 1856, for an account of one prison death.

166. *New York Daily Tribune,* Nov. 3, 1856.

167. UNION, in *St. Louis Daily Missouri Democrat,* Nov. 13, 1856.

168. ESSEX, in ibid., Nov. 17, 1856.

169. *Springfield Daily Republican,* Nov. 15, 1856.

170. *New York Daily Tribune,* Dec. 13, 1856.

171. UNION, in *St. Louis Daily Missouri Democrat,* Dec. 23, 1856.

172. Letter originally to *Cincinnati Gazette,* printed in *Boston Liberator,* Dec. 26, 1856.

173. *New York Independent,* Feb. 12, 1857.

174. Speech of Andrew Reeder, Sept. 19, 1856, in *New York Daily Tribune,* Sept. 22, 1856.

175. *New York Daily Tribune,* Feb. 21, 1857.

176. See Reynolds, *John Brown,* 210–213.

177. James Davis and others, in *St. Louis Daily Missouri Democrat,* Apr. 28, 1857; *New York Daily Tribune,* May 4, 1857.

178. T, in *St. Louis Daily Missouri Republican,* Sept. 26, 1856.

CHAPTER SIX

1. *Louisville (Ky.) Daily Journal,* Dec. 4, 1855.

2. Ibid., Sept. 4, 1855.

3. *New Orleans Daily Picayune,* Nov. 30, 1856.

4. Ibid., Oct. 8, 1856.

5. Ibid.

6. *New York Daily Times,* Mar. 25, 1854.

7. Unidentified Baltimore newspaper, n.d. [Oct. 1855], in Thomas W. Webb scrapbooks, New England Emigrant Aid Company collection, Kansas State Historical Society, Topeka, Kansas, 6:116.

8. *Mobile (Ala.) Daily Tribune*, n.d. [Oct. 1855], in ibid., 6:116.

9. *Charleston (S.C.) Mercury*, in ibid., 6:231–232.

10. *Charleston Mercury*, Apr. 1, 1856.

11. *Washington (D.C.) Union*, June 5, 1857.

12. *Daily Richmond (Va.) Enquirer*, Mar. 29, 1856.

13. *Richmond (Va.) South*, Apr. 7, 1857.

14. Ibid., May 2, 1857.

15. *Macon Georgia Telegraph*, May 12, 1857.

16. *Charleston Mercury*, Aug. 25, 1857.

17. *Columbus (Ga.) Times & Sentinel Tri-Weekly*, Sept. 8, 1857.

18. *Chicago Daily Tribune*, Apr. 12, 1858.

19. *Louisville Daily Journal*, Jan. 26, 1854.

20. Thomas Higginson, in *Boston Liberator*, June 12, 1857.

21. *Macon Georgia Telegraph*, Apr. 4, 1854.

22. *Washington (D.C.) Daily Union*, Apr. 30, 1854.

23. Quoted in *New York Herald*, Jan. 11, 1857.

24. *Washington Union*, Mar. 21, 1857.

25. *New Orleans Daily Picayune*, July 3, 1857.

26. Leonard Richards, *The Slave Power: The Free North and Southern Domination, 1780–1860* (Baton Rouge: Louisiana State University Press, 2000), 2, 26–27.

27. *New York Daily Tribune*, Feb. 2, 1854.

28. *New York Daily Times*, Mar. 1, 1854.

29. *Washington (D.C.) National Era*, June 25, 1857.

30. *New York Daily Tribune*, Dec. 7, 1855.

31. *Detroit Evening Tribune*, Jan. 23, 1856, in Webb scrapbooks, 8:183–184.

32. Ibid., Jan. 5, 1856, in Webb scrapbooks, 8:45.

33. *San Francisco Daily Alta California*, Mar. 14, 1854.

34. *Detroit Daily Free Press*, Dec. 25, 1856.

35. Ibid., Dec. 10, 1856.

36. Ibid., Sept. 1, 1854.

37. *New York Herald*, May 10, 1855.

38. Ibid., Jan. 14, 1856.

39. Speech of G. W. Jones, Apr. 16, 1856, in *Congressional Globe*, 34th Cong., 1st sess., appendix, 406–407.

40. Speech of G. E. Pugh, May 26, 1856, in ibid., 612–618.

41. Speech of R. M. T. Hunter, Feb. 24, 1854, in *Congressional Globe*, 33rd Cong., 1st sess., appendix, 226.

42. Speech of P. S. Brooks, Mar. 15, 1854, in ibid., 374.

43. Speech of G. S. Brown, Feb. 24, 1854, in ibid., 230.

44. Speech of T. L. Clingman, Apr. 4, 1854, in ibid., 491–492.

45. Speech of A. H. Stephens, June 28, 1856, in *Congressional Globe*, 34th Cong., 1st sess., appendix, 728.

46. *Washington Daily Union*, Oct. 4, 1855.

47. A SOUTHERNER, in *New York Daily Times*, Mar. 16, 1854.

48. Charles Stearns, in *Boston Liberator*, Oct. 5, 1855.

49. *Charleston Mercury*, Feb. 2, 1856.

50. *St. Louis Daily Missouri Democrat,*
Feb. 20, 1856.

51. *New Orleans Daily Picayune,* Mar.
22, 1856.

52. *Daily Richmond Enquirer,* Mar. 29,
1856.

53. *Mobile (Ala.) Daily Tribune,* n.d.
[Oct. 1855], in Webb scrapbooks, 6:116.

54. David Davis, *The Slave Power Conspiracy and the Paranoid Style* (Baton
Rouge: Louisiana State University Press,
1969), 3, 10, 20.

55. Franklin Pierce, message to Congress, Jan. 24, 1856, in *New York Daily Times,* Jan. 26, 1856.

56. *New York Daily Times,* Jan. 26,
1856.

57. *Albany (N.Y.) Atlas,* Jan. 28, 1856,
in Webb scrapbooks, Jan. 28, 1856,
8:229.

58. *Chicago Daily Tribune,* Jan. 29,
1856.

59. Speech of Henry Wilson, Feb. 18,
1856, in *Congressional Globe,* 34th Cong.,
1st sess., appendix, 90.

60. *New York Daily Tribune,* Mar. 14,
1856.

61. Nichole Etcheson, *Bleeding Kansas: Contested Liberty in the Civil War Era* (Lawrence: University Press of
Kansas, 2004), 97–98.

62. A good place to track the detail is
Daniel Wilder, *The Annals of Kansas,
1541–1885* (Topeka: T. Dwight Thacher,
Kansas Publishing House, 1886). This is
not, however, a volume for light recreational reading, or one that garners
points on style.

63. U.S. Congress, Senate, *Affairs of Kansas,* SR 34, 34th Cong., 1st sess.,
Mar. 12, 1856 (Serial 836), 7–8, 24–25;
Etcheson, *Bleeding Kansas,* 97.

64. U.S. Congress, Senate, *Affairs of Kansas,* 42, 45, 61.

65. Speech of William Seward, Apr.
9, 1856, in *Congressional Globe,* 34th
Cong., 1st sess., appendix, 399–405.

66. Charleston newspaper, Apr. 26,
1856, in Webb scrapbooks, 9:170–171.

67. *Daily Richmond Enquirer,* May 6,
1856.

68. This information came from
www.abebooks.com., an Internet compilation of the offerings of rare-book
dealers.

69. All quotations from Sumner's
speech, May 19–20, 1856, are from *Congressional Globe,* 34th Cong., 1st sess.,
appendix, 529–540.

70. "Heroic Lawrence," in *Philadelphia Daily Enquirer,* May 30, 1856, in
Webb scrapbooks, 12:247.

71. *New Orleans Daily Picayune,* May
28, 1856.

72. Ibid., June 17, 1856.

73. *Congressional Globe,* 34th Cong,
1st sess., appendix, 544–545.

74. A CLEVELANDER, in *Daily Cleveland Herald,* May 24, 1856.

75. *New Orleans Daily Picayune,* May
27, 28, 1856.

76. *London Times,* June 27, 1856.

77. Speech of A. H. Stephens, June
28, 1856, in *Congressional Globe,* 34th
Cong., 1st sess., appendix, 723–726.

78. *New York Herald,* July 4, 1856.

79. Ibid., July 2, 25, 1856.

80. *Springfield (Mass.) Daily Republican,* July 11, 1856.

81. Speech of J. Stewart, July 23,
1856, in *Congressional Globe,* 34th Cong.,
1st sess., appendix, 989–992.

82. Ibid.

83. *Charleston Mercury,* Aug. 11,
1856.

84. *Columbus Times & Sentinel Tri-Weekly,* Mar. 7, 1857.

85. *Washington Union,* Mar. 31, 1857.

86. *St. Louis Daily Missouri Democrat,* Nov. 26, 1856.

87. *New York Daily Tribune,* Jan. 3, 1857.

88. *Washington (D.C.) Union,* July 15, 1857.

89. *Hartford (Conn.) Daily Courant,* Feb. 10, 1858.

CHAPTER SEVEN

1. *Chicago Daily Tribune,* June 18, 1857; *Hartford (Conn.) Daily Courant,* Dec. 23, 1857.

2. KANSAS, in *St. Louis Daily Missouri Democrat,* June 8, 1857.

3. SAXON, in *Chicago Daily Tribune,* June 3, 1857; *Washington (D.C.) Union,* June 6, 1857; P. H. C., in *New York Daily Times,* June 6, 1857.

4. JUNIUS, in *Chicago Daily Tribune,* June 1, 1857.

5. *Chicago Daily Tribune,* June 13, 1857.

6. *Richmond (Va.) South,* June 5, 1857.

7. *Washington (D.C.) National Era,* Aug. 6, 1857.

8. Ibid., June 15, 1857.

9. *Macon Georgia Telegraph,* June 16, 1857.

10. *Washington Union,* June 27, 1857.

11. JACOBIUS, in *St. Louis Daily Missouri Democrat,* Aug. 1, 1857.

12. *Washington Union,* June 27, 1857.

13. JACOBIUS, in *St. Louis Daily Missouri Democrat,* Aug. 1, 1857.

14. Sara Robinson, *Kansas: Its Exterior and Interior Life. . . .* (Boston: Crosby, Nichols, 1856), 117.

15. *Washington Union,* June 27, 1857.

16. JACOBIUS, in *St. Louis Daily Missouri Democrat,* Aug. 1, 1857.

17. *New York Daily Tribune,* July 30, 1857.

18. JACOBIUS, in *St. Louis Daily Missouri Democrat,* Aug. 1, 1857.

19. Ibid.

20. *Pittsburg Daily Dispatch,* Dec. 4, 1857.

21. *Providence (R.I.) Daily Post,* Dec. 15, 1857.

22. *Washington National Era,* Aug. 6, 1857; *Chicago Daily Tribune,* Aug. 10, 1857.

23. *Washington Union,* Dec. 20, 1857.

24. *Columbus (Ga.) Enquirer Tri-Weekly,* Jan 16, 1858.

25. *Hartford Daily Courant,* Mar. 17, 1858.

26. Homer Socolofsky, *Kansas Governors* (Lawrence: University Press of Kansas, 1990).

27. *Boston Post,* Dec. 14, 1854; *Detroit Daily Free Press,* Jan. 30, 1856.

28. S. F. Tappan, in *Kansas City (Mo.) Enterprise,* Oct. 28, 1854, in Thomas W. Webb scrapbooks, New England Emigrant Aid Company collection, Kansas State Historical Society, Topeka, Kansas, 1:206–208.

29. *Boston Post,* Oct. 31, 1854.

30. *San Francisco Daily Alta California,* Feb. 3, 1855.

31. Paul Gates, *Fifty Million Acres: Conflicts over Kansas Land Policy, 1854–1890* (Ithaca, N.Y.: Cornell University Press, 1954), 39–40.

32. *New York Herald,* May 3, 1855.

33. *Boston Liberator,* May 4, 1855.

34. *Washington (D.C.) Daily Union,* May 11, 1855.

35. *New Orleans Daily Picayune,* Aug. 14, 1855.

36. *Washington Daily Union,* June 19, 1855.

37. *New Orleans Daily Picayune,* June 26, 1855; *New York Daily Times,* Apr. 30, 1855; William Unrau, *Mixed-Bloods and*

Tribal Dissolution: Charles Curtis and the Quest for Indian Identity (Lawrence: University Press of Kansas, 1989), 44. Unrau's book is outstanding on the subsequent history and influence of these parcels.

38. *Springfield (Mass.) Daily Republican*, July 31, 1855, and *Keene New Hampshire Sentinel*, Aug. 10, 1855, are among many editorial comments on the removal. For Reeder's account of his defense before Pierce, see A. H. Reeder, in *New York Herald*, July 23, 1856. For Manypenny's account, see George Manypenny, in *Kansas City Enterprise*, Aug. 23, 1856.

39. *St. Louis Daily Missouri Republican*, July 18, 1855.

40. *New York Herald*, quoted in *Charleston (S.C.) Mercury*, Aug. 2, 1855.

41. *Daily Cleveland Herald*, Nov. 30, 1855, in Webb scrapbooks, 7:22.

42. *Albany (N.Y.) Atlas & Argus*, Sept. 29, 1856.

43. Socolofsky, *Kansas Governors*, 37; *New York Daily Tribune*, Aug. 11, 1855.

44. Socolofsky, *Kansas Governors*, 38–43.

45. J. R., in *Boston Liberator*, Aug. 31, 1855.

46. *New York Herald*, Sept. 15, 1855.

47. *Albany (N.Y.) Atlas*, Sept. 15, 1855, in Webb scrapbooks, 5:175.

48. *Detroit Daily Free Press*, Sept. 16, 1855; *Lynchburg Virginian*, Sept. 21, 1855, in Webb scrapbooks, 5:191.

49. *Springfield Daily Republican*, Sept. 18, 1855.

50. LITERAL, in *New York Daily Times*, Dec. 17, 1855.

51. Wilson Shannon to C. S. Holliday and others, May 28, 1856, in *Albany Atlas & Argus*, June 6, 1856.

52. L, in *Milwaukee Daily Sentinel*, July 3, 1856.

53. Socolofsky, *Kansas Governors*, 46, 50.

54. *New York Daily Tribune*, Aug. 16, 1856.

55. Good detail is in *St. Louis Daily Missouri Republican*, Oct. 2, 1856.

56. *St. Louis Daily Missouri Democrat*, Sept. 19, 1856.

57. *New York Weekly Herald*, Sept. 27, 1856.

58. *New York Daily Tribune*, Oct. 18, 1856.

59. John Gihon, *Geary and Kansas . . .* (Philadelphia: Chas. C. Rhodes, 1857), 125–131, 134, 158–161, 195, 260.

60. *Hartford Daily Courant*, Jan. 30, 1857.

61. Accounts are in Thomas Goodrich, *War to the Knife: Bleeding Kansas, 1854–1861* (Mechanicsburg, Pa.: Stackpole Books, 1998), 190–193; Gihon, *Geary and Kansas*, 227–243; *New York Daily Tribune*, Mar. 4, 1857; *Springfield Daily Republican*, Mar. 5, 1857.

62. *New York Daily Tribune*, Feb. 28, 1857.

63. *St. Louis Daily Missouri Democrat*, Mar. 17, 1857.

64. *Charleston Mercury*, Mar. 18, 1857.

65. *New York Daily Tribune*, Mar. 21, 1857.

66. *New York Daily Times*, Mar. 23, 1857.

67. *New Orleans Daily Delta*, Mar. 25, 1857.

68. John Geary, address at Lecompton, Mar. 10, 1857, in Gihon, *Geary and Kansas*, 293–299.

69. *New York Herald*, Mar. 27, 1857.

70. *New Orleans Daily Picayune*, Apr. 9, 1857.

71. *Chicago Daily Tribune,* Apr. 11, 14, 1857; *Pittsburg Daily Dispatch,* Apr. 18, 1857.

72. *New York Herald,* Apr. 27, 1857.

73. *Kansas City Enterprise,* May 2, 1857.

74. *Chicago Daily Tribune,* May 4, 8, 21, 1857.

75. JUNIUS, in ibid., May 6, 1857.

76. The entire text of Walker's address is in Gihon, *Geary and Kansas,* 328–348.

77. *New York Daily Times,* June 8, 1857.

78. *New York Daily Tribune,* June 8, 1857.

79. *Albany Atlas & Argus,* June 8, 1857.

80. *Chicago Daily Tribune,* June 17, 1857.

81. *Louisville (Ky.) Daily Journal,* June 15, 1857.

82. *Chicago Daily Tribune,* June 18, 1857.

83. *Louisville Daily Journal,* June 20, 1857.

84. *Columbus (Ga.) Times & Sentinel Tri-Weekly,* June 27, 1857.

85. *Albany Atlas & Argus,* June 24, 1857.

86. *Jackson Mississippian,* quoted in *Charleston Mercury,* July 20, 1857.

87. *New Orleans Daily Picayune,* July 14, 1857.

88. *New York Daily Tribune,* July 14, 1857.

89. *Charleston Mercury,* July 15, 1857.

90. *New York Daily Tribune,* July 22, 1857.

91. *Washington Union,* July 22, 1857.

92. *New York Daily Tribune,* July 22, 23, 1857.

93. *Daily Cincinnati Commercial,* July 23, 1857.

94. *New York Daily Tribune,* July 27, 1857.

95. *Chicago Daily Tribune,* Aug. 26, 1857.

96. RANDOLPH, in *St. Louis Daily Missouri Democrat,* July 25, 1857.

97. *Boston Liberator,* July 31, 1857.

98. JACOBIUS, in *St. Louis Daily Missouri Democrat,* Aug. 1, 1857.

99. RANDOLPH, in ibid., Aug. 10, 1857; *Springfield Daily Republican,* Aug. 11, 1857.

100. *Daily Cincinnati Commercial,* Aug. 10, 1857.

101. Quoted in Goodrich, *War to the Knife,* 155.

102. George Barns, *Denver, the Man: The Life, Letters and Public Papers of the Lawyer, Soldier and Statesman* (Wilmington, Ohio: George Barns, 1949), 205, 207.

CHAPTER EIGHT

1. These events can be well followed in outline in Daniel Wilder, *Annals of Kansas, 1541–1885* (Topeka: T. Dwight Thacher, Kansas Publishing House, 1886). The Lecompton Constitution is printed there in full on 177–190. Other useful accounts, in varying detail, are Nicole Etcheson, *Bleeding Kansas: Contested Liberty in the Civil War Era* (Lawrence: University Press of Kansas, 2004), 139–189; Allan Nevins, *The Emergence of Lincoln,* vol. 1, *Douglas, Buchanan, and Party Chaos, 1857–1859* (New York: Scribner, 1950), 161–175, 259–304; Craig Miner, *Kansas: The History of the Sunflower State, 1854–2000* (Lawrence: University Press of Kansas, 2002), 72–74; David Potter, *The Impending Crisis, 1848–1861* (New York:

Harper & Row, 1976), 297–352; Kenneth Stampp, *America in 1857: A Nation on the Brink* (New York: Oxford University Press, 1990), 267–331.

2. Stampp, *America in 1857*, 267.

3. "The Great Struggle," in *Pittsburg (Pa.) Daily Dispatch*, Feb. 4, 1858.

4. *Providence (R.I.) Daily Post*, Oct. 29, 1857.

5. *Concord New Hampshire Patriot & State Gazette*, Jan. 5, 1857.

6. SPILMAN, in *St. Louis Daily Missouri Democrat*, Mar. 5, 1857.

7. *New York Daily Tribune*, Jan. 28, 1857.

8. *Concord New Hampshire Patriot & State Gazette*, Jan. 21, 1857.

9. *Albany (N.Y.) Atlas & Argus*, Feb. 27, 1857.

10. Charles Robinson to editor, Jan. 28, from Boston in *Boston Daily Atlas*, Jan. 30, 1857.

11. Charles Robinson, quoted in *Washington (D.C.) National Era*, Apr. 2, 1857.

12. H. C. P., in *St. Louis Daily Missouri Republican*, Jan. 17, 1857.

13. *Chicago Weekly Times*, Apr. 9, 1857.

14. JUNIUS, in *Chicago Daily Tribune*, Apr. 20, 1857.

15. *Concord New Hampshire Patriot & State Gazette*, Apr. 22, 1857.

16. *Washington National Era*, Apr. 23, 1857.

17. *Providence Daily Post*, Mar. 31, 1857.

18. JUNIUS, in *Chicago Daily Tribune*, June 16, 1857.

19. Charles Robinson, quoted in *St. Louis Daily Missouri Democrat*, June 17, 1857.

20. JACOBIUS, in *St. Louis Daily Missouri Democrat*, July 27, 1857.

21. *New Orleans Daily Delta*, July 2, 1857.

22. Ibid., May 22, 1857.

23. *Charleston (S.C.) Mercury*, July 6, 1857.

24. CATO, in ibid., July 30, 1857.

25. Z, in ibid., Aug. 13, 1857.

26. Laurence Keitt, in ibid., July 10, 1857.

27. OCCIDENT, in *Chicago Daily Tribune*, July 16, 1857.

28. *Richmond (Va.) South*, Aug. 11, 1857.

29. *Washington (D.C.) Union*, Aug. 27, 1857.

30. Ibid., Sept. 3, 1857; *New York Herald*, Sept. 4, 1857; *New York Daily Times*, Sept. 4, 1857; *Charleston Mercury*, Sept. 7, 1857; *New York Daily Tribune*, Sept. 11, 1857; *Daily Richmond (Va.) Enquirer*, Sept. 5, 1857; *Boston Post*, Sept. 5, 1857; *New Orleans Daily Picayune*, Sept. 10, 1857; *Chicago Weekly Times*, Sept. 17, 1857. The *Washington Union*, Sept. 12, 1857, contained a selection from newspaper reaction around the nation.

31. *New York Herald*, Sept. 7, 1857.

32. *Boston Post*, Sept. 5, 1857.

33. *New York Citizen*, quoted in *Washington Union*, Sept. 12, 1857.

34. George Curtis, *The Duty of the American Scholar to Politics and the Times*. . . . (New York: Dix, Edwards, 1856), 7–8, 45.

35. *New York Daily Times*, Sept. 30, 1857; *Richmond (Va.) Enquirer* (semiweekly), Oct. 2, 1857; *Richmond South*, Oct. 3, 1857.

36. *St. Louis Daily Missouri Democrat*, Oct. 22, 1857.

37. X, in *St. Louis Daily Missouri Republican*, Oct. 26, 1857; *Daily Cincinnati Commercial*, Oct. 29, 1857; *New Orleans Daily Picayune*, Nov. 11, 1857.

38. *New York Daily Times*, Oct. 27, 1857.

39. *Philadelphia Press*, Oct. 7, 1857.

40. Ibid., Nov. 2, Dec. 3, 1857; Homer Socolofsky, *Kansas Governors* (Lawrence: University Press of Kansas, 1990), 62.

41. *St. Louis Daily Missouri Republican*, Nov. 9, 1857.

42. ALEXIS, in *Chicago Daily Tribune*, Nov. 9, 1857.

43. *Washington Union*, Dec. 25, 1857.

44. J, in *Chicago Daily Tribune*, Nov. 24, 1857; ALEXIS, in ibid., Nov. 9, 1857.

45. *Providence Daily Post*, Oct. 30, 1857.

46. *New York Daily Tribune*, Nov. 16, 1857.

47. *New York Daily Tribune*, Nov. 16, 1857; *St. Louis Daily Missouri Democrat*, Nov. 30, 1857.

48. *New York Daily Times*, Nov. 16, 1857.

49. *Daily Cincinnati Commercial*, Nov. 18, 1857.

50. *New York Herald*, Nov. 18, 1857.

51. *Detroit Daily Free Press*, Nov. 20, 1857.

52. *Le Constitutionnel*, quoted in *Philadelphia Press*, Jan. 15, 1858.

53. *Chicago Daily Tribune*, Nov. 24, 1857.

54. S. C. P., in *St. Louis Daily Missouri Democrat*, Jan. 21, 1858.

55. *Daily Cincinnati Commercial*, Nov. 20, 1857.

56. *Philadelphia Press*, Nov. 23, 1857.

57. Ibid., Dec. 3, 1857.

58. A Kentucky Subscriber, in *New York Daily Times*, Nov. 28, 1857.

59. *New Orleans Daily Picayune*, Dec. 20, 1857, and *Charleston Mercury*, Dec. 31, 1857, summarize this position.

60. *Charleston Mercury*, Nov. 23, 1857.

61. *St. Louis Daily Missouri Democrat*, Nov. 23, 1857.

62. *Richmond (Va.) Enquirer* (semiweekly), Dec. 1, 1857.

63. Ibid., Feb. 2, 1858.

64. *Macon Georgia Telegraph*, Jan. 12, 1858.

65. *Eufaula (Ala.) Spirit of the South*, quoted in *Charleston Mercury*, Dec. 7, 1857.

66. *New York Daily Tribune*, Dec. 3, 1857; *New York Daily Times*, Dec. 4, 1857.

67. *Dayton (Ohio) Daily Empire*, Mar. 24, 1858.

68. ALEXIS, in *St. Louis Daily Missouri Democrat*, Dec. 23, 1858; *Washington Union*, Dec. 27, 1857; *New York Daily Tribune*, Dec. 28, 1857; *Boston Post*, Dec. 30, 1857; *Chicago Daily Tribune*, Dec. 31, 1857; *St. Louis Daily Missouri Democrat*, Jan. 2, 1858; *Providence Daily Post*, Jan. 7, 1858; *New York Daily Tribune*, Jan. 8, 1858. The details are beside the point for this history. A good contemporary source is William Tomlinson, *Kansas in Eighteen Fifty-Eight, Being Chiefly a History of the Recent Troubles in the Territory* (New York: H. Dayton, 1859). See also Thomas Goodrich, *War to the Knife: Bleeding Kansas, 1854–1861* (Mechanicsburg, Pa.: Stackpole Books, 1998), 213–225.

69. *St. Louis Daily Missouri Republican*, Dec. 27, 1857; Jan. 7, 1858.

70. Ibid., Jan. 4, 5, 1858.

71. *Cincinnati Enquirer*, quoted in *Boston Post*, Jan. 2, 1858.

72. *St. Louis Daily Missouri Democrat*, Feb. 2, 1858.

73. *New York Daily Times*, Jan. 8, 1858.

74. *Boston Post*, Feb. 26, 1858.

75. Ibid.

76. *Chicago Daily Tribune*, Feb. 9, 1858.

77. *Springfield (Mass.) Daily Republican*, Feb. 6, 1858.

78. *Providence Daily Post*, Feb. 22, 1858.

79. Ibid., Feb. 20, 1857.

80. *Columbus (Ga.) Times & Sentinel Tri-Weekly*, Feb. 16, 1858.

81. *Providence Daily Post*, Feb. 20, 1857.

82. George Bancroft, quoted in *Chicago Weekly Times*, Feb. 25, 1858.

83. *Chicago Daily Tribune*, Jan. 19, 1858.

84. James Buchanan, message to Congress, in *Washington Union*, Feb. 3, 1858.

85. *Philadelphia Public Ledger & Daily Transcript*, Feb. 3, 1858.

86. *New York Daily Tribune*, Feb. 3, 1858.

87. *Washington Union*, Feb. 6, 1858.

88. The *Washington Union* of Feb. 7, 1858, gives a good summary of newspaper quotations from around the country in favor of Lecompton.

89. Particularly subtle are arguments in the *Philadelphia Press* and the *Boston Post*, both Northern, antislave, but also Democratic Party newspapers.

90. *Bangor (Maine) Union*, quoted in *Washington Union*, Feb. 7, 1858.

91. *Richmond South*, Feb. 9, 1858.

92. *Columbus Times & Sentinel Tri-Weekly*, Feb. 4, 1858.

93. Ibid., Feb. 25, 1858.

94. *Louisville (Ky.) Daily Journal*, Feb. 8, 1858.

95. *Milwaukee Daily Sentinel*, Feb. 9, 1858.

96. OBSERVER, in *New York Independent*, Feb. 4, 1858.

97. *Chicago Weekly Times*, Feb. 4, 1858.

98. Speech of H. M. Phillips, Mar. 9, 1858, in *Congressional Globe*, 35th Cong., 1st sess., appendix, 71–72.

99. Speech of G. Pugh, Mar. 15, 1858, in ibid., 106.

100. *Chicago Daily Tribune*, Mar. 13, 15, 16, 1858.

101. Speech of H. Wilson, Mar. 15, 1858, in *Congressional Globe*, 35th Cong., 1st sess., appendix, 102.

102. Speech of Daniel Clark, Mar. 15, 1858, in ibid., 107–108.

103. Speech of R. Toombs, Mar. 18, 1858, in ibid., 124.

104. Speech of H. Wilson, Mar. 20, 1858, in ibid., 168.

105. Speech of M. Taylor, Mar. 29, 1858, in ibid., 231–233.

106. Speech of J. Gilmer, Mar. 31, 1858, in ibid., 283–284.

107. Speech of G. Pugh, Apr. 28, 1858, in ibid., 350.

108. TYPHIA, in *Charleston Mercury*, Mar. 26, 1858.

109. Ibid.

110. *New York Herald*, Jan. 6, 1858. See also ibid., Jan. 7, 1858.

111. All quoted in *New York Herald*, Jan. 13, 1858. See also *Richmond Enquirer* (semi-weekly), Jan. 12, 1858.

112. R. J. Walker, quoted in *New York Daily Tribune*, Apr. 1, 1858.

113. *Detroit Daily Free Press*, Feb. 13, 1858.

114. *Providence Daily Post*, Jan. 15, 1858.

115. *New Orleans Daily Delta*, Jan. 13, 1858.

116. *New York Herald*, Jan. 24, 1858.

117. *Columbus Daily Ohio Statesman*, Mar. 18, 1858.

118. *Detroit Daily Free Press*, Jan. 31, 1858.

119. *Charleston Mercury*, Feb. 22, 1858.

120. *Chicago Daily Tribune*, Mar. 25, 1858.

121. *Columbus Times & Sentinel Tri-Weekly*, Apr. 15, 1858.

122. *New York Daily Times*, Feb. 1, 1858.

123. Ibid., Mar. 15, 1858.

124. Ibid., Mar. 17, 1858.

125. Ibid., Mar. 23, 1858.

126. *New York Herald*, Feb. 7, 1858.

127. Ibid., Mar. 13, 1858.

128. Ibid., Mar. 24, 1858. See also ibid., Apr. 19, 1858, for an even more extreme diatribe against the "criminal" Congress.

129. *Washington Union*, Mar. 28, 1858.

130. *New Orleans Daily Delta*, Mar. 30, 1858.

131. *Daily Cincinnati Commercial*, May 3, 1858.

132. Charles Robinson, in *Milwaukee Daily Sentinel*, Mar. 19, 1858.

133. *Washington Union*, Mar. 31, 1858; see also *New York Daily Tribune*, Apr. 2, 5, 1858.

134. *New Orleans Daily Delta*, Apr. 10, 1858.

135. Etcheson, *Bleeding Kansas*, 176; *New York Daily Tribune*, Apr. 15, 1858.

136. *New York Daily Times*, Mar. 29, 1858.

137. *Charleston Mercury*, Apr. 5, 1858.

138. *New Orleans Daily Delta*, Apr. 6, 1858.

139. *Washington Union*, Apr. 8, 1858.

140. *New Orleans Daily Delta*, June 12, 1858.

141. *Charleston Mercury*, July 5, 1858.

CONCLUSION

1. *New Orleans Daily Delta*, Feb. 26, 1858.

2. *Daily Richmond (Va.) Enquirer*, Feb. 2, 1857.

3. The story has recently been well retold for a popular audience in Deborah Cadbury, *Dreams of Iron and Steel: Seven Wonders of the Nineteenth Century, from the Building of the London Sewers to the Panama Canal* (New York: Fourth Estate, 2004), 1–40. See the *Philadelphia Press*, Mar. 16, 1858, for a typical contemporary description and comment.

4. *Richmond (Va.) South*, Feb. 26, 1858.

5. *Washington (D.C.) Union*, Apr. 30, 1858.

6. Don Fehrenbacher, quoted in James Rawley, *Race and Politics: "Bleeding Kansas" and the Coming of the Civil War* (Philadelphia: J. B. Lippincott, 1969), 227.

7. Jean Baker, *James Buchanan* (New York: Henry Holt, 2004), 147.

8. *New York Daily Tribune*, May 1, 1858.

9. Ibid., Apr. 24, 1858.

10. *Louisville (Ky.) Daily Journal*, Apr. 24, 1858.

11. *Chicago Daily Tribune*, Apr. 24, 1858.

12. *Daily Cincinnati Commercial*, Apr. 24, 1858.

13. *Springfield (Mass.) Daily Republican*, Apr. 24, 1858.

14. *New York Daily Times*, May 1, 1858.

15. *New York Daily Tribune*, Apr. 26, 1858.

16. *Daily Cincinnati Commercial*, May 1, 1858.

17. *Charleston (S.C.) Mercury*, May 1, 1858.

18. *Dayton (Ohio) Daily Empire*, Apr. 28, 1858.

19. *Hartford (Conn.) Daily Courant*, May 1, 1858.

20. *New York Daily Times,* May 1, 1858.

21. *Columbus (Ga.) Times & Sentinel Tri-Weekly,* May 11, 1858.

22. *New York Herald,* June 5, 1858; *New York Daily Tribune,* June 8, 1858.

23. *Detroit Daily Free Press,* June 12, 1858.

24. Ibid., July 7, 1858.

25. *Washington Union,* quoted in *Montpelier Vermont Patriot & State Gazette,* May 21, 1858.

26. *New York Daily Times,* quoted in *Daily Ohio Statesman,* Oct. 24, 1858.

27. *New Orleans Daily Delta,* Apr. 9, 1858.

28. Michael Davis, *Wonderlust: Ruminations on Liberal Education* (South Bend, Ind.: St. Augustine Press, 2006), 68.

29. *Washington Union,* Apr. 8, 1858.

30. *Eufaula (Ala.) Spirit of the South,* quoted in *Charleston Mercury,* Mar. 3, 1858.

31. "The Case for Disunion," *New Orleans Daily Picayune,* Feb. 4, 1858.

32. *New York Christian Inquirer,* Feb. 27, 1858.

33. A. C. Monk, quoted in *Boston Liberator,* May 1, 1857.

34. G. from Northfield, in *Concord New Hampshire Patriot & State Gazette,* Feb. 10, 1858.

35. George Steiner, *In Bluebeard's Castle: Some Notes towards the Redefinition of Culture* (New Haven, Conn.: Yale University Press, 1971), 20–21.

36. *Albany (N.Y.) Atlas,* June 26, 1855, in Thomas W. Webb scrapbooks, New England Emigrant Aid Company collection, Kansas State Historical Society, Topeka, Kansas, 4:183.

37. *London Times,* Jan. 14, 1856.

38. Ibid., June 25, 1856.

39. Ibid., May 17, 1856.

40. *Boston Daily Courier,* June 20, 1856, in Webb scrapbooks, 13:156.

41. An unidentified Charleston newspaper, Apr. 26, 1856, in Webb scrapbooks, 11:170–171.

42. *Daily Richmond Enquirer,* May 2, 1856.

43. *Washington (D.C.) Daily Union,* Mar. 21, 1857.

44. *Philadelphia Public Ledger & Daily Transcript,* Oct. 7, 1857.

45. Quoted in Menahem Blondheim, *News over the Wires: The Telegraph and the Flow of Public Information in America, 1844–1897* (Cambridge, Mass.: Harvard University Press, 1994), 1.

46. *Boston Post,* Sept. 26, 1856.

47. Rush Welter, *The Mind of America, 1820–1860* (New York: Columbia University Press, 1975), 387.

48. *Washington Union,* Apr. 22, 1858.

49. *New Orleans Daily Delta,* May 1, 1858.

50. James Lowell, "E Pluribus Unum" (1861), in *The Complete Works of James Russell Lowell,* 16 vols. (New York: Houghton Mifflin, 1904), 6:62, 65.

51. Quoted in Glen Atschuler and Stuart Blumin, *Rude Republic: Americans and Their Politics in the Nineteenth Century* (Princeton, N.J.: Princeton University Press, 2000), 153.

52. Denton Snider, *The American Ten Years' War: 1855–1865* (St. Louis, Mo.: Sigma, 1906), 51.

53. R. G. Elliott, *Footnotes on Kansas History* (Lawrence, Kans.: Journal Company, Printers, 1906), 27–28.

54. *Philadelphia Press,* Aug. 3, 1858.

BIBLIOGRAPHY

NEWSPAPERS AND PERIODICALS

Newspapers are dailies, 1854–1858, unless otherwise indicated.

American Railway Times
Amherst (N.H.) Farmer's Cabinet
Austin Texas State Gazette
Bangor (Maine) Daily Whig & Courier
Bellows Falls, Vermont, Chronicle
Boston Christian Watchman & Reflector
Boston Congregationalist
Boston Daily Atlas
Boston Independent
Boston Liberator
Boston Post
Boston Zion's Herald & Wesleyan Journal
Buffalo (N.Y.) Evening Bulletin
Charleston (S.C.) Mercury
Chicago Daily Tribune
Chicago Weekly Times
Columbia Daily South Carolinian
Columbus (Ga.) Enquirer Tri-Weekly
Columbus (Ga.) Times & Sentinel Tri-Weekly
Columbus Daily Ohio Statesman
Concord New Hampshire Patriot & State Gazette
Daily Albany (N.Y.) Argus (title changed to *Atlas & Argus* in February 1856)
Daily Chicago Times
Daily Cincinnati Commercial
Daily Cleveland Herald
Daily Richmond (Va.) Enquirer
Dallas Herald (weekly)
Dayton (Ohio) Daily Empire
DeBow's New Orleans Review
Detroit Daily Free Press
Fayetteville (N.C.) Observer

Hartford (Conn.) Daily Courant
Indianapolis State Journal
Indianapolis State Sentinel (weekly)
Kansas City (Mo.) Enterprise (1855–1857)
Keene New Hampshire Sentinel
Kickapoo (K.T.) Pioneer (weekly; 1854)
Lawrence (K.T.) Herald of Freedom (weekly)
Louisville (Ky.) Christian Observer
Louisville (Ky.) Daily Journal
Macon Georgia Telegraph
Milwaukee Daily Sentinel
Montgomery (Ala.) Advertiser & State Gazette (weekly)
Montpelier Vermont Patriot & State Gazette
Natchez (Miss.) Daily Courier
New Orleans Daily Delta
New Orleans Daily Picayune
New York Christian Inquirer
New York City Evening Mirror
New York Daily Times
New York Daily Tribune
New York Evangelist
New York Herald
New York Independent
New York Observer & Chronicle
New York Weekly Herald
New York Weekly Tribune
Philadelphia Press (1857–1858)
Philadelphia Public Ledger & Daily Transcript
Pittsburg Daily Dispatch
Pittsfield (Mass.) Sun
Providence (R.I.) Daily Post
Putnam's Monthly Magazine of American Literature, Science & Art
Richmond (Va.) Enquirer (semi-weekly)
Richmond (Va.) South (1857–1858)
Ripley (Ohio) Bee
Salt Lake Deseret News
San Francisco Daily Alta California
Savannah Daily Georgian
Springfield (Mass.) Daily Republican
St. Louis Daily Missouri Democrat
St. Louis Daily Missouri Republican
Stockton (Calif.) Weekly San Joaquin Republican
Thomas W. Webb scrapbooks, 1854–1856. 17 volumes. New England Emigrant Aid
    Company collection, Kansas State Historical Society, Topeka, Kansas

Times (London)
Tuskegee (Ala.) South-Western Baptist (weekly; 1854–1856)
Washington (D.C.) National Era
Washington (D.C.) Union (from 1854 to 1856 the title was the *Daily Union*)

PRINTED MATERIAL

[Beecher, Henry Ward]. *Defense of Kansas by Henry Ward Beecher.* Washington, D.C.: Buell & Blanchard, Printers, 1856.
[Douglas, Stephen A.]. *Kansas, Utah, and the Dred Scott Decision: Remarks of Stephen A. Douglas, Delivered at the State House at Springfield, Illinois on the 12th of June, 1857.* N.p. Special Collections 4300, Ablah Library, Wichita State University.
[Holbrook, John]. *Our Country's Crisis: A Discourse Delivered in Dubuque, Iowa, on Sabbath Evening, July 6, 1856, by Rev. John C. Holbrook, Pastor of the Congregational Church.* N.p., n.d. Published as part of Gale Group microfiche antislavery pamphlets. Louisville: Lost Cause Press, 1962.
[Marshall, S. S.]. *The Real Issue—Union or Disunion: Letter Hon. S. S. Marshall on the Parties and Politics of the Day to the Freemen of the Ninth Congressional District of Illinois.* Washington, D.C.: Union Office, 1856.
Moffette, Joseph. *The Territories of Kansas and Nebraska: Being an Account of Their Geography, Resources, and Settlements, etc., etc., etc.* New York: J. H. Colton, 1855.
U.S. Congress. *Congressional Globe.* Washington, D.C., 1854, 1856, and 1858.
U.S. Congress. House. *Report of the Special Committee Appointed to Investigate the Troubles in Kansas. . . .* HR 200. 34th Cong., 1st sess. Washington: Cornelius Wendell, Printer, 1856.

ARTICLES

Harlow, Ralph. "The Rise and Fall of the Kansas Aid Movement." *American Historical Review* 41, no. 1 (October 1935): 1–25.
Miner, Craig. "Stereotyping and the Pacific Railroad Issue." *Canadian Review of American Studies* 6, no. 1 (Spring 1975): 59–73.
Pierson, Michael. "'All South Society Is Assailed by the Foulest Charges': Charles Sumner's 'The Crime against Kansas' and the Escalation of Republican Anti-Slavery Rhetoric." *New England Quarterly* 43 (December 1995): 531–557.
Schmeller, Erik. "Propagandists for a Free-State Kansas: *New York Times*' Correspondents and Bleeding Kansas, 1856." *Heritage of the Great Plains* 23, no. 3 (Summer 1990): 7–14.
SenGupta, Gunja. "Bleeding Kansas: Review Essay Series." *Kansas History* 24, no. 4 (Winter 2001–2002): 318–341.
Waldron, Jeremy. "What Would Hannah Say?" *New York Review of Books,* March 15, 2007.
Wood, Gordon S. "*The Rise of American Democracy:* A Constant Struggle." Review of *The Rise of American Democracy: Jefferson to Lincoln,* by Sean Wilentz. *New York Times Book Review,* Nov. 13, 2005.

BOOKS

Applegate, Debby. *The Most Famous Man in America.* New York: Doubleday, 2006.

Atschuler, Glen C., and Stuart M. Blumin. *Rude Republic: Americans and Their Politics in the Nineteenth Century.* Princeton, N.J.: Princeton University Press, 2000.

Ayers, Edward. *What Caused the Civil War? Reflections on the South and Southern History.* New York: W. W. Norton, 2005.

Baker, Jean. *James Buchanan.* New York: Henry Holt, 2004.

Barker, Nicholas. *Double Fold: Libraries and the Assault on Paper.* New York: Random House, 2001.

Barns, George. *Denver, the Man: The Life, Letters and Public Papers of the Lawyer, Soldier and Statesman.* Wilmington, Ohio: George Barns, 1949.

Blondheim, Menahem. *News over the Wires: The Telegraph and the Flow of Public Information in America, 1844–1897.* Cambridge, Mass.: Harvard University Press, 1994.

Brewerton, Douglas. *The War in Kansas: A Rough Trip to the Border among New Homes and a Strange People.* New York: Derby & Jackson, 1856.

Brown, Christopher L. *Moral Capital: Foundations of British Abolitionism.* Chapel Hill: University of North Carolina Press, 2006.

Bruce, Lenny. *How to Talk Dirty and Influence People.* Paperback ed. Chicago: Playboy Press, 1967.

Burton, Orville Vernon. *The Age of Lincoln.* New York: Hill & Wang, 2007.

Burrows, Edwin, and Mike Wallace. *Gotham: A History of New York City to 1898.* New York: Oxford University Press, 1999.

Cadbury, Deborah. *Dreams of Iron and Steel: Seven Wonders of the Nineteenth Century, from the Building of the London Sewers to the Panama Canal.* New York: Fourth Estate, 2004.

Cawardine, Richard. *Lincoln: A Life of Purpose and Power.* New York: Alfred A. Knopf, 2006.

Conkin, Paul. *American Originals: Homemade Varieties of Christianity.* Chapel Hill: University of North Carolina Press, 1997.

Cordley, Richard. *A History of Lawrence, Kansas, from the First Settlement to the Close of the Rebellion.* Lawrence, Kans.: Lawrence Journal Press, 1895.

Cox, Samuel S. *Three Decades of Federal Legislation, 1855 to 1885.* Providence, R.I.: J. A. & R. A. Reid, 1894.

Cronon, William. *Nature's Metropolis: Chicago and the Great West.* New York: W. W. Norton, 1991.

Curtis, George. *The Duty of the American Scholar to Politics and the Times. . . .* New York: Dix, Edwards, 1856.

David, Donald. *Inhuman Bondage: The Rise and Fall of Slavery in the New World.* New York: Oxford University Press, 2006.

Davis, David. *The Slave Power Conspiracy and the Paranoid Style.* Baton Rouge: Louisiana State University Press, 1969.

Davis, Michael. *Wonderlust: Ruminations on Liberal Education.* South Bend, Ind.: St. Augustine Press, 2006.

Dean, Virgil, ed. *Kansas Territorial Reader.* Topeka: Kansas State Historical Society, 2005.

Eickhoff, Diane. *Revolutionary Heart: The Life of Clarina Nichols and the Pioneering Crusade for Women's Rights.* Kansas City, Kans.: Quindaro Press, 2006.

Elliott, R. G. *Footnotes on Kansas History.* Lawrence, Kans.: Journal Company, Printers, 1906.

Etcheson, Nicole. *Bleeding Kansas: Contested Liberty in the Civil War Era.* Lawrence: University Press of Kansas, 2004.

Fehrenbacher, Don. *The Dred Scott Case: Its Significance in American Law and Politics.* New York: Oxford University Press, 1978.

Fermer, Douglas. *James Gordon Bennett and the "New York Herald": A Study of Editorial Opinion in the Civil War Era, 1854–1867.* New York: St. Martin's Press, 1986.

Freehling, William. *The Road to Disunion.* Vol. 2, *Secessionists Triumphant, 1854–1861.* New York: Oxford University Press, 2007.

Fromm, Eric. *Escape from Freedom.* New York: Reinhart, 1941.

Garsten, Bryan. *Saving Persuasion: A Defense of Rhetoric and Judgment.* Cambridge, Mass.: Harvard University Press, 2006.

Gates, Paul. *Fifty Million Acres: Conflicts over Kansas Land Policy, 1854–1890.* Ithaca, N.Y.: Cornell University Press, 1954.

Gihon, John. *Geary and Kansas . . . .* Philadelphia: Chas. C. Rhodes, 1857.

Gladstone, Thomas. *Kansas; or, Squatter Life and Border Warfare in the Far West.* London: G. Routledge, 1857.

Goodrich, Thomas. *War to the Knife: Bleeding Kansas, 1854–1861.* Mechanicsburg, Pa.: Stackpole Books, 1998.

Harnett, Stephen John. *Democratic Dissent and the Cultural Fictions of Antebellum America.* Urbana and Chicago: University of Illinois Press, 2002.

Harris, Brayton. *Blue and Gray in Black and White: Newspapers in the Civil War.* Washington, D.C.: Brassey's, 1999.

Higginson, Thomas. *A Ride through Kansas.* New York: Anti-Slavery Society, 1856.

Holloway, J. N. *History of Kansas from the First Exploration of the Mississippi Valley to Its Admission into the Union.* Lafayette, Ind.: James, Emmons, 1868.

Holt, Michael. *The Rise and Fall of the American Whig Party: Jacksonian Politics and the Onset of the Civil War.* New York: Oxford University Press, 1999.

Johnson, Samuel. *The Battle Cry of Freedom: The New England Emigrant Aid Company in the Kansas Crusade.* Lawrence: University Press of Kansas, 1954.

Juhnke, James, and Carol Hunter. *The Missing Peace: The Search for Nonviolent Alternatives in United States History.* 2nd ed. Kitchener, Ontario: Pandora Press, 2004.

Kent, Gregory. *Framing War and Genocide: British Politics and News Media Reaction to the War in Bosnia.* Creskill, N.J.: Hampton Press, 2006.

Kimball, Gregg. *American City, Southern Place: A Cultural History of Antebellum Richmond.* Athens: University of Georgia Press, 2000.

Lewis, R. W. B. *The American Adam: Innocence, Tragedy, and Tradition in the Nineteenth Century.* Chicago: University of Chicago Press, 1955.

Lippmann, Walter. *Public Opinion.* New York: Harcourt, Brace, 1922.

Lowell, James. "E Pluribus Unum" (1861). In *The Complete Works of James Russell Lowell.* 16 vols. New York: Houghton Mifflin, 1904.

Maihafer, Harry. *War of Words: Abraham Lincoln and the Civil War Press.* Washington, D.C.: Brassey's, 2001.

Malin, James C. *The Nebraska Question, 1852–1854.* Lawrence, Kans.: Privately printed, 1953.

Martin, George. *The First Two Years of Kansas. . . . An Address.* Topeka, Kans.: State Printing Office, 1907.

Marx, Leo. *The Machine in the Garden: Technology and the Pastoral Ideal in America.* New York: Oxford University Press, 1964.

Mayer, Henry. *All on Fire: William Lloyd Garrison and the Abolition of Slavery.* New York: St. Martin's Press, 1998.

McCloskey, Deirdre. *The Bourgeois Virtues: Ethics for an Age of Commerce.* Chicago: University of Chicago Press, 2006.

McLuhan, Marshall. *Understanding Media: The Extensions of Man.* New York: McGraw-Hill, 1964.

Menand, Louis. *The Metaphysical Club: A Story of Ideas in America.* New York: Farrar, Straus & Giroux, 2001.

Miner, Craig. *Kansas: The History of the Sunflower State.* Lawrence: University Press of Kansas, 2002.

Miner, Craig, and William Unrau. *The End of Indian Kansas: A Study of Cultural Revolution, 1854–1871.* Lawrence: Regents Press of Kansas, 1978.

Neeley, Mark, Jr. *The Union Divided: Party Conflict in the Civil War North.* Cambridge, Mass.: Harvard University Press, 2002.

Nevins, Allan. *The Emergence of Lincoln.* Vol. 1, *Douglas, Buchanan, and Party Chaos, 1857–1859.* New York: Charles Scribner's Sons, 1950.

———. *Ordeal of the Union.* Vol. 2, *A House Dividing, 1852–1857.* New York: Charles Scribner's Sons, 1947.

Nichols, Alice. *Bleeding Kansas.* New York: Oxford University Press, 1954.

Nichols, Roy. *The Disruption of American Democracy.* New York: Macmillan, 1948.

Nord, David. *Communities of Journalism: A History of American Newspapers and Their Readers.* Urbana and Chicago: University of Illinois Press, 2001.

Parker, Theodore. *Theodore Parker: An Anthology.* Ed. Henry Steele Commager. Boston: Beacon Press, 1960.

Peterson, Merrill. *John Brown: The Legend Revisited.* Charlottesville: University of Virginia Press, 2002.

Phillips, William. *The Conquest of Kansas by Missouri and Her Allies.* Boston: Phillips, Sampson, 1856.

Pocock, J. G. A. "Working on Ideas in Time." In *The Historian's Workshop,* ed. L. P. Curtis, 151–166. New York: Alfred A. Knopf, 1970.

Poole, Stephen. *Unspeak: How Words Become Weapons, How Weapons Become a Message, and How That Message Becomes Reality.* New York: Grove Press, 2006.

Potter, David. *The Impending Crisis, 1848–1861.* New York: Harper & Row, 1976.

Ratner, Lorman, and Dwight Teeter. *Fanatics and Fire-Eaters: Newspapers and the Coming of the Civil War.* Urbana and Chicago: University of Illinois Press, 2003.

Rawley, James. *Race and Politics: "Bleeding Kansas" and the Coming of the Civil War.* Philadelphia: J. B. Lippincott, 1969.

Ray, Orman. *The Repeal of the Missouri Compromise.* Cleveland, Ohio: Arthur H. Clark, 1909.

Reynolds, David. *John Brown, Abolitionist: The Man Who Killed Slavery, Sparked the Civil War, and Seeded Civil Rights.* New York: Alfred A. Knopf, 2005.

Reynolds, Donald. *Editors Make War: Southern Newspapers in the Secession Crisis.* Nashville, Tenn.: Vanderbilt University Press, 1970.

Richards, Leonard. *The Slave Power: The Free North and Southern Domination, 1780–1860.* Baton Rouge: Louisiana State University Press, 2000.

Robinson, Charles. *The Kansas Conflict.* New York: Harper & Brothers, 1892.

Robinson, Sara. *Kansas: Its Exterior and Interior Life. . . .* Boston: Crosby, Nichols, 1856.

[Ropes, Hannah]. *Six Months in Kansas. By a Lady.* Boston: John P. Jewett, 1856.

Sachsman, David, S. Kittrell Rushing, and Debra Reddin van Tuyll, eds. *The Civil War and the Press.* New Brunswick, N.J.: Transaction, 2000.

Saum, Lewis. *The Popular Mood of Pre–Civil War America.* Westport, Conn.: Greenwood Press, 1980.

Schlesinger, Arthur, Jr. *The Age of Jackson.* New York: Little, Brown, 1945.

Seitz, Don. *The James Gordon Bennetts, Father and Son: Proprietors of the New York Herald.* Indianapolis, Ind.: Bobbs-Merrill, 1928.

SenGupta, Gunja. *For God and Mammon: Evangelicals and Entrepreneurs, Masters and Slaves in Territorial Kansas, 1854–1860.* Athens and London: University of Georgia Press, 1996.

Sewell, Richard. *Ballots for Freedom: Anti Slavery Politics in the United States, 1837–1860.* New York: Oxford University Press, 1976.

Shapiro, Michael, ed. *Language and Politics.* New York: New York University Press, 1984.

Smith, Henry Nash. *Virgin Land: The American West as Symbol and Myth.* Cambridge, Mass.: Harvard University Press, 1950.

Snider, Denton. *The American Ten Years' War: 1855–1865.* St. Louis, Mo.: Sigma, 1906.

Socolofsky, Homer. *Kansas Governors.* Lawrence: University Press of Kansas, 1990.

Spring, Leverett. *Kansas: The Prelude to the War for the Union.* Boston: Houghton Mifflin, 1885.

Stampp, Kenneth. *America in 1857: A Nation on the Brink.* New York: Oxford University Press, 1990.

Starr, Paul. *The Creation of the Media: Political Origins of Modern Communications.* New York: Basic Books, 2004.

Steiner, George. *After Babel: Aspects of Language and Translation*. New York: Oxford University Press, 1975.

——. *In Bluebeard's Castle: Some Notes towards the Redefinition of Culture*. New Haven, Conn.: Yale University Press, 1971.

Stilgoe, John. *Metropolitan Corridor: Railroads and the American Scene*. New Haven, Conn.: Yale University Press, 1983.

Striner, Richard. *Father Abraham: Lincoln's Relentless Struggle to End Slavery*. New York: Oxford University Press, 2006.

Thayer, Eli. *The Kansas Crusade*. New York: Harper & Brothers, 1889.

Tomlinson, William P. *Kansas in Eighteen Fifty-Eight, Being Chiefly a History of the Recent Troubles in the Territory*. New York: H. Dayton, 1859.

Transactions of the Kansas State Historical Society. First and Second Biennial Reports. Topeka, Kans.: George W. Martin, Kansas Publishing House, 1881.

Unrau, William. *Mixed-Bloods and Tribal Dissolution: Charles Curtis and the Quest for Indian Identity*. Lawrence: University Press of Kansas, 1989.

Welter, Rush. *The Mind of America, 1820–1860*. New York: Columbia University Press, 1975.

Wildavsky, Aaron. "A Cultural Analysis of the Role of Abolitionists in the Coming of the Civil War." With Ellis Richard. In *Cultural Analysis: Politics, Public Law, and Administration*. New Brunswick, N.J.: Transaction, 2006.

Wilder, Daniel. *The Annals of Kansas, 1541–1885*. Topeka: T. Dwight Thacher, Kansas Publishing House, 1886.

Wilentz, Sean. *The Rise of American Democracy*. New York: W. W. Norton, 2007.

Williams, Robert. *Horace Greeley: Champion of American Freedom*. New York: New York University Press, 2006.

Wills, Gary. *Lincoln at Gettysburg: The Words That Remade America*. New York: Simon & Schuster, 1992.

INDEX

Smith, Gerrit, 52, 83, 101, 122
Smith, Henry Nash, 8
Snider, Denton, 4, 251
Springfield Daily Republican, xi
  on Atchison, 141
  on Howard report, 188
  on Kansas-Nebraska bill, 57, 64
  on Lane's request for statehood, 144
  on political leadership, 70
  and role of the press, 41
  on territorial violence, 150
Squatter Sovereign, 2, 93, 94, 105, 245
"squatter sovereignty," 61, 90, 181, 222
Stampp, Kenneth, 211
Stanton, Frederick, 194, 201–202, 210,
  223, 230
Starr, Paul, 6
states' rights, 70, 92, 249
Stearns, Charles, 36, 118, 140, 179
Steiner, George, 242
Stephens, Alexander, 3, 72, 99, 178,
  187
Stewart, James, 188–189
Stewart, John, 114–115
Stilgoe, John, 8
St. Louis Daily Missouri Democrat, xi, 36,
  152
  on Kansas issue, 34–35, 179
  on Lecompton Constitution, 219
  on popular sovereignty, 60
  on Sharps rifle, 109
  on territorial governors, 199, 206,
  207
St. Louis Daily Missouri Republican, xi,
  19, 35, 60, 150
Stringfellow, Benjamin F., 3, 48, 93,
  135–136, 196. See also *Squatter
  Sovereign*
Stuart, Charles, 228
Sumner, Charles, 3
  beating of, 11, 16, 117, 145, 149, 184
  "Crime against Kansas" speech by,
  46, 184–186, 187

  and Kansas-Nebraska debates, 51, 71,
  73–74
  and Lecompton Constitution, 229

Taylor, Miles, 227
Thayer, Eli, 37, 79, 80, 255n33
Thirty-fourth Congress (1855–1856)
  and army appropriations bill,
  154–155
  Douglas's report to, 181–183
  factions within, 187–188
  Kansas as dominating issue of,
  179–180
  Pierce message to, 180–181
  press reports on, 179, 181, 182,
  183–184, 186–187, 188, 189–190
  proposals for Kansas, 187–188
  Seward speech, 183, 184
  Sumner address to, 46, 184–186,
  187
Titus, Henry, 105, 152, 160, 199
Tomlinson, William, 24
Toombs, Robert, 187, 226, 229
Topeka Constitution
  drafting of, 97–98
  proposals for statehood under, 143,
  182, 184, 187
  replacement of, 211
Topeka government
  criticism of, 96, 98, 188–189
  1855 convention, 96, 105, 167
  (image)
  1857 convention, 163
  as free-state faction, 15–16, 96, 97,
  101
  national attention on, 98, 101
  in the press, 97–98, 104, 218, 204,
  245
  Robinson as governor of, 15–16, 105
  support for, 96
  treason charges against, 159–160
  U.S. troops and, 17, 101, 153
Tuskegee South-Western Baptist, 64